LAWRENCE HENRY GIPSON

AUTHOR

JARED INGERSOLL: A STUDY OF AMERICAN LOYALISM
IN RELATION TO BRITISH COLONIAL GOVERN-
MENT

STUDIES IN CONNECTICUT COLONIAL TAXATION

THE MORAVIAN INDIAN MISSION ON WHITE RIVER

LEWIS EVANS

THE BRITISH EMPIRE BEFORE THE AMERICAN REVO-
LUTION

*Every considerable library on American and British history
will require Mr. Gipson's volumes as an indispensable work
of reference, and most readers will be so captivated by the
lively reports of this intelligent and humane historical sur-
veyor as to look forward with impatience to future volumes.*

SAMUEL ELIOT MORISON

THE BRITISH EMPIRE
BEFORE THE AMERICAN REVOLUTION

VOLUME VIII

THE GREAT WAR FOR THE EMPIRE

THE CULMINATION

1760–1763

THE BRITISH EMPIRE
BEFORE THE AMERICAN REVOLUTION
VOLUME VIII

THE GREAT WAR FOR THE EMPIRE

THE CULMINATION, 1760–1763

BY

LAWRENCE HENRY GIPSON

M.A. (OXON.), PH.D., D.LITT., L.H.D., LL.D., F.R.HIST.S.

RESEARCH PROFESSOR OF HISTORY EMERITUS, LEHIGH UNIVERSITY

AND ONE TIME HAROLD VYVYAN HARMSWORTH PROFESSOR

OF AMERICAN HISTORY, THE UNIVERSITY OF OXFORD

MCMLIV
ALFRED A. KNOPF
NEW YORK

L. C. catalog card number: 36–20870

THIS IS A BORZOI BOOK,
PUBLISHED BY ALFRED A. KNOPF, INC.

COPYRIGHT 1953 BY ALFRED A. KNOPF, INC.

FIRST EDITION

*Manufactured in the United States of America
Published simultaneously in Canada by McClelland & Stewart Limited*

THIS BOOK IS DEDICATED *to the* OXFORD
EIGHTEENTH CENTURY GROUP *in recollec-*
tion of my happy and fruitful association
with it in a quest for a deeper under-
standing of the period.

Preface

THIS volume will hardly be of interest to those whose views of the progress of events between the years 1754 and 1763 have been firmly fixed by a tradition that has embodied the idea that what American history textbooks call "the French and Indian War" was a somewhat localized North American conflict which, in view of the great preponderance of population and wealth possessed by the British continental colonies when contrasted with such assets in French Canada, was inevitably to leave at its termination the destiny of the North American continent in the keeping of the English-speaking people. Nor will those who refuse to make a distinction between the Seven Years' War in Germany and the nine years of hostility between the British and French empires be much more interested in its contents. I am therefore obliged to address those whose minds have not as yet been committed, but are open to a fresh approach to an understanding of the history of the momentous three years that extend from 1760 to 1763 and that are here considered. For the events of these years were to determine the outcome of the war and with it the terms of the treaty of peace agreed upon between Great Britain and France and Spain, providing as they did for a new political configuration of the continent of North America and of India. Indeed, it is not going too far to assert that no war in modern times down to the beginning of the twentieth century had, by reason of the manner of its termination, consequences so permanent and profound in their nature over so large a part of the world.

Basic misconceptions and distortions of history are encouraged by, and almost inevitably arise out of, careless, faulty nomenclature. I have long been persuaded that this has been particularly true with respect to the war we are here considering as the result of the unfortunate use of names applied to it. Consistent with this view and not with any love of novelty, I have — as I have already indicated in the prefaces of earlier volumes of this *British Empire before the American Revolution* series — felt impelled to call it the Great War for the Empire, in order to introduce into the titles as well as the contents of my last three volumes as much accuracy as possible — the touchstone of all historical work of quality. This title, I conceive, conveys the real significance of the war: the broad objectives of the government of Great Britain in the first instance in committing the nation to the conflict, and its equally broad objectives as these were finally embodied in the treaty of peace accorded to vanquished France and Spain — a peace settlement that would, as intimated, determine for generations to come the place to be occupied by the English-speaking people in world affairs.

In relating in some detail the story of the dramatic culmination of the Great War for the Empire, it has at the same time seemed proper, by reason of its close relation to the Seven Years' War in Germany, to deal at least briefly with the leading events having to do with the latter conflict. The reader, therefore, while following the major theme, will be made aware of these other developments.

The gathering of the material for the writing of this volume has carried me to many places. As is indicated in the footnotes, I have drawn upon the manuscripts in the Public Record Office, the British Museum, the Library of the former India Office in the Commonwealth Relations building in London, the Bibliothèque Nationale, the Canadian Archives, the Clements Library at Ann Arbor, the Huntington Library at San Marino, the Library of Congress, the Newberry Library of Chicago, the Lehigh University Library, and the libraries at Oxford. The task of completing the writing of it, I may also add, has been greatly facilitated as the result not only of grants by the Rockefeller Foundation, Lehigh University, and the United States Educational Commission for the United Kingdom, but of my sojourn during the previous academic year at the University of Oxford as the Harold Vyvyan Harmsworth Professor of American History. In now presenting it to the public I can only express the hope that those who have found of interest its predecessors in the series will not feel, upon laying it down, that they have read it without some reward.

L. H. G.

Rotha,
Rydal, Pennsylvania
April 12, 1953

Contents

CHAPTER II

BRITISH CONTINENTAL COMMITMENTS, 1759–60

CHAPTER III

THE NEW KING AND THE GERMAN SEVEN YEARS' WAR

CHAPTER IV

PRIVATEERSMEN AND NEUTRALS

Chapter V

ISLAND HOPPING IN THE FRENCH WEST INDIES, 1759

CHAPTER VI

THE WAR SPREADS TO INDIA

CHAPTER VII

DISASTER OVERTAKES THE FRENCH IN THE CARNATIC

Chapter VIII

SENEGAL, BELLE–ÎLE–EN–MER, AND MARTINIQUE

Chapter IX

FAILURE OF PEACE NEGOTIATIONS
AND THE FALL OF PITT

CHAPTER XI

THE BURSTING OF THE SPANISH BUBBLE

CHAPTER XII

THE RETURN OF PEACE

Maps and Plans

CHRONOLOGY

1756

| June | 20 | The capture of Calcutta by the Nabob. |
| | 21 | The Black Hole incident. |

1757

Jan.	2	The British recapture of Calcutta.
March	23	The French surrender of Chandernagore.
June	23	The Battle of Plassey.
	29	Mir Jafar becomes Nabob of Bengal.

1758

April	29	The first Pocock-d'Aché naval engagement.
May	1	The surrender of Senegal to the British.
June	2	Lally captures Fort St. David.
Aug.	3	The second Pocock-d'Aché naval engagement.
Dec.	6	Pitt's public guarantee to Britain's allies.
	29	The British capture Goree.

1759

Feb.	16	The siege of Madras raised by the British fleet.
April	9	The storming of Masulipatam.
	13	The British defeat at Bergen.
May	2	The French surrender of Guadeloupe.
July	5	Rodney's attack on Le Havre.
Aug.	1	The French defeat at Minden.
	10	The death of Ferdinand of Spain and the accession of Charles III.
	12	Frederick's defeat at Kunersdorf.
	17	Boscawen's victory over de la Clue.
	18	Destruction of the French ships at Lagos.

Sept.   10   The third Pocock-d'Aché naval engagement.
Nov.   20   The decisive Battle of Quiberon Bay.
         21   The Prussian defeat at Maxen.

1760

Jan.   22   Coote defeats Lally at Wandiwash.
Feb.   20   Thurot captures Carrickfergus.
         28   The destruction of Thurot's ships.
Oct.   25   The death of George II and the accession of George III.

1761

Jan.   17   The French surrender Pondicherry.
Feb.   12   The fall of Mahé.
April   5   The capture of Gingy, last French stronghold in India.
June   6   The French surrender Dominica.
          7   The British conquest of Belle-Île-en-Mer.
Aug.   15   The Bourbon Family Compact signed.
Oct.   4   The resignation of Pitt.
Nov.   19   The British ultimatum to Spain.

1762

Jan.   4   Britain declares war on Spain.
          5   The death of Elizabeth of Russia and the accession of
              Peter III.
Feb.   16   The French surrender Martinique.
May   18   Portugal declares war on Spain and France.
June   27   The French gain possession of St. John's, Newfoundland.
July   18   The death of Peter III of Russia and the accession of Cath-
              erine.
         30   The British storm El Morro Castle.
Aug.   13   The surrender of Havana.
Sept.   18   The surrender of the French force at St. John's.
Oct.   6   The British storm Manila.
         30   The Spaniards surrender the Philippine Archipelago.

1763

Feb.   10   The termination of Britain's Great War for the Empire.
         15   The termination of the German Seven Years' War.

THE BRITISH EMPIRE
BEFORE THE AMERICAN REVOLUTION
VOLUME VIII

THE GREAT WAR FOR THE EMPIRE

THE CULMINATION

1760–1763

CHAPTER I

A French Attempt to Conquer the British Isles

IN THE preceding volume emphasis was placed on the fact that
France, in seeking to guard its great overseas interests, was
obliged to face among other things the fatal handicap of inade-
quate sea power. This meant that too few ships could be detached
to operate in the Far East, as will be subsequently indicated, in view
of the desperate need for them in the North Atlantic and the Mediterranean. Further, it may be noted that the fair equality of the
British and French naval forces operating in the New World in 1757
had disappeared the following year. The squadron sent to help defend Louisbourg, as we have seen, was destroyed in the harbour of
that seaport and was never replaced despite French efforts to that
end. On the other hand, the British shipyards both public and private continued to turn out great numbers of fighting vessels. According to a detailed enumeration of the ships of the British navy
made at the beginning of 1758, there were in commission — including ten captured French ships — one hundred and thirty-six, of between one hundred guns and fifty guns, and all but thirty-three of
them carried sixty guns or more and were therefore standard ships
of the line. By June of that year ten more warships were launched;
by the beginning of 1759 thirty more were on the stocks; and by the
fall of 1761 a total of over three hundred and fifty men-of-war and
frigates were in service.[1]

What had the French by the year 1759 to match the more than

[1] London advices to the *Pennsylvania Gazette*, August 24, 1758, February 22 and
May 31, 1759, and January 14, 1762.

one hundred and thirteen British ships of the line that were in fighting condition — not to mention the array of other lesser vessels? Apparently, they could muster not more than half as many of the line, in a position to operate — making the most liberal allowances as to the number of these ships.[2] But this disparity does not tell the whole story of French naval weakness. A good navy embraces more than ships that can sail and that possess adequate armament: it comprehends experienced sailors eager to fight; even more, it includes officers of high and low rank capable of making the best use of their knowledge of naval strategy and tactics under given conditions. Ship for ship, there is no denying the fact that the French vessel was the equal in fighting power of that of the British of the same class. That was demonstrated more than once in the course of the war. But crew for crew, it is equally certain that British seamanship and battle morale were by and large superior and that commander for commander, especially in the higher echelons of sea command, the British also possessed a very great advantage stemming from a long tradition of successful warfare on the high seas.

Facing overwhelming odds on the water and yet still possessed of transoceanic interests of transcendent value, the ministers of His Most Christian Majesty very logically turned their attention to the possibility of striking such a blow against the British Isles as would bring the war, despite previous reverses, to a triumphant end. The Maréchal Belle-Isle had in 1756 developed a plan for the invasion of England, but this had been put aside. It was now, early in 1759, revived with great seriousness under the mysterious designation *"d'expédition particulière."* [3]

The daring project provided for the movement of an expeditionary army of twenty-six battalions of foot soldiers, four squadrons of horse, and an artillery park — comprising some twenty thousand troops in all — out of the ports of Brittany in ninety vessels of from two hundred to four hundred tons' burden, which would be convoyed by six ships of the line under the command of Bigot de Morogues. This force was to be commanded by the Duc d'Aiguillon, victor of the Battle of Saint-Cas in Brittany the preceding Septem-

---

[2] In arriving at these figures of French naval strength I have made use of the tables presented by Robert Beatson in his *Naval and Military Memoirs of Great Britain from 1727 to 1783* (London, 1804), Volume III, Appendix.

[3] See *Vie privée de Louis XV* (London, 1781); Lacour-Gayet's *Le Marine militaire de la France sous le règne de Louis XV* (Paris, 1910).

ber. At the most favourable moment the armada was to proceed out into the Atlantic, and would thereupon swing round Ireland and then descend upon the estuary of the Clyde, the great shipbuilding and commercial center of Scotland. With Glasgow in Aiguillon's possession, he was then, according to his instructions, to march upon Edinburgh and get possession of the castle. Thus once in control of the Lowlands he could, he was told, anticipate receiving support from the Highlands, which had revolted in 1745, and by this means would be in a position greatly to expand his army in moving upon England.[4] In this connection, it was anticipated that negotiations in progress with Sweden would also result in the sending of from ten to twelve thousand Swedes to join the expeditionary corps. With Great Britain thrown into panic by the appearance of this force in the north, two other French army corps, commanded respectively by Soubise and Chevert and totalling some twenty thousand men, would move directly across the Channel in flotillas of great flatboats, each carrying four hundred men and armed with two twenty-four-pounders. One was to move out of the ports of Normandy, and the other from those of Flanders, with the purpose of seizing the southern coast of England and then converging on London.

As a guarantee of the success of the expeditions it seemed of the highest importance to the French that they should catch the British people unaware of their danger until too late. Preparations for it must therefore be made as secretly as possible. Moreover, it was considered absolutely essential to concentrate at Brest a sufficiently large naval force to provide a superiority over the British home fleet, should the latter attempt to interfere with these movements. This called for a Brest fleet of at least thirty-five or forty ships of the line, which, under command of Admiral Conflans, would, it was hoped, be able to seize temporary control of the Channel.[5]

To deny that this plan of invasion presented a real danger to Great Britain is to underestimate the possibilities implicit in it, especially under certain given conditions and circumstances that might have rendered British sea power off the coast of France and in home waters either nonexistent or at least ineffective for a period of days or even for a critical day or two.[6] But in practice certain essentials

---

[4] For Aiguillon's instructions, see Richard Waddington, La Guerre de Sept Ans, III, 364–5.

[5] J. S. Corbett, England in the Seven Years' War (London, 1907), II, 19.

[6] Corbett quotes with approval Newcastle's statement regarding the French design

for its most effective execution were lacking. In the first place, a copy of the letter of the King's Minister, the Duc de Choiseul, to the French Ambassador at Stockholm, Havrincour, dated May 31 and containing the Belle-Isle plan, came into possession of Newcastle the middle of June while the French were still busy with their preparations.[7] This put the British thoroughly on the alert. Again, an enormous difficulty was presented in the proposal to concentrate at Brest all the best fighting units of the French navy, and especially those at Toulon. For the British not only had a strong fleet under Sir Edward Hawke, which was blockading Brest itself, but another in the Mediterranean that was patrolling the waters in front of Toulon, the naval base there. Further, the invasion plans called for the expenditure of vast sums of money, the use of vast resources, and the display of great energy and capacity on the part of those charged with the responsibility not only of gathering together all the requisites for an invasion but of launching it. But the funds in the Treasury were exhausted. Choiseul, writing to his kinsman at the court of Vienna on October 21, 1759 declared despondently:

> "Our credit which formed the great arm of our power is annihilated: we are obliged to sustain ourselves alone by revenues. But as they have been consumed in advance of collection the King will be required to enter into some kind of bankruptcy. . . . The new imposts have not produced an actual enlargement; no group has been found that is able to make advances upon these impositions. We are therefore reduced today in the Council [of State] to press for the payment of the troops to the month of November, to send the silver service of the King and of individuals to the mint and to give in exchange bills which you may well judge, will not be strongly sought after. The King is paying absolutely nothing more than his troops, which at the moment are in need, and the subsidies agreed upon by the Treaties." [8]

Beyond the problem of financial paralysis lay that of securing essential supplies for the building and arming of ships and boats sufficient for the invasion. The Baltic states had the materials, and mer-

---

of invasion that it was "extremely well laid"; at the same time he proceeds to show (*ibid.*, II, 19–21) that the latest modification of the plan — providing, as this did, that the French grand fleet would escort the Channel expeditions rather than seeking out the British fleet in order to destroy it — was faulty, in that it sought success by evasion of the enemy and not by overwhelming him.

[7] *Ibid.*, II, 18.
[8] Waddington, *op. cit.*, III, 457–8.

chants there were induced to advance them to the account of the court of France. But the attempt to evade the blockade and to use Dutch ships, ports, and thoroughfares for transporting them to France was hardly successful, as will be noted somewhat at length in a subsequent chapter of this volume. It may be pointed out here, however, that a Dutch ship carrying lumber to Le Havre was seized by the British during this period, as were other ships bringing munitions.[9] Moreover, on September 28 Major General Joseph Yorke, British envoy at The Hague, presented to the States General a memorial against the efforts of French agents, employing, incidentally, Dutch merchants, to bring to France overland through Holland cannon, munitions, and other matériel, procured in the Baltic.[10] This came at a time, as we shall see, when the government of the United Netherlands was seeking by every means to moderate the policy of Great Britain regarding the seizure and condemnation of scores of Dutch "neutral" ships engaged in trade to the French West Indies. Yorke's protest was therefore especially effective in halting the flow of supplies.

Granting that under these circumstances great financial as well as extraordinary obstacles had to be faced in implementing the plan for invading England, it was, nevertheless, felt by those in authority in France that the time had come for desperate measures involving the gravest risks. Therefore, utilizing whatever means were at hand, they moved ahead with the daring project during the spring and summer of 1759. Large numbers of troops — some sixty-three battalions under command of the Prince of Condé, the Prince of Soubise, eight lieutenant generals, twelve major generals, and eighteen brigadier generals, it was reported [11] — were actually concentrated in the coastal area of Normandy and Brittany facing England across the Channel. At the ports where they were to embark, there was also intense activity at the docks and stocks in the construction of flatboats and in other preparations. Such proceedings could not escape the attention of the British. In fact, on May 30 William Pitt communicated to Parliament a message from the King to the effect that since advices had been received that the French court was making preparations to land an army in England, it was imperative, in order to ward off "the imminent danger of such an invasion," that

---

9 London advices, *Pennsylvania Gazette*, December 20, 1759 and January 24, 1760.
10 For the above memorial see the *Annual Register*, 1759, pp. 255–7.
11 John Entick, *General History of the Late War* (London, 1770), IV, 244–5.

the militia should be drawn out, embodied, and prepared to march as the occasion might require.[12] To this the House of Commons replied in pledging unanimously its "utmost efforts to repel all insults, and effectually enable his majesty, not only to disappoint the attempt of France, but, by the blessing of God, to turn them to their own confusion." [13]

Pitt, moreover, was not disposed to await the arrival of the enemy in home waters but rather to take the initiative against him before he was prepared to move. Dunkirk and Le Havre were manifestly two of the principal French embarkation points for the projected invasion of the British Isles. At the former, the daring privateersman Captain François Thurot was at anchor with a squadron, prepared at the favourable moment to descend upon Ireland. To hold him in check, Commodore William Boys (Boyce) had already been sent with a sufficient number of ships from the home fleet to patrol the entrance of that port and the Flemish coastline, and another squadron under Sir Peircy Brett had been strategically stationed in the Downs. At Spithead a third now came into existence that was designed for offensive action. This, placed by Pitt under command of George Brydges Rodney, a highly talented and seasoned officer recently promoted Rear Admiral of the Blue, was ordered at the suggestion of the First Lord of the Admiralty, Lord Anson, to move against Le Havre to destroy not only the flatboats that were being massed there, but also its marine magazines, including the great powder magazine.[14]

Le Havre, located at the mouth of the Seine, was at the time a well fortified town numbering some thirty thousand inhabitants. In addition to enjoying the protection of walls containing four bastions and five half-moons, there was a citadel located just east of it, now embodied in the modern town. Its harbour within the walls was spacious enough to contain three hundred sail; but the entrance to it provided by the river was narrow and dangerous, especially for larger ships without competent pilots. To the west of the harbour is the great roadstead, and to the east a lesser one where vessels of moderate displacement could ride at anchor. In the town itself was located one of the six general marine arsenals of France; it possessed also one of the most important docks for the building of war-

---

12 *Parliamentary History* (ed. T. C. Hansard, London, 1813), XV, 940.
13 *Ibid.*, XV, 940–1.
14 Corbett, *op. cit.*, II, 25; Entick, *op. cit.*, IV, 247–9.

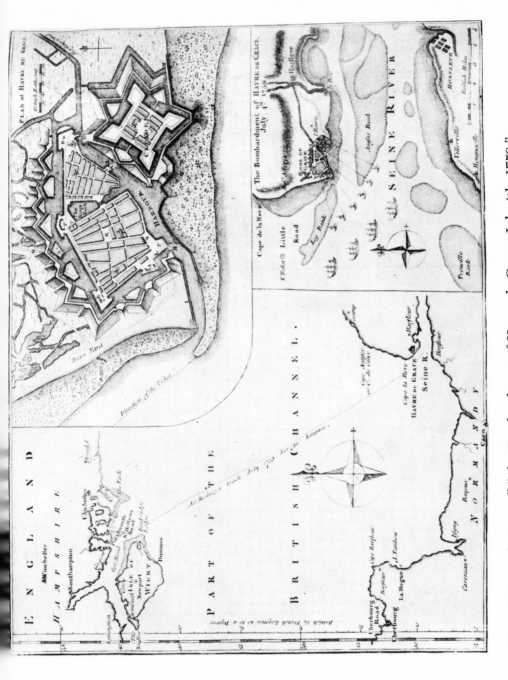

"Plan of Havre de Grace." "The Bombardment of Havre de Grace, July 4th, 1759."

(From the *Gentleman's Magazine*, 1759)

A portion of "A New and Correct Chart of the Seat of War on the Coasts
France, Spain, Portugal and Italy...." (From the *Annual Register, 176*

ships where numerous flatboats had already been built or were under construction. The place was therefore a logical British military objective.[15]

On June 6 Rodney received his definite instructions to prepare to proceed against the town. To his squadron of five warships and six frigates were now added six bomb-ketches and some fire-ships. Impatient to depart on his mission, he was nevertheless held in port during the remainder of the month by adverse winds. Then, with a change in the weather, he was able at length to set sail on July 2 and anchored the next day before the town. For an effective bombardment of its docks and magazines it was still necessary to get his bomb-ketches much closer to them; for royal docks in the Vauban Basin and the chief warehouses were located some distance to the rear of the entrance to the harbour.

Thanks to the efforts of the energetic Captain Samuel Hood — the future Viscount Hood of the Revolutionary War — and other naval officers, these vessels were carried up the Honfleur, or south channel of the Seine, within bomb range of their objectives. Supported by the frigates, they opened fire on July 4 and maintained for a period of fifty-two hours a heavy bombardment. Although the distance — some two thousand eight hundred toises (about six thousand yards) — was too great to inflict the maximum of injury on Le Havre, most of its inhabitants left in panic, a number of houses and vessels were struck and destroyed or damaged, and the magazine stores intended for the invasion were set afire and burned furiously for hours, despite the efforts of hundreds of people to extinguish the flames. Nor did the French guns planted on the fortifications prove to be very effective inasmuch as most of those that could be trained on the British ships did not have the desired range.[16] Some of the bomb-ketches, nevertheless, were struck by shells.

Since it was quite impossible to enter the Le Havre harbour itself, Rodney, feeling that the main purpose of his visit had been accom-

---

[15] For a contemporary description of Le Havre see Robert Beatson, *Naval and Military Memoirs of Great Britain* (London, 1804), III, 241–4. As to the location of the Vauban Basin, where the warships were built, the citadel, and the harbour of Le Havre, see the nineteenth-century plan of the town in the *Encyclopædia Britannica* (Cambridge, Eng., 1910), VIII, 354.

[16] Rodney to the Admiralty, July 6, 1759, Beatson, *op. cit.*, II, 323–4; see also Waddington (*op. cit.*, III, 366), who quotes from a contemporary French report on the action: "*Récit du bombardement du Havre.*"

plished and needing to refit, ordered his ships out of the Honfleur channel and on July 8 returned to Spithead.[17] Having completed his preparations, the rear admiral again visited the town late in August expecting once more to bombard it. But the weather was bad and the tides adverse. What was more serious, Rodney found that, profiting by their recent unhappy experience, the defenders had placed two floating batteries and two flat-bottomed vessels, all provided with heavy guns, in such a position in shoal water to the west of the Honfleur channel that while his own ships could not approach them in safety, they could easily rake the bomb-ketches should the latter attempt to move into their former positions. Further he noted that within the harbour of Le Havre and secure behind a great sand bank, four galleys, each provided with a gun of large calibre at the prow, were so stationed as to rake the ketches from the east whenever they should approach. In view of the almost certain destruction of his vessels, were they to come within range of this enfilading fire, the rear admiral, with the unanimous approval of his officers — including, it may be noted, not only Hood, mentioned earlier, but Thomas Graves and Samuel Barrington, both of whom, like Hood, were to figure prominently in naval affairs during the Revolutionary War — decided not to take the risks. He therefore wrote to Pitt early in September making clear his dilemma and at the same time pointed out that he had secured information that almost all the flat-bottomed boats designed for the invasion and constructed there — some one hundred and twenty in number — were now well out of reach up the Seine at Rouen, the capital of Normandy.[18] The contemplated attack was thereupon turned into a blockade, which, in the words of a correspondent, was so tight "that a Boat cannot go in or out of the River Seine unnoticed by him." [19]

One important consequence of the Rodney attack on Le Havre was the realization on the part of the French that an invasion of England by slow-moving flat-bottomed boats must await the establishment of some sort of sea control of the Channel, temporary as this might be. But this did not apply to the swift-sailing French

---

[17] According to Horace Walpole's Memoirs of the Reign of George II (London, 1846), III, 187, Rodney threw such a number of bombs at the enemy targets that he "almost melted his own mortars; but the flat-bottomed boats, which were not finished, proved to be out of his reach."

[18] Rodney to Pitt, September 3, 1759, Correspondence of Chatham (ed. W. S. Taylor and J. H. Pringle, London, 1838), I, 420–2.

[19] London advices, September 22, Pennsylvania Gazette, December 6, 1759.

ships that had been congregated at such western seaports as Bay-
onne, Bordeaux, La Rochelle, and Nantes. Could these, armed *en
flûte*, find their way to Brest and then, after being loaded with the
soldiers and military supplies already concentrated there, sail for
England under convoy of the grand fleet at Brest, reinforced by the
Toulon squadron and that of Bompar from the West Indies, success
might still crown the plan for invasion. It is therefore desirable to
turn now to a consideration of the French effort to implement this
project and the British counter-effort to thwart it.

Needless to say, British naval strategy accepted as a primary
point the necessity of maintaining, in so far as was possible under
given weather conditions, a rigid blockade of Brest. This task was
again assigned to Hawke, who was also instructed to keep an eye
out for the West India squadron. Leaving Torbay, he arrived off
Brest on May 24. But hard gales drove him away more than once;
yet he would doggedly return as soon as the weather cleared, in order to watch closely the movements of the French fleet there and
also the port of L'Orient, not far to the southeast.[20] While the blockade of Brest was thus proceeding, there was important activity in
the Mediterranean, and later off the coast of Portugal. Admiral Edward Boscawen, who had distinguished himself in the operations off
Cape Breton Island that led to the capture of Louisbourg in 1758
and had received the thanks of the House of Commons on December 6,[21] early in February of the new year not only was sworn to the
Privy Council but was soon afterward rewarded with the command
of the Mediterranean squadron that previously had been under the
command of Vice Admiral Henry Osborne, who had returned to
England for his health and in doing so had left Vice Admiral Thomas
Brodrick in temporary charge. Leaving the Isle of Wight on April 14
with seven ships of the line — including the *Namur*, which had been
his flagship in the preceding campaign — two frigates, and three
fire-ships, a month later the admiral was able to join Brodrick, who
with the squadron was patrolling the French base of Toulon. In
taking over the command, he proceeded to carry out his several orders, which were "to annoy the enemy, secure Gibraltar, and pro-

---

20 Corbett, op. cit., II, 28.

21 *Parliamentary History*, XV, 935–6. In John Campbell's *Lives of the British Admirals . . .* (London, 1814) VI, 413, the statement was made that in the capture of
Louisbourg "the Navy had little or nothing to do in it." This is quite erroneous, as has
been indicated in Volume VII of the present series.

tect the trade." [22] This he was able to do in view of the fact that he now possessed thirteen ships of the line, two fifties, and twelve cruisers, as well as the fire-ships.[23] His chief immediate concern was the maintenance of a close blockade of Toulon, where Admiral de la Clue was resting with his fleet. In June two French frigates sought to slip into the port and, failing to do so, thereupon took refuge in a near-by bay protected with batteries. An unsuccessful attempt to capture them entailed severe damage to three of his ships of the line. Nevertheless, Boscawen continued at his station until about the beginning of July; then, badly in need of water, provisions, and repairs, he raised the blockade and, after proceeding directly to Salobreña in Spain for fresh supplies, moved on to Gibraltar, where he arrived early in August in order to refit.[24]

De la Clue now at last had the opportunity that he had vainly sought to leave Toulon and to carry his squadron to Brest in accordance with his orders. On August 5 with twelve ships of the line and three frigates he raised anchor and moved into the Mediterranean. Taking a course that would bring him along the Barbary Coast of Africa, by the evening of the 16th he was, according to his report, ready to sail through the Straits of Gibraltar. His ships, moving in two columns, proceeded without incident in the darkness, keeping together by means of lanterns in the sterns. By two o'clock in the morning of the 17th they had all passed by Cape Spartel, the last African headland of the Straits, and all were still together.[25] It seemed that the attempt to elude Boscawen was to succeed. But the latter had taken the precaution to station one of his cruisers off Malaga, and another, the *Gibraltar*, off Ceuta. Captain McCleverty of the latter discovered the presence of the French squadron at nightfall on the 16th and before eight o'clock in the evening, by using all the sail he could crowd, was close enough to Gibraltar to signal with his cannon an alarm to the fleet. The signal was caught by someone on the *Namur* and then relayed. But the ships were not prepared for instant action, with their sails unbent and some of them still undergoing repair, and many of the officers were ashore, including Boscawen himself, who was dining with the Governor of San Roque. The alarm, nevertheless, spread like wildfire. Sailors and

---

[22] Corbett, *op. cit.*, II, 32.
[23] Beatson, *op. cit.*, III, 235.
[24] *Ibid.*, II, 313–14.
[25] De la Clue to the Minister, December 21, 1759, Waddington, *op. cit.*, III, 361.

officers in eager confusion clambered on board whatever vessel was most handy to ready it for sea and battle action. Before ten o'clock the admiral was able to set sail with eight of his capital ships and was soon followed by Brodrick with the rest of them.[26]

Warned by the *Gibraltar's* distant gun signals that the presence of his fleet had been detected, all of de la Clue's ships might have found safety in Cádiz had the wind been more favourable. Instead of this he extinguished his lanterns after giving orders to "sail large on the starboard tack" (*la bordée au large*) in the direction of Cape St. Vincent. Great was his surprise at daybreak on the 17th to see but six of his other ships. At six o'clock, however, according to the ship's "Journal," the outlooks reported that eight vessels were to the windward. Thinking that they were the rest of his squadron, the admiral waited for them with sails lowered. Their number, however, kept increasing, so that eighteen could at last be counted.

Now painfully aware that it was the enemy that was bearing down upon him,[27] de la Clue changed direction so as to take every advantage of the wind and, giving his sails their fullest possible spread, signalled to his other ships to follow the *Océan*. But the slow movement of one of his seventy-fours, the *Souveraine*, "a heavy sailer," caused a fatal delay, which was responsible for the fact that the enemy was able at length to come up to him.[28] At half past two in the afternoon his rearmost ship, the *Centaur*, a powerful seventy-four, was attacked by the *Culloden*, a ship of equal strength; soon afterward she was under fire from both port and starboard, as were the *Guerrier*, the *Souveraine*, and his own ship, the *Océan*. Although a calm set in while Boscawen was trying to move up, he was able to bring the *Namur* into action about four o'clock, and a half-hour

---

[26] Corbett, *op. cit.*, II, 34–5. There is confusion among writers as to the date of the naval battle and the termination of the struggle at Lagos Bay. I am following de la Clue's chronology of events in this account. Dr. John Campbell in his "Memoirs of Admiral Boscawen" is so careless as to give the date of the sea engagement as August 28, the events at Lagos as August 29, and Boscawen's arrival at Spithead as September 7 (*Lives of the British Admirals*, VI, 416–17).

[27] The explanation of Boscawen's ability to follow the course of the French squadron apparently lies in the fact that the *Gibraltar*, the speedy cruiser that had brought the warning of de la Clue's approach, continued to tag the ships of the latter throughout the night and from time to time sent up rockets and fired her signal guns so as to direct the course of the British fleet (Captain Diamond's report, *Pennsylvania Gazette*, November 1, 1759).

[28] De la Clue to Comte de Maria, August 28, 1759, Entick, *op. cit.*, IV, 257–9. "*Journal de l'escadre*," Lagos, August 27, 1759, Waddington, *op. cit.*, III, 361.

later came alongside of the *Océan*. The latter had already submitted to a good deal of battering and was only an eighty, whereas
the *Namur* had not been in action and was a ninety. Nevertheless,
after receiving the *Namur's* broadside, which tilted her, she replied
with such effect that the *Namur's* mizzenmast as well as her main
and fore topsail-yards were shot away and her sails torn to shreds.
The admiral was therefore impelled to sheer off. But in doing so he
now came abreast of the stricken *Centaur*, which had been obliged
to endure the fire of four of his other ships and which at length surrendered to him. It should be added that her commander, M. Sa-
bran-Grammont, wounded in eleven places, gave up the unequal
struggle and the ship only after her hull had been pierced by eighty
shots below the water line, and her crew of eight hundred had suffered such casualties in dead and wounded that only two hundred
and ten effectives remained on board.[29]

Although seriously wounded and burdened with a heavily damaged ship, de la Clue availed himself of the opportunity afforded by
the crippling of the *Namur* to endeavour to shake off the enemy.
The other serviceable ships, when signalled, immediately broke off
the engagement and departed from the scene of action with all the
sail they could carry — leaving the *Centaur* to its fate. Boscawen,
having transferred his flag to the *Newark*, once again ordered a pursuit. This was continued the whole night, during which two of the
French ships, the *Guerrier* and the *Souveraine*, by altering their
course, made their escape and finally reached Rochefort, in France.
As a result, with the coming of dawn on the 18th, only four of the
enemy vessels were in sight, trying in vain to round Cape St. Vincent in Portugal. There was now no escape. But, rather than surrender, de la Clue ran the *Océan* into the breakers near the port of
Lagos; soon after, the *Redoutable* followed suit; the *Téméraire* and
the *Modeste*, the two remaining capital ships, sought refuge under
the guns of the fort at Lagos. But the reaching of neutral soil did
not protect any of them. Captain Kirk in the *America*, under the admiral's orders, moved upon the *Océan*, now demasted and all but
deserted; after receiving the surrender of the ship from her captain,

---

[29] *Ibid.* Additional details are also provided in an account from French sources that
appeared in the *Pennsylvania Gazette* of December 13, 1759 and that is very critical of
Admiral de la Clue. A description of the engagement from British sources is to be found
in Sir W. L. Clowes's *The Royal Navy* (London, 1897–1903), III, 212.

the Comte de Carne,[30] he set fire to her; the *Redoutable*, no longer seaworthy, and deserted by her crew, was soon afterward likewise burned by Brodrick's orders; finally, the *Téméraire* and *Modeste*, neither of which had suffered greatly in the sea fight, were boarded with little resistance from the dispirited crews, and upon surrender joined the captured *Centaur* in the British line.

The remainder of the French squadron — three of the sixty-fours, two fifties, and three frigates — by altering their course in the night of the 17th and thereby eluding the British, were able to enter Cádiz harbour on the 19th. Writing on the 28th of the month to the French Ambassador at Lisbon, Comte de Marie, de la Clue referred to this disappearance of a part of his fleet as an "unaccountable fatality" and later accused the captains of changing directions without our orders.[31] Certainly their failure to support him placed him at a fatal disadvantage. Nor were they able to make any subsequent contribution to the French cause. In fact, although enjoined to resort to Brest at the first favourable moment, their one thought seems to have been to return to Toulon in safety.[32] For months, however, they were so closely watched by Brodrick that this was not possible. In fact, only after a severe storm had compelled the British squadron to go to Gibraltar to refit were they able to slip out and, fortu-

---

[30] Boscawen to Cleveland, August 20, 1759, *London Gazette Extraordinary*, September 7, 1759. The wounded de la Clue had before this been transferred to shore (Beatson, *op. cit.*, II, 317). Beatson, generally very accurate, mistakenly declared that he died at Lagos; he not only recovered from his wounds but in 1764 was awarded the rank of lieutenant general (Waddington, *op. cit.*, III, 364).

[31] De la Clue to Comte de Marie, August 28, 1759, Entick, *op. cit.*, IV, 257–8; Waddington, *op. cit.*, III, 363. According to purported testimony of ten French officers who remained with de la Clue and who arrived in Cádiz from Lagos shortly after the engagement there, the admiral after passing the Straits had opened his sealed instructions and discovered that he was ordered to proceed with seven ships of the line and three frigates directly to Rochefort, and that the rest of his squadron was to make for Cádiz (advice from Cádiz, August 22, *Pennsylvania Gazette*, December 6, 1759). This would seem to imply that de la Clue was powerless to use his discretion, and conflicts with his statement in the letter quoted above.

[32] It may be noted that at the time the French ships took refuge in Cádiz harbour, twenty-one sail of Spanish warships were at anchor there preparing to go to Naples in order to bring the new King Charles to Spain. It was reported that the French captains applied to the Spanish admiral to take them under convoy through the Straits, to which he replied that he could not protect them should they meet the British fleet; as a result, they determined to await a better opportunity to leave the port (Advices brought by Captain Diamond, who at the time was in Cádiz harbour, *Pennsylvania Gazette*, November 1, 1759).

nately, unobserved by the enemy, to return to the Mediterranean and to Toulon, where they proceeded to pay off their crews and dismantle their ships.[33]

Thus ended de la Clue's futile attempt to carry his ships to Brest; thus ended also at the high tide of achievement Boscawen's command of the Mediterranean squadron.[34] Following his latest instructions he turned it over to Brodrick as soon as the repairs could be made to the damaged vessels, and set sail for England with seven of his ships of the line, the three French prizes, and some smaller vessels with which to strengthen the home fleet.[35]

Despite the disaster that had befallen de la Clue's squadron and the bombardment of Le Havre by Rodney, with the subsequent movement of the flat-bottomed boats up the Seine to Rouen, the French persisted in their plans to invade England. Nor were the English less disposed to resist such an attempt when a letter purporting to have been written by the Duc de Belle-Isle to the Prince of Soubise appeared in translation in the press. According to it, the Maréchal, in tendering advice to the commander of the expedition in the name of the King, recommended that Soubise follow

> "the Example of William of Normandy, a Vassal of France, who having conquered England, forced them to part with their Freedom and estates; which as I hope your Highness will have the Glory of doing, under his Majesty's Authority, he distributed among his faithful Followers."

Moreover, in his treatment of the English and their property, the Prince was further recommended, in view of "the Perfidy of those *Islanders*, and their implacable Disposition toward our Nation," to take the great Turenne as his model, who proceeded in his Palatinate campaign "indiscriminately with Fire and Sword against the Enemies of France, because none, who are so, can be innocent."

---

[33] Corbett, *op. cit.*, II, 87–8.

[34] Soon after Boscawen's return to England he was appointed General of the Marine Forces with a salary of £2,000 a year, and continued in this service until his death some two years later (Beatson, *op. cit.*, II, 414–19).

[35] On June 29 secret orders were issued to Boscawen that in case the French squadron got out of the Straits and was bound for any Atlantic port, he was to return to England with a portion of his fleet. After waiting for two days off Cape St. Vincent — where he took station as soon as the French ships at or near Lagos had been disposed of — and finding no sign of the remainder of de la Clue's fleet, he judged that these ships had been able to get into the Atlantic and acted accordingly (Corbett, *op. cit.*, II, 33, 39).

Even complaints of the conquered were therefore to be severely punished; although the King, to show his clemency toward those who had not actually acted in a hostile manner, had willed that such offenders should be reserved "for his Gallies," if able-bodied. Finally, he was admonished that as hunger was the readiest way to bring a people into subjection he was — after securing ample supplies for his army and in order to bring on a famine — to spread a veritable desolation over the country "without regard to the Properties of such of the Inhabitants as shall profess themselves to be the most attached to your Interest." [36] One may add that whether this published letter was authentic — something that I have not been able to determine — it laid down a line of action that was thoroughly realistic, nothing short of which would doubtless have broken the spirit of a proud and free people. If nothing more than a bit of British propaganda designed to stir up the people, which would seem likely, it fully served that purpose.[37]

But the British were far better prepared and far more determined to resist to the bitter end than their enemies anticipated. As has already been noted, they did not propose to await the unfolding of events. Hawke was cruising off Brest with a powerful battle fleet that desired nothing so much as to bring Conflans there into decisive action. In order to watch more clearly every movement of the enemy and yet at the same time to guard against contingencies, he divided his fleet into two squadrons — a small one for close reconnoitring work under Commodore the Hon. Augustus Hervey, and the main one, embracing his own flagship and that of his second in command, Sir Charles Hardy, as well as all the other most powerful ships, which took station off Ushant to the west of Brest in bad weather, and in good weather much closer to the great French naval base. The strain on men and ships of a prolonged blockade was very great in the days of the sailing vessel. Relief had to be supplied from time to time as the weeks wore on. In June the admiral had under his command some twenty-five ships of the line, which for battle purposes were to operate in three divisions and were supported by frigates and fire-ships.[38] Between that month and the mid-

---

[36] "The exact Translation of a Letter from the Maréchal Duc de Belle-Isle, to the Prince of Soubise, upon the intended Conquest of England," *Westminster Journal*, September 8, 1759.

[37] For a so-called letter of Conflans actually written by a British naval officer serving on the *Torbay*, see Burrow's *Life of Hawke*, p. 412; see also Corbett, *op. cit.*, II, 56.

[38] For a list of Hawke's ships in June 1759 see Beatson, *op. cit.*, III, 239–40.

dle of November he also received reinforcements, among which was the squadron brought home by Boscawen. Confident of victory, he used various methods in vain in the course of the summer to lure Conflans out of his safe harbour. In line with this policy Hervey even exposed some of his ships of the inner squadron to the danger of capture.[39]

In August, with no sign of activity on the part of Conflans, Hawke became concerned lest the French, by pinning down his fleet before Brest, could be free to concentrate their troops and transports to the southward at suitable points along the Bay of Biscay, such as Nantes, and then, with what naval support could be gathered, head for the British Isles without warning or interference. To anticipate this danger, a third or southern squadron now came into existence. Although some sixty vessels from Nantes and Bordeaux succeeded in slipping into Quiberon Bay in the direction of Brest in order to take on troops and supplies, Robert Duff, now acting as Commodore of the Southern Squadron, settled down to watch them and also the activities at near-by L'Orient. In anticipation that M. de Bompar, returning from the West Indies, would try to enter one of the ports still farther to the south, Hawke organized a fourth squadron made up of seven ships of the line under Francis Geary to move down the Bay of Bascay as far as Rochefort to wait for him. But this was disapproved by the Admiralty, which directed him to give his chief attention to Brest and Quiberon Bay.[40] In fact, Bompar was destined early in November not to move into Rochefort but to join Conflans at Brest.

As for the preparations at Brest, Conflans faced the greatest difficulty in manning his ships. But his superior Berryer could not aid him. Writing in July to the admiral, he declared regretfully:

> "With the exception of some fishermen, aged people or children mostly and the feeble from the crews of coast craft, all the sea people of the kingdom are actually employed in the King's service." [41]

This was not the only discouragement he had to face. The middle of September he received orders to form a division of six ships of the line under Bigot de Morogues and send it down to the Morbihan in

---

[39] *Ibid.*, II, 325–6.
[40] Corbett, *op. cit.*, II, 29, 43–4.
[41] Berryer to Conflans, July 11, 1759, Waddington, *op. cit.*, III, 367; the letter is misdated as printed.

Quiberon Bay, where the Duc d'Aiguillon was waiting with his troops to be convoyed to his objective, the Clyde. Although this division of the fleet seemed very dangerous to Conflans, he was compelled to yield. Nevertheless, his judgment was vindicated when Morogues attempted to fulfil his mission. For the latter was soon driven back into Brest by Hervey. Therefore, on October 14 the full responsibility of going out with his whole fleet to break the blockade and of escorting the Morbihan flotilla was placed on the admiral's shoulders by the King, with the injunction that the safety of the flotilla was a matter of primary consideration.[42] Although Hawke at this juncture was driven off Ushant by a hard storm and forced to proceed to Plymouth, yet Conflans did not move out. He still needed additional sailors and stores for his ships, and especially provisions — the storeships containing the latter had been driven by British cruisers into a port a hundred miles away.

Although the grand fleet was not destined to sail from Brest until the middle of November in order to participate in the invasion of Great Britain, it is of interest to note that the great storm in the middle of October that drove Hawke from Ushant into Plymouth also drove Commodore Boys from his station off Dunkirk and afforded an opportunity to the dashing privateersman M. François Thurot to move out of that port on the 15th. The latter now had a commission from the King to command three frigates and three corvettes upon which were embarked some twelve hundred men under Brigadier General Flobert to be used for a descent upon Ireland — a movement that was an integral part of the broad plan for the conquest of the British Isles.[43] But before turning to the history of the almost fantastic adventures of this little squadron, it is desirable to continue our account of the movements of Conflans that were to end in irretrievable disaster and the shattering of French naval power.

October passed into November and the sea became ever more boisterous, and with it came an increasing wear and fatigue to both ships and men that formed the blockading force before the great French naval base. It seemed clear that before long Hawke would have to withdraw. Conflans may well have calculated on this event and the freedom of movement that he would enjoy as a result. In

---

[42] For the King's orders of October 14, 1759, see Lacour-Gayet, *Marine sous Louis XV*, Chap. XX.

[43] Waddington, *op. cit.*, III, 377. A Mr. Wallace, writing to John Cleveland of the Admiralty on November 20, 1759, stated that Thurot started his expedition with seven vessels (B.M., Add. Mss. 32900, f. 78).

fact, Hervey's ship, the *Monmouth*, became so foul and leaky that the commodore was obliged to give up his advanced station and withdraw to England. Hawke likewise early in November was again driven off Ushant by a series of storms and on the 9th took shelter at Torbay. His disappearance at the time luckily gave Bompar, who at last was nearing Brest with his West India squadron, the chance to enter it without the slightest interference.[44]

Under the above combination of favouring circumstances Conflans could not afford to hesitate a moment longer. It is true that Bompar's ships would not again be fit for service until they had been cleaned and refitted; nevertheless, his sailors were available to meet one of the admiral's most pressing needs. Therefore on November 14 the latter, at long last, moved out of Brest with what was now doubtless the most powerful fleet — at least in appearance and on paper — which up to that date was ever sent by France into the Atlantic. Indeed, despite the absence of de la Clue's squadron, it possessed a fire-power that far surpassed any other hitherto assembled under the ensign of a French admiral and therefore carried with it the hopes of France in these days of gloom and repeated reverses. As fate would have it, Hawke left Torbay that very day and on the 16th received the news from a British supply ship that Conflans had been seen to the west of the island of Belle-Île-en-Mer and was headed eastward, undoubtedly for Quiberon Bay and the Morbihan shore.[45] This was true.

Feeling that now, if ever, was the time — with Hawke absent from his Ushant vigil — to crush Commodore Duff's squadron still hovering about the Morbihan and thus free Aiguillon and his army to carry out their amphibious operation in Scotland, Conflans had proceeded down the Bay of Biscay. Although time was of the essence, he was compelled on the 17th, by the force of adverse winds, to make a wide sweep out into the open sea and as a consequence found himself becalmed on the 19th still far, it seemed, from his objective. The next day, however, he discovered at a distance the sails of Duff's squadron and gave chase. When about to overtake it, his outlooks signalled that from another quarter they detected the presence of twenty-three ships of the line, some of which appeared to have three decks. At first the astounded admiral could not believe it. He then came to the startling realization that, instead of having

[44] Beatson, *op. cit.*, II, 326–7.
[45] Corbett, *op. cit.*, II, 52–3.

only a weak squadron to deal with, he was, despite all his calculations, face to face with Hawke's main fleet.[46]

Hawke, after receiving the warning, had sailed all night long with
a full spread of canvas despite the fact that his fleet was battling a
violent wind — so eager were he and his men to come in contact
with the French, now that they had finally left their protecting
shore batteries.[47] What is more, he was followed at a distance in his
pursuit of Conflans by Admiral Geary from Plymouth with three of
the line and by Sir Charles Saunders in the *Somerset*, accompanied
by the *Devonshire* and the *Vanguard*, returning with these ships
from the St. Lawrence after the capture of Quebec.[48] Although neither of these commanders was able to join Hawke by the 20th, he
possessed without them a fighting force of tremendous power when
he bore down upon the French fleet. In addition to his twenty-
three ships of the line, carrying from one hundred to sixty guns, he
had four fifties and six cruisers, as against twenty-one French ships
of the line of from eighty to sixty-four guns, and four smaller vessels.[49] In view of the fact that the French eighty-gun ships had a
complement of from 1,200 to 1,000 men and the sixty-fours had 750,
as against 880 men on the *Royal George*, Hawke's flagship and the
only one-hundred-gun ship, and but 420 on the British sixty-gun
ships, there was, theoretically, little advantage on either side.

Indeed, had the French fleet enjoyed full freedom of action and
the benefit of a personnel that possessed the capacity, the experience with sea fighting, and the morale that characterized its opponent from top to bottom, history would doubtless have recorded —
in view of the tremendous stakes involved for the two nations in the
outcome of the conflict — one of the greatest sea battles ever waged
by sailing ships. But the aging Conflans, as Waddington has stressed,
did not have some of the essentials of a great commander: he had
neither a fighting heart nor the high competence with which to meet

[46] *Ibid.*, II, 57–61. "*Rapport de Conflans,*" November 24, 1759, Waddington,
op. cit., III, 369.

[47] Hawke to the Admiralty, November 17, 1759, *ibid.*, III, 370.

[48] Corbett, *op. cit.*, II, 55.

[49] Beatson, *op. cit.*, III, 244–6. The French *Hebé*, a forty-gun frigate, though a part
of Conflans's fleet, was not present during the engagement and is therefore not counted.

Newcastle, when the news reached England of Hawke's pursuit of Conflans, in writing to Rigby indicated — a view that must have been held by most people in the government — that the British admiral, supported by Geary's ships and Duff's squadron,
would command "a force sufficient to blow Mr. Conflans, & His 21 Ships of the Line
out of the sea" (B.M., Add. Mss. 32899, ff. 113–18).

the emergency that faced him. He had already, it seems quite clear
— in spite of some statements that he made to the contrary — determined to avoid a decisive engagement with Hawke, overestimating
as he did the Englishman's actual strength.[50] Neither were his chief
officers — brave men as some of them proved themselves to be when
put to the ordeal — any match for their British opponents, having
had little recent experience or possessing little expertness in navigation and naval action and little understanding of both the qualities and the defects of the ships they were called upon to command.
Nor were his crews — recruited to a great extent from agricultural
workers and coast guards — skilled either in the handling of the
great ships or in gunnery.[51]

Such was the situation when Hawke's flagship, the *Royal George*,
and seven other ships constituting the British van bore down upon
the French about nine o'clock of the morning of the 20th after the
British admiral had given orders to form in line of battle and to attempt to hold Conflans until the arrival of the rest of the fleet. But
the Frenchman, in view of a resolution already formed not to risk
his ships in a fight with the main British squadron, departed for the
Morbihan shore with a full spread of sail and with Hawke in hot
pursuit. The sea was very high; there were squalls and every indication of the brewing of a great storm. About a half hour after two
o'clock the British van was close enough to the enemy — now south
of Belle-Île sailing in one line eastward — to begin firing on his rearmost ship.[52]

In bearing down upon the Morbihan shore the two fleets entered
an expanse of dangerous reefs. Conflans's great ship, the *Soleil Royal*,
sailing at the head of the line, pushed beyond the great rocks called
the Cardinals and through the narrow entrance into Quiberon Bay
and was followed by the rest of the ships of the van and centre. But
the rear ships, moving without formation, soon found themselves,
when at the very entrance to it, heavily beset by Howe, Keppel,
and others in the British van. Hearing the firing, the French admiral attempted to re-form his ships within the bay and come out to
their assistance; but this ended in the greatest confusion. In the

50 Conflans to Aiguillon, November 10, 1759, Waddington, *op. cit.*, III, 368.

51 *Ibid.*, II, 369; Lacour-Gayot, *Marine sous Louis XV*, p. 329.

52 Hawke to Cleveland, November 24, 1759, Beatson, *op. cit.*, II, 334–8; "Rapport
de Conflans," Waddington, *op. cit.*, III, 370–1.

words of an officer of the *Inflexible*, another ship in the van that had followed the *Soliel Royal* into the bay:

> "There was frightful disorder when the vanguard of which I was a part was desired to heave to [that is, to go about]; for some of the ships could not possibly do it; we were, as it were, in a veritable funnel all mixed up with rocks on one side and ships on the other. As a result we anchored." [53]

Left to their own fate the French rear guard fought back desperately, The *Formidable*, carrying the flag of Rear Admiral Saint-André du Verger, was almost battered to pieces and struck only after both the rear admiral and his brother, the second in command, had succumbed; the *Héros*, completely demasted, was impelled to do likewise; [54] and the *Juste*, after having lost both of her commanding officers, in attempting to escape, sank at the mouth of the Loire. The *Magnifique*, under Captain Bigot de Morogues, alone of the rear guard did not apparently get deeply involved in the fighting and thus managed to regain the high seas again and reach the security of Rochefort.[55] But disaster was not limited to the rear-guard ships of the line. The *Thésée* and the *Superbe* — both of the centre and well within the bay — caught by surprise by a heavy squall with port-holes open, sank beneath the waters, carrying with them their crews, only a handful of whom were rescued.

With darkness intervening and in the face of an adverse wind that carried his vessels toward the reefs of the dangerous shore, Hawke wisely ordered all of his vessels to cast anchor where they were. During the darkness, with the British thus at rest, some eight of the French ships within the bay, among them Beaufremont's *Tonnant*, managed to slip out of it and even succeeded in joining de Morogues's ship at Rochefort. Thereupon, after being relieved of their heavy guns, they mounted the Charente River, and thus were beyond Hawke's grasp. As for Conflans's flagship, it was discovered very early the next morning that in the darkness and the storm she had unknowingly cast anchor in the very midst of Hawke's ships. Slipping out of this dangerous position the admiral sought to gain the protection of the batteries in near-by Croisic to the east, but, un-

---

[53] "*Lettre d'un officier*," *ibid.*, III, 371.

[54] By reason of the heavy sea, Howe in the *Magnanime* could not take possession of the *Héros* before she was beached by her captain.

[55] *Ibid.*, III, 371–2.

happily, the *Soleil Royal* grounded on the shoals near where the *Héros* had stranded late the preceding day. The remainder of the fleet within the bay succeeded on the 21st, despite the bad weather, in entering the Vilaine River, which flows into the bay, but only, it may be added, by throwing overboard their heavy impedimenta in order to cross the shallow bar at its mouth. With the dawning of the 22nd the weather had so moderated that Hawke was able to take further action. In the shallows to the southeast of him were, as indicated, the two stranded French warships, and he ordered Duff to take his vessels of light displacement and destroy them. As for the *Soleil Royal*, Conflans saved him that exertion; for upon Duff's approach the French admiral ordered his own sailers to set fire to the noble but now deserted ship.[56]

Thus ended the dream of the French conquest of England — with the great Brest fleet a thing of the past. One of Conflans's ships had been captured; three of them had foundered and sunk; two had been destroyed by fire after being beached; a part of the rest had fled up the Vilaine and the remainder up the Charente, having, with the jettisoning of their armament, lost, in common with those on the Vilaine, their character, for the time being, of fighting ships. A French witness to this humiliating disaster explained the reason for it succinctly in the following words:

"Imbecility, ineptitude, blundering, ignorance of manœuvring and of all sea tactics are the exclusive causes of our loss." [57]

It is now incumbent upon us to trace the movements of the little squadron that under the command of François Thurot issued from Dunkirk in the middle of October and thereupon disappeared into the North Sea. As previously indicated, the project of the French invasion of the British Isles also envisioned the plan to enlist the military support of friendly Sweden. It is therefore not without interest that Thurot should first of all resort to the shore of that country, doubtless hoping to receive aid. Whatever hopes he may have had to that end were not destined to be realized outside of the securing of needed stores. In fact, the only noteworthy thing that occurred while he was anchored in the harbour of Gothenburg (Göteborg) was the development of a sharp conflict between him and

---

[56] Hawke to Cleveland, November 24, 1759, Beatson, *op. cit.*, II, 334–8; Waddington, *op. cit.*, III, 373.

[57] "Correspondance de Vannes," November 24, 1759, *ibid.*, III, 373; Admiralty Office to Newcastle, November 30, 1759, B.M., Add. Mss. 32899, ff. 85–9.

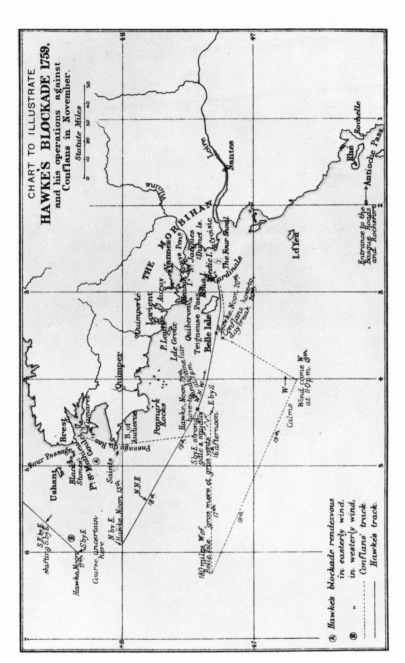

Hawke's blockade of Brest and his operations against Conflans in November 1759.

(From J. S. Corbett: *England in the Seven Years' War*, with the permission of Longmans, Green & Co.)

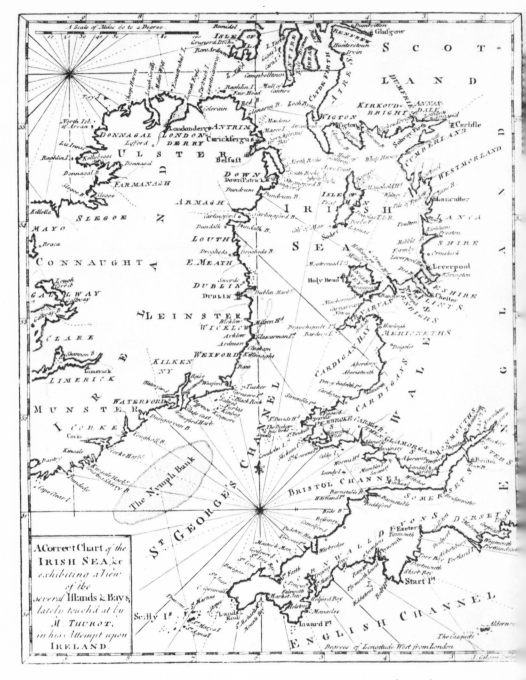

"A Correct Chart of the Irish Sea . . ." to illustrate M. Thurot's attempt up[on] Ireland.

(From the *Gentleman's Magazine*, 17[...])

his subordinates. Authoritarian in nature, violent in temper when crossed, daring to the point of bravado, and determined in purpose, he would not bend before those who questioned the soundness of his ideas and therefore who hesitated to act in accordance with them.[58] From Gothenburg the little flotilla moved up to Bergen in Norway on November 17 and in doing so had to face a terrible storm that so damaged one of the best of the vessels, the *Begon*, that she was obliged to return to France. After the others had been repaired at the Norwegian port, they proceeded to the Faroes, arriving there December 28. By this time the squadron had been reduced to four ships.[59]

Still Thurot would invade Ireland — despite the bitter opposition of the captains of two of his remaining vessels, the *Blonde* and the *Amaranth*. On January 25 he and his men got their first view of the northern Irish coast and of the town of Londonderry, which he expected to seize. But another great storm broke upon his ships, which were thereupon separated. The captain of the *Blonde*, in order to save her, was obliged to throw overboard some of her larger guns; while the captain of the *Amaranth*, disgusted with the enterprise, seized the opportunity to head for France and, in the face of great hardships and the necessity of fleeing frequently from enemy pursuers, at length arrived in great distress at Saint-Malo.

Now with only three small ships, Thurot still persisted in attempting to accomplish what he had been ordered to do. In vain the captains of the *Blonde* and the *Terpsichore* pleaded with him to give up the mad enterprise and to return to France. Instead, he now sailed for the island of Islay, off the coast of Scotland, where his men were restored to health with fresh meat and his flagship, the *Maréchal de Belle-Isle*, which was drawing too much water, was brought to a heel, and the other two ships repaired. While there, he seems to have happily impressed the inhabitants of the islands by his uniform courtesy, correctness of behaviour, and even generosity.[60] Although while at Islay he learned of the fate of Conflans's fleet, he did not alter his plans. Even if left alone, he would still strike a blow for the honour of France.

---

[58] Waddington, *op. cit.*, III, 377.

[59] Mr. Wallace at Bergen to Cleveland of the Admiralty, November 20, 1759, B.M., Add. Mss. 32900, f. 78; Beatson, *op. cit.*, II, 408–9.

[60] *Ibid.*, II, 409–11; "Deposition of Lieut. Malcolm Campbell," February 20, 1760, B.M., Add. Mss. 32902, ff. 320–3.

Leaving Islay on February 19, the three ships appeared the following day in Carrickfergus Bay — toward the head of Belfast Lough — where Thurot, abiding in his resolve, proceeded to land his soldiers and sailors, to the number of one thousand men, some two and a half miles from the town of Carrickfergus. As Brigadier Flobert moved upon it he met with some resistance from a small body of regulars and militia that Lieutenant Colonel Jennings, in charge of the castle there, had assembled. Forced to give up the gates of the town, Jennings retreated with his force to the half-ruined castle, which he succeeded in holding until Flobert brought up two pieces of artillery and began to batter the dilapidated structure. With his own ammunition exhausted, Jennings thereupon surrendered.[61]

Although in this action Brigadier Flobert and many others were seriously wounded and still others were killed, it had ended in an initial success. Thurot, now master of an Irish town, proceeded to levy upon it. He also succeeded in capturing two vessels going down the bay to Belfast loaded with flour and herrings, and even, on demand, secured food supplies from the Belfast authorities, who were in some little panic.[62] But when he sought to extend his conquest to Belfast, the wounded Flobert categorically refused to give him any further assistance from the soldiers.[63] Realizing that he had now gone as far as he possibly could with the trifling resources at his command — especially in view of the fact that he and his men had not been received in Ireland with open arms, as he doubtless felt they might be — he set sail for France on the 26th. It was high time.

When the news of the French landing was carried to Dublin, the Duke of Bedford, Lord Lieutenant of Ireland, took steps to march a strong body of horse and foot under command of the Earl of Rothes against the invaders; [64] he also sent expresses to all the leading seaports of the island to warn the captains of warships that might be there of the presence of the French ships. The news reached Kinsale in southern Ireland on the 24th. Resting in the harbour at the time were three frigates: the *Æolus*, Captain Elliot, the *Pallas*, Captain Clements, and the *Brilliant*, Captain Logie. With-

[61] B.M., Add. Mss. 32903, f. 39, for the terms of surrender; see also Major General Strode to Bedford, Belfast, February 22, and Bedford to Pitt, March 2, 1760, *Correspondence of the Duke of Bedford* (London, 1843), II, 408, 410–11.

[62] *Ibid.*, and Corbett, *op. cit.*, II, 89–90; B.M., Add. Mss. 32902, ff. 364–6.

[63] Waddington, *op. cit.*, III, 378.

[64] Bedford to Rothes, February 25, 1760, *Bedford Correspondence*, II, 407.

out waiting for orders, the three vessels immediately cleared and moved at full speed up St. George's Channel and into the Irish Sea. When off Dublin on the 26th, Elliot sent word to Bedford that he was moving up the coast to Carrickfergus in order to meet Thurot. Arriving at the entrance of the bay that very evening, he could not get into it because of a contrary wind. Thurot, however, had by this time already left and was, in fact, proceeding through the Irish Sea toward France, having left behind at Carrickfergus his wounded, among them Flobert.

Thurot sailed without incident until very early the morning of the 28th, when near the Isle of Man his ships were detected by Elliot, who gave chase. By nine o'clock the latter was alongside Thurot's flagship, and the action, once begun, became general and lasted for an hour and a half. The *Æolus*, of thirty-two guns and 220 men, was now pitted against the *Maréchal de Belle-Isle*, of forty-four guns and 545 men (including troops on board), according to Elliot's report.[65] The fight was indecisive until one of the other British ships joined in the fray. Only when his ship had four feet of water in her hold and her decks covered with ninety men killed or wounded did Thurot give orders for her to strike her colours. Unfortunately, the intrepid commodore, before this could be done and before the firing ceased, was killed. As to the remaining French vessels, though they sought safety in flight, the manœuvring of them was so bad that they were soon overhauled and, after a feeble resistance, also surrendered.[66] Thus ended the final phase of the grandiose project of the government of France to bring about the conquest of the British Isles.

The events described in this chapter, however, cannot be considered in isolation. They were closely related to developments in the New World, with which the preceding volume has been concerned, and also to those in the heart of Europe, in the West Indies, and in the Far East. We must therefore now turn our attention to these other areas in order to secure a proper comprehension of the vast implications that the failure of France to overwhelm the British in the course of the Great War for the Empire was to have for the future of the world.

---

[65] Elliot to Bedford, February 29, 1760, Beatson, op. cit., II, 413.
[66] Ibid., and Waddington, op. cit., III, 378–9.

CHAPTER II

Britain's Continental Commitments, 1759-60

THE PRECEDING CHAPTER has been concerned with a phase of the Great War for the Empire — the history of the French attempt to conquer the British Isles in 1759 — that has not been greatly stressed by most historians but that certainly has a direct, not to say important, bearing upon the course and outcome of other phases of that war, being waged as it was simultaneously on many fronts in widely separated parts of the world. For example, the British successes in 1759 in North America — already described at some length in Volume VII of this series — to a considerable extent were due to the fact that French designs against Great Britain, as well as home-defence needs undoubtedly limited the amount of available resources that could be devoted to the protection of Canada, without respect to the logistical problem of getting such resources across the Atlantic and up the St. Lawrence. What was true of Canada and its needs was equally true of other geographical areas where France had developed great interests which likewise were in need of protection from British attack, as will be noted in the progress of the present volume. Before turning to these developments, however, it is desirable to give our immediate attention to the unfolding of events in Germany. In doing so, a point earlier emphasized in this series must again be stressed: in the minds of contemporary statesmen the Anglo-French maritime and overseas war on the one hand, and the German war on the other, were two very distinct wars and yet, as the result of treaties of alliance, were closely intertwined. The outcome of one would likely, as a result, affect that of the other. Therefore the future of North America, with all that this might imply in terms of the future of the English-speaking peoples in the New World, would, in spite of the surrender of Canada by Governor General Vaudreuil and its military occupation by Major General Amherst in the fall of 1760, necessarily be to a great extent ultimately determined by the outcome of the issues at stake in Europe and elsewhere beyond the western hemisphere. To a consideration of these we shall therefore now turn.

Just as in the First and Second World Wars of the twentieth century the United States felt impelled to subsidize its associates and allies in Europe, so Great Britain in the Continental war of 1756–63 was obliged to perform that essential service. In each instance both the government of the United States and that of Great Britain, before making large European commitments, had been strongly isolationist in sentiment, which attitude gave way only in the face of what seemed to be hard facts involving the national welfare that could not easily be ignored. Indeed, Woodrow Wilson up to 1917 was not more reluctant than was William Pitt up to 1758 to throw the strength of his nation into the Continental balance; and yet, once this was done, both Wilson and Pitt became veritable symbols, as it were, of a policy of firm co-operation with the nation's associates or its allies both in the waging of the war and in the conclusion of hostilities.

As has already been noted in Volume VI of this series,[1] during the early months of the year 1758 up to May, Parliament, under the dynamic leadership of Pitt, was led to make a series of grants, amounting to over £1,800,000, to support the war in Germany in bolstering the armed forces of Prussia, Hanover, Hesse-Cassel, Brunswick, and Saxe-Gotha; on June 8 £800,000 was also voted, out of which the extraordinary contingencies of the Hanoverians and Hessians could be met;[2] and finally, on December 18 and 19 of that same year, almost £2,000,000 was voted for the next year's campaign in the Continental war.[3] Between November 27, 1759 and April 29, 1760 the appropriations to support it amounted to over £3,250,000,[4] and from November 29, 1760 to March 7, 1761 they

---

[1] See Chapter V of Volume VI.

[2] *Annual Register . . . of the Year 1758* (London, 1761), p. 131; C. W. Eldon, *England's Subsidy Policy toward the Continent during the Seven Years' War* (Philadelphia, 1938), pp. 108–11.

[3] *Annual Register*, 1759, pp. 172–3.

[4] *Annual Register*, 1760, pp. 182–9.

reached over £3,750,000.[5] Of the total of the £10,800,000 specifically made available to this end, hard-pressed Prussia received four grants each of £670,000, or an aggregate of £2,680,000.[6]

All this, it must be emphasized, took place during Pitt's tenure of office as chief minister and in face of his earlier record of bitter opposition to British Continental alliances and their subsidization. Not only was this true, but the Great Commoner went further than had his predecessors in office in assuring the country's European allies that his interest in a peace advantageous to them would be placed, if need be, even above the interests of the British Empire. On December 6, 1758, when a motion of thanks to Major General Jeffrey Amherst and Vice Admiral Edward Boscawen for the capture of the great fortress of Louisbourg and the conquest of Cape Breton Island was before the House of Commons, he took occasion, according to Horace Walpole, to announce that "it was too early to decide on what we would or would not restore." He then went on to state:

> "The Duke of Marlborough [in the War of the Spanish Succession] had acquired superiority; the peace of Utrecht gave it away. And then (whether equity or flattery dictated the declaration) he [Pitt] protested, that at the peace he would not give up an iota of our Allies for any British consideration." [7]

In view of this pledge, it is clear that Pitt had definitely linked the fortunes of the British Empire with those of Britain's Continental allies. This portentous commitment would not be forgotten in the years to come and was undoubtedly to have an important influence upon the minister's political career.

---

[5] *Annual Register*, 1762, pp. 151–8.

[6] The student will note that in the Appendix to Eldon's volume (*op. cit.*, pp. 161–2) the totals given as subsidy payments during the above four years do not nearly equal the sums presented in the *Annual Register* as appropriated for the German war. The explanation, of course, lies in the fact that much money, over and beyond the subsidies, was spent in the support of the British contingents on the Continent which was not treated as a subsidy. In fact, it is far from clear that the sum of £10,800,000 definitely appropriated to support the Seven Years' War was all that found its way to the direct support of the Continental conflict, since much money was appropriated during these years to the general war effort.

[7] Horace Walpole, *Memoirs of the Reign of King George the Second* (London, 1846), III, 150. The Prussian embassy reported from London on December 8 that Pitt had declared that "he would not sacrifice any fraction of the interests of the allies to secure a peace in favor of British claims" (Albert von Ruville, *William Pitt, Earl of Chatham* [trans. H. J. Chaytor, London, 1907], II, 219).

"Bataille de Minden."   (From Jomini: *Guerres de Frederich*)

"A Compleat Map of Germany comprehending in one View the

Seats of the Present War, 1759." (From the *Gentleman's Magazine*, 1759)

As was emphasized in the preceding volume, the subsidy granted by Parliament in the early part of 1758 not only aided Frederick to equip his forces and thereby, as the result of his astonishing military achievements during the summer campaign of that year, to ward off the thrusts of the armies of Austria, Russia, the Empire, and Sweden which assailed him in every quarter. It also made it possible for Prince Ferdinand, commander-in-chief of the Army of Observation, to pursue back across the lower Rhine the demoralized French army that under the Comte de Clermont had occupied Hanover and to strike it at Crefeld before he was obliged to retire in order to cover Hesse-Cassel and Hanover from the threatening moves of the French southern army under the Prince of Soubise. As the year came to a close, in Germany there was not the slightest disposition in evidence on the part of any of the belligerents to seek peace.

The balance sheet showed that in the west of Germany the French still occupied the Duchy of Cleves and other possessions of the King of Prussia on the Rhine, and that in the east the Russians remained in possession of the Kingdom of Prussia proper, which they had earlier overrun. Frederick, nevertheless, still controlled Silesia, wrested from the Empress of Austria in 1740, and Saxony, seized from the King of Poland in 1756, and the resources of these countries more than made up for his losses. As the new year dawned, he was still faced by the same powerful coalition against which he had successfully contended in the campaigns of 1758. But his superb army during the past three years of fighting had been sadly depleted of its veterans, both officers and troops of the line. Moreover, his once bountiful treasury was all but a thing of the past and to keep his forces in the field he was now compelled to rely largely on the British subsidy, on heavy contributions that he exacted from such states as Saxony and Mecklenburg, and on the systematic plunder of other hostile states.

With his resources thus limited and strained, Frederick therefore was obliged in the ensuing campaign, in order to save himself from irretrievable disaster, to use much more caution than he had previously displayed, to act in the main on the defensive, and, when he took the offensive, to concentrate in so far as possible on limited objectives. To keep the Russians from taking the field at an early date in 1759, he ordered a force from Silesia to march late in February into Poland to destroy the magazines of immense supplies that the

Russians had established at Posen and elsewhere to supply the Czarina's troops. This was fully accomplished. Further, to check the movement of the Austrians against him, the King — after leading Count Daun to centre his attention upon Silesia — ordered his brother, Prince Henry, in April to move from Saxony southward into Bohemia on the same sort of mission of magazine destruction, which was equally successful. Then in May the Prince, to discourage the Imperial army cantoned in Franconia, southwest of Saxony, from attempting to join forces with Daun, turned upon it and with its retreat to Nuremberg gathered a vast quantity of booty in the plunder of the bishopric of Bamberg and other places.[8] It was not until August, in fact, that the King himself took the field. But before dealing with this campaign it is desirable to consider developments in western Germany.

Early in the year the French general, the Prince of Soubise, by means of a stratagem that involved perfidy, succeeded in surprising and gaining possession of the free, neutral, German city of Frankfurt am Main. This gave the enemy a great advantage by placing the control of the Main as well as the Rhine in their hands, thus opening up an unobstructed communication and permitting them thereby to pivot their armies on that city either in threatening Hesse-Cassel or Hanover to the northeast or in co-operating with the army of the Imperials in Franconia to the southeast. In fact, the danger was now so great to the allied cause that Prince Ferdinand felt that it was absolutely necessary to make an effort to dislodge the French from this strategic centre. In April, with some thirty thousand picked troops, he moved in that direction and was confronted by a mixed army of French and Germans under the Duc de Broglie at Bergen, northeast of Frankfurt. There on the morning of the 13th a great effort was made to dislodge the enemy, but without success.[9] It was necessary, therefore, for the Prince not only to leave Frankfurt in their hands but also to extricate his army from a difficult situation. This was done the following night after a sustained bombardment

---

[8] Œuvres Posthumes de Frédéric II, Roi de Prusse (Berlin, 1789), III, 6–7; John Entick, The General History of the Late War (London, 1765), III, 454–9; Annual Register, 1759 (London, 1760), pp. 9–10.

[9] In this effort to gain possession of Bergen the British troops involved showed great valor, according to the author of The Case of the British Troops serving in Germany . . . (London, 1761), pp. 18–21. For an excellent account of the Battle of Bergen see Richard Waddington, La Guerre de Sept Ans (Paris, n.d.), III, 5–17.

of Broglie's lines and the shifting of troops as though preparing for a renewed attack.[10]

Brilliantly successful as was Ferdinand's retreat, it was nevertheless a withdrawal to his defensive lines. Even these did not hold when the French army on the lower Rhine under Contades and that on the upper Rhine under de Broglie were put into motion in May. Cassel, the capital of Hesse-Cassel, opened its gates to Broglie; Minden with vast magazine stores was taken by assault by Contades; and Münster also fell to him after a siege. The mixed forces under these two generals, having united and concentrated at Minden on the west bank of the Weser, were now in position at the favourable moment to cross this river and to overrun Hanover, as had been done in 1757. To prevent that misfortune the allies' commander-in-chief established a chain of posts near Minden. Flushed with the late success, Contades was impelled to give battle to break through these defences and, in doing so, to order his troops out of their strong entrenchments. This led on August 1 to the Battle of Minden, which was the most important engagement in which the British forces in Germany were involved in the course of the war and therefore deserves more than passing notice.[11]

As was related in the preceding volume of this series, in the summer of 1758 four regiments of foot and five of horse were — as the result of Pitt's reversal of policy with respect to the German war — sent to the Continent under the Duke of Marlborough and Lord George Sackville to support Prince Ferdinand in the defence of the Electorate of Hanover. This force was from time to time augmented. With the death of Marlborough in the fall of 1758, Sackville was commissioned to command all the British forces, both horse and foot, "serving on the Lower Rhine or to be there assembled with the allied army under the command of Prince Ferdinand of Brunswick . . ." and by the terms of this commission was subject to the orders of the latter. The day of the battle six British regiments of foot [12] were employed as well as fourteen British squadrons of horse. In fact, the British regiments supported by two Hanoverian bat-

---

[10] Dispatch of the Duc de Broglie to Count d'Affry, French Ambassador at The Hague, received at The Hague April 16, 1759, *Pennsylvania Gazette*, July 12, 1759; *London Gazette*, April 24, 1759.

[11] For the Battle of Minden see Waddington, *op. cit.*, III, 46–68.

[12] The 12th, Napiers's, the 20th, Kingsley's, the 23rd, Huske's, the 25th, Home's, the 37th, Stuart's, and the 51st, Brudenell's.

talions constituted Ferdinand's centre under his personal direction; his left wing was made up of various German units under the Prince of Holstein; and his right wing, of highly mobile British and Hanoverian cavalry, was commanded by Lord George.

In advancing upon the allies under orders from Contades, Broglie was under necessity to move through a large morass and at length found himself hemmed in by the Weser, the morass, and the allied army, which, to his great surprise and as the result of Ferdinand's tactical arrangements, faced him in full force. There was nothing left for him to do but to fight. The allied artillery, however, as soon as he came in range checked his advance. Thereupon Ferdinand hurled his centre of British troops against the French centre, made up largely of cavalry. By all accounts, the conduct of the British troops was magnificent. The French cavalry, after advancing, retired in confusion, as did two regiments of Saxon foot supporting it. Nor did Broglie's right wing fare any better. His army was, indeed, facing destruction. At this critical juncture Ferdinand ordered the right wing — Sackville's cavalry — to support the centre, now well in advance, by moving obliquely through fairly open woods so as to fall in behind the foot. In place of this, the English commander — habitually inclined to be "haughty in official intercourse and of an exacting temper" and apparently confused and also not in the best of condition at the time — ignored the urgent request repeatedly made, alleging as he later did without proper basis that the orders were not clear and were even contradictory. Nor would he permit Lord Granby, second in command and eager to join in the battle, to move the squadrons until he himself had consulted in person the commander-in-chief. By reason of these delays the golden opportunity of disposing of the flower of Contades's army passed.[13] But

---

[13] That Lord George Sackville was at the time under the influence of liquor may be indicated by the testimony of Lieutenant Colonel Sloper of Bland's regiment of dragoons, who deposed at the court martial that after Captain Ligonier had given Prince Ferdinand's orders to Sackville without effect, he (Sloper) said to Ligonier: "For God's sake, Sir, repeat your orders to that man . . . that he may not pretend not to understand them; for it is near half an hour ago that he received orders to advance, and yet we are still here, . . . but you see the condition he is in" (Entick, op. cit., IV, 56). According to Mr. Hans Stanley, sent to Paris in 1761 to try to negotiate peace, the French generals thought Sackville afraid to fight and were of the opinion "that the defeat at Minden would have been decisive if the French army had not been saved by Lord George Sackville's cowardice" (Stanley to Pitt, June 3, 1761, Frances Thackeray, A History of the . . . Earl of Chatham [London, 1827], I, 512). Yet, there are indications that cowardice was not a factor but that the English general deeply resented the

the matter was not permitted to rest. As a result of the Prince's well-grounded basis of complaint against the English general, Sackville was recalled home, dismissed from the army, and later, in 1760, as the result of the conclusions of a court martial, which he himself demanded, was disqualified to serve his country in any military capacity.[14]

Incomplete as was the victory of Minden, its importance, nevertheless, must not be minimized. The enemy not only lost the heavy baggage, the military correspondence, the Saxon military chest, and a series of magazines filled with provisions, but was obliged to evacuate Minden and then, soon afterward, Cassel. Although Contades was replaced by Broglie as chief commander of the French northern army, Münster, late in November after a siege, was also obliged to surrender — thus wiping out every gain that had been made after the allies' reverse at Bergen in April and Ferdinand's retreat.[15] Moreover, the Electorate, as well as Hesse-Cassel, was safe for the remainder of the year from the reach of the enemy, with Ferdinand at length establishing his headquarters well in advance of the latter principality, at Marburg in Nassau.

If the allied army fared well enough during the summer campaign in western Germany as the result of the "miraculous victory" of Minden, the same cannot be said of the forces of the King of Prussia. The year had opened, as already related, with the successful destruction of a series of great magazines in Poland designed to support the Russian army in its next drive against Brandenburg; then came Prince Henry's equally successful destruction of Austrian magazines established in Bohemia to meet the needs of Marshal Daun's army, followed by the Prince's rout of the Imperialists concentrating in northern Bavaria. The only immediate concern of Frederick

---

fact that he was subordinate to Ferdinand and sought means to displace him as the commander-in-chief of the allied forces in Germany (A. von Ruville, *William Pitt*, II, 244–5). The author of *A Letter from a British Officer now in Germany* . . . (London, 1761) wrote (p. 10): "As to lord G[eorge], cowardice was not the cause of his inaction; I am afraid it proceeded from a worse motive. M. Broglie now commands the French army because Contades was defeated: and if, on the contrary, we had been defeated, there is a moral certainty that lord G. S. would have been our present commander-in-chief."

[14] The verdict of the court martial is printed in the official *London Gazette* of April 26, 1760. The trial, including the testimony of witnesses, is given in great detail by Entick, *op. cit.*, IV, 35–82; see also *Proceedings of Sir George Sackville's Court Martial* (London, 1760).

[15] Waddington, *op. cit.*, III, 73–110.

now seemed to be the presence of Marshal Daun, strongly entrenched near Königgrätz in Bohemia, who was in a favourable position to move into either Saxony or Silesia. With a purely defensive campaign in mind, the King from his headquarters at Landshut in Bavaria therefore kept his eyes fastened upon every movement of his very deliberate but dangerous opponent, who twice had almost destroyed the Prussian army — in 1757 at Kolin and the following year at Hochkirch.

But Daun was in no hurry to move out of his powerful defences and the summer might possibly have passed without notable developments in the eastern area had not Czarina Elizabeth, furious at the loss of her magazines in Poland, determined to use every resource at her command so that the movement of her armies westward would not be delayed. By the end of April, in fact, Russian troops were pouring across the Vistula and inundating the frontiers of Pomerania, Brandenburg, and Silesia in such force that Frederick was under necessity to order various detachments scattered in the north to concentrate and to move into Poland under command of Count Dohna in order to strike at the main Russian army, entrenched at Posen. But Dohna, in moving up to attack, found the enemy's defences too powerful to attempt to break and fell back across the Oder. When the news of this retrograde movement reached the King, he severely criticized his subordinate, who now retired from the service, and ordered General Wedel, who had driven the Swedes from Prussian Pomerania the preceding year, to take command as dictator and with his little army of thirty thousand men to attack the Russian Soltykov with a force of over seventy thousand. For the enemy, by his movement in the direction of Crossen on the upper Oder, seemed bent on forming a contact with Daun, still at Königgrätz. Wedel carried out these commands and engaged the Russians in battle on July 23. The first news of it to reach the King told of a great Prussian victory.[16] But further advices changed the victory into a costly reverse. The situation, indeed, became daily more critical. Frankfurt an der Oder fell to the Russians, and then Crossen. Moreover, Daun now sent twelve thousand of his best horse and eight thousand foot under General Laudon to strengthen the Russians, who were especially weak in cavalry. The question

---

[16] Œuvres Posthumes de Frédéric II, III, 19–22; Andrew Mitchell, British Minister to the King of Prussia, writing to the Earl of Holderness on July 24 from Frederick's headquarters, London Gazette, August 7, 1759.

arose in the minds of men, could Brandenburg and Silesia now be saved?

Leaving Prince Henry to watch Daun, Frederick with ten thousand troops, "the flower of his army," moved rapidly eastward into Silesia and then early in August joined Wedel and thereupon took personal command, but not before the Austrian reinforcements had joined the Russians. As a result the King with an army of hardly more than fifty thousand was obliged to move upon a greatly superior force of ninety thousand well fortified and heavily supported by artillery. In doing so he attempted to succeed under conditions equally unfavourable with those that brought defeat to Wedel. The battle was joined on the 12th at Kunersdorf, not far from Frankfurt. At first it looked as though a great victory was in the making, with the Russian left wing giving way to the impetuous charge of the Prussian battalions. "Madam, we have beaten the Russians from their entrenchments; in two hours expect to hear of a glorious victory," declared the King in an exalting dispatch to the Queen at Berlin.[17]

But the King's impetuosity got the better of his judgment. Instead of remaining satisfied with an incomplete victory, as he wisely had been at Zorndorf the preceding summer, which had netted him great advantages, and even against the advice of his most competent officers, he risked everything in an effort to destroy the enemy by dislodging Soltykov from a really impregnable position — an eminence that could not be reached with the Prussian artillery because of the broken ground where, however, the Russian artillery had been massed. Driving his exhausted grenadiers again into motion, he sent them into what proved to be a horrible massacre, which was only increased when his tired horse in support of the foot was shattered by Laudon's fresh Austrian cavalry. Broken in spirit, the Prussian army at last fled in panic.

With some twenty-five thousand of his men killed, wounded, or taken prisoner, among them his best generals, and with but ten thousand troops remaining intact as an operating unit at the end of the wild retreat, Frederick suffered at Kunersdorf the most decisive defeat that he was ever to experience at the hands of an enemy.[18] Despondently, he wrote to his minister Finkenstein, after he had reached the Oder with the remnants of his army: "I have no more

---

[17] Annual Register, 1759, p. 26.
[18] For Frederick's own account of the Battle of Kunersdorf see Œuvres Posthumes de Frédéric II, III, 25–9.

resources and, to tell the truth, I believe everything is lost." There was every indication that this was so. For it seemed only a question of time before Berlin would be occupied by the Russians. Not only was the King's army shattered and the great artillery train lost, but two days after the disaster across the Oder his military chest and great magazine at Torgau, near Leipzig in Saxony, were surrendered to the Imperialists, who soon afterward came into possession of Leipzig and Dresden also. The great coalition, it now appeared, had a strangle hold on the wily King of Prussia and was finally in a position to bring him to terms.

Soltykov, the Russian general, however, did not follow up his advantage and march boldly on Berlin. Instead, he swung into Silesia with a part of his army to join forces with Daun, and the war thus became one of movement, in which Frederick, after welding together another army, displayed all of his former skill as a strategist. He was, moreover, aided by the fact that the Russians, with no great magazines to draw upon, were impelled after some weeks to retreat to their own frontiers, leaving him to deal only with Daun and the Imperialists.[19] Thus, until late in November he and his brother Henry held their own, but his judgment again failed when after destroying a number of Daun's magazines he separated his forces in order to cut off the Austrian general's retreat into Bohemia. The latter thereupon fell with overwhelming force upon a detachment of some twenty thousand under the Prussian General Finck near Maxen in Saxony and compelled its surrender and then, avoiding further risks, took up his winter quarters not in Bohemia but in Saxony. Thus ended the year's campaign in Germany, with the victory of Minden, largely won by the hard-fighting British infantry, the only source of satisfaction left to the rather bewildered allies. It may be added that 1759, like the end of 1758, witnessed no break in the alignment of the powers, in spite of the fact that William Pitt had taken a hand in European diplomacy with a vain attempt to bribe Russia to withdraw from the struggle and to become a neutral, and to persuade Bavaria to desert Maria Theresa and espouse the allied cause by dangling

---

[19] There is also evidence that a misunderstanding developed between the Austrians and the Russians. The former apparently claimed the credit for the victory of Kunersdorf, which Soltykov resented. When urged by Daun to continue to act with vigor, he replied: "I have done enough for one year, Sir; I have gained two victories which have cost the Russians 27,000 men. Before I again put myself in action, I shall wait till you also have gained two victories. It is not fair that the whole business of the war should be performed by the troops of my sovereign alone" (Thackeray, op. cit., I, 408).

before the Elector of that principality the possibility, were he to do so, of securing the Imperial crown.[20]

In spite of the stalemate in Germany, nothing could disguise the fact that France by the end of 1759 had suffered a series of great defeats elsewhere. For the Kingdom was being rapidly stripped of its overseas empire as the result of the conquests effected by the British army and navy. In Canada the forces of His Most Christian Majesty — with the loss of Louisbourg and Fort Duquesne in 1758 and of Fort Niagara and Quebec the following year — had late in 1759 retired to those areas on the upper St. Lawrence and the Richelieu bordering on Montreal. They also, it is true, held the posts of the upper Great Lakes, the Illinois country, and the Province of Louisiana, none of which, however, had been subject to attack. In the West Indies, in Africa, and in India, as will be indicated further on in this volume, these forces had also experienced serious defeats, which brought about the loss of the rich island of Guadeloupe in the Lesser Antilles, Senegal, and the island of Goree on and off the coast of Africa, as well as the factories and other interests of the Compagnie des Indes in Bengal, the Northern Circars and Hyderabad in India. Again, the French merchant marine had by the beginning of 1760 been largely swept from the high seas and the navy, after meeting with disaster both at Lagos and at Quiberon Bay, could be protected from further attack and destruction only by keeping to the shelter of such posts as Brest on the Atlantic and Toulon in the Mediterranean.

Within the Kingdom itself, according to the French historian and economist Sismondé, there was at this juncture the strangest contrast between Paris and Versailles and the vast rural areas. On the one hand, immense riches in the hands of those who controlled the revenues of the state; the lavish expenditure of the produce of their great estates by the nobility gathered at the royal court; and the prodigality of other courtiers loaded with favours and engaged in extravagances surpassing those of the most brillant days of the reign of Louis XIV. On the other hand, out in the country agriculture was stifled under the weight of the *taille* and *gabelle*, and the labourers, loaded with exactions, miserably clothed and scantily fed, were forced to hide from their oppressors the little that they had.[21]

---

[20] Ruville, *op. cit.*, II, 218.

[21] *Chronique de la régence et du règne de Louis XV, ou Journal de Barbier* (Paris, 1766), VII, 134, footnote.

In the face of the growing economic paralysis and financial and administrative disorganization that the ruinous war was bringing to France and to her rapidly shrinking empire, the Abbé de Bernis, who had been one of the authors of the Convention of Versailles with Maria Theresa in 1756 and had become Minister of Foreign Affairs in 1757, by the spring of the following year had become strongly convinced that it was absolutely necessary to secure peace on the best terms available, and took preliminary steps in that direction.[22] But he had to face the bitter opposition of Maria Theresa and even of the Marquise de Pompadour, equally determined that the war should continue. Nevertheless, in negotiations with the Empress of Austria he did succeed in securing a reduction in the subsidy by one half paid to this court under the terms of the secret convention,[23] and the liquidation of the arrears of the subsidies already due, before he surrendered his office on November 1, 1758 and was exiled the following month to the provinces in view of his continued opposition to a continuation of the war.[24] His place was filled by Étienne François Choiseul, Comte de Stainville, Ambassador at Vienna, who was accorded the title of Duc de Choiseul and was destined to exercise a dominating influence for many years not only in the field of diplomacy but in military and naval affairs. Even before Bernis was impelled to give up his post in favour of a cardinal's hat, the intense dislike of the Marquise had deprived the country of the services of the energetic Minister of War d'Argenson and at the time of his disgrace in the summer of 1758 the very capable Minister of the Marine, Machault, who had displeased Louis XV on purely personal grounds, likewise had received his dismissal.[25] In the course of the next year or two the administration of these two posts thus fell to Choiseul, who became in fact what Bernis in anticipation had hoped to become, *the* King's Minister and therefore, next to His Most Christian Majesty, the most powerful man in France.

The new Minister of Foreign Affairs, strongly committed to the idea of continuing the war, proceeded to reverse Bernis's peace policies and on December 30, 1758 signed a convention with the Aus-

---

[22] Charles Lacretelle, *Histoire de France pendant le dix-huitième Siècle* (Paris, 1819), III, 345–7; "*Mémoires Secrets de Duclos,*" *Collection des Mémoires relatifs a l'histoire de France* (Paris, 1829), LXXVII, 164–5.

[23] *Mémoire* of Kaunitz to the French Ambassador, Waddington, *op. cit.,* II, 426.

[24] The letter ordering Bernis into exile, dated December 13, 1758, is to be found in *Mémoires et lettres du Cardinal de Bernis,* II, 346.

[25] *Mémoires de M. le Baron de Besenval* (Paris, 1805), I, 303–314.

trian Ambassador, the Comte de Stahremberg, for a still further modification of the terms of the secret treaty entered into between France and Austria. By it France was guaranteed important territorial acquisitions in the Austrian Netherlands in return for supporting Maria Theresa's claims to Silesia. These expected gains were now renounced by Choiseul. In fact, the new treaty, finally ratified in the month of May of the following year, was in most respects very advantageous to the Empress Queen.[26]

France, however, was given some relief in connection with the waging of the German war, in that Maria Theresa was guaranteed as an aid *either* an army of one hundred thousand men or in lieu of this the payment of the equivalent in money to the amount of about eight and one half million livres. Thus, with the choice made in favour of military aid, the French subsidy to Austria now lapsed. But even with this relief the treasury faced exhaustion and the public credit of the various French funds was nearing an end. It was obvious in face of this dangerous situation that glaring abuses of long standing must be remedied and other steps taken to bring order out of the chaotic finances of the Kingdom. To perform what would be a near miracle under given conditions, the King turned to M. de Silhouette, who had, as was emphasized in the fifth volume of this series, acted as one of the French commissioners in negotiations with the British before the declaration of war, and in March 1759 the King entrusted him with the portfolio of Comptroller General of Finances. Silhouette entered upon his office on a wave of popularity and succeeded in bringing into the treasury considerable sums by none too drastic reforms, even persuading the King to set a laudable example of sacrifice by sending the royal silver table service to the mint. Even so, his bold project of reorganizing the revenue system of France — by substituting for the older taxes, such as the *taille,* which bore very unevenly on the nation, with large classes enjoying exemptions from it, other levies, such as a graduated income tax, which would fall upon all — aroused such a storm of indignation from privileged groups that after eight months in office the King was forced to retire the now hated but well-intentioned minister.[27] His successor, M. Bertin, while overturning the system of Silhouette em-

---

[26] The treaty, stripped of its diplomatic verbiage, is to be found in *Politique de tous les cabinets de l'Europe pendant règnes de Louis XV et de Louis XVI* (Hamburg, 1794), I, 427–36.

[27] *Journal de Barbier,* VII, 138, 154–60, 199–207.

bodying a "general subvention" and heavy taxes on luxuries, was compelled, in order to provide for the needs of the military forces, to secure by edict a temporary doubling of the capitation tax and an increase in the so-called *"vingtième"* tax on all property — both under title of extraordinary aids to run not later than the year 1762.[28] These, together with government borrowing and the stoppage of the payment on loans already matured, were temporary expedients that with skilful juggling with the finances made it possible to continue hostilities, in spite of the fact that this great and wealthy Kingdom was headed for ultimate national bankruptcy.

As for Great Britain, with the year 1760 signs were not lacking that the power of the Great Commoner both within and without the government was being shaken. While all men applauded his successful prosecution of the Great War for the Empire, the criticism of his policies with respect to the German war now became vocal. It had been assumed that with British aid, hostilities on the Continent would soon be brought to a happy conclusion. When there were no signs of this, men of influence became disillusioned, especially as they saw the resources of the Kingdom, supplied almost without stint, disappearing into what seemed to be an unfathomable abyss of expense. For example, Horace Walpole, though an admirer of Pitt, was nevertheless very critical of Pitt's irresponsibility in the field of public finance. With reference to the minister's policy at this juncture, he wrote:

> "He staked our revenues with as little management as he played with the lives of the subjects [of the King]; . . . he lavished the last treasures of this country with a prodigality beyond example and beyond excuse. . . ."[29]

Moreover, faith in the military prowess of the King of Prussia, which had been so high, particularly after the campaigns of 1758, had been badly shaken as a result of the costly reverses his armies had suffered in 1759. The *Annual Register* for that year (but published in 1760) reflected this attitude, in contrasting somewhat caustically Frederick as a general with Prince Ferdinand of Brunswick, wholly to the latter's advantage:

> "The king of Prussia rapid, vehement, impatient often gives decisive blows; but he often misses his stroke and wounds himself.

---

[28] *Ibid.*, VII, 235–6.
[29] *Memoirs of the Reign of King George the Second* (London, 1846), III, 173.

Prince Ferdinand is cool, deliberate, exact and guarded; he sees every possible advantage, he takes it at the moment, pursues it as far as it will go, but never attempts to push it further. . . . In him we do now see a person who is a great soldier; it is the idea of a perfect general; it is a general in the abstract. . . . Prince Ferdinand is famous for never committing a fault. The king of Prussia is above all the world in repairing those he has committed. . . . He commits an error, he repairs it; he errs again, and again admonishes us by his manner of escaping. We should often condemn the commander, but we are always forced to admire the hero." [30]

But public criticism did not stop with reflections upon the wanton lavishment of the wealth of England on the German war and upon the shortcomings of Frederick of Prussia as a military leader. The London agent of Massachusetts Bay, Israel Mauduit, in his remarkable *Considerations on the German War*, published in 1760, launched a devastating attack against the further support of that war. Indeed, the importance of this pamphlet was so great in influencing public opinion in Great Britain that it must be given more than passing notice.[31] Taking as his starting-point the following words uttered by the King of Prussia in 1744:

"As no German prince has a right to meddle with the internal policy of Great Britain, nor with the constitution of its government; I have some reasons to hope, that the English nation will not meddle with the domestic affairs of the [Holy Roman German] Empire . . . because England has no reason to meddle with this quarrel from any consideration of its commerce, or otherwise"

Mauduit affirmed that Britain had no business to be concerned with the Continental war:

"The only war, which England is at this time engaged in, is the war with France. . . . So far are we from having declared war with any other state, that Britain has scarce a contest subsisting with any other power in Europe." [32]

---

[30] *Annual Register*, 1759, p. 29.

[31] Horace Walpole, in his *Memoirs of the Reign of George III* (Philadelphia, 1845, I, 31), declared that the pamphlet *Considerations* "was shrewdly and ably written, and had more operation in working a change in the minds of men, than perhaps ever fell to the lot of a pamphlet." Sir Denis Le Marchant, Bart., who edited the *Memoirs*, says of the *Considerations*: "It is a masterly production. The style is clear and persuasive, the tone calm, and the reasoning close and logical (*ibid.*, I, 31, footnote).

[32] *Considerations on the present German War* (third edition, London, 1760), p. 8.

The nation was therefore not fighting at this juncture to maintain
any balance of power in Europe, as it was in the War of the Spanish
Succession. In fact, the war with France, he properly pointed out,
"began with a contest about foreign settlements, and the colonies of
the two nations [in North America]. A matter in which the parliament declared, that the immediate and essential interests of these
kingdoms are concerned." He then asked:

> "Why then should we have desired to divert any of the course of it
> into a land war in Germany? It could not be, because we found our-
> selves the most pressed, and in danger of losing most at sea; for
> England is on that element superior to France, and has been in a
> continual course of victory. It could not be because our victories
> were fruitless; because we are gaining the very points we fought
> for. . . ." [33]

He therefore denied the now classic Pitt contention made later, in
1762, that Great Britain won the contest in the New World in Germany.[34] Far from it, he insisted "that the German war is no diversion at all" in an effort to get the better of the enemy, but in contrast "was a diversion of the French choosing . . . to draw the
British force into Germany, where they [the French] knew themselves to be invulnerable, and were always sure to be superior
to us." [35]

In other words, Mauduit's position was that when the government
decided to defend Hanover, it walked blindly into a French trap and
must extricate itself from this snare. Not until Louis XV's ministers
became convinced that French troops could not be carried out of
continental Europe by reason of British sea power, he argued, was
Hanover even threatened. Then it was — "when they were pre-
cluded from invading England; and their West-India Islands lay all
naked and exposed to us," and when they realized that their armies
must either remain at home unemployed or be sent into Germany,
"where they have nothing to lose, or be in fear for" — that this was
done.[36] Yet he asked: "Could the French pretend to say that the
Electorate had taken any part in the dispute between the two nations about our possessions in America? Who does not see then, that

---

[33] *Ibid.*, p. 123.
[34] Pitt declared on November 13, 1762 in debate in Parliament over the address
that "America had been conquered in Germany" (Walpole, *op. cit.*, I, 66).
[35] *Considerations*, pp. 127, 134.
[36] *Ibid.*, p. 42.

the single reason, when it is attacked, is because the French know, that we shall defend it?" [37]

With respect to the resolution passed by Parliament in 1755 to defend Hanover, the irony of it was not lost on the author of the *Considerations;* he pointed out that at the time it was a promise "to defend the Electorate against the King of Prussia and the French, the rest of the [Holy Roman German] Empire being with us." [38] But under the present circumstances the carrying out of this agreement had served the purposes solely of the King of Prussia. "We are not at war with the House of Austria, and he will tell us, he is not at war with France." [39] As for the Hanoverians themselves, they had only suffered from British interference in the affairs of Germany and even preferred "a quiet state of neutrality" under the terms of the Convention of Kloster-Seven to resuming hostilities, which they had been compelled to resume as the result of the insistence of Frederick after the victory he had gained at Rossbach.[40] This enforced connection between Hanover and him, moreover, had been bitterly resented by the other princes of the Empire, who felt, not without reason, that Frederick had become the chief menace to the tranquillity of their countries. For they "had with indignation seen the King of Prussia twice set all Germany in a flame, ravage some of the finest parts of the empire, and sacrifice the lives of his own subjects, and theirs, by thousands, to his ambition." [41] Mauduit, indeed, summarized his fundamental objections to further participation in the German war in alliance with Frederick in these words:

> "What then have we gained by this ally? Two things: the one is the being obliged to pay him money to enable him to fight his own battles, against enemies which Britain has no quarrel with: the other is the driving the rest of the German Princes into a closer union with France, and making ourselves obnoxious to Europe for supporting this ally: can it be supposed that Britain is the stronger for either of these?" [42]

While attempts were made on the part of the supporters of the administration to answer the *Considerations on the Present German*

---

[37] *Ibid.,* p. 38.
[38] *Ibid.,* p. 59.
[39] *Ibid.,* p. 47.
[40] *Ibid.,* p. 34.
[41] *Ibid.,* p. 35.
[42] *Ibid.,* p. 68.

War,[43] yet it is not without significance that its popularity was attested by the fact that it went through at least six editions and that it was supplemented in 1761 by the author's *Occasional Thoughts on the Present German War,* which was prepared as an answer to his critics and to reinforce his earlier effort.[44] Its arguments, moreover, were used on the floor of the House of Commons in December 1760 with such telling effect, it was asserted, that no answer to them was attempted.[45] Pitt, nevertheless, secured the passage of the Prussian subsidy for the year 1761 without difficulty, in spite of the lack of enthusiasm for it in the House.[46] This was destined to be the last financial aid that Frederick would receive at the hands of this particular minister, who was to leave office the following year as the result of an adverse vote of confidence on the part of his colleagues in the Cabinet Council over issues that will be later considered in some detail.

---

[43] See, for example, *A Full and Candid Answer to a Pamphlet, entitled Considerations on the Present German War* (London, 1760) and *The Conduct of the Ministry Impartially Examined. And the Pamphlet entitled Considerations on the Present German War Refuted from its own Principle* (London, 1760). A third pamphlet, while not referring to the *Considerations,* extolled the great merits and achievements of the King of Prussia and strongly supported the Pitt Continental policies. It appeared under title *Conjectures on the Present State of Affairs in Germany. Containing Remarks on the conduct of his Prussian Majesty; and the Probability of his concluding a safe and honorable Peace. By an Impartial Hand* (London, 1760).

[44] *Occasional Thoughts on the Present German War. By the Author of Considerations on the same Subject* (London, 1761).

[45] Richard Rigby, a member of Parliament from Devonshire, declared after a debate in December 1760: "If the author of the pamphlet was in the gallery and wanted conviction that his arguments were unanswerable he had it today to his satisfaction" (Rigby to Bedford, December 22, 1760, *Correspondence of John 4th Duke of Bedford* [ed. Lord John Russell, London, 1843], II, 426).

[46] *Journals of the House of Commons,* XVIII, 991.

CHAPTER III

The New King and the German Seven Years' War

WITH GREAT BRITAIN in the midst of the victorious Great War for the Empire and involved in this connection in the war in Germany, as the rival of France, and since 1758 as the ally of Frederick of Prussia, there took place a momentous change at the seat of government the morning of October 25, 1760 with the totally unexpected death of King George II.

The King, who had reigned for over thirty-three years and, more than that, had ruled with the aid of ministers chosen from among the leaders of the dominant Whig Party, had influenced profoundly the direction of the nation's foreign policy. Rather indifferent as he may have been regarding most matters of domestic concern within his kingdom and most matters relating to the British Empire, he had never been indifferent when it came to the problem of guaranteeing that he had a friendly House of Commons nor to developments on the Continent, especially such as might affect his beloved Hanover. Indeed, if his body remained in England during most of his long reign, his heart had always been in the land of his nativity, his ancestral Electorate. In outlook, in ideals, and in habits of conduct, he was as thoroughly a German prince as had been his father, George I. Always considered by his British subjects as a good deal of an alien, the King would have been the last to deny that this was true. Yet he had not been considered to be a poor ruler, not to say a bad one — little as he had succeeded in winning the affections of his British subjects. To his credit, he had fully accepted the constitutional results of the Glorious Revolution as binding upon himself and his ministers and therefore had bowed to the fact that the great crown powers now rested in his High Court of Parliament, a body that by its Act of Settlement had made it possible for him as well as for his father to ascend to the throne. Again, he had accepted the church established by law in England, and that in Scotland; further, he had never oppressed or even pressed his subjects in order to maintain an extravagant court; finally, he had stood as a barrier to the return of the Stuart line whose attempt to do so with French encouragement had aroused such deep dread in 1746. Therefore, while the nation could not love a very unlovable person, it had many reasons to be grateful to him and consequently had accepted him without question and with it the permanency of the Hanoverian dynasty.

That George II was far from a nonentity in government had been long clear to every person of discernment. For example, in 1754, with the beginning of hostilities between the colonials and the French at the forks of the Ohio, he had shown, according to the Duke of Newcastle, "an utter aversion" to sending British troops to America for fear that this might imperil the peace that he wanted to maintain. Only by the strongest urging on the part of his son, the Duke of Cumberland, that the colonials must not be left at the mercy of French regular troops was he finally persuaded to agree to the proposal of the Cabinet Council to send two regiments to Virginia under General Braddock. Nevertheless, once the die was cast, he was prepared at the beginning of 1755 to see appropriated whatever "Sum of Money it may be proper to ask of Parliament for the Assistance of His Majesty's Subjects in North America" — and this was done.[1] Late that same year, in anticipation that the French would turn their attention to Hanover, he secured a pledge from Parliament to assist him "against insults and attacks that may be made upon any of His Majesty's dominions, through not belonging to the Crown of Great Britain." [2]

His decisive influence upon British foreign relations was also evident when in 1757 he determined that Cumberland should be sent to the Continent to command the Army of Observation gathered to protect his Electorate. Further, to ensure the proper maintenance of this force, he consented to act on his son's demand that Pitt, the national idol, be removed from office. Moreover, only when the latter had been able to persuade him that he would do the King's "busi-

---

[1] See Volume VI of this series, pp. 51–61.
[2] *Ibid.*, VI, 379.

ness" was he again restored to his post. That the Great Commoner from that time on received George's firm support and was thereby permitted to continue to direct affairs can only be explained by the fact that he came to share the latter's views as to the vital importance in the Great War for the Empire of keeping Hanover out of the clutches of the French armies. Thus at the time of the death of the King, Britain was so deeply involved in war in Germany as the result of his own peculiar interests and of his influence in favour of these upon his Cabinet Council and Parliament, that an army of twenty-five thousand picked British troops was guarding the approaches to Hanover; vast financial commitments, in addition, had been made to support the Electoral troops and those of other German principalities that were engaged in the same task; and a treaty of alliance with the King of Prussia made in 1758 still held firm. The student should therefore be cautioned to view with more than suspicion the tradition embodied in British history that George II was lacking in interest in the affairs of the government of Great Britain and, as a result, pliantly yielded to the demands of his real master, the Whig oligarchy, which was thereby permitted to determine all serious matters of policy.[3]

With the coming of the grandson of the late King to the throne as George III there was no immediate break with the international policy that had been pursued. But that such a break might soon occur was not hard for contemporaries who had been closely in touch with the new monarch to prophesy. Just as George II had shown that he had a mind of his own, so his successor was to indicate that this was true of him as well.

About no other figure in the eighteenth century have there arisen so many and so sharply divergent views as about King George III. If one were to accept the verdict passed upon him by the Second Continental Congress in its Declaration of Independence of 1776, he was a brutal and tyrannical King, seeking for his own personal satisfaction and glory the sadistic triumph of enslaving his subjects in the American colonies. If, on the other hand, one were to accept a common verdict passed upon him after his death by the people of Great Britain, he was well entitled to be called, not without affection, "good King George" or "farmer George" — a man whose manifold virtues fairly glowed in comparison with those of his imme-

---

[3] This view is expressed by John Adolphus in his *History of England from the Accession to the Decease of King George the Third* (London, 1840), I, 12.

diate predecessor or immediate successor. Unfortunately, he has never had a great biographer and this is especially surprising in view of the vast accumulation of material that is available for the writing of his life.[4]

George III had a very lonely and unhappy boyhood. He was made fully aware of the hatred directed against his rather worthless

[4] The most recent important study having to do with the public life of George III is that by Professor Richard Pares entitled *King George III and the Politicians* (Oxford, 1953). Among other works that are directly concerned with this monarch are M. S. Guttmacher's *America's Last King: An Interpretation of the Madness of George III* (New York, 1941), which is by far the best study of the recurring malady of the King, but is not equally effective in other respects; C. E. Vulliamy's *Royal George* (London, 1937), which adds somewhat to our understanding of the King and his times, but is designed for the general reader; A. Mervyn Davies's Stanhope Prize study, *The Influence of George III on the Development of the Constitution* (Oxford, 1921), which though limited largely to printed works is, in spite of its brevity, of value for its discussion of constitutional questions. William Hunt's "George III," which appeared in 1908 in the *Dictionary of National Biography*, will be useful to the student, but shares the defect of Beckles Willson's *George III, as Man, Monarch and Statesman* (London, 1907), in that it does not comprehend much material that has come to light since its publication. Among older works are J. H. Jesse's *Memoirs of the Life and Reign of George III* (London, 1867) and Edward Holt's *The Public and Domestic Life of his late Gracious Majesty, George the Third* (London, 1820), each of which falls far short of being an adequate biography. L. B. Namier has, however, in his *England in the Age of the American Revolution* (London, 1930), brilliantly portrayed the political activities of George III, his ministers, and others during the brief period between 1760 and the close of 1762; this study was preceded by his illuminating but non-biographical *The Structure of Politics at the Accession of George III* (London, 1929). Namier also brought to light the numerous letters of King George to Lord Bute which, competently edited by Romney Sedgwick, were published in 1939 under the title: *Letters from George III to Lord Bute, 1756–1766*. They really fill a void that existed in the still more important work: *The Correspondence of King George the Third from 1760 to December 1783,* which, edited by the Hon. Sir John Fortescue and published in six volumes, appeared in 1927 and 1928. One should, however, use the Fortescue with caution and only in connection with Namier's *Additions to Sir John Fortescue's Edition of the Correspondence of King George the Third* (Manchester, 1937), which, based on an examination of the Bute, Grafton, Northington, and Shelburne manuscript collections, corrects a large number of errors in Volume I. To these sources must be added *Letters of George III* (ed. Bonamy Dobrée, London, 1935) and *The Correspondence of King George the Third with Lord North from 1768 to 1783* (ed. W. Bodham Donne, London, 1867), as well as selections of letters published in 1827 and edited by Henry Philpotts and another selection of them published in 1927 and edited by Fortescue, both relating to the period after the close of the War for American Independence. Beyond the works just mentioned that are concerned more specifically with George III, there are many contemporary memoirs and letters that throw much light upon his activities, as do, of course, the histories of his reign by such writers as Mahon, Adolphus, Massey, Lecky, and Hunt. Finally, students should consult Gerda Richards Crosby's "George III: Historians and a Royal Reputation," in *Essays in Modern English History in Honor of Wilbur Cortez Abbott* (Cambridge, Mass., 1941).

father, Frederick Prince of Wales, by George II and Caroline and shared the hatred that his father in turn bestowed upon the King and Queen.[5] Moreover, as a young prince George was very diffident and introspective; he was indolent and suspicious of the motives of people, especially those about the court, whom his mother taught him to shun; he therefore was reluctant to give his confidences to more than a chosen few. Among these few were his mother and his brother Edward. There was also John Stuart, Earl of Bute, who became a lord of his father's bedchamber in 1750 when George was in his thirteenth year. While there were dark whisperings as to the nature of the relations that developed between Bute and the mother of the new Prince of Wales, Augusta, after the death of Frederick in 1751 — all of which may be passed over by the historian, as it was by the Prince of Wales, as the most slanderous gossip — it is a matter worthy of emphasis that the Scottish nobleman gave to the prospective heir to the throne the sort of devotion that was only seldom to be met with in England, but had been traditional in his own country in the relations between clansman and chieftain. This devotion Prince George returned to the fullest extent.[6] It may be further added that while, under great political pressure, the intimacy between the two ceased after 1765, Bute never deviated from the deep sense of loyalty he had for his royal master, even in expressing in later years, when in practical exile, a feeling that the King had proved to be ungrateful. A man of wide reading and of refined tastes, a botanist of distinction, a connoisseur in the field of the fine arts, the Earl would seem to have won and held the friendship of such men as Bishop Warburton, Samuel Johnson, and Lord Mansfield, and was certainly culturally well equipped to impart a love of learning to the Prince. Bute introduced him to such works as Blackstone's *Commentaries on the Common Law*, still in manuscript and in the form of lectures that the great jurist had delivered at the University of Oxford in 1758, and the writings of Bolingbroke; and, with the example even of his grandfather George II always before the self-disparaging young man, Bute apparently did everything within his power to urge

---

[5] As Romney Sedgwick in his *Letters of George III to Lord Bute* points out (Introduction, pp. xi–xiii), this jealousy and enmity between the ruler and the heir to the throne was characteristic of the political system of Great Britain and of Europe in the eighteenth century.

[6] Albert von Ruville, *William Pitt, Earl of Chatham* (London, 1907), II, 315.

him to brace himself and to follow the admonition of his mother: "George, be King." [7]

That under this tuition the Prince gained in self-confidence and in understanding is clear.[8] It is equally clear that he had held before him constantly both the reality and the ideal of Great Britain as a limited, constitutional monarchy and that he accepted this system as the best possible form of government. In an essay that he wrote while preparing himself for his future role, he referred to the "noble and balanced constitution" of his country. To him it was "a constitution of free and equal laws, secured against arbitrary will and popular licence, a constitution in fine the nurse of heroes, the parent of liberty, the patron of learning and arts, and the dominion of laws." [9] In such a limited constitutional monarchy, still the monarchy of the Glorious Revolution, a king had his part to play; so had the ministers of state, and so had the Parliament — each with peculiar responsibilities that must not be ignored, or neglected, but, on the contrary, fully accepted and carried out. It was with this conviction that at the age of twenty-two the Prince ascended the throne.

All who have studied the life of George III seem to be agreed that from the time he became King he cast away his earlier slothfulness and that, in spite of recurring spells of insanity, he was, normally, perfectly lucid; that he was also extraordinarily conscientious in the performance of his royal duties, fixed in his judgments once he had formed them, temperate in his habits, domestic in his tastes, and deeply religious. With respect to the merits of his personal views on particular issues that arose during his reign, with respect also to the merits of the policies that he actively favoured and as a result promoted with unabated zeal — all of which will be considered in detail in subsequent volumes of this series — there has never been any unanimity of opinion among scholars or among men of practical affairs, nor is it likely that there will be in the future. That when he became King he found the old British Empire at the height of its glory and achievement cannot be questioned, nor can it be questioned that long before he ceased to rule he was

---

[7] J. Nicholls, *Recollections* (London, 1820), I, 11.

[8] For evidence of the development of Prince George see the letters, sixty in number, written to Lord Bute between May 1756 and October 1760 (*Letters from George III to Lord Bute, 1756–1766*, pp. 1–47).

[9] Quoted by Namier (*England in the Age of the American Revolution*, p. 95) from the Bute Manuscripts.

obliged to acknowledge the failure of policies that he strongly supported in the loss to the Empire by the successful revolt of thirteen
of the American continental colonies. Yet even after this colossal
reverse that he received — which brought with it a great and permanent loss of personal prestige and the ultimate constitutional
transformation of the kingship as well as Parliament through the
growth of political democracy — there was no widespread feeling
either that he had betrayed the nation or that he was unfit to occupy the throne. Indeed, before his death in 1820 it may be said
that his people, as a group, held him in greater affection and respect than they had done during the earlier years of his reign.

Doubtless one thing that gave him on most occasions until 1781
the firm support of the powerful middle class, especially with the
waning of the popularity of William Pitt after 1766, was the fact
that his very conservative views in the main coincided with theirs
on important public issues. Indeed, far too much emphasis has been
placed by certain writers upon the activities in Parliament of the
so-called "King's friends" — as though this was something unique
that had not characterized the functioning of the parliamentary
system under George's predecessors. For this does not account for
the sharp contrast, for example, between *his* great influence in the
direction of national policy up to the close of the American War for
Independence and the repudiation of James II by the nation within
three years after his coronation, in spite of the fact that when the
latter as an acknowledged Roman Catholic came to the throne in
1685, he could count on the aid of powerful contingents not only in
the House of Lords but in the House of Commons — of members
who could as truly have been called "the King's friends" as were
the men who were led to rally behind George and his ministers during the developing American crisis.

The government of Great Britain at the time that George III ascended the throne was, as has been suggested, strongly conservative; it was also aristocratic in spirit and composition and was to
remain so throughout his reign. That it did so was largely, as will
be stressed later in this series, because he would not have it different. In contrast to his grandfather, who had never been quite at
home in England, but was always so in Hanover, the new King,
born in London, was destined never to leave the country of his nativity even for a temporary sojourn in his Continental heritage, the
Electorate. Also in contrast to George II, he was thoroughly British

in his outlook on life and proudly affirmed in addressing his first Parliament from the throne:

> *"Born and educated in this country, I glory in the name of Brit-ain;* [10] *and the peculiar happiness of my life will ever consist in pro-moting the welfare of a people, whose loyalty and warm affection to me, I consider as the greatest and most permanent security of my throne.* [He then proceeded to declare:] I doubt not, but their steadiness in these principles will equal the firmness of my invari-able resolution to adhere to, and strengthen, this excellent constitu-tion in Church and State; and to maintain the Toleration inviolable. The civil and religious rights of my loving subjects are equally dear to me with the most valuable prerogatives of my crown. . . ." [11]

The sentiments as expressed above by the new King were a happy augury of the role he would play in his high position. He had reaffirmed the belief that he had had as a prince in the excel-lence of the constitution and had voiced his determination to ad-here to it and even to strengthen it.[12] He had also promised that the rights of his subjects would be equally dear to him with the pre-rogatives of his Crown. All this was surely voicing the national aspiration for the new reign. Further, in character and in appear-ance he measured up to the ideals of regality held by the best of his people. Horace Walpole gave expression to this in characteris-tic terms:

> "In the flower and bloom of youth, George had a handsome, open and honest countenance; and with the favour that attends the out-ward accomplishments of age, he had none of the vices that fall un-der the censure of those who are past enjoying them themselves." [13]

Yet among kingly accomplishments was one he did not have that every other English king from the days of Charles I had possessed:

---

[10] This is given in most, if not all, contemporary accounts as "Briton." But the holograph note in the handwriting of the King in the British Museum shows that he wrote "Britain" (C. E. Vulliamy, *op. cit.*, p. 64). It was changed by the Earl of Hard-wicke to read "Briton" before publication (P. C. Yorke, *Life and Correspondence of . . . Hardwicke* [Cambridge, 1913], III, 262).

[11] The address was drawn up by the Earl of Hardwicke and was amplified by the King, who introduced that part of it quoted above that is in italics (*Parliamentary His-tory of England*, ed. T. C. Hansard, XV, 982; *Annual Register*, 1760, p. 248; *Corre-spondence of the Earl of Chatham*, ed. Taylor and Pringle [London, 1838], II, 81–2).

[12] See the comment of Romney Sedgwick, former Fellow of Trinity College, Cam-bridge, and editor of the *Letters of George III to Lord Bute*, p. viii.

[13] Horace Walpole, *Memoirs of the Reign of George III* (Philadelphia, 1845), I, 15.

he was not a soldier, for he had never been in arms and had therefore never enjoyed the command of troops. That he had expressed
a deep desire to acquire experience in this profession, as Prince of
Wales in the summer of 1759 when twenty-one years of age, is well
known; it is equally so, that the request to that end made to his
grandfather was refused, in spite of the fact that Pitt favoured his
application.[14] That George's disappointment was very real Bute
could not hide from the Great Commoner when in writing to him
on August 7, the Earl declared: "I need not tell you that he complains bitterly of the extreme neglect he ever meets in any matter
(be it what it will) that immediately concerns himself." [15] But he
was destined never to lead troops in battle, as was true of his father, Frederick. In fact, that honour was enjoyed by no reigning
British monarch after the time of George II.

As to the Great War for the Empire, there is no reason to doubt
that George while still heir to the throne strongly approved it,[16] but
with respect to continued participation in the war in Germany —
that was quite another matter. He had been opposed to the sending of troops there in 1758 and expressed the fear, according to a
memorandum left by Newcastle, that "if this unhappy measure
should be taken we shall be drawn deeper in a Continent War than
ever." [17] After this had, nevertheless, been done, he seems to have
favoured the idea — something that Lord George Sackville apparently had much at heart [18] — of having the commander of the British
expeditionary army in Germany enjoy an independent command
so that he could limit his activities to those that were most directly
in line with British interests. With a dislike of the House of Brunswick ever since the time when his grandfather had attempted in
1755 to force him into a marriage with a member of it, he was, consistent with the above view, especially disposed to support Sackville, as against Prince Ferdinand, in the bitter controversy that

---

[14] "Tho' the Command in Chief was not named, or anything like it," wrote the
Duke of Newcastle, "the King took it to mean that; and indeed that did seem to be the
purport of the letter" (L. B. Namier, op. cit., pp. 115–16). It would appear that one
reason, perhaps the chief, for refusing the Prince was the King's fear of offending the
Duke of Cumberland — at least both Newcastle and Lady Yarmouth thought that this
was the case (ibid.).

[15] Correspondence of Chatham, I, 416.

[16] See his enthusiastic letter to Lord Bute of August 11, 1758, Letters to Bute,
p. 11.

[17] Prince George to Bute, July 2, 1758, ibid.

[18] Sackville to Pitt, November 11, 1758, Correspondence of Chatham, I, 367.

arose in 1759 over the latter's insubordination during the Battle of Minden [19] and, as the result of his influence, Lord George was "given leave" to return to England rather than being abruptly recalled from his command.[20] Nor, one may believe, was he, upon becoming King in 1760, any happier about the German war than he had been earlier. When the Privy Council assembled, as required by law, on October 25 in order to proclaim him King, in addressing the Lords he referred to it as "a bloody and expensive war" and was prevented from having it appear in print in these terms only by the intervention of Pitt, who was insistent that the words when published should be changed to "an expensive, but just and necessary war." Only most reluctantly did the young King agree to this.[21]

Indeed, the key to his speech [22] is to be found at its end, where he stressed the fact that to secure "an honourable and lasting peace" he would continue to prosecute the war against France.[23]

George, it should be made clear, had already disclaimed any responsibility for Britain's participation in "the German war" — a war, as already suggested, that he disliked. Again, some two years earlier he had expressed the feeling, as recorded by Newcastle, that as long as it continued, those who had brought the nation into it would have to remain in office — thus preventing him, should he meanwhile come to the throne, from selecting ministers of his own choice.[24] This he certainly had very much at heart.

The King was a constitutional, limited monarch, however, clothed only with those powers that remained after Parliament had stripped from the throne most of the great and fundamental prerogatives enjoyed by the rulers of England before the Revolution of 1688. He could not, therefore, in order to realize his aims, pit himself against

---

[19] Prince George to Bute, August 11, 1759, and two letters to the same, April 23, 1760, Letters to Bute, pp. 29 and 43; Horace Walpole, Memoirs of the Reign of George II (London, 1846), III, 256.

[20] Correspondence of Chatham, I, 417–18.

[21] King George to Bute, November 1760, Letters to Bute, p. 49; Horace Walpole, Memoirs of the Reign of George III, I, 17. According to Lord Melcombe, the King had intended in this address to refer to the German measures "in terms of coldness" (Adolphus, op. cit., I, 19).

[22] The documents relating to the proclamation of George III as King, including the address, are printed in Edward Holt's The Public and Domestic Life of his late Most Gracious Majesty, George the Third (London, 1820) I, 12–15.

[23] The final words of the address, "in concert with my allies," were another alteration in it that Pitt also insisted upon (Walpole, op. cit., I, 17).

[24] King George to Bute, November 1760, Letters to Bute, pp. 49–50; L. B. Namier, op. cit., p. 67.

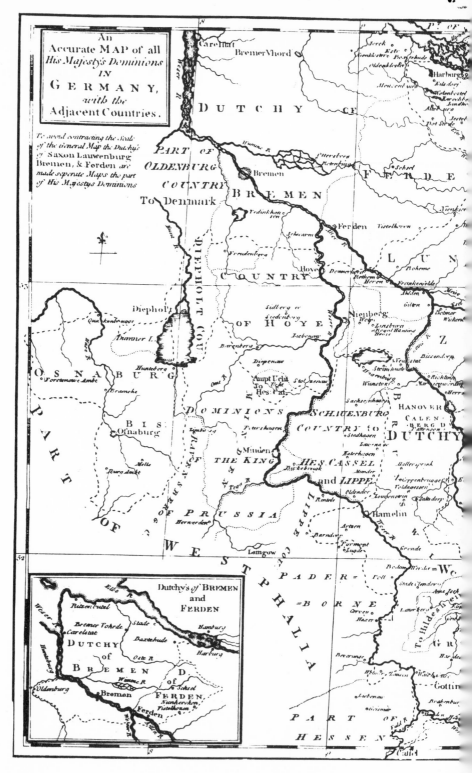

Within the map:

An Accurate MAP of all His Majesty's Dominions IN GERMANY, with the Adjacent Countries.

To avoid contracting the Scale of the General Map the Dutchys of Saxon Lauwenburg, Bremen, & Ferden are made seperate Maps the part of His Majestys Dominions

To Denmark

DUTCHY OF

PART OF OLDENBURG COUNTRY

BREMEN

Carelstat

BremerVhord

FERDE

Ferden

LUN

DIEPHOLT COUNTRY

COUNTRY OF HOYE

Diephol't

Hanover L.

Nienberg

Z

OSNABURG

DOMINIONS

SCHAUENBURG COUNTRY to

HANOVER

CALEN BERGD

DUTCHY

PART

BIS: Ofnaburg

OF THE KING

Minden

HES.CASSEL and LIPPE

Hamelin

OF PRUSSIA

Lemgow

WESTPHALIA

PADER BORNE

Dutchy's of BREMEN and FERDEN

Ritzenbutel

Bremer Vohrde Carelstat

Stade

Hamburg

Baxtehude

Harburg

DUTCHY of BREMEN

Oldenburg

Bremen

Ferden

Wamme R.

D of FERDEN. Nienkerchen Vistelhonem

To Hildesheim

GR

PART OF HESSEN

Gottin

"An Accurate Map of all His Majesty's Dominions in Germany. . . ."

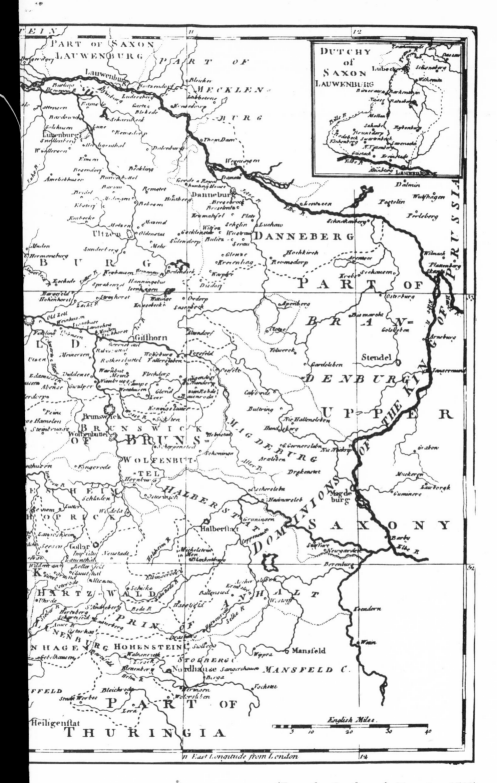

(From the *Gentleman's Magazine*, 1761)

that body in which was now concentrated the sovereignty of the Crown; he could only, if possible, control it. At the time of his accession Pitt's leadership within Parliament was unquestioned, and the Great Commoner was determined to support the Continental war along the lines that were in harmony with his previously announced policies. In his address to Parliament on November 18, to which reference has previously been made, George was therefore impelled for many good reasons to follow the line laid down by the Cabinet Council and to speak in praise of "the wise and able conduct of my general Prince Ferdinand of Brunswick" and of "my good brother and ally the King of Prussia" and to declare to the members:

> "I rely upon your zeal and hearty concurrence to support the King of Prussia and the rest of my allies; and to make ample provision for carrying on the war, as the only means to bring our enemies to equitable terms of accommodation." [25]

However, it is not without great significance that nowhere in the address is mention made of Hanover — "that horrid Electorate," as he had called it the preceding year [26] — to protect which George II, and finally Pitt, had gone to such great lengths. Indeed, the King had neither love for the Electorate nor, for that matter, for any of his grandfather's German connections. Lord Melcombe, who was a member of the court circle, was convinced that "the giving up of Hanover early in 1761 was his Majesty's own system," and therefore urged Bute to take the lead in proposing this, and felt that the ministry, outside of Pitt, would come into this plan whereby they would devote the money heretofore lavished by the nation upon the protection of the Electorate to distressing the French in other quarters so as to bring them to make peace. [27] That this was in line with his views at this period seems evident by the fact that George showed himself in such agreement with the caustic arguments of Israel Mauduit to that end, as expressed in his *Considerations on the German War* (reference to which was made in the preceding chapter), that he later bestowed upon the author a pension. [28]

---

25 *Parliamentary History*, XV, 983–4.

26 Prince George to Bute, August 5, 1759, *Letters to Bute*, p. 28. It is true that later, when he became afflicted with insanity, he came to idealize Hanover, though he never was to see it.

27 *Diary of George Bubb Dodington, Baron of Melcombe Regis* (London, 1809), pp. 375–9.

28 *History of the Late Minority* (London, 1765), p. 13.

The subsidies, nevertheless, for Prussia and the other German allies for their support during the following year were voted by Parliament in December 1760 with little argument, as has already been
indicated. But this was not to be the case when in November 1761
the question of these supplies was again raised, now by Lord Bute.
Although Pitt was no longer in office, he strongly favoured the continuance of the Prussian alliance and still enjoyed such vast popularity that even the King and those close to him felt that they could
not move against the tide. That, however, did not prevent a violent
opposition to the German war finding vent in the House of Commons before the subsidies for the year 1762 were finally approved.
In the words of Walpole:

> "The court support it, for they don't know how to desert it, nor care
> to be taxed with abatement of vigor; yet the temper of the House of
> Commons, and the tone even of the advocates of that war, were evi-
> dently repugnant to that measure." [29]

Indeed, Colonel Isaac Barré, who had fought in Canada, George
Grenville, Pitt's brother-in-law, Sir Francis Dashwood, Richard
Rigby, the Scot George Dempster, Richard Glover, Charles Thomas
Bunbury, and Sir F. B. Delaval, all now joined in denouncing either
the Prussian alliance or some other aspect of the Pitt European policy. Grenville, deploring the Prussian treaty, nevertheless, admitted that Britain was now so deeply involved as to make the grant
necessary. At the same time he denied that America had been conquered in Germany; rather, France had been fatally hampered in
the New World for want of men accustomed to a seafaring life –
and therefore by lack of sea power. Barré – a supporter of Fitzmaurice, who was strongly opposed to interference in the German
war – in assailing the treaty even turned upon Pitt, his erstwhile
friend, and berated him for his changes and contradictions in policy and did not hesitate to ridicule his public poses.[30] The Prussian
subsidy, though permitted by its opponents at length to pass without a division, was destined to represent the last appropriation

---

[29] Horace Walpole to Sir Horace Mann, December 12, 1761, *Letters of Horace
Walpole* (ed. Mrs. Paget Toynbee, Oxford, 1904), V, 152.

[30] *Correspondence of Chatham*, II, 169–70; Horace Walpole, *Memoirs of the Reign
of George III*, I, 79–80; *Correspondence of John, 4th Duke of Bedford* (ed. Lord John
Russell, London, 1842–6), II, 426; *Memoirs of the Marquis of Rockingham* (ed. Earl
of Albemarle, London, 1852), I, 71, 81; Lord Fitzmaurice, *Life of Shelburne* (London,
1875), I, 125–6.

made by Parliament to underwrite the military operations of Frederick, in spite of the fact that the needs of Hanover and Hesse-Cassel were still supplied for some time to come by reason of prior commitments.[31]

One explanation for the growing hostility in England to further participation in the Continental war was certainly the indecisive nature of the struggle there in contrast with the decisive victories gained in the Great War for the Empire. The military events in Germany in 1760, as well as those of the next two years, must therefore be considered briefly. Again, as in 1759, on all fronts throughout the year 1760 it was a war of movement, with the coalition powers maintaining great superiority in numbers and occupying Saxony, much of Silesia, as well as East Prussia and Frederick's possessions in the area of the Rhine. The plan of the enemy was to crush the King of Prussia and occupy Berlin by a simultaneous movement against him of three armies, one from Saxony, another from Silesia, and a third from the country east of the Oder. It seemed as though the plan would succeed.

In June the Prussian General Fouqué's (Fouquet's) army of some thirteen thousand was almost destroyed near Landshut in Silesia when marching under orders from Frederick to cover Breslau. Then in August the King penetrated deeply into Silesia and was almost surrounded by the Austrians and the Russians, but escaped the trap and near Liegnitz inflicted upon the Austrian Laudon a severe defeat and thereupon by a clever ruse brought about the retirement of a Russian army ready to close in upon him. Until early in October he continued to manœuvre in Silesia against Daun, until he was informed of the capture of Berlin by a combined force of Russians, Imperialists, and Austrians, the last from Saxony, all moving rapidly upon the place by prearrangement. With the news of his approach to his capital, however, the enemy departed after levying heavy contributions upon its inhabitants and destroying all military supplies. The Imperialists and Austrians moved to Torgau, to the north of Leipzig, where they were joined by Daun with the main part of his army. Determined to attack them, in spite of the inferiority of his forces, Frederick on November 3 ordered his Prussian grenadiers to march against the strong entrenchments of the

---

[31] As late as 1766 Parliament voted indemnification money to Hesse-Cassel. For a tabular statement of parliamentary subsidies, see C. W. Eldon, *England's Subsidy Policy toward the Continent during the Seven Years' War* (Philadelphia, 1938), pp. 161–2.

Austrian general, who had concentrated there some four hundred guns that poured upon them an annihilating fire. But fresh troops were thrown into the breach and the fight continued from two o'clock in the afternoon until, in the blackness of night, with Daun dangerously wounded, the Austrians withdrew. Even so the latter's losses were far less than those of Frederick, which amounted to thirty per cent of his army. After this great battle, which had shown the King of Prussia at his best as a strategist, the campaign in east Germany came to an end, still as inconclusive as were the campaigns of the preceding two years.[32]

Nor was there anything more decisive in the activities, during the same year, of Prince Ferdinand, commander-in-chief of the allied army in western Germany. The enemy remained greatly superior to it and was more easily supplied. Indeed, the English cavalry under Lord Granby suffered greatly for lack of forage, which was extremely scarce in an area that for years had been the scene of hostilities. During the late spring and early summer, as the result of the pressure of the French — moving under Broglie from Frankfurt am Main into Hesse-Cassel, and under St. Germain through Westphalia — Ferdinand slowly retired. At Corbach in July he suffered defeat at the hands of St. Germain; in the same month at Ziegenhagen his forces, however, fell upon a strong French contingent of Broglie's army and routed it. Then on the last day of the month at Warburg near Corbach he again routed the enemy. These engagements were especially characterized by the splendid showing made by the British cavalry, determined, as it were, to wipe out the disgrace of Minden. Yet in concentrating his forces against the French in Westphalia the Prince was obliged to leave Hesse-Cassel to its fate.

In September, to prevent the gathering of another French army on the lower Rhine, the Hereditary Prince of Brunswick suddenly moved westward with a part of the allied forces and not only laid siege to Wesel, a fortress at the confluence of the Rhine and the Lippe to the east of the Rhine, but passed rapidly over the Rhine River in an effort to recapture Cleves, long a possession of the house of Brandenburg, but now in the hands of the French. The latter were taken by surprise and had it not been for unprecedented rains that prevented the allied general from receiving reinforcements over the flooded river, his two objectives might have been

---

[32] John Entick, *History of the Late War* (London, 1763), IV, 420–5.

secured. As it was, he was able late in October, without too great
losses and in the face of an enemy growing hourly in superiority, to
retrace his steps and rejoin the main force under Ferdinand. The
latter, soon afterward, went into winter quarters with Hanover still
at his back and facing the French army, which in the form of a giant
crescent occupied Hesse-Cassel and extended its left flank to Wesel,
and its right to Göttingen.

If Torgau in 1760 added to the military reputation of the King of
Prussia, the year 1761 was one of humiliation for him in his weakness. Entrenched securely with his army in northern Silesia, pressed
by the Austrians, Daun and Laudon, and by the Russians who also
once more had entered that principality, he could only remain on
the defensive throughout the year in seeking to protect Breslau.
But in doing so he permitted the Austrians early in October to capture the great fortress of Schweidnitz to the southwest of that city,
and late in December he was practically cut off from the Baltic by
the loss to the Russians of the still more important fortified town of
Kolberg. It seemed quite evident that, without being able to risk a
single battle during the entire campaign, his power was crum-
bling away. Nor was Ferdinand, in western Germany, in a position
to make a much better showing now against the armies under Marshal Broglie and the Prince of Soubise. Nevertheless, in this so-called
petite guerre he did succeed in protecting most of Hanover and also
in saving Brunswick to the east of it from conquest, though obliged
to see Westphalia ravaged from one end to the other while holding
his position tightly in the general area of the Weser.

It was at the end of this campaign that officers in the British expeditionary force became so deeply dissatisfied with the role they
were forced to play that they became actively engaged in the war
of pamphlets over the interventionist policy of Pitt in the German
war. In *The Case of the British Troops Serving in Germany, Hum-
bly Submitted to the Consideration of Parliament*, published late in
1761, not only was the unhappy situation of the British army on the
Continent stressed, but the point was driven home that the quarrel
between Great Britain and France originally had nothing to do with
Europe, and that when the former had secured her chief object in
the war, the troops in Germany should have been withdrawn. This
also was the theme of *A British Officer now in Germany . . . Hum-
bly Recommended to the Perusal of the Legislature*, which appeared at the same period. The author of it insisted that the war

between England and France and that between Prussia and Austria were in the beginning "entirely independent of each other." He then went on to say: "I cannot help being of opinion that . . . we should have brought the French to terms much sooner if we had continued unconnected." For a variety of reasons, moreover, he deplored involvement in the German war — an involvement so unnecessary to Britain and so harmful rather than beneficial to the Germans. As to the war with France, he stated its cause succinctly:

> "France, not satisfied with her possessions in America, thought proper to encroach upon her neighbour, at a time when they were supposed to be friends . . . we not chusing to relinquish our lands, for no other reason, than because they happened to lie convenient for our natural enemy, fell to taking of their ships, because they would give no other satisfaction: declarations of war succeeded. . . . This I think is a true history of the cause of the present war between France and England."

Moreover, the author assured the reader that his views on the German war were those generally held by the expeditionary force.

Out of the gloom that thus enveloped the allies there came an unexpected gleam of light early in 1762 that, in fact, was to signalize a dramatic change in their fortunes. For Elizabeth of Russia, Frederick's bitter enemy, passed away on January 5 and was succeeded on the throne by her nephew Peter III, who had unbounded admiration for the King of Prussia. The young Czar, with a claim to the Duchy of Holstein which he ardently desired to make good at the expense of Denmark, took immediate steps therefore to end all hostilities with Prussia. A truce was signed on March 15, and on May 5 came the treaty of St. Petersburg. Not only did Russia summarily abandon her late confederates and agree to surrender her conquests, but an army was actually sent to aid Frederick in driving the Austrians out of Silesia. This amazing reversal was not lost upon the King of Sweden, who for his own security felt that his policies must be in accord with those of his powerful neighbour, and on May 22 in the Treaty of Hamburg he agreed to cease all hostilities with Prussia on the basis of a *status quo ante bellum*. With his northern and eastern frontiers no longer threatened and with a friendly and hard-fighting Russian army at his disposal, the King of Prussia could now feel free to turn again to aggressive warfare against the three armies of the Empress Queen cantoned in Silesia and in Saxony. While he was in the midst of preparations to this end, however, came the startling news of the deposition of the Czar early in July in favour of his wife Catherine II, and the recall of the Russian army destined to co-operate with him in the projected campaign. It first seemed to him that Catherine would renew the hostile policy of Elizabeth, but the new Czarina instead determined upon one of strict neutrality and therefore nonintervention in the war. In harmony with it she proceeded to fulfil the agreement Peter had made to evacuate all the conquered possessions.

Now with lightning speed Frederick moved in the direction of Schweidnitz, called "the key to Silesia," to retake it, routing an Austrian army under Laudon that sought to protect it. He then besieged the fortress, with its garrison of eight thousand, which was obliged to surrender in October. Late in the same month Prince Henry in Saxony, on being reinforced by his brother, dealt a heavy defeat to a combined army of Austrians and Imperialists at Freiberg. This, together with the slackening of the Austrian war effort, was disastrous to the Imperialists. Prussian forces raided Bohemia and moved rapidly into various other hostile states of the Empire, raising immense contributions, as at Nuremberg. Thus Frederick, by these means and through other drastic war measures, such as currency debasement, and also buttressed by the British subsidy voted late in 1761, was to emerge from the long period of hostilities far from bankrupt; on the contrary, not only was he financially solvent, but his treasury was full.

In western Germany during the same year the allies likewise more than held their own. Here the Marshal de Broglie was superseded as commander of the main French army by the Prince of Soubise and Marshal d'Estrées. The Prince of Condé also commanded an army on the lower Rhine. In spite of the continued numerical superiority of the enemy and their great efforts, most of Hanover still continued to remain beyond their grasp. What they had seized within the southern part of the Electorate, moreover, they were finally forced to relinquish as the result of the very able use that Prince Ferdinand made of his limited forces. Further, by outmanœuvring the French and even outfighting them, he gradually pushed his opponents out of most of Hesse-Cassel and in the course of the year's campaign, after a siege of fifteen days, secured the surrender of the city of Cassel, with its French garrison of ten thousand. Thus was the great hope of the French, their chief object, in fact, in becoming involved in the war in Germany — the conquest and holding of Hanover until by a peace it would be restored under terms advantageous to them — rudely blasted. The culmination of the war in Westphalia and elsewhere in western Germany in this fashion, as disadvantageous to them as it was advantageous to the allies, was only made possible, it may be affirmed, as the result of heavy and continued support by Britain. The record of the British expeditionary force under Lord Granby, in addition, was one of great gallantry. Embodying as it did some twenty-five thousand well-equipped troops, it gave to Ferdinand a hard-fighting, swift-moving, dependable nucleus. The rest of his troops, moreover, were paid, armed, and supported by British resources. Indeed, only by these means lavishly furnished could Hanover have been defended and have escaped being used as a pawn in the negotiations for peace between France and Great Britain.[33]

But we must now take leave of Europe in order to turn to a consideration of the course of events on the high seas, particularly in the Caribbean area.

---

[33] For the German Seven Years' War covering the years from 1759 to the end of 1762 see Richard Waddington's *La Guerre de Sept Ans*, Vols. III, IV, and V; A. Schäfer's *Geschichte des Siebenjährigen Krieges* (Berlin, 1874), Vol. II; and Emil Daniels, "The Seven Years' War," *Cambridge Modern History* (London, 1909), Chapter IX. For a contemporary account of the events dealt with in this chapter see Frederick II's *Histoire de la Guerre de Sept Ans*, in *Œuvres de Frederic le Grand* (Berlin, 1847), Vol. V. John Entick's *The General History of the Late War* . . . (London, 1770–2), Vols. IV and V, while made up largely of compilations from such accounts of the war as those contained in the *Annual Register* and other contemporary works, is still useful to the student. The best study of the military and other activities of Prince Henry of Prussia is Professor Easum's *Prince Henry of Prussia, Brother of Frederick the Great* (Madison, 1942).

CHAPTER IV

Privateersmen and Neutrals

LTHOUGH before the beginning of the Great War for the Empire the ultimate disposition of the so-called "neutral" West India islands of Dominica, St. Lucia, St. Vincent, and Tobago [1] was a matter of dispute between Great Britain and France and became the subject of extensive deliberations on the part of the Anglo-French Commission meeting in Paris between the years 1750 and 1754, as well as of rival memorials, this was not the issue that precipitated the outbreak of hostilities — except in so far as the conduct of the French authorities respecting the rival claims to the islands had convinced the government of Great Britain that France could not be trusted in *any* controversy to proceed in good faith. Indeed, during the earlier years of hostilities the area of the Caribbean Sea might be called the quiet sector, with comparatively little attention paid to it, except for the protection of the trade there and the encouragement of privateering. [2] In other words, the mighty conflict had its origin in North America involving issues that were particularly related to this continent, and for years really absorbed most of the energies and resources of the two powers that were available for overseas warlike activities. It should not be inferred, however, that from the point of view of either the British or the French the West Indies were unimportant.

France was entrenched on three islands that by 1754, especially with the growth of the sugar industry, had become perfect mines of wealth [3] — the fertile western portion of Santo Domingo, which por-

---

[1] For an analysis of the problem of the "Neutral Islands" of the West Indies see Volume V of this series, Chapter VII and pages 312–14 of Chapter X.

[2] Julian S. Corbett, *England in the Seven Years' War*, I, 351.

[3] For a study of the growth of the sugar industry in the French West Indies see Volume II of this series, Chapter IX.

tion the French called St. Domingue, ceded to them by Spain in 1697 in the Treaty of Ryswick, and, in the Lesser Antilles, Guadeloupe and Martinique. St. Domingue was considered to be the most valuable by far of the French possessions in the West Indies. By 1726 it is said to have had some thirty thousand white inhabitants and over one hundred thousand Negro slaves; some forty years later its sugar, indigo, cotton, and coffee, raised in profusion on rich lands and exported to France, were estimated to possess an annual value of well over one million pounds sterling, and its trade in European manufactures to the Spaniards, of some two million Spanish milled dollars.[4] The protection of this valuable colony in time of war was therefore a matter of first consideration on the part of the French government.

Guadeloupe, lying to the south of British Antigua and the largest of the Leeward Islands, was said to produce before the war more sugar than all of the British West India islands put together.[5] Martinique — some thirty leagues to the southeast of Guadeloupe, with the island of Dominica between them — while not nearly so great a sugar colony as was Guadeloupe, nevertheless, with its ten thousand white inhabitants aided by the labour of forty thousand Negro slaves, succeeded in raising crops the annual value of which was declared to amount on an average between the years 1747 and 1755 to some twenty-five million livres, or in terms of pounds sterling to over one million, according to a petition to the King by the Council of Commerce of France in 1762.[6] The island, moreover, was distinguished by the fact that the Governor General of the French Caribbean possessions had his residence there; that it also was the seat of the Superior Council, which had the responsibility of supervising the activities of all the French possessions in the West Indies, including St. Domingue; and that its Fort Royal was the naval base of the French islands in the Lesser Antilles. It was asserted that to serve the needs of the French West Indies the services of some fourteen hundred vessels were required before the outbreak of war.[7] The value of these islands when compared with Canada as a source of wealth to France may be measured by the fact

---

[4] M. Bruzen de la Martinière, Le Grand Dictionnaire géographique, historique et critique (Paris, 1768), V, 233–5; D. Fenning, J. Collyer, and others, A New System of Geography (London, 1765), II, 707.

[5] Ibid., II, 710.

[6] London advices, April 1, 1762, Pennsylvania Gazette, June 24, 1762.

[7] Ibid.

"An Accurate Map of the West Indies, with the Adjacent Coast."

(From the *Gentleman's Magazine*, 1762)

that during the year 1754 but forty-one ships ascended the St. Lawrence, including nine from the Caribbean Sea.[8]

Flourishing as these islands were in time of peace — in contrast
to the gradual decline in importance during the eighteenth century of the British West India possessions, outside of Jamaica, by
reason of soil exhaustion and the weight of taxation — their needs
for subsistence could not be met locally, at least economically. It
was estimated that land employed there for the raising of food and
wine for the support of ten people, if given over to the cultivation
of sugar, cotton, and other export staples, could support more than
fifty inhabitants.[9] Moreover, in the one instance their only value to
the mother country would be as an outlet for her population, while
in the other they not only added greatly to her wealth but supported
a large merchant marine, so necessary an adjunct to the protection
of the national interests. Their utter dependence upon outside
sources of supply, nevertheless, could not be fully met within the
French Empire. As a result they were obliged to look to the British
continental colonies, eager to exchange their flour, meat, fish, lumber, and many other commodities for the vast quantity of molasses
— a by-product of the sugar mills — that otherwise could not be
profitably sold because of the French preference for wine and
brandy to rum. The laws, also, forbade this base for the distilling
of rum to be imported into France. Out of this mutually profitable
exchange of articles of commerce with the continental colonies,
there developed a certain real economic interdependence that was
very adversely affected by the outbreak of hostilities in 1754 and a
declaration of war two years later.

As for American ship captains who had been accustomed to resort to the West Indies and to trade with the French there, one of
two courses now lay open to them should they continue to visit
these islands in time of war. One was to arm the vessel and as a
privateer raid the merchant ships of the enemy seeking either to
approach their ports or to depart from them. The other was to run
the risk of attempting to continue to trade with the inhabitants. In
either case success brought large personal rewards that had some
relation to the dangers involved. It may be noted in this connection
that at such American ports as New York privateering became a
leading occupation of the merchants established there, especially

8 Shelburne Papers, 64:169, Clements Library.
9 Article "Martinique," Bruzen de la Martinière, op. cit., IV, 122.

during the years 1756 and 1757. In 1756 forty New York vessels were commissioned to act as privateers; [10] and in 1757 there were fifty-nine petitions for commissions of marque and reprisal by owners of vessels at the same port.[11] Some of them, such as the ship *Blakeney* of fifty-four guns, carried a large complement of sailors and were capable of committing much havoc among the enemy shipping, while others, such as the *Anne* with only ten guns, could be used with effect, it is clear, only under the most advantageous circumstances as raiders and could be protected in turn against most of the French privateers only be superior sailing qualities. What was true of New York was equally characteristic of other American seaports such as Newport and Boston. As was mentioned in the preceding volume of this series, the sheriff of Newport County calculated in 1757 that ten thousand colonials were taken into the service of American privateers.[12] The lure of gaining a quick fortune was such, it is certain, as to lead many men to desert the army and the royal navy. In 1757 so many warships were made helpless in New York harbour as a result of the desertion of the crews preparatory to joining some privateer, that the Governor of the province, Rear Admiral Sir Charles Hardy, found that it was necessary to surround the city with regular troops and then make a house-to-house canvass to recover the secreted sailors to man the King's ships.[13] The Earl of Loudoun, writing to Pitt in the spring of 1757, estimated that already French prizes valued at two hundred thousand pounds sterling had been brought to that port alone.[14]

The Caribbean Sea, as a result of the zeal of colonial shipowners, swarmed with privateers ready to pick up individual French merchantmen — and, it may also be added, with French privateers almost as numerous and just as ready to fall upon individual merchantmen flying the British colours. In view of the hazards thus presented to trade in the West Indies, each side turned to the device

---

[10] It may be of interest to students of nautical affairs to note the types of vessels employed for this work. Of the forty that were commissioned, twelve were sloops, ten were ships, eight were snows, eight were brigantines, and, finally, there was one schooner and one dogger (New York Col. Mss., 83:88, 65–72, 117–60, 84:60, New York State Archives, Albany).

[11] See the "Calendar of Manuscripts in the Office of Secretary of State," Part II, Albany.

[12] Loudoun Papers, No. 2618, Huntington Library.

[13] Earl of Loudoun to William Pitt, May 30, 1757, *Correspondence of William Pitt*, I, 69.

[14] *Ibid.*

of convoys as in earlier wars. At Cap François, the chief harbour of French St. Domingue, or at Port-au-Prince on the same island, ships would assemble preparatory to the return to France, and then would be escorted by warships well out of the chief danger zone; thereupon most of the armed vessels would return to their regular station to guard this valuable possession, while others would continue the task of escort across the Atlantic. Likewise, the French merchantmen resorting to Guadeloupe and Martinique as well as to the settlements on the "Neutral Islands" were assembled and escorted well out into the ocean by the French squadron stationed at Fort Royal in Martinique and then left to the protection of such ships of war as were consigned to this duty. In like manner the merchantmen trading to the British West Indies were convoyed from two concentration points: Port Royal in Jamaica and English Harbour in Antigua.

The strategic position of the French Caribbean islands was superior to that of the British possessions in that vessels approaching either Cap François or Fort Royal were not obliged to skirt the enemy's shores and, by the prevailing trade winds, were under ordinary weather conditions wafted speedily and directly to their destination. On the other hand, ships seeking either the British Leeward Islands or Jamaica were compelled as a rule to run the gantlet. In order to reach the British Leewards they were generally obliged to skirt Guadeloupe as well as Martinique, where, as Corbett points out, the old race of French buccaneers still bred like flies, or, to arrive at Port Royal in Jamaica they were forced to move along the infested southern shore of St. Domingue.[15]

With both French and British privateers in large numbers haunting the West Indies, the newspapers — such as Franklin and Hall's *Pennsylvania Gazette* — were from 1756 onward to the very end of the war, in 1763, filled with reports of innumerable clashes between them, each, as a rule, cruising as a lone wolf in search primarily of richly laden, unarmed merchantmen of the enemy, but often bearing down upon a heavily armed adversary, who generally did not hesitate to give battle. With respect to these individual combats on the high seas, no clear generalizations can be made as to the superiority of one side over the other as fighters, when the ships were equally matched in fire-power. It should, nevertheless, be pointed out that figures collected for the year 1758 show that in various

---

[15] J. S. Corbett, *op. cit.*, I, 355.

ways the French lost forty-nine privateers and armed merchantmen as against the British loss of but seven privateers.[16] On the other hand, it may be asserted that the record of the French privateers was far superior to that of the French navy and gives one the impression that the more hardy, hard-fighting French seamen sought and secured service on board the French privateers rather than on the ships of war of that nation. In this connection may be noted the exploits of the romantic French privateersman Captain Chatelean — the terror of British shipping along the coast of the southern colonies.[17]

From what has just been stated the reader may gather that the navies of the two powers did not seek to destroy the merchant marine of their opponent. This is far from the truth. Frequently a convoy would be sighted by a squadron, which would bear down upon it and after disposing of the guardian warships would pick up all other vessels that could not easily escape. At the same time, it should be understood that the commanding officers of squadrons on either side were under their instructions seldom given the freedom to disperse in order to go in pursuit of individual merchantmen. Indeed, the strategic task that they were given to perform forbad their departure from strict tactical arrangements, which demanded that the ships act as a unit within view of the flagship so as to receive the orders sent out from time to time to the commanders of individual vessels.

How dangerous were the waters of the Caribbean Sea and also those of that part of the Atlantic lying directly to the northward of it to individual ships may be noted by the fact that of twenty-one heavily laden vessels that left Charleston, South Carolina, for England late in 1756, only two escaped capture; [18] in two months during the spring of 1758 twenty vessels, apparently unprotected, were captured near the British island of Antigua. Manifestly the system of convoy was the best solution of the problem. In 1757 that from Jamaica numbered one hundred and twenty ships and in 1758 it numbered one hundred and sixty-four; [19] from Plymouth, England, some two hundred merchantmen were protected by Admiral Holmes with

16 John Entick, *The General History of the Late War* (2nd ed., London, 1765), III, 399–401.
17 For some account of Chatelean's activities see the *Pennsylvania Gazette* for December 21, 1758 and January 11, 1759.
18 London advices, *Pennsylvania Gazette*, July 7, 1757.
19 *Ibid.*, August 1, 1757 and August 17, 1758.

a squadron destined to serve in the West Indies.[20] But sometimes the best-laid plans of escort went astray. In 1758 the Virginia tobacco ships, some ninety in number, sailing in a body under escort, were scattered as the result of a storm, with the result that many were lost apparently to the enemy.[21] In 1759, however, they were more fortunate, arriving, it appears, in the Downs under convoy of H.M.S. *Lynn.*[22]

It is clear that a much greater number of vessels flying the British flag were captured in the course of the war than those that belonged to the enemy, which may be accounted for by the fact that the sea-borne commerce of Great Britain and her colonies taken together was vastly greater than that of France. By the middle of June 1757, the French were credited with the capture of seven hundred ships from the beginning of the war, whereas the British who took some three hundred and fifty ships before an open declaration of war in 1756 — all as a reprisal for French aggression in North America — had by that date captured only some two hundred additional vessels.[23] This high rate of capture on the part of the French did not decline. According to Lloyd's figures, between June 1756 and June 1760 a grand total of some 2,539 British and colonial vessels fell victim to French raiders on the high seas, whereas up to the middle of 1760 a total of only 944 French vessels were lost to the British.[24]

Yet the simple fact remains that the French merchant marine was being inexorably swept from the seas, for ship-construction in France during the course of the war was but a fraction of that which took place within the British Empire, where replacements of losses continued to be made. Indeed, one important factor that accounts for the rather poor showing of the British and colonial privateers in comparison with those of France was that the French government in order to protect the nation from losses or to compensate for them turned to the policy of encouraging neutrals to undertake the tasks of both supplying the French colonies with necessities and carrying the products of the colonies to the ports of France, either directly or indirectly.[25]

---

20 *Ibid.*, May 29, 1760.
21 *Ibid.*, January 25, 1759.
22 *Ibid.*, February 14, 1760.
23 London advices, *ibid.*, September 1, 1757.
24 *Ibid.*, October 2, 1760.
25 How difficult it had become for the French West India planters to market their produce and supply France with sugar is indicated by an article published in *Owen's*

Among the powers that remained neutral in this war, the Dutch had by far the greatest merchant marine. Although it no longer enjoyed the proud pre-eminence that it had possessed in the early half of the seventeenth century, it was still impressive in size and naturally sought to profit by the situation, just as later the merchant marine of the youthful United States sought to profit as a neutral in the course of the Napoleonic Wars. In each instance the government of France, in order to bring relief to the inhabitants of her sugar islands, encouraged neutrals to bring food and other supplies to them and to carry away their great accumulation of sugar and other commodities. This seemed to present a golden opportunity to acquire wealth without undue risk on the part of the shipowners of the chief neutral carrying power, and they proceeded to act accordingly. As a result, hundreds of neutral ships became involved during each of these wars in this profitable business, as beneficial to one of the two belligerents as it was detrimental to the war aims of the other. The British thus saw the logical pressure of their superior sea power, designed to bring the enemy to terms, nullified by the activities of neutrals, which were now permitted by the French authorities to do in time of war what they could not possibly do legally in time of peace — in view of French decrees and ordinances governing the trade of their colonies. It is clear that the Dutch, in acting as a transporting agency for the French islands, received every inducement from the inhabitants of the latter. British vessels taken by French privateers were sold to Dutchmen "for little or nothing," according to the confession of Captain Sinclair of the *Three Brothers* of Boston, who, while engaged in trade with the enemy, was captured with his vessel by a British warship, the *Invincible*. Sinclair also declared that the planters and merchants of the French islands paid the Dutch the very high price of four shillings sixpence per hundred pounds for transporting their sugar to France.[26]

The Dutch, in fact, felt themselves in a rather secure position in that as a neutral nation their ships were free to roam the seas and

Weekly Chronicle, published in London, in the issue of December 23, 1758. According to one who had just arrived from France (presumably a neutral observer), loaf sugar, which was selling for tenpence a pound in London, was selling in Jamaica at twenty-four shillings per hundredweight, while on the French island it was sold to those engaged in the contraband trade at from eight shillings sixpence to twelve shillings per hundredweight.

[26] From the *Antigua Gazette* of March 22, 1757.

even to go to a belligerent port that was not actually blockaded. For the principle that "free ships make free goods" had been embodied in the temporary Anglo-Dutch treaty of 1668 and in the permanent treaty between the two powers in 1674, that was in turn clarified by the treaty of 1675, which was still held to be in force in 1756. In view of this situation, the question arose in the minds of both belligerents and neutrals, by what right could British warships or privateers flying the Union Jack interfere with this advantageous Dutch trade? The answer came in the promulgation of a new principle of international law as set forth by the British High Court of Admiralty and Court of Prize Appeals. This was the famous Rule of 1756, supplemented by the Doctrine of Continuous Voyage.[27]

Stated in its simplest form, the Rule of 1756 declared that while a neutral ship and its cargo could not be condemned for trading with the enemy *per se*, these could be condemned if it were found that the enemy authorities treated such a ship on terms that under the decrees and ordinances of that state only the ship of a national was privileged to enjoy. In other words, this principle, while accepting the Anglo-Dutch doctrine of "free ships make free goods" and regarding therefore the treaty of 1675 as intact and sacred, went beyond it in setting up the new doctrine that stated: "If a Dutchman in certain compromising circumstances was not a Dutchman at all, but a Frenchman, it was no violation of the treaty to condemn him, ship, cargo and all."[28] It was not, however, until the Court of Prize Appeals confirmed in the spring of 1759 the condemnation of the Dutch ship *America* and her cargo by the High Court of Admiralty on February 26 of that year, that we come to the decision of the Earl of Hardwicke, one of the Commissioners of Appeal, that gave to the Rule of 1756 its classical setting. In it he declared that the *America* — freighted on French account and sent to French St. Domingue, where her cargo, by express permission of the Governor there, had been delivered and where her homeward-bound cargo, the property of French subjects, had been, after official survey of the ship under terms of the French ordinances, placed on board and all export

---

[27] I am in agreement with the view of Professor Richard Pares, as set forth in his *Colonial Blockade and Neutral Rights, 1739–1763* (Oxford, 1938), pp. 180–204, that no effective precedent for the Rule of 1756 can be found earlier than the Anglo-Spanish war of 1739–48 and that in considering it in its matured form it will be found to have broken new ground in the field of international law.

[28] *Ibid.*, p. 197.

duties had been paid on it, according to French law — "ought by law to be considered in this case as a French ship. . . ." [29] As the result of this condemnation and that of other Dutch ships and their cargoes the following year, "as adopted French ships," the old maxim of "free ships make free goods," which still applied to Europe, became irrelevant with respect to the colonies of a belligerent, nor could papers purporting that the goods had changed hands and were the property of Dutchmen protect them.

As to the Doctrine of Continuous Voyage, this had its foundation in the Rule of 1756 and grew out of the efforts of the Dutch to circumvent the rule by receiving at their islands of St. Eustatius and Curaçao commodities from St. Domingue shipped in enemy vessels. The goods, while ultimately destined for France, would thereupon be placed on board Dutch vessels, which could then proceed to Europe in their role of neutrals. In face of this practice, the Earl of Holderness, Secretary of State, early in 1759 warned Sir Joseph Yorke, British Minister at The Hague, to make clear to the Dutch government: "That a voyage begun on a bottom that would render the cargo confiscable [that is, an enemy bottom], is not to be continued by the ship of a friend, but would still be confiscable as the continuance of the same voyage." [30] Upon the basis of the principle embodied in this declaration as well as upon the broad Rule of 1756, ships were freely condemned in courts of vice-admiralty. There is every reason to believe that this basis for the capture of Dutch ships as good prizes was greeted in the British colonial ports with delight. Nevertheless, there is a certain grim irony surrounding the laying down of these principles of maritime law, in that the time would come in the course of the Napoleonic Wars when American neutral vessels would be condemned in British vice-admiralty courts for their violation and that decisions of admiralty courts that were once applauded as right and proper by Americans would be bitterly denounced by their descendants.

The American privateers that roved the West Indies and those of English registration that haunted the English Channel, as well as British ships of war, had already laid a heavy hand on Dutch ship-

---

[29] *Ibid.*, p. 198. The Amsterdam owners of the *America* complained bitterly of this condemnation and an instruction by the States General to the Dutch Minister in London was framed protesting against it as in violation of the treaty of 1674, but all in vain. (For these instructions see the *Pennsylvania Gazette*, August 23, 1759.)

[30] Richard Pares, *op. cit.*, p. 223.

ping before the case of the *America* had been decided in February 1759. Indeed, it is clear that there was resentment among colonial shipowners and ship captains in search of prizes that by the middle of 1757, the French in the West Indies, as reported in the press, "Now lay up all their Merchant Ships as they arrive from Europe, except such as are fit for Cruizers, which they fit out, having left off shipping any of their Produce but in Dutch Bottoms and dutchified Prizes; all which our good Friends and Allies [the Dutch] get insured in England." [31] It is equally clear that already numbers of Dutch ships had been captured and that the Dutch in the West Indies — especially the Governor of the island of Curaçao — were protesting mightily, but uselessly.[32] New York and Rhode Island privateers working in a pack, for example, the following year (that is, in 1758) captured three Dutch vessels trying to enter a port in French St. Domingue, and privateers from the same colonies even carried to New York "two deep laden large Dutch ships," bound, at least according to their commanders, from Amsterdam to Curaçao.[33] Nor did the Dutch shipmaster find relief in sailing in company with numerous other ships flying the Dutch flag. In the spring of 1758 twenty of their merchantmen from a flotilla were carried as prizes to the Leeward Islands by their captors.[34] While the courts of vice-admiralty would not ordinarily condemn a Dutch ship moving to a Dutch possession from Holland, it was quick to settle the fate of such a ship should there be found papers — secreted in one instance in a ship buoy — showing French invoices and bills of lading.[35] By the summer of that year the Dutch merchants, in petitioning the government of the United Provinces to protect their property, declared that at least two hundred and forty of their ships had already been captured.[36]

As might have been conjectured, the seizure of Dutch vessels, especially of such a large number, led to a storm of indignation in Holland, with rumours that the government of the United Nether-

---

[31] *Pennsylvania Gazette*, August 4, 1757.

[32] *Ibid.*, August 18, 1757.

[33] *Ibid.*, March 16, 1758.

[34] *Ibid.*, May 4, 1758. Sometimes the Dutch ships were escorted by French warships (Julian S. Corbett, *op. cit.*, II, 6; Richard Pares, *op. cit.*, p. 383).

[35] *Pennsylvania Gazette*, May 11, 1758. One method employed to circumvent the privateers, according to the captured letter of a Martinique merchant to his correspondent in Bordeaux, was to consign the cargo to the captain of the Dutch ship; he would then claim to be the owner of it. The merchant claimed that the ruse worked in the case of four ships (*ibid.*, October 12, 1758).

[36] London advices, June 27, *ibid.*, September 14, 1758.

lands was on the point of breaking off relations with that of Great Britain.[37] But the Dutch were realists, and one writing from The Hague on December 22, 1758 with reference to the attitude of the States General declared "that their High Mightinesses in view of the weight of our national debt, the miserable state of our finances, and the wretched condition to which the poor inhabitants of these provinces are reduced will think seriously on a matter of so much importance notwithstanding the popular clamour." [38] Indeed, when Mr. Hop, the Dutch Minister accredited to the Court of St. James's, presented his protest to Secretary of State Pitt about this treatment of the Dutch merchant ships, we are told, the latter replied heatedly to him:

> "That the navigation and trade to the French islands were carried on for the account of the French though under borrowed names . . . that all the certificates, which attest upon oath that the vessels, merchandizes, and effects, destined for these islands [were Dutch], were found to be false and counterfeit, etc; that the merchants concerned in that trade preferred gain to their eternal salvation; and that by false oaths they had given up their souls to be eternally damned." [39]

It may be added that Holland was not the only neutral country to feel the effects of the West India and English privateers. For example, twelve Danish ships sailing from either Danish St. Thomas or St. Croix were seized, despite the fact that the papers of these ships seemed to be in order. But Holderness turned as deaf an ear to Danish protests as Pitt had done to those of the Dutch.[40] Although the Danish Prime Mininster Bernstorf sought to establish an entente of the neutral powers opposed to the drastic British policy, which would take the form of a union of armed neutrality, and, it would appear, approached the Dutch at The Hague to that end, he soon discovered that people in the United Netherlands were so divided in their sentiments, with a strong Orange pro-British party there, that nothing could be done along that line.[41]

The truth is that the Dutch had long since seen their best days as a naval power. While there was repeated talk of sending out ships

---

[37] See Owen's Weekly (London) Chronicle of December 30, 1758 for a long letter from The Hague dated December 22, which sets forth the situation in Holland.

[38] Ibid.

[39] Ibid.

[40] Richard Waddington, La Guerre de Sept Ans, III, 423–4.

[41] Ibid., III, 425.

of war to protect their trade,[42] there hung over the head of the nation
the threat of war if this were done, as was announced at The Hague.
It is true that late in February 1759 by a plurality of votes, but in
the face of violent protests, it was agreed to arm twenty-five ships
of the line.[43] But it was found that only three of them were ready
for the sea, and even these lacked the necessary sailors, though high
wages were offered.[44] Nevertheless, in the course of time, merchant
ships sailing in groups on missions clearly permitted by the treaty
of 1674 were escorted by some warships and without serious interference from the British navy. At the same time it is true that even
Dutch warships carrying military supplies to the French were compelled to strike their colours and were brought into the Downs together with merchantmen bent on the same mission.[45]

There seems little doubt, however, that during the course of the
Great War for the Empire the merchant marine of Holland was
greatly augmented. In the summer of 1760 it was estimated that the
shipping of the one province of Friesland alone had increased in the
last two years from two hundred and twenty vessels to some six
hundred; and also that instead of some forty-five Dutch vessels employed exclusively in the West India service before the war, the number was then, in spite of seizures, one hundred and fifty.[46] Indeed,
the immense trade of the Dutch, as the world's principal neutral
carrying power, seemed to be clearly indicated by one writer who in
the winter of 1761 reported the vast movement of ships out of the
Texel on a single day, January 26.[47] At the same time St. Eustatius,
which had enjoyed during the early years of hostilities unbelievable
prosperity as a free trading centre, by spring of the following year
(that is, by 1762) had lost all importance, so strictly was the movement of trade to and from it watched by British warships and colo-

---

[42] London advices, under date of January 30 in the *Pennsylvania* Gazette of April 12,
1759, stated that ninety Dutch merchantmen were about to sail to the French West
Indies escorted by four Dutch men-of-war.

[43] The Hague, March 2, *ibid.*, May 24, 1759.

[44] The Hague, February 9, *ibid.*, May 31, 1759.

[45] London advices of August 27, September 18, and September 27, *ibid.*, November 18 and 25 and December 9, 1762.

[46] Amsterdam, June 16, *ibid.*, September 11, 1760.

[47] According to the report, seventy-two vessels left the Texel on January 26 for
France (with, one must presume, non-contraband articles), twenty for Lisbon, twenty-
two for Cádiz, thirty for the Straits (that is, for the Mediterranean), ten for England,
eight for Curaçao, seventeen for St. Eustatius, seventeen for Surinam, and ten for the
East Indies, all under convoy of men-of-war (London advices, February 14, *ibid.*, May 7,
1761).

nial privateers. One writing from Antigua on March 10, in fact, indicated that stores on the Dutch island which once rented for three thousand pounds a year were now quite deserted.[48] The fall of Guadeloupe and then Martinique and the entrance of Spain, the historic enemy of the United Netherlands, into the war also changed drastically the situation of the Dutch in the West Indies as well as their attitude toward the struggle that was soon to terminate with the treaty of peace early in 1763.

Unhappily, the Dutch and the Danes were not the only people who sought to profit by the necessities of the French, who welcomed their ships to their West India possessions. Englishmen and British colonials were guilty of many unlawful practices. Lawless privateersmen, failing to lay their hands upon legitimate prizes, occasionally turned to piracy against the ships of still friendly powers.[49] They also were guilty of trading with the enemy in time of open war. Some of this traffic, it is true, was under cloak of legal intercourse — the so-called flag of truce for the purpose of either exchanging prisoners of war or releasing them, if there was no exchange, on a friendly shore. The practice was one that seems to have gone back to the fifteenth century.[50] Obviously, it had as a basis a humanitarian motive and also, it may be added, one that was economic, especially when food supplies in a country might be scarce and the support of prisoners costly. The usual practice was for someone in authority in the colonies, usually the governor or the assembly, to grant commissions to shipowners to convey prisoners of war under a flag of truce to some enemy port, with the expectation of receiving in return an equal number of nationals who had been captured.[51] But this was subject to grave abuses. Large profits in trade with the enemy seem to have

[48] Ibid., April 29, 1762.

[49] For example, the captain and some members of the crew of the English privateer Pluto were capitally convicted in London at the Old Bailey late in 1759 for "piratically and feloneously" robbing the captain of a Dutch vessel proceeding from Ostend to London (Owen's Weekly Chronicle, November 3, 1759). In America, one Haddon, master of the privateer Peggy of New York, was prosecuted in 1758 by the New York authorities for the robbing of a Spanish ship in the West Indies (Loudoun Papers, 81:3671, Huntington Library and New York Colonial Manuscripts 85:84; 86:15, 19, 95, New York Archives, Albany); likewise Nicholas Horton of the privateer Johnson was arraigned by the same authorities for the plundering of the Dutch ship Dolphin (ibid., 86:138-9).

[50] Richard Pares, War and Trade in the West Indies, 1739-1763 (Oxford, 1936), p. 446 note.

[51] Flags of truce were granted occasionally for other purposes. On February 10, 1759 the schooner Sussanah, Captain Wright, was commissioned by the Governor of New York in order to go to Cap François "to endeavor to recover the sloop Rebecca, belong-

motivated most of the men who secured these commissions. Indeed, it has been asserted that commercial intercourse with the French islands on the part of British colonials was actually greater and more lucrative than in time of peace.[52] In the case of the island of Bermuda, it was, it would appear, quite customary to distribute the prisoners of war among the merchantmen so that each of them, with perhaps one or two on board, could boldly move to St. Domingue, Guadeloupe, or Martinique without fear of capture, to exchange their cargoes of food and other supplies for West India products.[53] Moreover, the sale of flag-of-truce commissions by provincial governors, such as William Denny of Pennsylvania at twenty pounds sterling more or less, became a notorious scandal.[54] According to Deputy Governor Hamilton, Denny's successor, writing from Philadelphia to William Pitt late in the year 1760: "In Consequence of this iniquitous conduct . . . I found . . . a very great part of the principal merchants of this City, engaged in a trade with the French islands in the West Indies. . . ."[55]

Shipowners, in order to take advantage of the flag-of-truce trade, even went to the length of hiring Frenchmen to serve as prisoners of war. When carried to the West Indies as such, they would be secretly returned to the Continent to be further employed in this fashion.[56] Such intolerable abuses as the above inevitably led to the capture and condemnation of these flags of truce in courts of the vice-admiralty,[57] and when the Lords Commissioners for Prize Appeals finally upheld such condemnations, this unpatriotic type of

---

ing to Wm. Kelly & Samuel Stilwell, of New York merchants" (New York Col. Mss. 86:159, State Archives, Albany). The *Rebecca* was seized by the French while in the Spanish port of Monte Cristi.

[52] H. C. Wilkinson, *Bermuda in the Old Empire* (Oxford, 1950), p. 233.

[53] *Ibid.*

[54] Governor Hamilton to Pitt, November 1, 1760, *Correspondence of William Pitt* (ed. Miss Kimball), II, 351–2.

[55] *Ibid.*

[56] Richard Pares, *op. cit.*, p. 448.

[57] The French of course also made use of the flag of truce to cover up trade activities with the enemy. In June 1758 a French ship from St. Domingue carrying a few prisoners of war and much sugar to Philadelphia was seized, and in September of that year a French ship from the same island headed for New York and a Rhode Island vessel headed for French Port au Prince on St. Domingue were condemned in a vice-admiralty court at Williamsburg, Virginia (*Pennsylvania Gazette*, June 22 and September 21, 1758). It may, in this connection, be pointed out that a privateer commissioned by the authorities of one colony, while not hesitating to capture flags of truce belonging to another colony, was very reluctant to lay hands on a vessel commissioned by the same colony. The privateer *Hope* of New York, for instance, brought into port for condemna-

traffic was doomed.[58] Further, in 1761 the home government assumed responsibility for the management, expense, and disposition of prisoners of war and therefore left little if any legitimate basis for it on the part of private traders.[59]

But the flag of truce was but one means employed by shipmasters in their trade with the enemy in provisions and warlike stores. Sometimes vessels without this seeming protection sailed to enemy ports in the West Indies. For example, late in February 1757 a British sloop of war sent into the harbour of Charleston, South Carolina, for condemnation the Rhode Island *Charming Sally*, Captain Benjamin Church, loaded with gunpowder, muskets, etc., which had been caught hovering about the French port of Cap St. Nicholas, a port in St. Domingue.[60] Again, a ship loaded with a valuable cargo destined for the French might be sold to a neutral firm that would agree on delivery. Such was the case of the *Friendship*, of Philadelphia, cleared from that port for South Carolina with only ballast reported but actually loaded with thirteen hundred barrels of flour. Transferred with its cargo to a Spanish firm, De Costa & Co., it was attempting to enter Cap François when it was seized by the privateer *Hawke*, Captain Alexander, and carried for condemnation to Jamaica, where it was declared a good prize.[61] The most common practice, however, was to sail to some neutral West India island such as Dutch Curaçao or St. Eustatius or to Monte Christi on the northern coast of Spanish Santo Domingo, lying close to two French ports to the westward. There the cargoes could be transferred, perhaps after the formality of landing, to waiting enemy vessels which in turn had come loaded with the produce of the French West Indies. In 1759 it was declared after an investigation that the situation involving trade with the enemy was much worse than earlier in the war. As many as a hundred craft flying the British red ensign were observed at one time at Monte Christi.[62] Early in that year William Vassall, Esq.,

tion seven commissioned by Pennsylvania, Rhode Island, and the Bahamas respectively, but no New York vessel (Richard Pares, *op. cit.*, p. 452 note).

[58] *Ibid.*, p. 455.

[59] *Ibid.*, p. 449. Yet as late as the middle of June 1762 the flag-of-truce *Sea-Nymph* of New York was brought into Providence in the Bahamas and condemned (*Pennsylvania Gazette*, July 22, 1762).

[60] *Ibid.*, March 24, 1758.

[61] Henry Livingston to Henry Holland of New York, January 20, 1751, Loudoun Papers, 60:2686, Huntington Library.

[62] George Colebrooke to the Lords Commissioner of the Treasury, February 18, 1760, P.R.O., C.O. 323.

writing from Boston, affirmed: "The Colonies on the Continent carry on a prodigious great & very pernicious Trade to Monti Christo on Hispaniola. . . ." [63] Vice Admiral Thomas Cotes writing of the situation late in 1759 from his station off Jamaica referred to the "vile Illicit Trade that . . . carried on since the commencement of the present war is really and still remains infamous and barefaced." [64]

To Pitt the whole business of trade with the enemy was a monstrous travesty on decency. During the summer of 1760 he directed a letter to all governors of British colonies in the New World calling attention to the "illegal and most pernicious Trade . . . by which the enemy is, to the greatest Reproach . . . supplyed with Provisions, and other Necessaries, whereby they are, principally, if not alone, enabled to sustain, and protract, this long and expensive war." They were in the same letter directed to make the strictest inquiry into these "dangerous and ignominous" practices and to use every means to bring all the "henious Offenders to the most exemplary and Condign Punishment." [65]

But while the Great Commoner could thunder against colonial lawlessness, it was another problem to bring those guilty to justice. Powerful interests were arrayed against those who sought to do so. When one, George Spencer of New York, had attempted earlier in the same year to expose this nefarious intercourse with the enemy by an article in a local paper, the printer did not dare to publish it. In fact, for his pains Spencer was maltreated by a mob and thrown into jail on what he claimed was a false charge. Writing to General Amherst from his confinement on May 29, he made clear that he would have been freed long since had he not implicated two of the justices of the New York supreme court of judicature. [66] Certainly no local informer against those giving aid and comfort to the enemy for private profit would have been safer in either Boston or Rhode Island than in New York, were his identity known. Nor is it clear that in any of the trading colonies a court of common law acting with a jury would have convicted the most brazen offender. It is true that in Massachusetts Bay Governor Bernard sought earnestly to stamp out the evil. But the problem facing him was clearly indi-

---

[63] William Vassall to Messrs. Drake and Long, March 3, 1759, Chatham Mss., Bundle 96, P.R.O., Canadian Archives Transcripts.

[64] Cotes's letter of December 6, 1759 is also in C.O. 323.

[65] Pitt to the Governors in North America and the West Indies, August 23, 1760, Correspondence of William Pitt, II, 320-1.

[66] New York Colonial Manuscripts, 89:30, State Archives.

cated by General Amherst. Writing to Bernard early in the summer of 1762, he declared: "The Measures you are taking to Bring the Guilty to due punishment are Every thing that can be Expected from you, but I am afraid that this trade has already got to Such a height, that few Jurys will be found as free from connections as to be willing to Understand the Crime in its true light." [67] As for the traders of Rhode Island, Lord Loudoun, commander-in-chief of the Armed forces in North America in 1757, was impelled, in communicating with Pitt, to denounce them as "a lawless set of smugglers, who continually supply the Enemy with What Provisions they want, and bring back their goods in Barter for them." [68]

The most effective weapon, designed purely as a war-time measure, for putting a stop to this intercourse with the enemy was the use of the embargo. Even in 1762 Amherst was under necessity to employ it as British commander-in-chief in North America to keep supplies from flowing not only to the enemy settlements but to their fleets and troops in the New World. He therefore prohibited, in spite of evident hardships that it would entail upon British settlers, any shipmaster from carrying fish to the British West Indies and provisions to Halifax, Newfoundland, and Quebec. For, once on the high seas, vessels with false clearances would not fail to sail to their real destination.[69] Any relaxation of the embargo by the same military authority that laid it seems to have led immediately to the return of illicit trade with the enemy.[70] In other words, in the face of popular sentiment in the great American seaports of the middle and New England colonies civil government acting alone was powerless. The Great War for the Empire, the termination of which was to lay the foundation for the future power and greatness of American colonies, was therefore to be won even in the face of the opposition of many of those who with their descendants would become the greatest beneficiaries of its triumphant conclusion.

---

[67] Amherst to Bernard, June 10, 1762, P.R.O., War Office Papers, 34, Vol. 27, p. 499.

[68] Loudoun to Pitt, May 30, 1757, P.R.O., C.O., 5:48.

[69] Amherst to Governor Bernard, May 6 and 10, 1762, P.R.O., War Office, 34, Vol. 27, pp. 481–6.

[70] For information as to false clearances secured by certain New York merchants "charged with illegal communication with the King's enemies," see the Massachusetts Historical Society Collections (fourth series), IX, 469–73.

CHAPTER V

Island Hopping in the French West Indies, 1759

IN THE PRECEDING chapter emphasis was placed on the effective-
ness of the French privateers, particularly those operating in the
area of the Caribbean Sea. It has been calculated that in the
course of the Great War for the Empire as many as fourteen hundred British vessels were captured and brought to the island of
Martinique alone.[1] Prizes were also carried to St. Domingue and
Guadeloupe. While it was highly desirable as a military measure to
deprive the enemy of those bases for such operations, and for other
reasons, Pitt had determined, in taking over the direction of the war
in the New World, to concentrate British power against Canada and
her dependencies. In fact, it was not until the fall of Cape Breton
Island in 1758 that he permitted himself to consider the advisability
of proceeding against the French West Indies. After the news of
this event reached England, the West India sugar planter Alderman William Beckford wrote to him in August of that year urging
that Martinique should now receive attention. In doing so he avoided
the arguments that naturally would occur to one who had large personal West India interests that were adversely affected by the
swarming of French privateers there. Instead, he shrewdly stressed
the advantage that would accrue to Great Britain in the capture of
the island in that later it could be used as a basis for the return of
Minorca. As to Cape Breton Island, the Alderman would not permit himself to contemplate any reversion of this to France as was

---

[1] H. C. Wilkinson, *Bermuda in the Old Empire* (Oxford, 1950), p. 232.

done in 1748 in the Treaty of Aix-la-Chapelle, in view of the fact that to him it was the "Key of Canada" and as such must be kept.[2]

There is every reason to believe that Pitt was influenced by the argument of Beckford, his loyal supporter in Parliament, to alter his broad strategy respecting the war, with the idea, as advanced by Beckford, of securing Martinique to exchange for Minorca.[3] Up to this period not only had he given chief emphasis, as indicated, to the project of reducing Louisbourg and closing up the St. Lawrence with the aim of the conquest of Canada, but had also employed resources in carrying out raids against the coasts of France — much to the dislike of some of his colleagues in the ministry. According to Newcastle, early in September — while the expeditionary force was still intact and busy in France but after the second failure to capture Saint-Malo — Pitt began drawing up tentative plans with the aid of the Secretary of the Admiralty for a Martinique expedition.[4] Then came the news of the disastrous ending of the Bligh raid in Brittany, followed by a storm of public disapproval of any further use of raiding tactics.[5] Further, a second letter from Beckford, dated September 11, pleaded in the most urgent terms for an attack without a moment's delay against the French West India island. In this connection he affirmed:

> "The island . . . has but one town of strength: take that, and the whole country is yours; all the inhabitants must submit for want of food, for they live from hand to mouth, and have not victuals to support themselves and numerous slaves for one month, without a foreign supply. The Negroes and stock of that island are worth above four million sterling, and the conquest easy. . . . For God's sake, attempt it without delay and noise." [6]

If reports were true, the ability of Martinique to resist an enemy had certainly been greatly lessened during the preceding years of the war. According to a letter written by a resident of St. Pierre, the metropolis, to a merchant in Bordeaux in June of the same year

---

[2] Beckford to Pitt, August 26, 1758, Chatham Manuscripts, Vol. 19, P.R.O.

[3] J. S. Corbett, *England in the Seven Years' War* (London, 1907), I, 374; Albert von Ruville, *William Pitt, Earl of Chatham* (London, 1907), II, 222.

[4] J. S. Corbett, *op. cit.*, I, 373.

[5] For an account of Bligh's raids against Cherbourg and Saint-Malo see Volume VII of this series, pp. 134-7.

[6] Beckford to Pitt, September 11, 1758, *Correspondence of the Earl of Chatham* (ed. Taylor and Pringle, London, 1838), I, 353-4.

and entrusted to a Dutch vessel that was carried into Portsmouth to
be condemned, conditions there were very bad indeed:

> "This poor Country, which you once knew in a flourishing state has
> been afflicted within three years by two dreadful Hurricanes, which
> has for ever ruined one third of the Inhabitants; by a War, more
> dreadful than can be imagined; and to compleat our misery, by a
> Drought, which continued from the beginning of this year, ruins all
> the Plantations, and affords a very melancholy Prospect for the en-
> suing Year. May God have Mercy on us, and at least grant us a
> Peace, no matter on what Conditions!" [7]

Quick at making decisions, Pitt now determined to proceed
against the island at the earliest possible moment. In coming to
this resolution it is clear that he departed somewhat from certain
strategical principles that had had not only his own but the nation's
approval — the retention at home, or at least close at hand, of a considerable body of regular troops, which, supported by the navy,
could provide protection for the British Isles in case of an attempted
invasion. Forces engaged in raiding Brittany or Normandy could be
speedily recalled in case of necessity; but those consigned to an attack upon France's West India possessions would not be available
should a sudden need for them arise. Nevertheless, Pitt was apparently prepared to run whatever risks were involved in the new enterprise. After all, a powerful fleet would still be retained in the
home waters and only a portion of the regulars that had been held
as a reserve on the Isle of Wight and elsewhere need be utilized for
the expedition. Moreover there was the militia now available under
the terms of the act passed the preceding year, which could be
quickly mobilized; and finally, French naval power had greatly de-
clined during the past year, and with this the dangers of invasion
were thereby greatly lessened.

In advancing definite proposals for the conquest of Martinique it
was necessary for Pitt, it may be pointed out, to put at rest certain
serious doubts that arose in the minds of Lord Barrington, Secretary

---

[7] London advices, September 7, *Pennsylvania Gazette*, November 9, 1758.

That the French were well aware of the danger to this important colony in its weakness is clear in view of the fact that Choiseul wrote, on December 25, 1758, to Aube-
terre, French Ambassador at Madrid, that to ward off the dangers to the Spanish possessions, the court there should order twenty-four war vessels into the anchorages of
Martinique, which would be joined by Bompar's squadron (Alfred Bourguet, *Le Duc de
Choiseul et l'Alliance Espagnole* [Paris, 1906], p. 6).

at War, and Lord Anson, First Lord of the Admiralty. Barrington was disturbed at the proposal to utilize "only" or "chiefly" for this purpose new army corps, especially those which had never been out of England. "If some old regiments cannot be obtained," he wrote on September 20, "I wish some of the new ones, which have been on the [Bligh] expedition, might be sent, if it were only to show the others how to embark and disembark, to which they have been much used this summer." [8] As for Anson, he was fearful lest Pitt should send away all the best ships, which would therefore not be at hand when he himself might most need them. [9] As the rumour spread that an enterprise was on foot against some one of the French West India islands, there were others who became greatly concerned — perhaps in view of the unhappy ending of Admiral Vernon's expeditions against the New World Cartagena in 1740 and Santiago de Cuba in 1741. Horace Walpole, at the moment in a very critical frame of mind against Pitt, writing to his friend Conway respecting the intended expedition, the specific objective of which was not generally known, declared despondently: "Martinico is the general notion; a place the strongest in the world, with a garrison of ten thousand men. Others now talk of Guadeloupe, almost as strong and of much less consequence. Of both, everybody that knows, despairs. It is almost impossible for *me* to find out the real destination . . . and I would rather not be told what I am sure I shall not approve." [10]

To command the expedition the King's choice fell upon Major General Thomas Peregrine Hopson. Hopson was a veteran in the service. He had been in command of Louisbourg after its capture in the preceding war, had served for a brief period as Governor of Nova Scotia, had commanded the troops sent from Great Britain in 1757 to reinforce Lord Loudoun when the latter was planning a descent on Cape Breton Island, and previous to this had joined with Vice Admiral Knowles in drawing up an able memorandum indicating under what conditions an attack on the island might hope for success — a memorandum that undoubtedly wisely influenced the final decision of the commander-in-chief not to attempt an assault on Louisbourg under given unfavourable circumstances. A man of

---

[8] *Correspondence of Chatham*, I, 355–6.

[9] J. C. Corbett, op. cit., I, 374.

[10] Walpole to H. S. Conway, October 17, 1758, *Letters of Horace Walpole* (ed. P. Cunningham, Edinburgh, 1906), III, 182–3.

sound judgment, he was capable and energetic despite his years.[11] The force placed at his command — and in face of the Secretary at War's objection previously noted — were six "fresh" regiments,[12] together with a battalion of the Royal Highlanders, a part of a regiment on duty on the British island of Antigua, and, finally, an artillery train. To escort the transports that carried these contingents, eight ships of the line, headed by the *St. George*, a ninety-gun ship, were detached from service in the home waters. That no support should be lacking from the British established on Barbados and the Leeward Islands, Pitt wrote to the governors of these possessions calling upon them to render every assistance to the troops, particularly in furnishing provisions, refreshments, horses, and beasts of burden.[13] As a final precaution, Admiral Saunders with a large squadron of capital ships moved toward the western coast of France to see that no enemy fleet should come out from one of the ports to interfere with the expedition.[14]

After a false start late in October under very bad weather conditions, the armada of seventy-five vessels under command of Commodore Hughes finally sailed from Plymouth on November 12. It was composed of the eight ships of the line, with some frigates and bomb-ketches, and sixty-four transports carrying not only some six thousand British regulars but a large artillery train, and an adequate supply of small arms and ammunition.[15] Under Pitt's orders it sailed for Barbados for a general rendezvous in Carlisle Bay, where it arrived without incident on January 3. There Hughes turned over the command of the fleet as planned to Commodore Moore, who had been stationed in the area of the Leewards with a small squadron. With the two squadrons now combined there were some thirty men-of-war, twelve of which were of the line, and fifty

---

[11] Pitt personally favoured young Colonel John Barrington, a brother of the Secretary at War. Barrington, nevertheless, was placed second in command, with the temporary New World rank of Major General (J. S. Corbett, *op. cit.*, I, 377). For a draft of Hopson's Secret Instructions of October 16, 1758 see P.R.O., C.O., 5:215.

[12] The regiments were Elliot's, Barrington's, Armiger's, the Old Buffs, Watson's and Duroure's.

[13] Pitt to Governor Charles Pilford of Barbados and Governor George Thomas of the Leeward Islands, October 16, 1758, *Correspondence of William Pitt . . .* (ed. Gertrude S. Kimball, New York, 1906), I, 366–7.

[14] London advices, *Pennsylvania Gazette*, February 8, 1759.

[15] For an instructive account of the expedition against Martinique in 1759 see the article by Marshall Smelser, "The Insular Campaign of 1759: Martinique," *American Neptune*, VI, 290–300.

transports. On the 13th most of these vessels moved out of Carlisle Bay and sailed for Martinique, which is to the windward.[16]

Martinique, situated some distance northwest of Barbados, was colonized by the French in 1635. At first the settlers gave themselves to the cultivation of tobacco and cotton; but in 1650 sugar plantations made their appearance, and sugar soon became the most important crop produced on the island. In 1723 coffee was likewise introduced and was grown advantageously on the higher cultivated slopes, together with indigo, ginger, and many other commodities. This extension of cultivated lands called for an increase in slave labour. In fact, in 1723 it was estimated that there were sixty thousand blacks on the island and in the period under consideration the number of white people was put at ten thousand. The island, known today as "Queen of the Caribbees," is some forty miles in length and between ten and twenty miles in breadth and is of volcanic origin. Very irregular in form, with a sharply indented shore-line, it is traversed by innumerable rivers and lesser streams, many of which flow through precipitous ravines and become raging torrents in the rainy season. Its hills and the lower slopes of the mountains where cultivation has not taken place are shrouded with a bewildering variety of trees, vines, and other forms of tropical vegetation. On the northwestern part of the island, as a culmination of its mountainous backbone, towers Mont Pelée.

In 1759, while there were two settlements worthy of note on the eastern or windward coast — La Trinité and Cul-de-Sac Robert — the principal towns were on the western or leeward coast — St. Pierre, the metropolis, and Fort Royal, now known as Fort de France. St. Pierre, but a memory since its tragic destruction, with the death of more than thirty thousand people, in 1902 with the eruption of Mont Pelée, was the island's chief governmental, commercial, and social center. Here were to be found many impressive public and private buildings, including the quarters occupied by

---

16 The following ships were employed: the St. George, a ninety-gun ship; the Cambridge, Commodore Moore's flagship, an eighty; a seventy-four; a seventy, the Norfolk, with Hughes in command; four sixty-fours; two sixties; two fifties, and twelve smaller warships, including three bomb-ketches. Sixty transports carried the six regiments, the battalion of Highlanders, the contingent of regulars from Antigua, eight hundred marines, four hundred able Negroes for the hard labour, five thousand spare arms, as well as the artillery train ("Journal of an Officer," January 13–30, 1759, Correspondence of Pitt, II, 27; Captain Gardiner's An Account of the Expedition to the West Indies . . . [Birmingham, 1762], p. 4; "An Account of the Expedition against the Islands of Martinico and Guadeloupe, January, 1739," Loudoun Papers, Huntington Library).

the Captain General of the French Antilles, the Intendant for Martinique, and the principal merchants of the island; here also were
the Palais de Justice and the headquarters of the bureau of royal
domain for the Lesser Antilles, as well as the splendid Church of
St. Pierre, built by the Jesuits in the Doric style. Dominating the
town, which stretched for some two miles in a crescent along the
shore and the harbour, was the citadel, with its heavy walls, para-
pets, battlements, and two high towers of stone, all bristling with
artillery; and here at the Anchorage (*le Carenage*) privateers and
merchant ships assembled and rode in security as a rule, sheltered
from the hurricanes by the massive of Mont Pelée and the peaks of
Carbet. To the southward, some twenty-one miles distant, connected with St. Pierre by means of a road (little used, however,
because of the great inconvenience involved in traversing it), was
the chief naval base for the Lesser French Antilles and the town
of Fort Royal, theoretically the capital of the island, which in reality was St. Pierre. The fort protecting it was at this period located on a peninsula that projected into the bay and was supported
by outworks and numerous batteries.[17]

It was against Fort Royal that General Hopson now directed his
attack. This was logical. The number of inhabitants and therefore
potential defenders was much less than those of the metropolis; the
fort itself was not of heavy masonry as was that at St. Pierre, but
constructed chiefly of earthen works; and, finally, the chief depots
on the island for the reception of ammunition and provisions were
located not there but at the chief governmental centre; and once
cut off from these supplies by sea, the garrison of the place, to obtain them, would be forced to fall back upon the extraordinarily
difficult road winding northward to it.

On January 15 the fleet appeared off the harbour and started to
manœuvre into the bay. The garrison of the fort had been warned
and was on the alert. At the time there were within the inner harbour, protected by the guns of the fort, but one French ship of the
line, the *Florissant*, a seventy-four, and a single frigate. Another
frigate, the *Bellona*, had escaped in time and raced to reach France

---

17 "A Description of the Island of Martinico . . . ," *Naval and Military Memoirs
of Great Britain from 1727 to 1783* (ed. Robert Beatson, London, 1804), III, 360–3;
Abbé Raynal, *East and West Indies* (trans. J. Justamond, London, 1777), IV, 153–84;
D. Fenning, J. Collyer, and others, *A New System of Geography . . .* (London, 1765),
II, 710–12. The importance of Martinique to France has been stressed at the beginning
of the preceding chapter.

with the news of the invasion.[18] To gain possession of the town and
its fort Hopson realized that he must land his troops at some convenient point. To the northwest of it on the northern shore of the
Bay and almost out of gun range was Fort Negro, and still more
distant, also along the northern shore, was a French battery at a
place called Cas des Navires. With these in his grasp, this could
be done. Commodore Moore agreed to silence the guns of the two
batteries and on the morning of the 16th accomplished the task and
thereupon landed his marines at Fort Negro. The marines, unopposed, proceeded to spike the guns there before returning to their
ships.[19] While preparations were being made to land the troops
near it, the transports, on account of the effect of the bombardment from the main fort, were obliged to withdraw somewhat and
it was therefore found to be more convenient to make the landing
at Cas des Navires. With this achieved, a force of grenadiers and
Highlanders under direct command of Barrington marched through
the woods almost unopposed to Fort Negro and proceeded to raise
the English colours there.

So far Hopson's movements had met with success. But on the
17th the French began firing upon the troops from the shelter of
the heavy brush. Despite the fact that Highlanders and grenadiers
plunged into the thickets to get at the enemy and also erected a
battery on a hill beyond Fort Negro in the direction of Fort Royal,
they could not consolidate their position, since they could not be

---

[18] Captain Hood of the *Vestal*, of thirty-two guns, on February 21 intercepted the
Bellona on her way to France with dispatches from the Governor of Martinique. This
led to a bitter engagement of over four hours. Only when some forty members of her
crew had been killed and after the loss of her topmast and yard, with only her foremast
standing, did the French vessel surrender. She was thereupon brought to Spithead by the
Vestal, which had also suffered the loss of her mainmast (*Gentleman's Magazine*, XXIX
[1759], p. 143).

[19] "Journal of an Officer," January 13–30, 1759, sent to Pitt by Hopson as the official proceedings of the army, *Pitt Correspondence*, II, 27; Captain Gardiner, *op. cit.*,
pp. 6–8. Gardiner, a captain of the marines on board the *Rippon*, was apparently one of
the landing party.

The care the student must exercise in using original sources is illustrated by advices
from Antigua dated January 31 to the *Pennsylvania Gazette* (March 8, 1759) giving a
distorted account of the Martinique expedition by Lieutenant Cary of the privateer *Fly*,
who, according to his testimony, landed with the troops. Cary declared that seven thousand British troops were taken ashore, entrenched themselves, and were thereupon attacked by five or six thousand French troops from Fort Royal. The Highlanders then
counterattacked and, in the course of the battle, drove the enemy several miles, killing
between three and four hundred of them until "there was not a Frenchman for some
miles around."

protected from the continuous firing of the defenders from another hill, called Morne Tartenson. There the latter were well screened by underbrush and trees and held their own in the face of efforts to drive them from it. In the words of an unknown officer, "the Highlands of Scotland, for Woods, Mountains, Canes, and Ravines, is nothing to it." [20]

Another difficulty now appeared: the road that connected Fort Royal with St. Pierre ran well inland at this point and to reach it and then to traverse it in order to assault the French town and fort meant that a connecting road would have to be made by the engineers through this difficult country in order to transport the siege artillery, military stores, and other impedimenta, once these had been unloaded from the ships. If this were attempted it meant that even after the road was built, detachments, in order to hold the line of communication, must be stretched over six miles between the beachhead and the fort and must necessarily be dangerously weak at any point because of the limited size of the expeditionary force. Assuming as did Hopson that the French could stand an investment of some ten days, the question arose whether it would be possible during this period to offer any adequate protection to the troops engaged in the siege from those firing upon it from the fort and from the adjacent woods.[21] When Moore was called upon to find a landing-place for the artillery closer to Fort Royal, he replied that no place was available closer than Fort Negro; [22] nor was the commodore in a position to provide an adequate number of men out of the fleet to transport the guns under the protection of the soldiers.[23] Therefore, after a council of war held late the morning of the 17th and after a final futile appeal to Moore for a better landing site, Hopson decided to re-embark his troops. This was done without incident that very evening.[24]

Regarding the wisdom of this move, it is difficult to arrive at a valid conclusion. Unbeknown to Hopson, the Governor General of the French Windward Island, the Marquis de Beauharnais, in di-

---

[20] "Journal of an Officer," op. cit., II, 28; Richard Pares, War and Trade in the West Indies (Oxford, 1936), p. 247.

[21] Hopson to Pitt, January 30, 1758, Correspondence of Pitt, II, 21–2.

[22] Professor Smelser has neatly disposed of a contemporary account that the landing approaches to Fort Royal were mined by the French (American Neptune, III, 168–9).

[23] Hopson to Pitt, January 30, 1758, Correspondence of Pitt, II, 21–2.

[24] "Journal of an Officer," ibid., II, 28; Moore to Pitt, January 30, 1759, ibid., II, 30; Captain Gardiner, op. cit., pp. 9–14.

rect charge of the defense of Fort Royal, was actually contemplating the blowing up of the overextended fortifications there after the successful British landing [25] — something that might well have taken place had the attack against the French continued. News reports were also later received that Martinique merchants, fearful that the island was about to fall to the British, had sent three sloops to Eustatius loaded with effects valued at three hundred thousand pounds.[26] On the other hand, to the British leaders there seemed to be no evidence of panic among the defenders after the temporary withdrawal of the latter from the neighbourhood of Fort Negro and Cas des Navires on the 16th. Their harassment of the Highlanders and grenadiers on the 17th, if not continuous, was of such a nature — with casualties listed at a hundred — as would indicate a fighting spirit among them. The great difficulty, in face of this, of securing possession of the fort by traversing successfully miles of broken country with forces inadequate to maintain a supply line and to consolidate a position, once the troops had arrived in front of Fort Royal, was clearly recognized.

But Hopson, with his soldiers on board the transports again, was not prepared to give up his project of taking over the island without further effort. Early the morning of the 18th he called a meeting of his staff on board the *Cambridge*, Moore's flagship, to determine, in spite of the commodore's pessimism, the possibility of beating past the citadel in order to enter the inner harbour of Fort Royal. After questioning the pilots, the design was, however, found to be impracticable.[27] Thereupon he and Moore agreed to move up to St. Pierre for reconnaissance purposes to determine the feasibility of making a successful landing there, and the following day the fleet approached the bay upon which it was located. Here some forty merchant ships and privateers were riding at anchor under shelter of the guns of batteries located along the shore-line as well as of those of the citadel situated above and to the north of the "pretty looking Town along the bottom of the Bay." [28] To test out

[25] Richard Pares, op. cit., p. 247.

[26] Gentleman's Magazine, 1759, p. 145. Marshall Smelser (op. cit., VI, 298) also cites, as other evidence of French demoralization, the statement, embodied in Edward Cust's Annals of the Wars of the Eighteenth Century (London, 1862–9, II, 285), that the inhabitants of Fort Royal had actually assembled before the British withdrawal, for the purpose of sending deputies to the invaders to secure terms, whether with or without the approval of the military is not stated.

[27] Hopson to Pitt, January 30, 1759, op. cit., II, 22.

[28] "Journal of an Officer," op. cit., II, 28; Captain Gardiner, op. cit., pp. 14–15.

"A Map of Martinico, from the latest and best Authorities."   (From the *Gentleman's Magazine*, 1759)

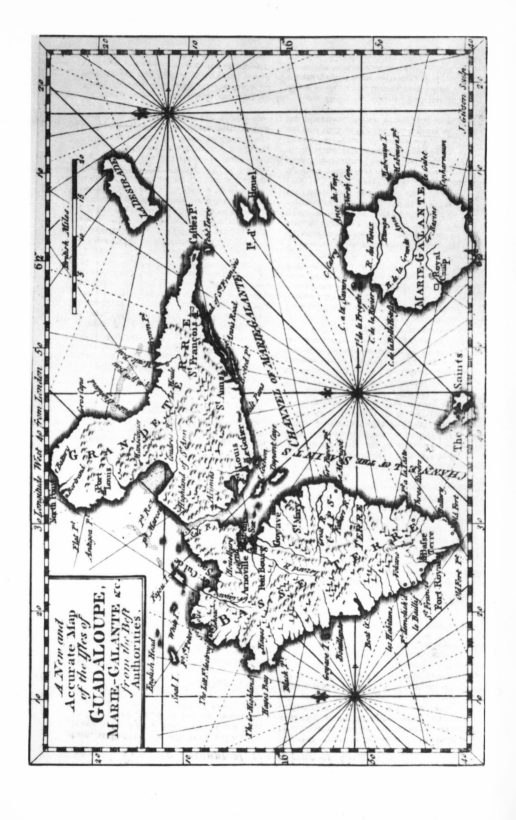

A New and
Accurate Map
of the Isles of
GUADALOUPE,
MARIE-GALANTE &c.
From the Best
Authorities.

the strength of the defences, Captain Jekyl of the *Rippon*, a sixty-gun ship, was ordered by Moore to lay in against a battery located a mile and a half to the north of the town. While he soon silenced it, anchored as he was at a distance of but a hundred yards from the shore, other batteries opened upon him and found a ready target. In vain he used both his broadsides simultaneously, together with his stern-chase guns against the enemy, who gave him their concentrated attention. To save the riddled ship, unfortunately held to the shore by a leeward breeze — an unusual phenomenon in these parts — the commodore finally ordered fifty of the crew to take to the boats, and with great exertion they towed the *Rippon* out of danger.[29] This was destined to be the only action at St. Pierre at this period.

While Jekyl was thus engaged north of the town, Hopson and Moore were holding a council of war. The commodore, after examining the forbidding coastline about St. Pierre, had already come to the conclusion that while an effective bombardment of the citadel and the town could be made such as to bring about their surrender, it would doubtless leave his squadron in such condition — by sustaining the enemy fire at close range — as to make it useless for any other immediate service. He accordingly had written to Hopson to that effect. The rough way in which the *Rippon* was handled by the enemy doubtless only confirmed his doubts of the wisdom of the attack. Instead, he recommended that the expedition avoid the hazard of moving into the bay and, instead, proceed against the town of Basse-Terre on Guadeloupe, by all accounts much less strongly protected than either Fort Royal or St. Pierre. In view of the fact that the general himself had doubts of his ability to garrison and supply St. Pierre after its capture, while occupied at the same time with the reduction of the other towns of the island,[30] he

---

[29] Beatson, *op. cit.*, II, 233–5; Captain Gardiner, *op. cit.*, pp. 15–20.

[30] There was an opinion current among people in London that Martinique was far too strong to capture, except by means of a very large expedition, such as was launched against it in 1762. Many thought therefore that the real destination of the expedition was against Guadeloupe: "For (say they) Fort St. Pierre, at Martinico, is greatly too strong to be taken by sea; and he [Commodore Hughes, who commanded the fleet that sailed from Plymouth] had not forces to besiege it by land, because there are 30,000 white people on the island, fit to bear arms, and near one third trained to the use of them; they allow indeed that he may land by surprise, in different parts of the back of the island, destroy some plantations, and perhaps carry off some of the Negroes, and that is all" (London advices, December 18, 1758, *Pennsylvania Gazette*, February 22, 1759). However, the Secret Instructions given to Hopson on October 16 to guide him do not men-

questioned whether the mere destruction of the town could be justified as a military measure. So it was agreed to continue northward
to Guadeloupe.[31]

The island of Guadeloupe, called by the British "the chief nest
of French privateers; constantly infesting the British [West India]
islands," [32] is really two islands: that of Guadeloupe proper, called
Basse-Terre, and Grande-Terre, separated by the very narrow
Rivière Salée. Taken together, their greatest length as well as
breadth is something over fifty miles. Basse-Terre, so called by reason of its leeward position with respect to the other island, is, inconsistently with its name, elevated and mountainous, capped by
the lofty volcano La Soufrière and watered by many streams;
Grande-Terre, on the other hand, is low-lying, with a limestone
rather than a volcanic base, and almost destitute of springs. In the
eighteenth century — in contrast to the present — most of the sugar
plantations were located on Basse-Terre; indeed, it was mistakenly
thought that the soil of Grande-Terre could not long submit to such
cultivation.[33] As a consequence, the majority of the population of
Guadeloupe was living in 1759 on Basse-Terre. The number of inhabitants of the two islands in 1755, according to the local regis-
ters, was 9,643 white people and 41,140 slaves, who did the labour

tion Guadeloupe, except by inference, but are concerned almost entirely with the conquest of Martinique. Hopson, it is true, was given discretion in case of failure against this
island to make an "Attempt on the other French Islands in those Parts" (P.R.O., C.O.,
5:215).

[31] The writer of the contemporary memoir relating to the Martinique expedition
(Bateson, op. cit., II, 233) is very critical of the decision of Hopson and Moore not to
attack the shipping in the harbour of St. Pierre. In view of the fresh breeze from the
leeward on the 19th, it is clear that the ships and bomb-ketches could have gone into the
harbour without tacking; but its deep water permitted the merchant ships to huddle
close to the land and well within the protection of both the shore batteries and the guns
of the citadel. Under these circumstances, with the wind unfavourable for a safe retirement, there is serious question whether the attacking vessels could have inflicted great
damage without the risk of being lost. The student should bear in mind that sound strategical as well as tactical principles opposed the use of warships by the commander of a
fleet, engaged in a special mission, for any purpose not directly connected with it — such
as for chasing enemy merchantmen on the high seas or for such an adventure as entering
the St. Pierre harbour for the destruction of enemy shipping. While not stressing these
views, both Corbett (op. cit., I, 379) and Pares (op. cit., pp. 294–5) would therefore
appear to be right in approving Moore's decision to safeguard all his ships for use in the
task that lay ahead.

[32] Gentleman's Magazine, 1759, p. 142. It would appear that most of the privateers
that moved out of Guadeloupe harbours to prey on the commerce of the near-by British
Leeward Islands were from Martinique (Abbé Raynal, op. cit., IV, 196).

[33] Ibid., IV, 192–3.

on some three hundred and fifty sugar plantations as well as on those devoted to the raising of cotton, coffee, indigo, tobacco, and cocoa.[34] The growth in wealth of the island during the preceding fifty years is indicated by the fact that in 1700 there were less than four thousand white people and less than seven thousand slaves who cultivated only sixty small sugar plantations and sixty-six where indigo was grown.[35] The quantity of sugar produced on the island during the period under discussion was far greater than on Martinique and was estimated to total annually between forty thousand and one hundred thousand hogsheads, as against but ten thousand.[36] This commodity, taken together with the relatively large quantity of cotton, coffee, indigo, and ginger grown and exported, had laid the basis for the prosperity of the island. Yet its commerce with the mother country was mostly by way of Martinique, the official trade entrepôt for the French Lesser Antilles, where the harbours were much better and could easily accommodate the largest merchant ships.[37]

Although there were numerous places where privateers and other ships could seek shelter, such as Petit Cul-de-Sac, the chief defence of Guadeloupe was Fort Royal and its supporting batteries, which were designed to protect the capital of the island, Basse-Terre. The town extended for a mile along a large, open bay on the island that bears the same name. At this period it possessed many handsome edifices, among these several churches, the Jesuits' College, and the residences of the royal officials, who were "sumptuously lodged." In addition, there were in the business quarter of the town numerous great storehouses into which the merchants gathered the produce of the island preparatory to its exportation as well as the imports from the outside world. Unfortunately, because of the shallowness of the water of the roadstead, there were no wharves at Basse-Terre, and ships that came, by reason of the great depth of the ocean water at not too great distance from the shore, were obliged to anchor rather dangerously close to it and run the risk of beaching in case of sudden storms.[38] In fact, the limitations of the

---

[34] *Ibid.*, IV, 185–6.

[35] *Ibid.* The importance of Guadeloupe to France has been emphasized at the beginning of the preceding chapter.

[36] D. Fenning, J. Collyer, and others, *op. cit.*, II, 710; Beatson, *op. cit.*, III, 211.

[37] Abbé Raynal, *op. cit.*, IV, 194.

[38] "A Description of the Town of Basseterre on Guadeloupe . . . by a person who was on the spot," *Pennsylvania Gazette*, April 12, 1759; Beatson, *op, cit.*, III, 211–13.

harbour remind one of that of Basse-Terre on the small British Lee-ward Island of St. Christopher, lying northwest of Guadeloupe. For in each it was and is still necessary to discharge and load merchant-men by means of boats and in each a heavy surf is likely to hamper seriously these operations. The fort, situated on an elevation south-east of the town and close to the shore-line, was irregular in form, with bastions and ravalines, and mounted about fifty cannon, some of large calibre, which commanded both the town and the bay as well as the road leading to the fort.[39]

Whether or not the so-called attack on Martinique was in reality little more than a mere feint to throw the enemy off their guard and to test out their strength on the island, there was an impression among officers who served on the expedition that this was the case.[40] For obvious reasons, had there been a secret understanding between General Hopson and Commodore Moore to that effect, it could not possibly be avowed by them in the light of their instruc-tions, which made that island their first objective. It is certain that in sailing for Guadeloupe on the 19th the army and navy had deter-mined upon real action.

The following day brought the expedition to the neighbourhood of the "neutral" island of Dominica, from which point the *Winches-ter*, a speedy fifty-gun ship, moved forward to Guadeloupe having on board both the chief engineer and the quartermaster general, who were sent ahead to reconnoitre. On account of calms, it was not until the morning of the 22nd that the rest of the fleet appeared off the Saints, a group of small islands just southeast of Guadeloupe, and then spent the rest of the day patrolling the waters that lay between them and the town of Basse-Terre in order to reconnoitre the shore. Despite the fact that the chief engineer, Colonel Cun-ningham, who had gone ahead of the fleet, as indicated, had ar-rived at the conclusion that the fort of Basse-Terre, on account of its elevation, was impregnable to ships, since their lower-deck great

---

[39] According to Captain Tyrrell of the *Buckingham*, there were mounted at the fort at the time of the attack "82 large Pieces of Cannon" (*Pennsylvania Gazette*, March 8, 1759).

[40] An officer serving under Captain Leslie in the *Bristol*, in writing from Basse-Terre on January 25 about the attack on Fort Royal in Martinique, declared: "All this was but to feint for we were intended for this place, which we now have in possession" (*ibid.*, March 8, 1759). Likewise, a letter from Antigua under date of February 5 addressed to a Philadelphia correspondent in the same vein affirmed: "Our Forces landed in Martinico, made a Feint, and then reimbarked . . . they immediately proceeded to Guadeloupe." (*ibid.*).

guns could not batter it,[41] Moore was determined to risk moving all his best ships but the *Buckingham* close to the town in order to submit the fortifications to an intensive bombardment. For this purpose he gave specific orders to the commanders of eight ships of the line. Each had a particular assignment: the *St. George*, a ninety-gun ship, the *Cambridge*, an eighty, and the *Norfolk*, a seventy-four, were to concentrate on silencing the fort; two others were to take care of the royal battery; and the remaining three were made individually responsible for disposing of one of the other three batteries.

Early the morning of the 23rd, after Moore had shifted his broad pennant from the *Cambridge* to the frigate *Woolwich*, a forty-four, the signal for the attack was made. By nine o'clock the *Lion* (*Lyon*), a sixty, was abreast her objective — a battery just south of the fort — and began firing. She was badly raked by the concentrated fire of this battery and by the guns in the fort, but persevered until the ships assigned to take care of the fort were able to go into action a half-hour later. Soon afterward the bombardment became general when six ships began reaching their targets and continued, despite damage sustained to their hulls and rigging, until late in the afternoon, when all the enemy's guns had been silenced.[42]

At first it was thought best to put the troops ashore without delay; but the order was countermanded. Instead, the bomb-ketches were ordered by Moore to move in toward the town, doubtless to prepare the way for the landing. Unhappily, contrary to his intentions, the bombs and carcasses had the unfortunate effect of igniting the wooden shingles of the warehouses loaded with rum and sugar. As a result fierce fires were started and were soon out of control. According to the commodore, by ten o'clock that night "this beautiful town blazed forth . . . a dreadful scene of conflagration." [43]

The afternoon of the following day the troops landed without opposition, moved through the wrecked and charred town, took possession of the fortifications, and thereupon raised the British colours

[41] Captain Gardiner, *op. cit.*, p. 23.

[42] Captain Gardiner, *op. cit.*, pp. 24–7.

[43] Moore to Pitt, January 30, 1759, *op. cit.*, II, 30; Hopson to Pitt, January 30, *ibid.*, II, 23; see also Beatson, *op. cit.*, II, 239. Marshall Smelser's "Insular Campaign of 1759: Guadeloupe," *American Neptune*, VII, 21–34, is especially recommended to students and forms a companion piece to his "Insular Campaign of 1759: Martinique," *ibid.*, VI, 290–8.

over the citadel, plans for its destruction by the French commander
having miscarried. As for the defenders of Basse-Terre — consisting
of some marine and militia companies assisted by slaves — when it
seemed apparent that the town was no longer tenable, they retreated some four miles northward to the Dos d'Ane, "the ass's
back" — a pass in the mountains leading to the eastern fertile settled part of the island — "of such difficult access that twenty resolute men may defend it against ten thousand." Here the Governor
of the island, Nadau d'Etreil [d'Etriel, Dutriel], gathered a large
body of militia and proceeded to entrench himself.[44] On the 27th in
this posture he received from Moore and Hopson a summons to surrender, with proposals for carrying it into effect. These he very
properly rejected.[45] Thereupon the British gave their immediate attention to putting the citadel as well as what remained of the town
in condition to serve as headquarters for subsequent operations on
the island. Writing to Pitt on the 30th, Hopson made clear his embarrassment in seeking to bring the enemy to terms — sickness had
already greatly reduced (by fifteen hundred) the number of soldiers
available; likewise, the number of Negroes for carrying out the task
of repairing the fort and pioneering work in general was also inadequate. He nevertheless assured the minister that whether he
concentrated on attacking the enemy's retreat or re-embarked
most of the troops in order to operate against the eastern, settled
section of Basse-Terre, known as Caps-Terre, he would "use the
utmost zeal and alacrity, and improve every possible Measure in
my power for the King's Service." [46]
    The general's final decision was against any attempt to dislodge
the enemy from the Dos d'Ane. This was undoubtedly wise — the
island could be gained without any such reckless use of ground
troops. Moreover, before proceeding with the campaign, Hopson
was faced by the immediate necessity of strengthening his position
at Basse-Terre. Another cause for delaying the next move in these
amphibious operations against the rest of Guadeloupe was the fact
that Moore's leading ships of the line had been roughly handled by
the enemy during the course of the bombardment on the 23rd. Un-

44 Beatson, op. cit., II, 242; III, 212; Gardiner, op. cit., pp. 31–2.
45 The summons was written on the 26th, but the officer who carried it was fired
upon and retired, with the result that it was forwarded the next day to d'Etreil by an inhabitant of the island.
46 Hopson to Pitt, January 30, 1759, op. cit., II, 24–5.

til they were placed in condition, it seemed unwise to bring about any dispersal of the fleet and also of the ground forces. General Barrington's offer to his superior, made three days after the troops landed, to take sixteen hundred of them to make an attack on the windward side of the island of Basse-Terre was therefore rejected.

Whether the refusal was wise or not is difficult to determine. Strong arguments for and against a moment's delay of the campaign may be advanced. It at least seems to be quite certain that Hopson acted in closest co-operation with Moore from the moment the expedition left Barbados. He therefore may well have based his decision on objections advanced by the Commodore — in anticipation of a series of vigorous moves against the French on Guadeloupe, with the town of Basse-Terre at last strengthened and the fleet again in fighting condition. They now drew up and published a declaration to the people of Guadeloupe making clear that at the time of the recent landing letters were addressed to the French Governor to the effect that if the inhabitants submitted peacefully to the British occupation of the island, both their persons and property would be fully protected. The offer was repeated in the proclamation, with the warning that should it be refused, the responsibility for what might take place would rest with them.[47] What gave added power to this guarantee of protection was the havoc that the privateers were creating all along the well-settled eastern coast of the western island from the most northern port, called Englishman's Head, downward. According to an account sent from Guadeloupe on February 15, "the privateersmen have hardly left a house standing near the sea, but have burnt and plundered all the coast." [48] Moreover, to keep supplies from reaching the island by way of St. Eustatius, lying northwest of it, so close a watch on the Dutch island was kept that, according to report, four thousand barrels of beef intended for the French on Martinique and Guadeloupe were held so long there that it spoiled.[49]

Toward the end of the first week in February the next definite

---

[47] Basse-Terre, Guadeloupe advices, February 15, *Pennsylvania Gazette*, March 29, 1759.

[48] *Ibid.* Advices from Barbados dated February 28 stated: "Several privateers arrived yesterday from Guadeloupe, laden with plunder" (*ibid.*). Captain Todd, arriving in New York from Antigua, also reported that vessels were daily arriving at Antigua and St. Kitts with their plunder (*ibid.*).

[49] Report brought to Charleston, South Carolina, from St. Croix, W.I., *ibid.*, March 22, 1759.

step was taken in the reduction of Guadeloupe. On the 6th Moore detached Captain Harman of the *Berwick*, a sixty-four, with four smaller vessels and two bomb-ketches, with orders to attack and reduce Fort Louis at Point Petre on the southwestern shore of Grande-Terre, the chief French stronghold on this island. With the squadron went also a detachment of marines and several companies of Hopson's Highlanders. Arriving in front of the place, Harman found that, on account of its situation, unless all the vessels moved directly into the harbour at the same time, no bombardment was likely to be effective. This move, however, involved so much danger to his squadron that without specific orders from Moore he was unwilling to risk its outcome. These were given upon application, and the *Panther*, another ship of the line, a sixty, was also sent to reinforce him.[50]

Boldly sailing into Point Petre harbour on the 14th, the squadron moved close to the fort and for almost six hours the heavy ships and cruisers hurled their broadsides against it while the bomb-ketches lobbed their carcasses upon it and into the town. With the enemy's fire at length silenced and the town in ashes, the Highlanders and marines landed and, with the retreat of the defenders, took possession of the place. The significance of the capture of Point Petre lay in the fact that it not only gave the British a foothold on Grande-Terre but provided them with an excellent harbour that would be useful for subsequent operations against the rest of Grande-Terre and the eastern part of Basse-Terre.[51]

Despite criticism by British contemporaries of the slowness of the campaign, the spirit of resistance of the French on Guadeloupe was being gradually undermined. It was quite evident to the enemy by the care given to the strengthening of the fortifications at Basse-Terre, which included a chain of posts three miles in extent, that the British intended to remain on the island. Now Fort Louis, the strongest place on Grande-Terre, was likewise lost to them, and the coast of Caps-Terre had become a scene of devastation, outside of the towns located there. Hopson, however, was on his own part seriously handicapped in following up the advantages already gained, on account of the continued prevalence of sickness among his soldiers. On February 16 he was obliged to send six hundred of them to Antigua to recuperate, and by the latter part of the month

---

50 Extract of a letter from Basse-Terre, February 12, *ibid.*, March 29, 1759.
51 Moore to Pitt, March 6, 1759, *Pitt Correspondence*, II, 54–5.

over fifteen hundred of them were in such condition that they had
to be evacuated from the island.[52] Faced with this situation he had
appealed to Governor Thomas of the Leeward for reinforcements,
which would be especially useful as the men on these islands were
accustomed to the climate.[53] In the midst of these important activities he was carried away by fever on February 27. Up to the time
of his death he had exhibited steadiness and reliability if not bril-
liance as a soldier. He was succeeded by Major General Barrington.

The new commander determined on a bold course of action. The
headquarters were transferred early in March from Basse-Terre to
Point Petre — after he had destroyed at the former place the remaining houses within the town proper and also the outlying batteries lately constructed with so much effort — leaving eight hundred soldiers and two ships of the line, the powerful *St. George* and
the *Buckingham*, to protect the citadel.[54] He was aided in his subsequent movements by the fact that his predecessor's call for aid
was answered by volunteers from Antigua, both whites and blacks.
On St. Christopher and Montserrat, likewise, many whites agreed
to go to Guadeloupe at the head of their Negroes. Three hundred
and fifty of these Leeward Islands volunteers arrived at Point Petre
on March 25, and others continued to appear, so that Barrington's
hands were thus materially strengthened.[55] Moreover, many of the
soldiers who had been sent from Basse-Terre to Antigua were soon
again fit for duty and rejoined their units.

While Barrington and Moore were thus developing their plans
for the reduction of the remaining portions of Guadeloupe, the ominous news reached them on March 12 that Maximin de Bompar,
commanding a French fleet of nine ships of the line and three frigates, had been seen near Barbados on the 8th heading for Fort
Royal, in Martinique.[56] The commodore immediately decided to
collect his ships and to sail for Prince Rupert's Bay in northwest
Dominica, which lies between Guadeloupe and Martinique, as "the
most convenient place for watching their [the French squadron's]
motions, giving assistance to the Army [on Guadeloupe] and pro-

---

[52] Barrington to Pitt, March 2, 1759, *ibid.*, II, 49; Gardiner, *op. cit.*, p. 39.

[53] Barrington to Pitt, March 6, 1759, *Pitt Correspondence*, II, 53.

[54] Beatson, *op. cit.*, II, 247; Antigua, March 10 and 21, *Pennsylvania Gazette*,
April 12 and 19, 1759,

[55] *Ibid.*

[56] For a list of these ships see Beatson, *op. cit.*, III, 220; see also Moore to Pitt,
April 11, 1759, *Pitt Correspondence*, II, 83.

tecting our Leeward Islands." [57] The move seemed to have been based on sound logistical, strategical, and tactical conceptions of the role that his fleet must play in the West Indies at this critical juncture.[58] Although Moore in concentrating his ships of the line was compelled to call in the *St. George* and the *Buckingham* from the Basse-Terre roadstead, he left Barrington a heavy cruiser, some bomb-ketches, and other smaller vessels, mostly sloops, which together with the transports would give the army mobility of action — especially as the new position of the British fleet would seem to guarantee that the enemy fleet could not reach either Basse-Terre or Fort Louis without the necessity of coming to grips with a superior naval force.[59]

With the departure of Moore on the 13th, Barrington proceeded energetically to strengthen the defences of Fort Louis and then, with his forces at hand mostly concentrated there and with the arrival of other transports with troops on board that after leaving Basse-Terre had been carried far off their course by the powerful trade-wind, he was ready to act. Detaching six hundred men in the best armed of the transports, he sent them against the towns of St. Anne and St. François, lying some distance eastward on the southern coast of Grande-Terre. Not only were these towns destroyed, but at the same time the French post of Grosier, slightly to the east of Fort Louis, was also stormed and burned by another amphibious attack.[60]

With the disappearance of the French from the southern coast towns on Grande-Terre — though the enemy still lurked in the woods, but without the support of artillery — Barrington felt that, while still holding his position at Fort Louis, he could at last proceed against the towns of the eastern shore of the island of Basse-Terre, which the American privateers had not attempted to disturb on their raiding expeditions. Although his plan to take by surprise

---

[57] *Ibid.*

[58] Captain Gardiner (*op. cit.*, pp. 46–7) is critical of Moore's move in sailing to Dominica rather than to Fort Royal. On the other hand Corbett (*op. cit.*, I, 384–5) develops a strong argument supporting Moore's decision; see also Richard Pares, *op. cit.*, p. 275 n.

[59] Assuming that Bompar would incorporate into his squadron the *Florissant*, stationed at Fort Royal, it would give him but nine real line-of-battle ships, plus a fifty-gun ship, as against Moore's ten ships of that class, plus three fifties; further, Bompar had but three cruisers, as against ten possessed by Moore, even after leaving one at Guadeloupe (Beatson, *op. cit.*, III, 220).

[60] Barrington to Pitt, May 9, 1759, *Pitt Correspondence*, II, 95–7.

three of the towns — Petit Bourg, Guoyave, and St. Marie — by moving upon them simultaneously, failed, a force under Brigadier Clavering, landing above Petit Bourg on April 12, carried a strong point fortified by the enemy and then proceeded southward against the town itself, protected by entrenchments across the river Lezard. By sending a detachment over it lower down the stream and by striking the French on the flank he compelled the latter to retreat into the town. Here Clavering received the support of a bomb-ketch, which proceeded to hurl its carcasses into the fort there with such effect as to compel the enemy to desert the place. In fact, the defenders of the fertile Caps-Terre had now lost all heart for fighting. Guoyave, southeast of Petit Bourg, fell with only the feeblest resistance, and when Brigadier Crump with seven hundred troops appeared before Le Marigot on Bay Mahout, some distance southward down the coast, they found the place deserted and proceeded to burn "an immense quantity of provisions that had been landed there by the Dutch." [61] Only St. Marie now remained, where the French hastily concentrated most of their forces that had retreated from the other places in Caps-Terre and where for a time it seemed as though they would stop Clavering's triumphant advance against it, which had begun on the 20th. But when the British by great effort got in their rear and then made a determined attack upon them posted on the heights near the town, they hastily abandoned all their artillery and, in fact, disintegrated as a military force.[62]

With the collapse of all armed resistance in Caps-Terre, and with the plantations there that were far enough inland from the coast to have escaped the plundering of the privateersmen now open to devastation, the end came likewise to the resistance of the French forces posted in the inaccessible Dos d'Ane, overlooking the roadway to Basse-Terre, where the British garrison at the fort had held its own despite attempts to dislodge it by means of the construction of French batteries near the ruined town. For Governor d'Etreil could not possibly continue to sustain his position when the inhabitants of the island had lost their will to fight. Indeed, the leading planters of Guadeloupe by the 24th now took the lead in asking for terms that Barrington might be prepared to grant, and by May 1 the capitulation had been signed for the surrender of the island of

---

[61] Clavering to Barrington, April 24, 1759, Gentleman's Magazine, XXIX, 273–5, and Gardiner, op. cit., pp. 53–7.

[62] Ibid.

Basse-Terre, and the following day that for Grande-Terre. Hardly had this been done when a messenger arrived at the camp with the news that Bompar's squadron, having eluded Moore, had landed at the burned town of St. Anne the Governor General of the French Lesser Antilles, the Marquis de Beauharnais, with six hundred regulars, two thousand Martinique buccaneers, and two thousand stands of arms, together with artillery and mortars for the support of the inhabitants of Grande-Terre. In view of the fact, however, that the planters were by no means prepared to run the risk of repudiating their surrender of the island, and without their support Beauharnais could do little, he proceeded to re-embark his forces. As for Bompar, with Moore's superior fleet liable to appear at any time, he was not, it is quite apparent, prepared to risk having any of his precious ships disabled by attacking either the towns of Basse-Terre or Fort Louis. The enemy fleet therefore as quietly and quickly departed as it had appeared.[63]

The capitulations that placed Guadeloupe in British possession were remarkable in more ways than one. In contrast to the capitulation signed at Montreal the following year and embodied in one document, there are two distinct documents: one comprehending the troops under arms; the other, the inhabitants of the two islands. The troops, including the detachments earlier sent from Martinique and Dominica, were, in the first, granted the right to leave Guadeloupe with all the honours of war and with no restrictions placed upon them as to subsequent military service. The inhabitants, in the second, received concessions that were all but unprecedented: they were permitted not only to enjoy all their property on the island, but perfect freedom of religion and the privilege of bringing in priests from France and of sending their children there to be educated. They were likewise to be governed by the laws, customs, and ordinances in force at the time of the invasion, with justice administered by Frenchmen who were in office at the time of the surrender; nor were their taxes to be other than those previously paid to the French King; nor were they liable, as were the inhabitants of the British colonies, to furnish barracks for the troops or, without the consent of the masters, slaves to work on the fortifications. They were, moreover, to enjoy all the commercial benefits that Britons possessed, with the simple reservation respecting the exclusive rights accorded to particular British trading companies and

[63] Barrington to Pitt, May 9, 1759, Pitt Correspondence, II, 100–5.

those embodied in the Navigation laws limiting trade to and from the island to British bottoms. Finally, upon taking an oath to maintain the terms of the capitulation, they were to be favoured by a grant of perfect neutrality.[64]

The capture of Guadeloupe was hailed as a matter of "infinite consequence" to Great Britain. General Barrington stated in this connection that he had been informed there was more sugar produced on it than "in all the [British] Leeward islands put together, besides great quantities of cotton and coffee." In fact, he described the Caps-Terre country as "the finest I ever saw, watered with good rivers every mile or two and [with] a port belonging to it, where all the navy of England can ride safe from hurricanes." [65] The task now was to hold it until the establishment of peace, when its ultimate fate would be determined. It could then be exchanged for Minorca, if the latter island was considered to be at the time of sufficient importance to the British and was still in the possession of the French; or it could be retained and embodied within the Empire. With its occupation and that of its near neighbour Marie Galante toward the end of May, the West India campaign for the year came to a close.[66] Barrington therefore returned to England in June, leaving Moore to keep his eyes on Bompar, who still loitered about the Lesser Antilles, always ready to seize some advantage but unwilling to risk his luck in an encounter with the British squadron.

---

[64] For the two capitulations see Beatson, op. cit., III, 215–20; they are given also by Gardiner (op. cit., pp. 60–9).

[65] Gentleman's Magazine, XXIX, 275–7.

[66] Moore to Pitt, June 24, 1759, Pitt Correspondence, II, 135–6.

CHAPTER VI

The War Spreads to India

THE FOUNDATIONS for British political control of India came, as is well known, as the result of the spread of the Great War for the Empire to this vast subcontinent. In Chapters viii and ix in Volume V of this series the commercial activities of the United East India Company for the period from 1750 to 1754 were considered in some detail, as were also its relations with the French Compagnie des Indes and the native rulers, especially in the Carnatic and the Deccan — that area embracing the Coromandel Coast and the region stretching westward and including the great central plateau of the peninsula. Certain facts became evident in this survey. Among these was the determination of the directorate of the English company, on the one hand, to limit its interest in India to trade and, on the other hand, to use every means at its disposal to prevent the French company or its servants from establishing political control there that would adversely affect this trade.

The position of the directors of the Company was logical enough. It was based on the view that the Portuguese and Dutch method of conquest in the Far East was in opposition to the idea that the free exchange of goods, without assuming any responsibility for the ruling of native peoples, was not only infinitely less complicated but also in the long run much more profitable. Further, it was fully in accord with the powers granted to it by the government to act, not as an empire-builder, but rather as a trading company. But its chief commercial rival in India, beginning with the year 1744, embarked on new and startling policies that compelled it to resort to counter-measures.

Had the French Compagnie des Indes been able to prosper to

the extent that the United East India Company had been able to do as the result of legitimate business transactions, it is likely that the history of India during the past two centuries might have been radically different. In default of great trade profits, the Compagnie, unhappily, permitted itself to become involved by its servants Dupleix and Bussy in the establishment of political spheres of influence and the winning of extensive territorial grants from the native princes, bringing with them theoretically at least the revenues of these possessions. In the face of such developments, which seemed destined to cut Madras off from its commercial contacts with the interior and even with native coastal cities in the Northern Circars, the servants of the United East India Company went into action.

They found in the clerk Robert Clive a man quick in decision, fearless, cool, and resourceful, who enjoyed to a remarkable extent the confidence of the native troops — the sepoys — in the employ of the Company. It was Clive who became the chief instrument, as was made clear, in undermining the grandiose French plan for India and of disillusioning the directors of the Compagnie des Indes, which led in 1754 to the recall of Dupleix to France in disgrace. In reverting to their earlier policy of non-interference in the quarrels of the native rulers, they replaced Dupleix with a M. Godeheu, who received instructions to enter into an agreement with the English company officials at Madras that would end the past ten years of turmoil in the Carnatic and would permit the two great companies to concentrate once again on trade rather than on the politics of power.

With the signing of a provisional peace treaty on December 15, 1754 by the representatives of the two companies at Madras, it seemed that an epoch of peaceful business activity was now to take the place of offensive alliances with native princes to counteract other offensive alliances and the hostile movements of European and native troops, with the besieging of towns and cities, and the clash of arms on the open field of battle — all to the disruption of the arts of peace. This happy anticipation, however, was not to be realized. Not only was the Marquis de Bussy left ominously entrenched in the Deccan at the court of the Subahdar, who claimed an overlordship over the Carnatic, but in the upper valley of the Ohio, in far-off North America, the embers of Anglo-French international rivalry had been fanned into a flame. The spreading conflagration was not to spare India. On the contrary, it led the servants of the English company in Bengal to follow the example of Bussy in the Deccan.

It was India's great misfortune at the beginning of the Great War for the Empire to have been the scene of political anarchy. The Great Mogul established at Delhi could no longer control the empire over which he was supposed to rule. In the eyes of Hindus he, a Mohammedan, was really a usurper, whose claim to power rested on the fact that Akbar, in the days of Elizabeth, had established himself among them by violence and conquest. Nor did this Moslem empire ever include all of India. Not even powerful Aurangzeb; who died in 1707, could conquer the southern parts, despite incessant effort, and his son, Bahadur Shah, who died in 1711, was the last of the strong Indian emperors. By 1754 the power of the Great Mogul, now Alamgir II, was indeed but a shadow. Dominated in his own palace by court officials and favourites, many of whom were not natives of India, his nominal authority beyond the environs of Delhi was, more frequently than not, ignored when it was not mocked. The Hindu Mahrattas of the Western Ghats, whose dominions for a brief interval of time during the period under consideration was to stretch in western India from the Indus River and Himalayan Mountains almost to the southern tip of India, plundered their neighbours at will; the viceroyalty of the Deccan ruled by the Moslem Subahdar Salabat Jang, Nizam of Hyderabad, had established its position as an independent principality for all practical purposes and with it an overlordship of the Carnatic; Bengal under the Moslem Nabob 'Ali Wardi Khan (Alivirdi Khan) was largely a law unto itself; and what was true of the Deccan and Bengal was equally true of almost every other principality within the theoretical confines of the empire — without reference to the quite independent states beyond its northern bounds as well as those that lay south of its pretended limits. Finally, the Great Mogul was repeatedly terrorized not only by the Mahrattas within India itself, but by the repeated incursions of the Afghans and Persians who swept in upon him from time to time through the passes of the Himalayas like swarms of locusts to scourge and loot and then to retire. Nor was Bengal, the richest province in Hindustan, permitted to remain in peace. During the rule of 'Ali Wardi Khan it was subject to repeated attack, especially by the Mahrattas.

Drained by the sluggish waters of the great Ganges flowing eastward and the Brahmaputra flowing southward out of Tibet, Bengal

"Bengal," based on Rennell's map.

(From S. C. Hill: *Indian Record Series. Bengal in 1756-1757*)

"Calcutta in 1756-1757."

(From S. C. Hill: *Indian Record Series. Bengal in 1756-1757*)

Road to the Salt Lakes

The Causeway

Road to Dum Dum

Dinga Bunga

Jan Bazar

Lal Bazar

Brojo Kishore's Bungalow

Buttaichutta Tree

Manik Tolla

Sham Bazar

Sobah Bazar

Umichund's Garden

Govind. Ram. Mistri's Garden

March of Clive's army on the 3ᵈ February 1757

Nawab's Camp (Retreating) (about two miles)

Maratha Ditch

S I M I L A

C A L C U T T A

MOLUNGA

SUTANATI

Burra Bazar

Portuguese Church

Armenian Church

Pagoda

Court House

Jail

St. Anne's Church

Play House

Rajah Walk

Rope Walk

Great Tank

Little Tank

Bazar

Park

Buzz Bazar

Great Ground

Old Fort William

Governor's House (Cruttenden's)

Perin's Redoubt

Chitpur Br.

Dum Dum or Cow Cross Bridge

BAGH BAZAR

C H I T P U R

Kelsalls Octagon

Mill Ground

Ferry Bridge

Clive's advanced Post

Clive's Camp 3ᵈ Feb. 1757

Chitpur Tank

Batteries

H U G G L I

R I V E R

Chandpal Ghat

Thakur's Ghat

Cooley Ghat

Cruttenden's Ghat

Coss's Ghat

Jackson's Ghat

Greatdue Ghat

Nabob's Ghat

Suttanity Ghat

(a) Ditches & Slight Works made in 1742

(b) Gates of the Bara Bazar

(a) Ditches & Slight Works made in 1742.
(b) Gates of the Bara Bazar.

then as now teemed with people whose cities and villages were clustered along the banks of these mighty rivers and those of their tributaries or estuaries. With respect to the cities on the Ganges, there was Murshidabad, the capital of the Nabob; lower down the river on its estuary, the Hugli, was Chinsura, where the Dutch East India Company had its principal factory; then four miles below it was the French Chandernagore; finally, twenty miles still farther down and about one hundred miles from the Bay of Bengal lay Calcutta, the chief centre of activity of the United East India Company in India. Despite the perpetual struggle going on to the westward for political power and with it economic control of north central India, conditions remained fairly quiet in the European trading settlements on the Hugli from the beginning of the eighteenth century until the year 1756. The explanation for this lies in the fact that none of the European trading companies departed in this area seriously from its primary objective. Not even the struggle in the Carnatic, in which the British at Madras and Fort St. David and the French at Pondicherry were deeply involved, disturbed too greatly the relative calm that prevailed along the Hugli.

As to Calcutta — the future metropolis of India, destined to number in our own days over two million people — from three small, disease-ridden villages located about tide-swept swampy land and purchased in 1698 by the Company, there slowly arose a city that at this time numbered perhaps a hundred and twenty-five thousand souls. As with Madras and Bombay, Calcutta had both its native and its European quarters. The latter, located just beyond the walls of Fort William, were adorned with attractive homes and gardens, most of them belonging to the employees of the Company, and beyond them stretching northward were those of wealthy Armenians, Portuguese, and natives, together with their places of worship; and southward those of the more humble class of native workmen. As was also true of Madras and Bombay, Calcutta not only had attracted Indian families of wealth and business capacity, but had become a refuge centre where, in fleeing from the anarchy of the interior of the country, people could find for themselves and their property a degree of security lacking in most other places. In this connection it may be noted that the Mohammedans up to this period had apparently settled there in such small numbers and had hitherto made so small a contribution to its progress that not even a mosque had been built as a place of worship before the year

1756. The heart of the city, Fort William, was a weak and inde-fensible place from a military point of view, but vastly important as the headquarters of one of the three so-called Presidencies that the United East India Company had established in India to super-intend its multifarious and widespread business activities and the conduct of its employees. Here the Council carried on its activities, presided over by Governor Roger Drake, certainly a man of busi-ness but not of outstanding heroic stature, as will be noted.

Until the middle of the eighteenth century the Calcutta Presi-dency had chiefly relied for its protection on a so-called *firman* or formal grant made at a cost of some one hundred thousand pounds to the Company by the Great Mogul Farrukh-siyar in 1717. This provided for a token annual payment to him of three thousand rupees for the privilege of establishing factories or trading houses in any city of Bengal, Orissa, or Behar and for the ample protection of its peaceful activities. In addition, the right to the continued use of the three villages — which were, as noted, purchased in 1698 upon the basis of the payment of a specified annual quit-rent and within the limits of which the city of Calcutta arose — was also solemnly confirmed.[1] As early as 1696, moreover, permission had been given to the Company by the Nabob of Bengal to build Fort William when it had determined otherwise to withdraw from the Ganges as the result of the insecurity of its position. Totally inade-quate as was the fort at any time to resist any determined move on the part of the Nabob of the province to possess it, it had been permitted to fall into decay, and even the garrison that was sup-posed, in case of emergency, to defend it, was but a handful of men, mostly foreigners, quite lacking in martial spirit.[2] It is true that during the Mahratta incursions into Bengal in 1743 and 1744 the Council was permitted by 'Ali Wardi Kahn to strengthen the fortifi-cations by digging a moat or ditch — called the Mahratta Ditch —

---

[1] For a copy of the firman of 1717 see *Indian Record Series. Bengal in 1756–1757* (ed. S. C. Hill, London, 1905), III, pp. 375–7. This important work will hereafter be cited as *Bengal Records*. As Hill has with vast industry included in it most important sources of information, consisting of 612 documents or miscellaneous accounts, some of them very extensive in nature, the task of the author of the present series, now con-cerned with the activities of the British in Bengal for the years 1756 and 1757, has been immensely lightened.

[2] Vice Admiral Sir George Pocock, writing to the Earl of Holderness on April 14, 1757 from the *Kent* off Calcutta, refers to the "shamefull neglect" of the Presidency in not providing "a well built Citadel with a proper Number of Land Forces," Pocock Letter Book, Huntington Library.

about Fort William, and that this was begun by the people of the native quarter and carried to a point so as to give a semblance of protection to the northern part of the city; but with the disappearance of the Mahratta scare the work was suspended and even the part that had been excavated was allowed to fill with mud.[3]

The Calcutta Council, in fact, was firmly persuaded that the peaceful activities of the Company in Bengal were so beneficial to all concerned that this would be its chief security. Its more important factories in this area numbered twenty-five, and in addition there were some subordinate factories, at all of which goods were contracted for and were received for processing and prepared for export, and where payments were made for them.[4] It was generally recognized at the period in question that the business of the United East India Company in Bengal surpassed in value and quantity that of all the other competing European companies there taken together. Its great exports, as well as those of the other companies, could only be met by payment in specie. In fact, in the first half of the eighteenth century, in the words of Alexander Dow, one who knew the country well, "the balance of trade was against all nations in favour of Bengal; and it was the sink where gold and silver disappeared without the least prospect of return."[5]

All this, according to the same writer, was due to the remarkable skill of the Hindus, the fertility of land, and the comparative mildness of the climate.[6] If there was widespread poverty in this land of opulence, as there was, there is every reason to believe that it was caused not only by the inhibitions of the fixed social system and the faulty distribution of wealth produced there in such abundance, but also by the fact that human fertility, under not unfavourable conditions for the survival of the individual, exerted under these circumstances continuous pressure on the means of subsistence even in this rich country and provided, as an inevitable consequence, an inexhaustible supply of cheap labour. From the fields of the husbandmen came rice, sugar, spices, tobacco, cotton, silk, fruits, vegetables, and many other articles; from the looms of the weavers poured the fine muslins of Dacca, the lovely silks of Cossimbazar,

---

[3] Hill, *Bengal Records*, I, Introduction, xxxi and xxxv.

[4] Kalikinkar Datta, *Studies in the History of the Bengal Subah, 1740–70* (Calcutta, 1936), I, Chap. ii.

[5] Alexander Dow, *The History of Hindostan* (London, 1772), I, ciii.

[6] *Ibid*

the printed Patna chintzes, and other beautiful and delicate fabrics designed for the export trade, as well as those for common use.[7]

Unhappily, the marauding of the Mahrattas in western Bengal was not conducive to the stability and maintenance of handicraft industry. In 1751 a letter from the Company factory of Cossim-bazar to the Calcutta Council stressed the effects of its decline "owing to the Mahrattas constantly entering Bengal, plundering and burning the people's houses and destroying the chief Aurungs [an establishment where articles were produced or collected for wholesale or export], from whence the workmen have fled to distant places, and not to any malpractice in the gentlemen there." [8] In referring to these invasions, Howell, a member of the Calcutta Council, declared: "Insecurity of person and property overwhelmed the merchants and weavers, and the manufacture of the country was greatly affected." [9]

The simple fact is that the government of Bengal as then constituted, and in view of the chaotic conditions that existed in Hindustan, was no longer able to provide the proper security to the inhabitants of the province and to their property — something that they deeply desired, while apparently little concerned, by and large, as to who it was that ruled over them, so long had they been accustomed to government by foreigners. Yet the Nabob 'Ali Wardi Khan — a Turkman whose progenitors had dwelt in Persia and who himself had seized the nabobship by violence and bloodshed — was a man of ability and also, it may be said, of considerable humanity, even if guilty of treachery. For ten years, from the beginning of his reign in 1741, he fought the Mahrattas with varying degrees of success; and in 1751, by ceding to them Orissa, a province lying south of Bengal, and agreeing to make them certain large annual payments, secured to the people temporary relief from harassment from that quarter.[10] Nor were his relations with the European com-

---

[7] K. Datta, op. cit., pp. 417–42. For a statement covering the varied Bengal investments for the year 1755 see the letter of the Select Committee of Fort William to the Company, under date of December 8, 1755, received in London on September 6, 1756 ("Abstracts of the General Letters: the Coast & Bay . . . have sent from 1754. India Office: HEIC's Coromandel Coast and Bay," 6:85–94. This Coast and Bay series and the later separate abstracts of the Bengal, Madras, and Bombay correspondence, covering the period from 1754 to 1775, are now available to students in America at the Library of Congress in microfilm form and have been utilized in preparing this volume).

[8] Datta, op. cit., p. 437.

[9] Ibid., p. 436.

[10] Hill, Bengal Records, I, Introduction, xxvii.

panies of an unfriendly nature. He forbad them to make war against one another when hostilities between the French and English took place in the Carnatic. If he made large demands upon them for special gifts in times of stress, these were not without justification and were generally met, at least by the servants of the United East India Company.[11] For they realized that it was of the utmost importance to their trade and to the permanence of their Bengal establishments to prevent the ruin of the province, already exhibiting grave signs of industrial decay, as previously noted.

Here, in brief, is the background for presenting an analysis of developments in Bengal that were to lead to the establishment of the British *raj* not only in that province but ultimately throughout the length and breadth of India.

In the spring of 1756 the venerable 'Ali Wardi Khan died at the age of eighty-two, leaving as a successor his great-nephew, carrying the promising name Siraj-ud-daula, which means "the Lamp of the State." This young man in his twenty-third year, handsome in appearance, was, unfortunately, of very unstable character. The Indian historian Ghutam Husain Khan, in his work entitled *Seir Mutaqherin*, referring to the new Nabob declared that in indulging himself he made

> "no distinction between vice and virtue, and paying no regard to the nearest relations . . . carried his defilement wherever he went, and, like a man alienated in his mind . . . made the houses of men and women of distinction the scenes of his profligacy. . . . In a little time . . . people on meeting him by chance used to say, God save us from him."[12]

Before mounting the throne he had already treacherously disposed of certain powerful men who had opposed him. Depending on his changing humour, he would sacrifice a friend as quickly as an enemy; and those compelled to have dealings with him were made to realize how faithless were his promises.[13] Had he possessed the firmness of purpose and stability of character of his predecessor,

---

[11] Robert Orme, *A History of Military Transactions of the British Nation in Indostan* (London, 1778), II, 45–6; "Evidence of Mr. Richard Becher," 1772, Hill, *Bengal Records*, III, 287–90. Becher served the Company during this period at Dacca.

[12] Quoted by Hill, *Bengal Records*, I, Introduction, xxviii.

[13] Luke Scrafton, one of the Company servants who negotiated with Siraj-ud-daula, declared that the Nabob's mind was affected (*Reflections on the Government of Indostan* [London, 1770], p. 50).

there is little likelihood that events would have taken the course that they now took. Under 'Ali Wardi Khan the Company had been permitted through the Nabob's neglect to stretch the privileges that it enjoyed by the imperial firman to a point where abuses became evident and needed to be checked. In dealing with the causes leading to Siraj-ud-daula's attack upon Calcutta, a ship captain, David Rannie, in a memorandum drawn up in the summer of 1756 while in Indian waters, states those of a general as well as those of a specific nature. He stressed the alarming example of the Coromandel Coast, where the English and the French in supporting rival nabobs had, to all appearances, divided the country; again, he mentioned the "trickery" of Siraj-ud-daula in seizing the Company's factory at Cossimbazar, located near his capital, Murshidabad; and he referred to "our [the Company servants] acting unjustifiably by the Moors [that is, the Mohammedan rulers]." With respect to the last point, he wrote:

> "The injustice to the Moors consists in that being by their courtesy permitted to live here as merchants, to protect and judge what natives were their servants, and to trade custom free, we under that pretence protected all the Nabob's subjects that claimed our protection, though they were neither our servants nor our merchants, and gave our *dustucks* or passes to numbers of natives to trade custom free, to the great prejudice of the Nabob's revenue, nay more we levied large duties upon goods brought into districts from the very people that permitted us to trade custom free, and by numbers of . . . impositions (framed to raise the Company's revenue) some of which were ruinous to ourselves, such as taxes on marriages, provisions, transferring property etc., caused eternal clamour and complaints against us at Court." [14]

With respect to the illicit trade, referred to above — which had long been permitted by the Company's servants to the loss of the Nabob's revenue — Rannie does justice to Governor Drake in stating that the latter had before the attack on Calcutta already taken steps that had stopped most of it. [15] So there only remained for correction other abuses of the privileges accorded to the Company, including domicile provided for those who fled to Calcutta for protec-

[14] "Causes of the loss of Calcutta by David Rannie, dated August, 1756," Hill, *Bengal Records*, III, 383–4.
[15] *Ibid.*

tion.[16] In this connection the charge that domicile had been granted to one Krishna Das, a son of the financial officer of the Nabob's very wealthy uncle, Muhammad Khan, who had died at Dacca the preceding December, was the chief ostensible reason for Siraj-ud-daula's march upon the city. But the fact remains that when Krishna Das, who had come down the river to Calcutta with his family, was once again in the power of the new Nabob, instead of being punished as a fugitive from justice, he was given marks of honour,[17] which would seem to indicate either that the charge against Das was an excuse for a plan to plunder the Company or that the Nabob came to realize that Das, accorded the protection of the English flag, had not, in reality, been guilty of any wrongdoing. Finally, there remained the charge, not mentioned by Rannie, but important as a motivating cause for ensuing hostilities, that the Company servants at Calcutta "had built strong fortifications and dug a large ditch . . . contrary to the established laws of the country." [18]

This last complaint was to some extent true. With news arriving of hostilities between the English and French in the New World and on the high seas that seemed to indicate an open declaration of war in the near future and in view of the general chaotic condition in India, the Council at Calcutta had during the long illness of 'Ali Wardi Khan begun to make preparations for eventualities in Bengal and in this connection proceeded to take steps to clean out the old Mahratta Ditch and to place in repair the decaying fortifications of Fort William. Further, at the great bend of the Ganges north of the city and as a protection to the native quarter from a surprise attack

---

[16] In a letter to Governor George Pigot of the Madras Presidency, dated June 30, 1756, Siraj-ud-daula, while calling Governor Drake "a very wicked and unruly man," only levied the charge against him that he "began to give protection to persons who had accounts with the *Patcha* [or sovereign] in his *Koatey* [factory]" (*ibid.*, I, 196). It is true that the Nabob, in writing to a wealthy Armenian merchant at Hugli named Coja Wajid on June 1, also mentioned the Company abuses in the tolls, which, as noted above, had been dealt with by Drake, and said that it "had built strong fortifications and dug a large ditch . . . contrary to the established laws of the country" (*ibid.*, I, 4–5).

[17] *Ibid.*, I, Introduction, xliv.

[18] Siraj-ud-daula to Coja Wajid, June 1, 1756, *ibid.*, I, 4–5; H. H. Dodwell, in the *Cambridge History of India* (Cambridge, 1929, Vol. V, 142), gives the chief cause of the Nabob's resentment as due to the fact that the Company had strengthened its military position in Bengal. Little in this direction, however, had been done by the close of 1755 (see letters of September 3 and December 8 of the Fort William Select Committee, India Office, HEIC's Coast and Bay, 6:84 and 91).

from Chandernagore, a small redoubt was newly erected.[19] It was for these various stated offences that the Nabob now determined to "extirpate" the English in Bengal unless they agreed not only to surrender their prized imperial firman, but also to destroy all of their fortifications — which they had been given the right to erect at Calcutta as early as 1696 — and to rely from this time forward wholly upon his protection and upon whatever privileges he might from time to time permit the Company to exercise.[20]

Therefore, when Governor Drake refused to turn over Das on demand and also refused to permit the Nabob's messenger to remain in Calcutta, which he had entered secretly, and, instead, wrote to Siraj-ud-daula questioning the latter's additional demand that the Calcutta fortifications be destroyed,[21] the Nabob acted quickly against the English company. He sent troops to Cossimbazar, near his capital, where it had long maintained a fortified factory defended by some fifty troops, and invested it. Then under a pledge of safe conduct he laid his hands on its chief agent, William Watts, and soon afterward took possession of the factory. This occurred at the beginning of June 1756, and on the 7th the news of its loss reached Calcutta. Already — as the result of disturbing reports sent by Watts in May that Siraj-ud-daula had been advised that Calcutta could not be defended and therefore would be easily conquered and its supposed immense wealth placed at his disposal — preparations had been begun at Fort William to prepare for a possible attack.[22] But little could be done. Having been lulled with a feeling that the city was too important to the welfare of the rulers of Bengal to suffer injury from them, the bastions of the fort had by 1756 become almost useless in case of an assault by land. Not only had they suffered de-

---

[19] Governor Drake's "Narrative," July 19, 1756, Hill, *Bengal Records*, I, 118–63; J. Z. Holwell to the Court of Directors, November 30, 1756, *ibid.*, II, 1–52.

[20] Siraj-ud-daula to Coja Wajid, June 1, 1756, *ibid.*, I, 4–5.

[21] No copy of this letter has survived. Drake, however, declared — when later defending his conduct in a long statement addressed to the Fort William Council on January 25, 1757 — that it had contained no threat to the Nabob; that, on the contrary, it had indicated that the only threat to the peace in Bengal came from the danger that, with war impending between France and England, Calcutta might be captured by the French as Madras was during the late war, and that it had, finally, charged that the report that new fortifications were being built was the work of enemies (*ibid.*, II, 134–56). Drake, nevertheless, signed the Select Committee's letter to the Company of September 3, 1755, which referred to plans for works "designed to repel Country Forces" (India Office, HEIC's Coast and Bay, 6:84).

[22] Governor Drake's "Narrative," July 19, 1756, *Bengal Records*, I, 118–62.

cay, but houses and even a large church, St. Anne's, had been built just outside the walls and obstructed the line of fire from the fort and even commanded the bastions in a military sense.[23] When the further news reached Calcutta that the Nabob with a large army was actually marching on Calcutta, Captain Alexander Grant recommended to the Select Committee that these costly structures be levelled so that a proper defence could be made. But the owners of the homes, mostly servants of the Company who could not believe that the danger was great, protested vigorously at the idea of the destruction of their homes and even demanded that these be included within the line to be defended.[24] Yet the military force available for this purpose was fantastically small to cover the miles that must thus be contained.

Against the many thousands of natives and a small force of European mercenaries embodied in Siraj-ud-daula's army, there were on hand at Fort William a total of five hundred and fifteen men, including all the Company servants capable of carrying a gun. Of this number there were but one hundred and ninety soldiers, a greater part of whom were Portuguese, and of these troops, if Holwell is correct, "there were not five who had ever, I believe, seen a musket fired in anger." [25] In addition, the militia of the city, now placed under arms, amounted to two hundred and fifty men, most of them either Portuguese or Armenians, and so little versed in the use of weapons as — again quoting Holwell — scarcely to know "the right from the wrong end of their pieces"; [26] further, the ammunition on hand for their use was scanty, the powder poor in quality, and the gun-carriages so rotten as scarcely to bear the weight of a gun; [27] finally, their commanding officer, Captain-Commandant George Minchin, an indolent man, was utterly incapable of rising to such an occasion and at the most crucial point in the defence of the fort, as will be noted, weakly left it to seek safety on board a ship. Here we have a picture of the military might of the East India Company in Bengal — outside of the fact that there was perhaps a total of some two hundred more soldiers, equally competent, doing police duty at

---

[23] H. H. Dowell, op. cit., V, 143.

[24] Captain Grant's Account of the Capture of Calcutta, July 13, 1763, Hill, *Bengal Records*, I, 73–88.

[25] J. Z. Holwell to the Court of Directors, November 30, 1756, *ibid.*, II, 1–52.

[26] *Ibid.*

[27] *Ibid.* See also Holwell's letter of July 17 to the Governor and Council of Bombay (India Office, HEIC's Coast and Bay, 6:113–15).

the other factories, such as at Cossimbazar, Dacca, Luckipore, and Balasore! [28]

On June 13 the Nabob's army — composed of from thirty to fifty thousand men, one hundred and fifty elephants, as well as camels, and an artillery train manned by over two hundred Europeans and native Portuguese — was reported to be in the vicinity of Calcutta.[29] As it was by no means clear that the city could be held, the Council now decided to seize and hold, if possible, a strong fort located on the right bank of the Hugli at Tanna, just below Calcutta, as a possible place of refuge. Despite the fact that the native garrison was driven out, it was found to be impossible to keep possession of the Tanna fort on the approach of a large contingent of the Nabob's army. It was therefore clear that Fort William must be defended to the uttermost, unless the Council was prepared to order its evacuation by at least the Europeans, who in safety could thereupon move down the Hugli to some such place as Balasore near its mouth by using the shipping still at hand. But this weak course was not seriously considered at the time. In fact, the feeling among the Europeans was that the Nabob was really more interested in a generous bribe to call off his army than in a fight, and that everything would end quietly, with the peaceful return of Siraj-ud-daula to his capital. Still, as a precaution, on the 16th the British women were brought into the fort enclosure when an attempt was made by the enemy to force the Mahratta Ditch. But soon the northern native quarter of the city was flooded by thousands of the Nabob's troops and camp followers who came to plunder. On the 18th the first attack was delivered against the line — which included all the European residences. It was soon pierced on the southeast, in spite of heroic resistance on the part of the handful of English defenders, and the invaders proceeded to occupy many of the spacious houses, most of which possessed strong walls of masonry called *pucca*, which resisted even cannon-fire.

Only at the end of the first day of real fighting, with the new defence line now narrowed to the houses located immediately in the neighbourhood of the fort, did the British realize the full gravity of

---

[28] "Account of Military at Bengal, 29 February, 1756," *Bengal Records*, III, 408.

[29] For different estimates of the strength of the Nabob's army see J. Z. Holwell to the Councils of Bombay and Fort St. George, July 17, 1756, *ibid.*, I, 109–15; Governor Drake's "Narrative," July 17, 1756, *ibid.*, I, 118–62; W. Tooke's "Narrative," April–November 1756, *ibid.*, I, 248–300.

the situation. Added to this was the fact that when a battery of heavy guns had been outflanked at a place in the city where a jail was located, and was deserted, the spiking of them had been so imperfect as to permit the French artillerymen in the service of the Nabob to put them to the most effective use against the fort itself and especially its outlying defences.[30] That evening the Council met and decided to put the women on board ship. This was done during the course of the night and very early the following morning.[31] Also about two o'clock of the 19th Governor Drake and a number of others held an informal conference.

Upon the basis of the existing situation, with the ammunition nearing exhaustion, the militia drunk, mutinous, out of control, and the rest of the defenders too weak to check the progress of the enemy, it was decided to abandon the fort and retreat to the ships.[32] Still further efforts, however, were made to rally the soldiers to defend the fort, where, among other people, a large number of Armenian and Portuguese women and children, natives of India, was being given protection. Then about ten o'clock in the morning, as the rumour spread that the ammunition was quite exhausted and the enemy was cutting off means of escape to the ships, a wild stampede took place to the Company's near-by wharf, in the course of which many were drowned in the river. It was in the midst of the general fright that Commandant Minchin, "without the least concern to anyone," and numerous other gentlemen fled to the boats, and they were soon followed by Governor Drake and Adjutant Grant, the latter "esteemed the best officer in the service." [33] Up to that moment the two had supported the defence with resolution. Drake claimed that through worry and lack of sleep he had become confused in the panic, and as a consequence had been impelled to enter a boat to seek safety in flight to the ships now dropping down the river, thinking that all resistance to the enemy had now ended.[34]

After the panic there was little activity the rest of that day on the

---

[30] Holwell to the Court of Directors, November 30, 1756, ibid., II, 1–52.

[31] Captain Alexander Grant's "Account of the Capture of Calcutta," July 13, 1756, ibid., I, 73–88.

[32] Governor Drake's "Narrative," July 19, 1756, ibid., I, 118–61.

[33] "Fulta Consultation," August 20, 1756, ibid., I, 200–1. For Grant's explanation of his retirement to the ships, as presented to the Select Committee on August 20, 1756, see ibid., I, 89–95.

[34] For Drake's explanation of his conduct see his letter to the Council of Fort William of January 17–25, 1757, ibid., II, 134–56.

part of the men who were left behind in the fort. The remaining members of the Council, however, proceeded to suspend Drake and others of that body who had gained the ships and elected Holwell to Drake's place for the period of the emergency.[35] One hundred and seventy soldiers — without counting the Armenians and Portuguese, who were no longer anxious to fight — was the total force now remaining. It was agreed that retreat was absolutely necessary, but the effort to get the ships — now out of range of gunfire down the river — to return was unavailing, and a vessel that might have taken them off, the *Prince George*, grounded above the fort and was burned by the enemy. That day the great Company warehouse just south of the fort went up in flames, as well as other houses. Many of the common soldiers made desperate by their plight now broke into the officers' quarters and consumed quantities of liquor and again got out of control. Although the assaults on the morning of Sunday, the 20th, were repulsed by those who remained at their place of duty, it was realized that the end had come. In the afternoon a flag of truce was hoisted and soon afterward, ignoring it, the enemy poured through the western gate facing the river and scaled the walls on all sides.[36] With resistance ended, the Nabob entered the fort and, in an interview with Holwell, promised that no harm would befall him, in this connection placing all the blame for what had happened upon Drake.[37]

Fort William, as well as the city of Calcutta, was now in possession of the Nabob. He proceeded to rename the latter Alinagar and ordered a mosque to be erected there in honour of his triumph. How many in his army were destroyed in the fighting it is impossible to indicate with accuracy, though figures of from seven to fifteen thousand have been given.[38] At least it is clear that his soldiers sought revenge for their heavy losses, and when those belonging to the Company, while still drunk, assaulted some of the natives, Siraj-ud-daula was prevailed upon to order them and all the other Europeans

[35] According to William Lindsay, a Company servant, Holwell himself sought to get away, but the boat that he had reserved for himself had meanwhile been appropriated by two other gentlemen (Lindsay to Robert Orme, July 1756, *ibid.*, I, 163–73).

[36] Holwell to the Court of Directors, November 30, 1756, *ibid.*, II, 1–52.

[37] Watts and Collet to the Fort William Council, July 14, 1756, *ibid.*, I, 97–8.

[38] M. Durand, in the French Compagnie des Indes service, says that the Nabob's losses were computed at between twelve and fifteen thousand men (Durand to la Motte, July 2, 1756, *ibid.*, III, 77–81); Holwell writing to the Councils of Bombay and Fort St. George (Madras), July 17, 1756, declared that by their own confession the enemy's losses in killed were over five thousand (*ibid.*, I, 109–16).

as well to be placed in the guardhouse — familiarly known as the Black Hole. As a result, Governor Holwell and one hundred and forty-five people on the evening of the 20th were crowded into a little room less than eighteen feet square, provided with but two small windows, and designed for the accommodation at most of a handful of unruly soldiers. The heat was terrific. Men fought with one another for a breath of air; in their agony they either taunted or begged the guard outside to shoot them; they trampled one another to death, or died from suffocation, or went mad in their raging thirst. By six o'clock the following day only twenty-three of the inmates were still alive, including Holwell and a woman who had accompanied her husband.[39]

As early as May 25 the Council of Calcutta had written to that of Madras of the threatening attitude of the Nabob. Other letters followed, calling for aid, especially letters written on the 7th and 8th of June.[40] The news of the loss of the Company factory at Cossimbazar arrived at Fort St. George on August 3, and on the 17th of that month came a letter telling of the fall of Calcutta.[41] Although a small relief force had already been dispatched to the Ganges, it was realized, with the news of the fall of Cossimbazar, that something much more effective must be done to remedy the situation in Bengal. When the Council thereupon consulted Admiral Watson, in charge of the British squadron on the Coromandel Coast, he advised delay so that the main expeditionary force might avoid the debilitating rainy season.[42] At the same time he promised full support. His advice was accepted. To provide the necessary troops, the Council, even in the face of the danger of the capture of Madras by the French should they seize the opportunity, now "drained all the garrisons on the

---

[39] The most detailed account of the Black Hole tragedy is given by Holwell in a very long letter to William Davis, Esq., dated February 28, 1757 (Gentleman's Magazine, February 1758). On July 17, 1756, on release from his imprisonment, he wrote to the Bombay Council that between one hundred and sixty-five and one hundred and seventy people were "crammed altogether into a Small Prison in the Fort called the Black hole wherein all but sixteen were Suffocated" (India Office, HEIC's Coast and Bay, 6:114). Many other accounts of the Black Hole are printed in Hill's Bengal Records. J. H. Little in his Bengal Past and Present (London, 1915, 1916), seeks to throw doubt on the Black Hole incident. However, H. H. Dodwell (op. cit., V, 156) has shown with what unreliable materials this writer has sought to do so.

[40] For these letters of June 7 and 8 see Hill, Bengal Records, I, 12–14.

[41] Watts and Collet to the Council of Madras, Chandernagore, July 2, 1756, ibid., I, 45–8.

[42] Watson to the Council, August 25, 1756, ibid., I, 206.

Coast to strengthen the detachment preparing for Bengal." [43] At the head of this they finally decided to place Colonel Robert Clive, who had returned to England in 1755 after his exploits in the Carnatic, which have already been considered in this series, and was now again in India with the King's military commission as lieutenant colonel and the Company's commission as Deputy Governor of Fort St. David. He was, moreover, in this emergency given full powers to act in all military matters under general instructions furnished him by the Madras Council, even to the exclusion of the authority of that of Calcutta, but in close co-operation with Admiral Watson. [44]

When the expedition finally sailed from Madras on October 16, it carried about six hundred European troops and some twelve hundred of Stringer Lawrence's hard-fighting sepoys. Its purpose was not only to recapture Calcutta and to secure the restoration of the other factories, together with all the privileges guaranteed by the imperial firman, but to obtain ample reparations to the Company for its losses in Bengal. To this end Clive was authorized, if need be, to go so far as to overthrow Siraj-ud-daula by giving his support "to any Powers in the provinces of Bengal that may be dissatisfied with the violences of the Nabob's Goverment, or that may have pretensions to the Nabobship." [45] Here, in other words, was provided the basis for the first phase of the revolution that was soon to take place in Bengal and was to end in the establishment there of the political power of the United East India Company.

Owing to adverse winds, it was not until early in December that the ships beating up the Bay of Bengal finally approached the Hugli, and then on the 12th the first of them arrived at Fulta — located some distance up the river and only thirty-two miles from Calcutta — where the British Calcutta survivors had established themselves and where the Fort William Council was acting once more under Governor Drake, despite the protest of Holwell, [46] who, having been released from the Black Hole, had found his way to Chandernagore

---

[43] The Select Committee of St. George to the Select Committee of Fort William, February 21, 1757, *ibid.*, II, 232–6. An expedition to be led by Clive against Bussy and Salabat Jang in Golconda was about to leave Madras (India Office, Home Series, Misc., Vol. 191:11–29).

[44] *Ibid.* See also the letter of the Select Committee of October 11, 1756 that pointed out the difficulties in giving the command to Clive in face of Colonel Aldercron's attitude (India Office, HEIC's Coast and Bay, 6:123).

[45] The Select Committee of Fort St. George to the Select Committee of Fort William, October 13, 1756, *Bengal Records*, I, 237–41.

[46] For the Holwell protest of August 13, 1756 see *ibid.*, I, 202–3.

and later to Fulta. Then, on December 27, after Watson and Clive had held consultations with the Select Committee of the Fort William Council and after taking other preparatory steps, the expedition began its movement up the river. At Budge Budge and at Tanna it brushed aside all opposition and on January 2 it approached Calcutta. Clive thereupon landed his troops, including the sepoys, who proceeded to march upon Fort William; at the same time two of Watson's ships bombarded it. Terrified with the roar of the great guns from the *Kent* and *Tyger*, the defenders, after remarkably little resistance, fled, and the following day the admiral was able to place the keys of the heavily damaged fort in the hands of the Calcutta Council.[47]

The city was in ruins. Many of the fine structures within it, such at St. Anne's Church and Government House, had been burned; the wooden wharves along the river had been destroyed, and the native quarters had become a scene of desolation. In the words of the Dutch Council at Hugli:

> "There now is that beautiful place, whose blooming and flourishing condition caused every one to admire it, and from which the English Company drew a . . . princely income. The Fort and all the other costly buildings have been pulled down, the shops . . . plundered, and the timber wharfs destroyed, the place renamed Alingar, and put under the government of a Faujdar." [48]

In other words, Calcutta — outside of the destruction of some of the fortifications to make way for a mosque — remained as it had been left six months earlier with the departure of the Nabob for his capital soon after his triumph. In fact, it seems to be clear that Siraj-ud-daula, when at last he had possession of Calcutta, did not know what to do with that once thriving place. But it is equally clear that, after what had taken place, he did not want the English Company again in control there, despite the fact that so little effort was put forth to ensure that this would not happen. Now it had come to pass. What is more, on January 3 both the Company Council and Admiral Watson issued open declarations of war against him in recounting his misdeeds and his violation of their imperial firman "contrary to

---

[47] In this chapter the friction that developed between Clive on the one hand and Watson and the Calcutta Council on the other, over the question of Clive's powers, will be passed over, since it will be emphasized subsequently in this series.

[48] Dutch Council at Hugli to Supreme Council at Batavia, July 5, 1756, *Bengal Records*, I, 53–6. Fort William was not pulled down, however, as stated in this letter.

all justice and equity." [49] In preparation for a new attack on the part of the Nabob, all the remaining houses about the fort were ordered destroyed by the Select Committee. Further to frustrate his movements, Clive and Watson agreed to send an expedition up the river to the city of Hugli — located above the principal Dutch factory at Chinsura — where the Dutch had another factory and where Sirajud-daula had collected large supplies for his army. By the 19th the mission had been accomplished with the destruction of all the Nabob's granaries and his forts in that area, and the detachment had returned to Calcutta.

Siraj-ud-daula, with the news of the attack on Hugli, again moved slowly down the river with his army. While preparing to fight, he at the same time enlisted the aid of the French and certain prominent Hindus, such as the Seth brothers, great merchant princes of Murshidabad, to bring the British to a peaceful agreement. The latter were asked to state their terms, and in reply Clive sent proposals for a termination of all hostilities upon the basis of four demands: reparation for all damage suffered by the Company in Bengal from the Nabob and his army; the restoration of all its facilities throughout the province; the unrestricted right to fortify all its factories; and, finally, the privilege of erecting a mint at Calcutta [50] with the same privileges as those possessed by that in his own capital.[51] As the Nabob seemed desirous of spinning out the negotiations while continuing to approach the city,[52] other demands were added to the above to provide more specifically for the full protection from any molestation of the people of Calcutta, as well as the boats and goods belonging to the Company.

Clive, meanwhile, in anticipation of an attack on Calcutta, had strongly entrenched himself on the bank of the Hugli above the limits of the city. On February 3 the army of the enemy began passing

---

[49] For the declaration of war see *ibid.*, II, 83–7.

[50] The Company enjoyed the privilege of a mint at Madras, and the Nabob on January 30 promised the French at Chandernagore a mint (*ibid.*, II, 185–6). On September 3, 1755 the Select Committee wrote the Company, respecting a mint, that "they will take the first Opportunity to obtain a Grant for one" (India Office, HEIC's Coast and Bay, 6:84).

[51] For these terms see *Bengal Records*, II, 126.

[52] On January 30 the Nabob wrote to Clive most reassuringly of his desire to come to a full agreement with the Company, and the same day wrote to the French at Chandernagore that the English were "a people without faith" (see *ibid.*, II, 184–5 for these letters; see also his letters to Watson of the last of January and to Clive of February 1, *ibid.*, II, 203–4, 208).

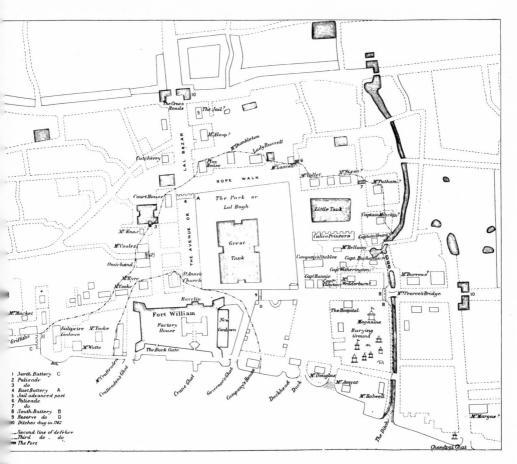

he Environs of Fort William."

(From S. C. Hill: *Indian Record Series. Bengal in 1756-1757*)

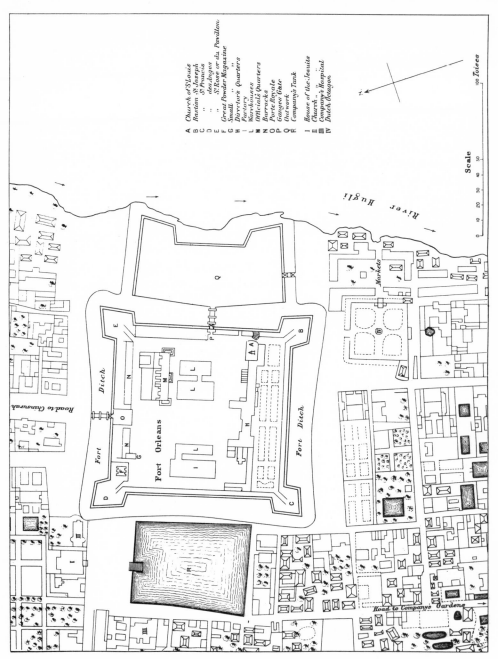

REFERENCE

A Church of St. Louis
B Bastion St. Joseph
C .. St. Francis
D .. des Anges
E .. St. Rose or du Pavillon
F Great Powder Magazine
G Small ,,
H Director's Quarters
I Factory
L Warehouses
M Officials' Quarters
N Barracks
O Porte Royale
P Ganges Gate
Q Outwork
R Company's Tank

I House of the Jesuits
II Church ,,
III Company's Hospital
IV Dutch Octagon

Scale

0 10 20 30 40 50   100 Toises

River Hugli

Road to Chinsurah
Road to Chinsurah

Fort Ditch

Fort Ditch

Fort Ditch

Fort Orleans

Markets

Road to Company's Gardens

"Plan of Chandernagore made by M. Mouchet 15 Dec., 1749."

the camp at a distance of half a mile. According to Captain Eyre
Coote, it contained forty thousand horsemen, sixty thousand foot
soldiers, fifty elephants, and thirty pieces of cannon.[53] To oppose it
was a British battalion of somewhat over seven hundred men, thirteen hundred sepoys, fourteen field pieces — and Clive.[54] Still the
Nabob outwardly seemed disposed to negotiate, though some of his
army began plundering the outskirts of the city, where he himself
now encamped just outside the Mahratta Ditch.[55]

There appeared to be abundant evidence that Siraj-ud-daula had
treacherous designs, with the result that the colonel determined to
attack him before his own forces and the vice admiral's squadron,
for lack of provisions, would be compelled to withdraw.[56] Having
received early the next morning from Watson, on request, a reinforcement of some five hundred and sixty sailors, he started for
the camp of the Nabob before daybreak with the purpose of seizing the latter's artillery and then attacking his headquarters. But a
fog so enveloped everything that, though the British marched right
through the camp and a good deal of confused fighting took place,
nothing decisive occurred. Siraj-ud-daula, nevertheless, was badly
frightened, and his army proceeded to retire a distance of some
eight miles.

From the new vantage point the Nabob now wrote to Clive. He
offered to place the Company in possession of everything granted
by the imperial firman, with full liberty to fortify Fort William,
and also to permit it to establish a mint in Calcutta.[57] This was confirmed by specific articles agreed to, signed, and sealed on February 9, in connection with which Siraj-ud-daula solemnly affirmed:
"God and His Prophets are witnesses, that I never will deviate from
the terms of the treaty." [58] By this formal instrument he granted
every request made of him; while in turn the Council of Fort William covenanted to transact the Company's business as formerly;
never to do violence to any person without cause or to offer protection to any of the Nabob's officials or to murderers or robbers, and

---

[53] "Journal of Sir Eyre Coote," covering the period from October 17, 1756 to
July 3, 1757, ibid., III, 39–55.
[54] Ibid.
[55] Lord Clive's "Evidence," 1772, ibid., III, 307–18.
[56] Clive to the Secret Committee in London, February 22, 1757, ibid., II, 237–41.
[57] Clive to the Select Committee of Fort St. George, February 6, 1757, ibid., II,
214–15.
[58] For the treaty see ibid., II, 215–17.

to keep inviolate the terms of the agreement.[59] But the treaty needed clarification at certain points, and Watts, the agent at Cossimbazar, was deputed to go to Murchidabad to undertake this task, which would test Siraj-ud-daula's sincerity.[60]

A new factor was now introduced into the problem of restoring tranquillity to Bengal. The British were demanding that the French there agree to a strict neutrality regardless of whatever was happening elsewhere in the world, and that the Nabob enforce it; otherwise Clive was quite prepared to attack Fort d'Orléans at Chandernagore. Such action seemed to be imperative, for the British were informed that M. Bussy was marching into Bengal from the Deccan to reinforce the French there.[61] When the Nabob protested at this contemplated British action and also voiced the fear that he himself would be attacked, both Watson and Clive in separate letters agreed that there would be no further hostilities in the region if the French would consent to a "solid treaty of Neutrality." But the truth is that Siraj-ud-daula was not looking for peace. At this juncture he wrote to Bussy requesting him to provide two thousand troops under good officers to join with his own to act against the English.[62] As for Vice Admiral Watson, he felt that under the circumstances to avoid hostilities in Bengal it was necessary that the authorities at Pondicherry, whose jurisdiction in India extended to Chandernagore, should approve this neutrality that the French in Bengal offered — which would involve, however, many weeks of delay.[63] At the same time he opposed any hostile movement against the French factory without the Nabob's express permission.

Clive was thus faced with a cruel dilemma. He had orders from the Madras Council, under whom he was acting, to return with his troops after settling matters with the ruler of Bengal; but he was deeply alarmed for the safety of Calcutta should he do so before

---

[59] "The Governor and Council's Agreement with the Nabob of Bengal," ibid., II, 217.

[60] The Select Committee to Watts, February 16, 1757, ibid., II, 225–7.

[61] Clive to the Secret Committee in London, February 22, 1757, ibid., II, 237–41. In January the Select Committee had agreed to the principle of neutrality, with the French, rather than war with them (the Committee to the Company, January 26, 1757, India Office, HEIC's Coast and Bay, 6:142).

[62] The Nabob to Bussy, February 1757, Bengal Records, II, 264–5.

[63] Watson to the Select Committee of Fort William, March 3, 1757, ibid., II, 268–70. The Select Committee had almost settled on a neutrality with the French when Watson refused to confirm the articles based upon the above considerations (India Office, HEIC's Coast and Bay, 6:145).

making the French in the valley of the Ganges powerless to act as
they had done in the Carnatic against Madras in the preceding war.
Writing to the Select Committee of Fort William on March 4, he
agreed, were he authorized by it to do so, to march immediately
against the French fort; otherwise, he informed them, he must return without delay to the Coromandel Coast.[64] But this latter al-
ternative the Committee would not consider and — little as most of
the members of the Council wanted the colonel, as the representative of the Madras Presidency, to mix further in their affairs — with
the arrival of Bombay reinforcements and even in the face of the
Vice Admiral's reluctance to be personally involved, Clive went
ahead with his preparations for reducing Chandernagore. By this
time it was known to both Watson and Clive that the government
of Great Britain, with the French attack on Minorca, had issued a
declaration of war that embodied an order to all the King's officers
"to distress the enemy as far as it is in their power." [65] Both of them,
in possession of royal commissions, were therefore responsible for
carrying out this general order. The last obstacle to the Vice Admiral's willingness to co-operate disappeared when on March 10
the Nabob was led, as the result of the activities of Watts at Murshidabad, to give a provisional consent for Watson, as the King's
leading representative, to launch an attack on the French fort.[66]

Clive, meanwhile, was already beginning to move against the
French Fort d'Orléans. On March 12, when but two miles from it,
he summoned the commandant, M. Renault, to surrender. This was
refused.[67] On the 14th a preliminary attack was made to feel out the
strength of the enemy and then on the 19th, despite low water,
boats from Watson's ship got possession of the French shipping
lying in the Hugli above the fort. The walls of the fort were too
strong to be much affected by Clive's field artillery; but by the 23rd,
after Clive had stormed a shore battery, two British warships, the
Tyger and the Kent, were at last in position to begin a bombardment. When the fort was not delivered upon Watson's demand,

---

[64] Clive to the Select Committee, March 4, 1757, Bengal Records, II, 271–3.

[65] Watson to Clive, March 6, 1757, ibid., II, 273–4; Select Committee to the
Company, March 26, 1757 (India Office, HEIC's Coast and Bay, 6:146).

[66] After calling upon Watson to show generosity to the French commandant, the
Nabob at the same time agreed that "you must be well satisfied of the innocence of
his intentions, if not, whatever you think right, that do" (the Nabob to Watson,
March 10, 1757, Bengal Records, II, 279).

[67] See Clive's "Military Journal," covering the period March 2–25, ibid., III, 62–5.

after notification to Renault that a state of war existed between France and Great Britain, the broadsides were delivered with devastating effect even in the face of heavy damage to the ships and of great loss of life on board them. To continue resistance under these circumstances — with most of the European soldiers dead or wounded, with no hope of aid in sight, and faced by overwhelming superiority in forces — was quite useless.[68] The French commandant therefore raised the white flag and before the day was over signed a capitulation — the terms of which were drawn up by him and his staff and amended by Watson and Clive.[69] By its terms the French were obliged not only to desert Chandernagore but also to place all their other factories in Bengal at the disposal of the Nabob and the British; the officers of the garrison became prisoners on parole, and the common European soldiers simple prisoners of war. Further, when Renault and other members of the late Chandernagore Council, upon removing to Dutch Chinsura, continued to act as officials in corresponding with the French elsewhere, their paroles were revoked and they were confined at Calcutta for some two months before their release after agreeing not to serve against the British.[70] With respect to Fort d'Orléans, since troops were lacking to hold it, the decision was made to destroy it.[71] This decision was thereupon carried out.[72]

The fall of Chandernagore, bringing with it ultimately that of the other French establishments at Cossimbazar, Dacca, and elsewhere in Bengal, was a momentous event in the history of that great province and of India in general. With no other European power at the time ready to interfere, the British were now able to face Siraj-ud-daula with renewed confidence. Their program, moreover, was very actively supported at his court by both Watts and Luke

---

[68] Renault's total force, including native troops, numbered 794 (Renault to the Superior Council of Pondicherry, October 26, 1758, ibid., III, 265–83; see also ibid., III, 256–63 for a detailed French account of the attack). According to exaggerated reports brought by refugees from Chandernagore to the Dutch factory at Hugli, the French total losses during the siege were 500 Europeans, besides those of native troops (Johannes Ross to M. Vernet, March 23, 1757, ibid., II, 290–2).

[69] For the articles of capitulation of Chandernagore see Robert Beatson, Naval and Military Memoirs (London, 1804), III, 156–7.

[70] Clive to Watson, April 13, 1757, Hill, Bengal Records, II, 327–8; Renault to Dupleix, September 7, 1757, ibid., III, 242–52.

[71] Pocock to Holderness, April 14, 1757, Pocock Papers, Huntington Library.

[72] For an account of Chandernagore after the destruction of Fort d'Orléans and the French warehouses see Hill, Bengal Records, III, 256–60.

Scrafton. The latter, in his *Reflections on the Government of Indo-stan*, recorded the mercurial changes in the attitude of the ruler from day to day.[73] Watts also in his *Memoirs* noted the Nabob's extreme trepidation during the course of the siege of the French fort.[74] Although he wrote to Clive on March 26 indicating his "inexpressible pleasure" at the British victory over the French,[75] Siraj-ud-daula at the same time was communicating with Bussy as his ally — welcoming his rumoured arrival in Orissa with a powerful army and denouncing the perfidy of the English.[76] Further, while the Nabob openly banished M. Law, the French agent at his court, he secretly kept him in his pay and refused to give his consent to the British to take over the French factories. Moreover, he failed to fulfil the treaty that he had signed in February and was pointedly reminded of that fact by Clive in the month of April.[77]

In view of the utter unreliability of the Nabob, a confederation was formed against him — with the encouragement, it is needless to add, of Watts — among a group of influential natives, including the Seth brothers of Murshidabad itself, with the object of placing on the throne Mir Jafar Ali Khan, a brother-in-law of the late Nabob, 'Ali Wardi Khan, and also the generalissimo of the army.[78] According to the Frenchman Jean Law, Mir Jafar had borne a reputation for bravery and uprightness; as the result of insults heaped upon him by the fickle Siraj-ud-daula, however, he at last secretly agreed to a revolution in his name and accepted the support of the Seths and the British.[79] This seemed to be a happy solution of the problem, for, in the words of Rear Admiral Pocock, Mir Jafar was "held in great Esteem by all Ranks of the People." [80] On May 1 the Calcutta Select Committee voted in general terms to aid him, as it was

---

[73] Luke Scrafton, *op. cit.*, p. 73.

[74] William Watts, *Memoirs of the Revolution in Bengal, A.D., 1757* . . . (London, 1766), p. 48.

[75] The Nabob to Clive, March 26, 1775, Hill, *Bengal Records*, II, 295.

[76] For these letters see *ibid.*, II, 313–14.

[77] Clive to the Nabob, April 10, 1757, *ibid.*, II, 320–1. Rear Admiral Pocock was convinced that the reason for the nonfulfilment of the treaty was that the Nabob had been persuaded by the French at his court that a large force had arrived at Pondicherry from France which would soon appear to co-operate with him against the English in Bengal (Pocock to Holderness, April 14, 1757, Pocock Papers).

[78] Renault, writing from ruined Chandernagore in September, declared that "the whole of the Nabob's Darbar, or Royal court, was won over to the conspiracy" (Renault to Dupleix, September 7, 1757, Hill, *Bengal Records*, III, 252–521).

[79] For Law's long memoir see *ibid.*, III, 160–215.

[80] Pocock to Holderness, July 16, 1757, Pocock Papers.

unanimously of the opinion that no further trust could be placed in the ruling Nabob.[81] In the view of Rear Admiral Pocock, who was active in the affair, this appeared to be "the most effectual way of establishing a peace in the Country and Settling the English on a good and Solid Foundation." [82] Therefore, on the 19th, after considerable negotiation, the committee laid down the specific terms of its support of the revolution, which included not only all that had been agreed to in the treaty with Siraj-ud-daula in February but in addition the following points: that all the French factories would be delivered into the hands of the English; that not only would the Company receive a liberal compensation for its losses, amounting to the sum of one hundred lakhs, but individuals as well, for theirs; that the new Nabob would, in addition, pay the expenses of British troops when he needed them to defend himself; that he would also agree to erect no fortifications on the river below the city of Hugli, and that he would enlarge the jurisdiction of Calcutta.[83] This was finally signed by Mir Jafar on June 4.[84]

At this point it is necessary to deal with one aspect of this plan for the overthrow of the Nabob that would seem to reflect discredit on Robert Clive and the Select Committee of the Calcutta Council. A native of India by name of Omichand — whose people were of the Punjab race and who himself had dwelt in Calcutta for forty years, a man of wealth and possessing great influence in Bengal — had become a party to the move to displace Siraj-ud-daula, but had favoured a candidate for the nabobship other than Mir Jafar, the latter supported by the powerful Seth brothers. It is said that Omichand began his career as the Calcutta agent for the Seths, then broke with them and afterward entered the employ of the Calcutta Council as its agent for the purchase of goods for export. After serving in that capacity for some time, he was displaced. But he did not lack resources, possessing as he did a monopoly for the purchase of opium. Whether he played a part in bringing the Nabob down upon Calcutta was never proved, but this was charged by Governor Drake, who imprisoned him.[85] Holwell also emphasized

[81] For the proceedings of the Select Committee of May 1, 1757, see Hill, *Bengal Records*, II, 370–1.

[82] Pocock to Holderness, July 16, 1757, Pocock Papers.

[83] "Proposed articles of Agreement between Jafar Ali Khan and the Company," May 19, 1757, Hill, *Bengal Records*, II, 383–5.

[84] For the final agreement as signed see Robert Beatson, *op. cit.*, III, 158–9.

[85] The above charge was made against Omichand by Governor Drake in his long

the fact, in his narrative of the Black Hole incident, that Omichand was a vindictive person who "can never forgive." [86] He was, nevertheless, subsequently employed by the British in negotiating with Siraj-ud-daula; but the Seths thoroughly distrusted him and, as plans for the revolution developed, refused to be a party to any change in the government of Bengal were he associated with it. After tricking the Nabob, as a loyal subject, out of a large sum of money, according to Watts, who was, as indicated, at Murshidabad, Omichand now demanded as the price of his support of Mir Jafar that he be paid "5 *per cent.* on all the Nabob's treasure, which would amount to two *crore* [twenty million] rupees, besides a quarter of all his wealth." [87]

With this development both Clive and the Select Council became persuaded that the man was so thoroughly unscrupulous and at the same time so dangerous that they would be justified in circumventing his ambitions by using the same type of weapon against him that he himself had employed so successfully against others. At the colonel's suggestion, therefore, two agreements with Mir Jafar were drawn up: one that included Omichand's exorbitant demands and that would be shown to him; the other, the real agreement, leaving those demands out, which would be signed and sealed by Mir Jafar. That this indirection was a departure from the standards of conduct of the Company's representatives in Bengal seems to be clear. Even Omichand in February had in the presence of Siraj-ud-daula taken an oath, while touching a Brahman's foot, "that he had lived under English protection these forty years, [and] that he had never known them to break their engagement" [88] — a statement in no way surprising respecting the activities of a great company that could only continue to prosper through the years, as it had done, by maintaining a record of fair dealing. As for Clive, he continued to defend his conduct on this occasion, especially in view of the fact that Omichand had by blackmail threatened to betray the whole plan to the Nabob if he were not thus bribed.[89] In

letter of January 17–25, 1757 to the other members of the Fort William Council, Hill, *Bengal Records*, II, 134–57.

[86] "Holwell's Genuine Narrative of the Black Hole," *ibid.*, III, 131–54.

[87] Watts to Clive, May 14, 1757, *ibid.*, II, 380–2.

[88] Watts to the Select Committee, February 21, 1757, *ibid.*, II, 231–2.

[89] See the testimony of Francis Sykes, Esq., of Cossimbazar, who was told by Watts in much agitation that "Omichund had been threatening to betray them to Sirajah Dowla and would have them all murdered that night unless . . . the sum promised (by Mr. Watts) should be made good" (*ibid.*, III, 306–7).

1772 he declared before a parliamentary committee that when he heard of this threat, which would have involved the death of Watts, he "thought art and policy warrantable in defeating the purposes of such a villain . . . in such a case." [90] It may be added that neither the colonel nor the members of the Council personally benefited by this stratagem.

A week after the treaty with Mir Jafar was signed, Watts and the other Englishmen at Murshidabad left the city, under pretext of going hunting, and on June 14 succeeded in joining Clive, who was at Chandernagore. Siraj-ud-daula by this time had been informed that there was a plot against him. While he suspected that Mir Jafar was a party to it, he probably did not realize the extent of Mir Jafar's involvement. For he went to the generalissimo, sought to wipe out the past misunderstanding, and secured Mir Jafar's promise to join him as a friend in an expedition against the English which he had now determined upon.[91] This warlike step seemed to be imperative in view of Clive's threatening letter of the 13th in which he not only accused the Nabob of treacherous correspondence with both Bussy and Law but notified him that he was marching to Murshidabad to submit these and other complaints to the chief nobles there, including Mir Jafar and the Seths.[92] That very day, in fact, Clive started on his memorable expedition at the head of some one thousand Europeans and two thousand sepoys with an artillery train of eight six-pounders.[93] By the 19th he was in possession of Katwa (Cutiva), called the "Key to Murshidabad," where the Mahrattas had been defeated by the late 'Ali Wardi Khan. There he placed before a council of war the question whether an immediate advance should be made or whether it would be best to remain at Katwa, with its strong fort, until Mir Jafar would openly support them and also until the monsoon was ended. It is certain that Major Eyre Coote, later to win great fame in the Carnatic,

[90] "Evidence of Lord Clive," 1772, ibid., III, 307–21.

[91] Mir Jafar to Clive, June 16, 1757, ibid., II, 414.

[92] Clive to the Nabob, June 13, 1757, ibid., II, 405–7.

[93] The above figures were given by Clive to the Select Committee of Fort St. George in his letter of July 2, 1757 (ibid., II, 439–43); Eyre Coote in his "Evidence," 1772 (ibid., III, 321–3) was more specific, giving 750 men in the battalion, 2,100 sepoys, and 150 in the artillery train. While Vice Admiral Watson refused to have any part in the overthrow of the Nabob, Rear Admiral Pocock, stationed at Chandernagore, willingly loaned Clive 50 of his seamen to serve as gunners (Pocock to Holderness, July 16, 1757, Pocock Papers).

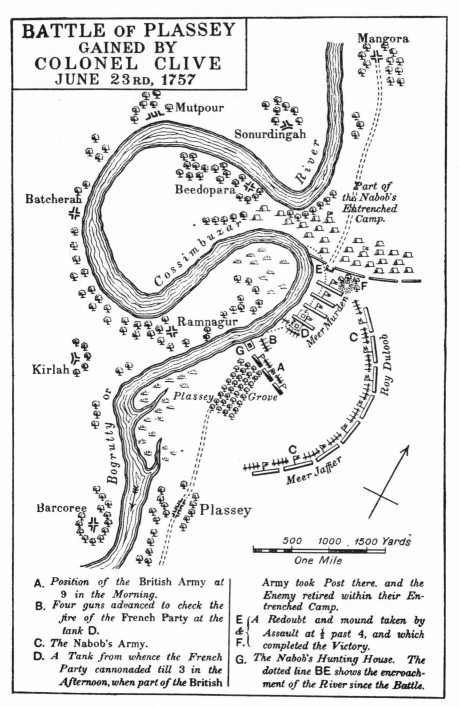

BATTLE OF PLASSEY
GAINED BY
COLONEL CLIVE
JUNE 23RD, 1757

Mangora

Mutpour

Sonurdingah

Part of the Nabob's Entrenched Camp.

Batcherah

Beedopara

Cossimbuzar River

E

F

Ramnagur

Meer Murden

C

Kirlah

B

Roy Duloob

G

A

Plassey Grove

C

Meer Jaffer

Bogrutty or

Barcoree

Plassey

500   1000   1500 Yards
One Mile

A. *Position of the British Army at 9 in the Morning.*
B. *Four guns advanced to check the fire of the French Party at the tank D.*
C. *The Nabob's Army.*
D. *A Tank from whence the French Party cannonaded till 3 in the Afternoon, when part of the British*

Army took Post there. and the Enemy retired within their Entrenched Camp.

E & F. *A Redoubt and mound taken by Assault at ½ past 4, and which completed the Victory.*

G. *The Nabob's Hunting House. The dotted line BE shows the encroachment of the River since the Battle.*

The Battle of Plassey.

(From V. A. Smith: *The Oxford History of India*, with the permission of the Clarendon Press)

urged immediate action. Although in the voting Coote was in the minority and had Clive against him, the latter soon changed his view and determined to march without delay against the Nabob.[94]

Siraj-ud daula had concentrated his forces in the neighbourhood of the village of Plassey, located on a branch of the Ganges above Katwa and but some thirty-two miles from Murshidabad. These troops included fifteen thousand cavalry, thirty-four thousand foot, war elephants, camels and forty pieces of cannon — from nine-pounders up to thirty-two-pounders — serviced by a body of some fifty French artillerymen. After a seven hours' forced march and a crossing of the river, Clive's little army on the morning of the 23rd arrived at the village, took possession of a grove close by that was protected by the mud banks of two so-called "tanks" or small reservoirs, and prepared for action.

What now greeted their sight was deeply impressive, to say the least, to the beholders. An unknown author of a military journal of the expedition declared: "The enemy approached apace, covered a fine extensive plain in front of us as far as the eye could discern from right to left. . . ."[95] Indeed, it seemed inconceivable that, were the Nabob's troops disposed to fight, they could not overwhelm the puny force arrayed against them and cut it off almost to a man. Even Clive, it is recorded, in viewing this mighty array bearing down upon him, admitted to a fellow officer: "We must make the best fight we can during the day, and at night sling our muskets over our shoulders and march back to Calcutta."[96] The enemy's heavy artillery, however, which outranged by far the British six-pounders, when it was brought into action did not seriously disturb the veteran British and native troops behind the mud banks. Later in the morning a large body of the enemy cavalry appeared on Clive's right flank — really Mir Jafar's friendly troops — and seemed to be preparing to make a charge, but soon retired out of range of the British artillery. Then came a heavy downpour, and with it the cannonading of the Nabob's heavy guns slackened. At two in the afternoon a body of British grenadiers moved forward and seized an eminence from which the enemy had previously been firing upon

---

[94] Hill, Bengal Records, III, 321–3.

[95] "Journal of Military Proceedings on the Expedition to Murshidabad," ibid., III, 65–8.

[96] Quoted from the Orme Manuscripts by H. H. Dowell, op. cit., V, 150.

them. A still more advanced post was shortly afterward taken, and at last Clive's six-pounders — now but some three hundred yards from the entrance of Siraj-ud-daula's camp — were played with such effect upon the enemy that the latter found it impossible to bring out again its own artillery, moved by oxen. When a body of horsemen and foot soldiers advanced out of the camp, they in turn were checked with severe losses and retired. This success led to an assault on the entrance of the camp itself, and when it was once gained, the battle was won; for a general panic seized the Nabob's army, which fled from the camp and was pursued by the British for a distance of six miles.[97]

But Plassey — described by the Frenchman Jean Law as the "famous battle which put Bengal and its dependencies, so to say, in the power of the English" [98] — was not won merely as the result of the valor of the British grenadiers and the Madras sepoys, whose losses were really trivial.[99] The simple truth is that Siraj-ud-daula's camp was full of treason. Mir Jafar, who commanded the cavalry on the left wing of the Nabob's army, and Rai Durlabh, another leading commander, who likewise was a party to the conspiracy, while refraining from marching over to the British camp, kept their troops out of the battle; even Siraj-ud-daula's own attendants, we are told, gradually deserted his tent until he was left quite alone.[100] One man upon whom he had placed especial reliance had been Mir Madan, who was in personal command of his military household. But Madan, commanding that part of the army which advanced against Clive, had been fatally wounded by a cannon ball and soon died; and the paymaster of the army, one Hazarry, who had also remained faithful to the Nabob, had likewise been killed in action,

---

[97] I have followed in this account of the Battle of Plassey the "Journal of Military Proceedings on the Expedition to Muxadavad [Murshidabad]," Hill, Bengal Records, III, 65–8; see also a "Description of the Battle of Plassey," dated June 29, 1757 (ibid., II, 433–6), which emphasizes other aspects of the fight. Clive's own account is given in his letter of July 2, 1757 to the Select Committee of Fort St. George (ibid., II, 439–43). At one stage of the battle Major Kilpatrick made an advance without command from Clive and was sharply reprimanded for not waiting for his orders. Clive, however, held to this position and, taking personal charge, was able two hours later to storm the Nabob's camp (A Letter from John Walsh, Esq., one "constantly near the person of the Commander-in-Chief during the whole of the engagement," 1763, ibid., III, 403–4).

[98] "Memoir of M. Jean Law," ibid., III, 215–41.

[99] According to Pocock, Clive's total losses were nineteen Europeans and thirty sepoys either killed or wounded (Pocock to Holderness, July 16, 1757, Pocock Papers).

[100] Luke Scrafton, op. cit., p. 86.

together with some other men of distinction.[101] Thereupon — after making a final personal appeal to Mir Jafar not to desert him, which the latter, swearing on the Koran, agreed not to do,[102] yet failed to order his troops into battle — the Nabob was convinced that all was lost. Mounting a swift camel, he fled from the camp and back to Murshidabad, where he arrived at midnight and where he was soon joined by a portion of his thoroughly demoralized army.

Siraj-ud-daula's end was not long in doubt. After the rout, Mir Jafar and other conspirators appeared in Clive's camp, uncertain as to the nature of the reception they would receive in view of the fact that they had not earlier deserted to the English. But they were welcomed. Mir Jafar then affirmed his fidelity to the treaty he had made and also assured the Englishmen that the leading *jamadars*[103] had promised him "that the Nabob shall not escape."[104] With a force of three thousand, the new claimant to the throne therewith marched upon the capital. Upon hearing the news of his arrival there, the Nabob, already in hiding in his own house, sought to escape in disguise, taking with him as much of his treasures as he could convey, apparently with the idea of joining Jean Law, who with a force of some two hundred European troops was at Patna, far to the northwest of Murshidabad, and who continued to have the most confidential relations with Siraj-ud-daula as an ally in his pay.[105] But at Rajmahal the flight ended. The once all-powerful Siraj-ud-daula was recognized beneath his mean clothing, placed under arrest, and sent back to his capital before Law, hurrying forward, could rescue him.

Meanwhile, even in the face of warnings by Watts of treachery on the part of certain high officials, Clive marched into Murshidabad on June 29 with two hundred Europeans and three hundred sepoys. In the afternoon of that day he entered the palace to wait upon Mir Jafar and, finding that the latter had hesitated to occupy the royal cushion, the *musnud*, took him by the hand, seated him upon it, and then saluted him as Nabob. The colonel also assured

---

[101] Clive to the Select Committee of Fort William, June 24, 1757, Hill, *op. cit.*, II, 427–8; Mir Jafar to Clive, n.d., *ibid.*, II, 423–4.

[102] *Ibid.*

[103] Indian military officers.

[104] Clive to the Select Committee of Fort William, June 24, 1757, *ibid.*, II, 427–8.

[105] Pocock to Holderness, July 16, 1757, Pocock Papers; see also the "Memoir of M. Jean Law"; Mir Jafar to Clive, June 25, 1757; and Clive to the Select Committee of Fort St. George, July 2, 1757, Hill, *Bengal Records*, III, 10–215; II, 428, 439–43.

him and his followers that with such a ruler it was felt by the English that the country would again be quiet and would permit them again "to attend solely to commerce, which was our proper sphere and our whole aim in these parts." [106] Thereupon, Mir Jafar was accorded, we are told, "the usual Homage . . . by all Ranks of the people as Subah of the Provinces of Bengal, Bahar, and Orixa." [107] As for Siraj-ud-daula, soon after his return to his late capital and despite his most abject pleas for mercy, he was — quite unknown to Clive, who supposed that he would simply be imprisoned for life — put to death by orders of Miran, the son of the new Nabob, whether with or without the knowledge of his father is unknown.[108]

The revolution in Bengal, it seemed, was now complete. Little did Clive or the Council of Fort William or the Directors of the United East India Company in London realize that this was but its first phase. Its progress, however, must be reserved for further consideration, since it is now necessary to turn our attention to the stirring events that took place in the Carnatic and were to lead to the elimination of all French influence there as completely as it had been in Bengal by the end of 1757.

---

[106] Watts and John Walsh to Clive, June 27, 1757, and Clive to the Select Committee of Fort William, June 30, 1757, ibid., II, 431–2, 437–9.

[107] Pocock to Holderness, July 16, 1757, Pocock Papers.

[108] William Watts, op. cit., p. 108; Clive to the Select Committee of Fort William, July 4, 1757, Hill, Bengal Records, II, 444.

CHAPTER VII

Disaster Overtakes the French in the Carnatic

IN ANY LISTING of those who helped to lay the foundations for British military and political supremacy in India in the eighteenth century, the names of Robert Clive, Stringer Lawrence, "father of the Indian Army," George Pocock, and Eyre Coote must stand at the top. The last two men had certain things in common. Each was the son of a minister of the Gospel, each entered the calling in which he was to attain high distinction at a tender age — one on the high seas, the other on land. Each therefore upon attaining a position of great responsibility had behind him long years of active service, had become thoroughly imbued with the ideals of that service, and was a professional in every sense of the word; each, ordered to India in 1754, arrived in time to participate in the campaign in Bengal, as has been noted in the preceding chapter, and, as a result, each came to his task off, or on, the Coromandel Coast equipped with experience and an understanding of peculiar local conditions that might either facilitate or limit his ability to achieve his objectives. Finally, each, commissioned by the King rather than by the United East India Company, looked to the government of Great Britain for his orders and for final approval of his acts performed in line of duty.

Pocock, who attained the rank of commodore in 1747 after twenty-nine years of naval service, left for the East Indies with that rank. But his promotion became rapid thereafter. In 1755 he was gazetted as Rear Admiral of the White; late in 1756 he became Vice Admiral of the White; and upon his return to England in 1761 he not only was made Admiral of the Blue, but a Knight of the

Bath. Serving in Indian waters as second in command of the squadron under Watson, when that excellent naval officer died in Bengal on August 16, 1757, Pocock succeeded him. By the beginning of the new year he felt that he could with reasonable safety to British interests in that province leave the Hugli and sail for Madras. For quiet had been restored where violence had ruled, with Clive in firm control of the situation. The small force of Frenchmen that had operated about Patna on the upper Ganges under M. Jean Law had now been dispersed, as had those few natives who continued actively to oppose the authority of the new Nabob, Mir Jafar. Writing to William Pitt on November 18 from the *Tyger* off Calcutta, Pocock declared:

> "Nothing is now wanting to make this a most Flourishing Province and very beneficial to the Nation and Company but a Proper Government, Fort William fortified, and a sufficient Number of Troops well disciplined to keep out the French, and maintain the Company in their very extensive Possessions and Privileges, granted by the Nabob, which if properly done must be extremely advantageous, being informed that the Revenues will more than maintain Fifteen Hundred Men, exclusive of great advantages in trade to what the Company ever enjoyed heretofore." [1]

But if Bengal seemed to be at peace again and fairly secure from enemy threats, the same could not be said for the British interests on the Coromandel Coast. In September, Pocock received alarming news that a French squadron of some twelve vessels had arrived off that coast with fourteen hundred troops — the Lorraine regiment — under the command of the Chevalier de Soupire. What the designs of the enemy might be could only be surmised. That his own squadron must be in a position to help protect either Fort St. George or Fort St. David from attack was, nevertheless, clear to him and impelled him therefore to give up his plans for carrying his ships to Bombay, on the western coast of India, for refitting, despite their bad condition.[2] However, he only left the mouth of the Hugli on February 5, 1758, after taking the precaution of sending out a vessel to reconnoitre, which returned without evidence

---

[1] Pocock Letter Book, Huntington Library.

[2] *Ibid.* According to the letter sent by the Select Committee of Fort St. George to the Company, under date of October 13, 1757, the French had on the Coast 2,900 European soldiers, not including Bussy's army in the Deccan, as against 1,718 British soldiers stationed in that area (India Office, "Abstracts of the General Letters: The Coast & Bay," 6:177. Library of Congress microfilms).

that the French squadron was in the neighbourhood of that river. As the wind was favourable, he arrived without incident at Madras on the 23rd. He found upon landing there that the Select Committee of Fort St. George was deeply disturbed by reports that the French Compagnie des Indes had armed twelve of its ships at L'Orient, its port in France, and that these, joined by six large ships of war from the French royal navy, and carrying four thousand land troops under command of Comte de Lally, were expected any day on the Coast.[3]

The truth is that the French forces in the Carnatic —without taking into account the anticipated arrival of powerful reinforcements from home — were already so superior to those of the British that the latter, after the dispatch from Madras of Clive with the expeditionary army to Bengal, could not take the field and were therefore obliged to assume a purely defensive position at Fort St. George, where there were seven hundred European soldiers provided with an artillery train, and at Fort St. David, defended by half that number — without reference to sepoys in the service.[4] It is therefore clear that the interests of the United East India Company along the Coromandel Coast were in the greatest peril, especially should it not be possible for Pocock to prevent the French squadron from arriving. He had under his command at the time of his appearance before Madras only five vessels, among them the *Cumberland* in such bad condition as to be almost unseaworthy. With this weak squadron it was obvious he could do little against the French fleet when it would appear. Nevertheless, he was anticipating the arrival of Commodore Charles Steevens,[5] who had been sent out to India the preceding year but had been obliged to stop at Bombay and refit. The commodore, fortunately, late in March succeeded in reaching the Madras Road with four warships that were in good condition. Consequently, Pocock now felt that he was in a position to challenge the French and, taking the *Yarmouth*, one of the new arrivals, as his flagship, left the road on April 17 in order to get to the windward not only of Fort St. David to the south but also of the enemy fleet when it sailed through the Ceylon passageway.[6]

---

[3] Pocock to Holderness, March 13, 1758, Pocock Letter Book.

[4] *Ibid.*

[5] In August 1758 Steevens was gazetted as Rear Admiral of the Blue (Robert Beatson, *Naval and Military Memoirs of Great Britain* [London, 1804], II, 92).

[6] Pocock to Pitt, July 22, 1758, Pocock Letter Book.

At this point it should be emphasized that in the autumn of 1756, with the declaration of war by Great Britain against France, the court of Versailles decided to send to India a naval force and corps of troops of sufficient strength to be able to sustain the Compagnie des Indes in these parts. For it was realized that the agreement of 1754 between the local authorities of Pondicherry and Madras, to which reference has been made in Volume V of this series, was at best only a truce. In fact, it apparently determined to send out a much larger number of troops than the four battalions that actually left France. The fleet sailed in two divisions, The first, of twelve ships under M. Lozier de Bouvet, left on December 30, 1756 and arrived with the two battalions of the Lorraine regiment at Pondicherry on September 8, 1757. After landing the troops under the command of the Chevalier de Soupire, Bouvet sailed for Île de France, now Mauritius. Soupire, assuming command of all the French forces in the Carnatic, almost immediately took the field and within a period of two months succeeded in capturing three native towns [7] lying to the northwest of Pondicherry, the rulers of which had shown unfriendliness toward the French. The British, their allies at Madras, were now too weak to prevent this action. What might have now happened had Soupire been free to continue his campaign in the direction of this stronghold can only be surmised. But he was obliged to retire not only by reason of the sickness of his troops but because of the exhaustion of the treasury at Pondicherry.[8]

As for the second division of the India reinforcement, this did not leave France until May 1757. Arriving at Île de France in the latter part of the year with many of the soldiers and sailors ill, the expedition did not leave this island until late in January 1758. The squadron of nine vessels, under the command of Comte d'Aché, carried the Comte Thomas Arthur Lally, Baron de Tollendal, and the Lally regiment of two battalions.

By April 26 d'Aché had reached Karikal, and three days later he was in the neighbourhood of Fort St. David, where he was sighted

---

[7] Chettiput (Chettaput, Chillyput, Chittapette), Jinge (Ginge), and Trinomely (Fort St. George Select Committee letters of October 20 and November 10, 1757, India Office, HEIC's Coast and Bay, 6:177–8).

[8] Writing from Pondicherry on February 15, 1758 to d'Argenson, Soupire declared his funds were exhausted and called on d'Argenson to send out each year at least ten million livres to cover the expense of the yearly campaign (Richard Waddington, La Guerre de Sept Ans, III, 382).

by Pocock.[9] The French commander had, unfortunately for him, weakened his force by sending one of his ships of the line, a seventy-four, and a frigate to Pondicherry to deposit Lally, so that when the engagement began that day he did not possess the superiority that he otherwise might have enjoyed.[10] Further, among his vessels only one, the *Zodiaque*, his flagship, was of the French royal navy; the others — with one exception, a thirty-six gun frigate — were converted two-deck merchant ships belonging to the Compagnie des Indes. D'Aché, nevertheless, did not try to avoid a fight and moved out into the open sea.

It was not until three o'clock in the afternoon of the same day that the British squadron was able to get into line and within random shot of the enemy. With the *Yarmouth* using her full canvas and sailing on the windward side and also parallel to the *Zodiaque* and a little ahead of the latter, the French vessel now opened fire; but Pocock did not give the signal to engage until his own ship was within half-musket-shot of his opponent. He then signalled to the other ships to move in close to the enemy, which order was obeyed at least by the ships in the van. For an hour and a half a running fight took place. Thereupon the *Zodiaque* suddenly, after an explosion on board, broke the French line, shot up under the lee quarter of the ship ahead of her, and then put before the wind coming from the south, and was soon followed by the rest of the French squadron.

Although Pocock immediately ordered a general chase, it was not possible to carry it out in view of the fact that the French fire had been directed principally against the rigging of the British ships and that four of them, including the *Yarmouth*, had sustained so

---

[9] Waddington (*ibid.*, III, 383), who is generally very accurate in his statements, is in error when he writes that Steevens only joined Pocock at Madras five days previous to April 29. The date of his arrival is recorded as March 24 by Pocock in his letter to Pitt of July 22, referred to in an earlier footnote. Waddington's further statement therefore falls to the ground that had d'Aché "appeared some days sooner on the Coast he could have prevented the reunion of his adversaries or perhaps beaten Pocock before the arrival of Stevens [Steevens]" (*ibid.*).

[10] "*Rapport sur la Campagne*," October 30, 1758, quoted by Waddington (*ibid.*). Pocock, on the other hand, stated in his account (Pocock to Pitt, July 22, 1758, Pocock Papers) that in running down to Fort St. David from Madras he observed seven enemy ships in the roadway there, with two more French ships cruising in the offing, and that in giving chase he saw the two join the seven in line of battle. If the last statement is correct, the French had nine ships to oppose Pocock's eight. If d'Aché is correct, they had but seven.

much damage to the masts, yards, and sails as to make it impossible to enter effectively into pursuit. But the French did not escape unscathed. The *Bien-Aimé*, a seventy-four-gun ship, was so much damaged in her hull that she was no longer seaworthy. In the attempt to beach her near Sadras, she rolled on her side and stranded.[11] To offset this, it should be pointed out that two of Pocock's cruisers that were sent out to gain information were caught in Fort St. David roadway by d'Aché before the engagement and, to keep them from falling into his hands, were burned by their captains.[12] Thus the end of the indecisive engagement left the opponents on a basis of fair equality.

Two reflections may be made respecting this sea fight. As has been emphasized in the preceding two volumes of this series, French naval commanders were under constant instruction — by reason of French naval inferiority — not to run unnecessary risks and especially to avoid, if possible, decisive engagements with a British fleet if the larger strategical objectives could otherwise be achieved. The accepted French practice of concentrating their fire on British rigging was a tactical means to this end. By thus disabling the enemy, pursuit could be made very difficult for the latter, while freedom of action for the former was gained — without running the great hazard of fighting at close quarters with fire directed against the hull of the opponent, which was a canon of British naval practice. This rule d'Aché observed. On the other hand, Pocock held just as tenaciously to his "Fighting Instructions" in calling on all his ships from van to rear to close with their respective opponents, rather than attempting to crush the enemy van or to cross the "T." [13] In this connection it must be borne in mind that he could not have been easily relieved from England were his squadron to suffer seriously in seeking a crowning victory, and as a consequence the vitally important strategic services that he was called upon to render British interests not only along the Coromandel Coast but in the Bay of Bengal could not therefore be performed. In view of the great stakes involved, he was, under the circumstances, doubtless properly cautious not to over-commit himself.

---

[11] Waddington, *op. cit.*, II, 96–9 and III, 173; Pocock to Pitt, July 22, 1758, Pocock Letter Book.

[12] *Ibid.*

[13] *Fighting Instructions, 1530–1816* (ed. J. S. Corbett, London, 1905), Navy Records Society Pub., XXIX, 192; J. S. Corbett, *England in the Seven Years' War* (London, 1907), I, 347.

As it was, the French suffered many more casualties than did the British — over 400 according to French reports, as against but 118.[14]

Again, some commanders of vessels on each side showed timidity in action. At the end of the conflict it was therefore necessary for both d'Aché and Pocock to take disciplinary measures against them for failure to do their duty. On the one hand, D'Aprée de Mannevillette, in command of the *Duc de Bourgogne* was *mit à pied* for unwillingness to move his ship into the line of battle and for sheltering it during the action behind other vessels, between the masts of which he fired on the enemy. On the other, Captain Vincent of the *Weymouth* was dismissed from command of his vessel, Captain Legge of the *Newcastle* was cashiered, and Captain Brereton, temporarily in command of the *Cumberland*, was sentenced to the loss of a year's service as a post captain — all for failure to obey Pocock's signals.[15]

The fact that when the French squadron was first sighted by Pocock it was in the roadway of Fort St. David was sufficient indication to him that the enemy had designs upon that important British trading post. The vice admiral therefore used the greatest haste in repairing his rigging damaged in the engagement and by May 7 was able to take to sea in order to assist in its defence. But moving southward at this time of year in the teeth of strong adverse winds was a slow task indeed. Having touched land on the 26th, the vice admiral was informed that Fort St. David was being invested; continuing down the coast to save it, if possible, on the 30th he appeared off Pondicherry and two days later he saw the French squadron of ten sails come out of the roadstead. But despite the fact that he was to the leeward of it and therefore gave d'Aché every opportunity to bear down upon him, the latter was in no mood at the time to renew the fight and by keeping close to the wind plied away so rapidly that the British ships, held back by the leaky *Cumberland*, could not successfully give chase. Still moving southward with greatest difficulty, Pocock was informed by the Select Committee of Fort St. George on June 6 of the fall of Fort St. David and was asked to return immediately to Madras to help defend it.[16] This he proceeded to do.

---

[14] Pocock (*op. cit.*) said it was reported by several French officers, as well as by the Dutch, that d'Aché had six hundred killed and as many more wounded.

[15] *Ibid.*

[16] *Ibid.*

Turning now to the French activities on land along the Coromandel Coast, it should be emphasized that when Lally was appointed Commissioner General by the Ministry and the Council of the Compagnie des Indes, he was furnished with instructions which, while calling upon him to retire from all engagements made with the native princes, at the same time made clear to him — in view of the fact that a state of war now existed between France and Great Britain — that the capture of Cuddalore (the French Gondelour) and Fort St. David, lying close by on the river Gadilam, should be his immediate military objective. With this accomplished, he was to seize all other British seaports along the coast, ignoring at the time all factories possessed by the enemy in the interior.[17] With a military force of some seven thousand men, one half of whom were Europeans, it seemed that — considering the weakness of the enemy — the utter destruction of British power in the Carnatic could be achieved. Landing at Pondicherry on the very day of the naval engagement, Lally left by land the next day for Cuddalore, only thirty miles south of the French city. There he joined Brigadier Comte d'Estaing (later to acquire fame as a naval commander in the American Revolutionary War), who had preceded him with a contingent. This place was easily captured on May 3, and then the real task of carrying the near-by British fort was begun, with the French forces thus committed numbering some thirty-four hundred Europeans, supported by an artillery train and native soldiers.

For St. David, before its destruction as the result of the French attack, was not only a fort with strong bastions erected by the United East India Company at very considerable expense at the estuary of the Godilam; it was also a district, the centre of wealth and fruitful activity. Within its bounds, which extended eight miles along the waterfront and four miles inland — an area sold to the company in 1690 by the native ruler — there were many fine villas and a great concentration of skilled native artisans who dwelt there in their villages and produced quantities of long cloth, chintzes, calicoes, and muslins for export. Indeed, in the eyes of the French it was "the most important European establishment on the Coast," [18] and in view of this they had long sought to deprive the British of

---

[17] For Lally's instructions, dated December 11, 1756, see Waddington, op. cit., III, 380–1.

[18] Ibid., III, 385.

it and to that end had made a great but unsuccessful effort in the preceding war. They were at last now to succeed.

In the course of the month's siege the overextended British outworks in the form of trenches were overrun; by the latter part of May three French batteries had been erected close enough to play upon the main fortifications; and by the beginning of June a partial breach at least had been made in the wall of the waterfront bastion. Within the fort Major Paul Polier de Bollens, British commanding officer, had at his disposal, according to Pocock, over six hundred Europeans, including some two hundred sailors, as well as sepoys. Since his forces were protected by works of very considerable strength, it was felt by the vice admiral, who, as has been noted, was attempting in vain to beat his way down the coast to bring aid, that he was capable of making a prolonged defence. But Polier failed to use his limited supply of powder judiciously, and by the beginning of June it was nearing exhaustion. Further, when the wells at the fort, which were the only means of water supply for the garrison, were much damaged in the course of the siege, he did not take steps to place under the most rigid regulation the use of arrack and other potent liquors drawn from the storehouses and used freely by his men, with baneful effects, as a substitute for water. Finally, he showed distrust of the troops and was distrusted by them. Therefore, in the face of the general demoralization of his European soldiers, the desertion of his sepoys, the depletion of his ammunition, and no aid in sight from Pocock, he called for a council of war on June 2, which unanimously agreed to surrender under terms that were therewith drawn up and presented to Lally.[19]

By the final articles of capitulation, the troops as well as the local council of the Company were made prisoners of war, with the understanding that they would be exchanged for French prisoners held at the great mountain fortress of Trichinopoly, a native stronghold located on the Cauvery some distance inland from Fort St. David. But the fort together with its stores came into the hands of Lally, who proceeded to destroy it, according to his instructions, and also the villas and even native villages located within its pre-

---

[19] *Ibid.*, III, 385–6; Fort St. George Select Committee to the Company, May 20 and August 10, 1759, India Office, HEIC's Coast and Bay, 6:218; Pocock to Pitt, July 22, 1758, Pocock Letter Book; Beatson, *op. cit.*, II, 100–4; H. H. Dodwell, *Dupleix and Clive* (London, 1920), p. 162.

serves. This last act, together with other high-handed displays of temper and lacking of understanding of the Hindus, was, it may be noted in passing, to earn him their hatred throughout the Coromandel Coast.[20]

The news of the fall of Fort St. David brought only dismay to Madras. Well it might, in view of the fewness of its defenders and of the strength of the French and their freely expressed determination to root out all British establishments along the coast, and especially Fort St. George.[21] Most fortunately for the British, when Lally, returning from his conquest, proposed to the Pondicherry Council an immediate attack upon Madras, that body unanimously opposed it.

The crux of the French difficulty was the shortage of funds in the treasury, to which reference has previously been made. It seems that d'Aché and Lally brought with them little silver and there was a crying need for it. Soldiers had to be paid, as did those native rulers who furnished sepoys; provisions and other military supplies had to be purchased. One source for replenishing the treasury with rupees for the projected campaign was pointed out to Lally: the King of Tanjore, under great military pressure in 1749, had given a note to pay to the French Company seventy-five lakhs. It was therefore now determined to require him by a display of force to hand over at least fifty-five of them (equal to somewhat over three hundred thousand livres).[22] On June 18, at the head of some twenty-five hundred regulars and a considerable body of disciplined se-

---

[20] After the surrender of the fort a court of inquiry was held at Madras, which, while commending Bollens's personal behavior, impeached his judgment for attempting to defend the outposts with his limited forces; the court was also of the opinion that the place might have held out much longer and that the articles of capitulation were shameful in view of the fact that the enemy had not mastered the outward covered way, had made no effective breach, and had a wet ditch to fill up and pass before the fort could be assaulted (John Entick, *History of the Late War* [London, 1765], III, 286–7).

[21] When, after the surrender of Fort St. David, Pocock wrote to Lally asking for the exchange of the seamen made prisoners of war, the latter refused and gave as his reason "that he was resolved to besiege Fort St. George therefore it would be unnatural for him to do it" (Pocock to Pitt, July 22, 1758, Pocock Letter Book; see also Fort St. George Select Committee to the Company, October 5, 1758, India Office, HEIC's Coast and Bay, 6:294).

[22] Entick (*op. cit.*, III) says that it was seventy-five lakhs that Lally demanded of the King of Tanjore; Pocock (Pocock to Pitt, August 22, 1758, Pocock Papers) that it was seventy-two lakhs, based on Captain Caillaud's report to him; Beatson (*op. cit.*, II, 194) in his *Memoirs* gives the figure as seventy; and Waddington (*op. cit.*, III, 367), as but fifty-five.

poys, Lally left Pondicherry and, after some pause along the way, marched into Tanjore, called "the Garden of Southern India," located on the rich alluvial lands of the lower Cauvery and some distance southwest of Fort St. David. The Mahratta Rajah was prepared to bargain with him, but became infuriated not only by the plundering of the French army but by Lally's indirection in the negotiations that ensued. Having received military support from Captain Caillaud, the British commander of Trichinopoly — located, as already indicated, on the upper Cauvery — he determined to resist in his own capital. With other reinforcements arriving, furnished by another Mahratta ruler near Trichinopoly, which helped to cut off the flow of supplies to the invaders, and with the latter at last in a serious if not a desperate condition, he ordered on August 9 a sally from the capital, which was conducted with such fury and was so successful in its results that to escape this veritable hornets' nest Lally, after suffering five hundred casualties, was reduced to the humiliating necessity of spiking the guns of his batteries at night and retreating in the darkness to Karikal on the coast, and from there reached Pondicherry the latter part of August without the desired rupees and with a decided loss of prestige.[23]

Another opportunity to fill the empty treasury of Pondicherry likewise slipped from the French when the apprehensive Council there prevailed upon d'Aché — in view of the fact that most of the troops were with Lally in Tanjore — to remain in the roadstead there as a protection, rather than to cruise in the Bay of Bengal. For three heavily laden ships with supplies and much treasure — sent out the preceding year by the English Company — after reaching Bengal were thus enabled to make their way in perfect safety down the coast to Madras, arriving there early in July. In fact, it was not until the opportune arrival in the fall of a ship from France with specie to the value of one hundred thousand rupees that Lally was in a position to march against Fort St. George. So dependent, indeed, were the French in India, as well as the British there, on maintaining an oceanic connection with their respective homelands that any serious stoppage of it would mean nothing less than the utter ruin of their enterprises. Herein lies the supreme importance of the activities of the little squadrons of d'Aché and Pocock along

<hr>

[23] Fort St. George Select Committee to the Company, August 10 and October 5, 1758, India Office, HEIC's Coast and Bay, 6:219, 291–2; Waddington, op. cit., III, 367–87, 391–2; Entick, op. cit., III, 296–9.

the Coromandel Coast — trivial as their encounters and other movements may seem to be when viewing the matter superficially.

Pocock, at this juncture, had received information that a French vessel, the *Centaur*, coming from Mauritius, was expected to arrive any moment on the Coast where d'Aché's ships were at the time anchored "close in with the Surff under the Guns of Pondicherry." [24] Doubtless with the hope of picking up the French vessel and of protecting any Company ships bound for the Coast, the vice admiral moved out of the Madras roadstead on July 25; two days later he was in the neighbourhood of Pondicherry, where the French squadron was still at rest. The news of his appearance compelled d'Aché in turn to take to the sea in order to frustrate British plans, whatever they might be. The French admiral, instead of moving against his opponent, still to the north of him, turned southward and kept well to the windward. On August 1 Pocock in steady pursuit came in view of him off Tranquebar and, after some manœuvring, the two fleets formed in line of battle and it seemed that an engagement would take place. But the Frenchman, still avoiding a fight and easily outsailing his opponent, particularly in light of the bad condition of the *Cumberland*, disappeared to the southward, and it was not until very early the morning of the 3rd that he again came into view off Nagapatam. By now Pocock had succeeded in getting the weather gauge of him and soon afterward, with some of the ships of the two fleets within musket-shot of one another, the firing began, with the French ships moving in the formation of a half-moon. For an hour the running fight continued. The *Comte de Province*, a seventy-four and the enemy's leading ship in the line of battle, having lost her mizzenmast and fighting a fire that broke out on board, then put before the wind. The *Zodiaque*, also having to fight fire and with a broken rudder, followed by the *Condé* and *Moras*, both badly damaged, began veering away to the leeward and was joined by the other French ships seeking to break off the engagement. Pocock's vessels, this time all in action, meanwhile continued to rake the enemy until the latter finally moved out of gun range and, sailing northward, sought the shelter of Pondicherry.[25]

---

[24] Pocock to Pitt, July 22, 1758, *op. cit.* In this letter the vice admiral discounted the assertion that the French at Pondicherry "confidentally give out that they expect the *l'Orient* with five more Ships and two Battalions."

[25] Pocock to Pitt, August 22, 1758, Pocock Papers; Waddington, *op. cit.*, III, 392–3,

Indecisive as was this victory, Pocock deserved great credit for his conduct in the action. D'Aché was superior in number of ships, having eight ships of the line as against his seven; he also had two seventy-fours, two sixty-fours, two sixties, and two fifties as against the Englishman's two sixty-fours, two sixties, one fifty-six, and two fifties.[26] However, the British thirty-two-pounder guns were used to great effect and proved superior to the heaviest French broadsides, and it also may be added that the British sailors, all from the royal navy, acted with much greater co-ordination than did the sailors aboard the French ships, who in the main were enlisted by the French Company. This helps to account for the greater damage sustained by d'Aché's squadron than that received by Pocock's and also for the fact that almost five hundred Frenchmen were killed or wounded in the fight as against less than two hundred of the British. Once again, however, in thinking in terms of casualties, account must be taken of the fact that the rigging of the British ships was the chief target of the French admiral, whereas Pocock directed his fire at the decks and hulls of the enemy's. In fact, not long after reaching Pondicherry, d'Aché wrote to the Superior Council in France indicating the extent to which he had become incapacitated:

> "The greater part of my sailors are dead, or attacked with scurvy or blood fluxes; without sailors one can neither manœuvre nor fight; all my masting has been ruined by the shots that pierced it, all my rigging spliced and in a sad condition; many of my vessels have rudder trouble and others have much water in the hulls. . . . I have come to the decision to go to Île de France to refit my vessels and put myself in condition to await aid from Europe." [27]

Despite Lally's insistence, supported strongly by the Pondicherry Council, that the squadron should remain on the Coast, and the General's offer of the loan of fifteen hundred men to man the ships, d'Aché was determined, upon the advice of his captains, to go to Mauritius, and he set sail early in September. Arriving there the second week in October, he found a French frigate with a supply of money on board amounting to a million livres, sent out by the Company. This he immediately dispatched to Pondicherry. In writ-

based upon d'Aché's Rapport sur la Campagne de 1758, October 30, 1758, Ms., Archives de la Guerre; Beatson, op. cit., II, 109–12.

[26] Ibid., III, 173–4.

[27] D'Aché to the Conseil Supérieur, August 18, 1758, Waddington, op. cit., III, 393.

ing home at this period, he deplored the fact "of having in one despotic, passionate, violent man [Commissioner General Lally] so much consolidated power." [28] Likewise he made clear that a bitter feud between the French army and navy — as previously illustrated in the preceding volume of this series by the situation that developed earlier the same year at Louisbourg — again had blazed forth. The admiral charged that upon his return to Pondicherry after the battle, his wounded were grossly neglected, that "M. de Lally, hating the navy, believing it useless or at least desiring it were, has continued to check me in my operations and to oppose me" and that he sought to retain "the squadron on the Coast at the risk of having it succumb under fire of the enemy or to perish there." [29] It may be added that with the disappearance of d'Aché from the Coast, Pocock was now free to leave for Bombay to refit his own ships and left Madras on August 20; on September 2 he sighted the French fleet off Ceylon, but was unable to approach it, as it sped away to Île de France.[30]

The unfortunate expedition against the Rajah of Tanjore had been undertaken by Lally, as noted, to secure a supply of money for paying his troops in order to launch his proposed campaign against Madras. He now was led to adopt the view that the booty to be secured from Madras were it captured would be adequate to care for his needs in rounding out his military objectives in India. But before turning to this next phase of his campaign consideration should be given to developments in southern India, which have not yet been discussed.

Commissioner General Lally showed deep hostility not only toward the men of the navy, as has been noted, but also toward the Company Council of Pondicherry and particularly toward Governor General Leyrit, and even openly threatened to overthrow the Compagnie des Indes before leaving India unless it employed better people in its service.[31] At the termination of the campaign against Fort St. David, he also turned his attention to the Marquis de Bussy, who since the year 1751 had been playing a key role in the Deccan at the court of the Viceroy, Subahdar Salabat Jang, in Aurangebad. Having, with the aid of the small but highly disci-

---

[28] D'Aché to Moras, October 30 and November, 1758, ibid., III, 394.
[29] Ibid.
[30] Beatson, op. cit., II, 115.
[31] Waddington, op. cit., III, 388.

plined French army at his command, freed Jang from the clutches of his rivals for power there, Bussy for all practical purposes, except in form, became the ruler of a vast area and as such used his authority to enrich himself as well as to further French interests over a wide area. Thus securely entrenched, he received from Lally a letter so remarkable for its lack of understanding of the realities of the situation that it must be quoted in part. In calling upon the Marquis to leave the Deccan with his troops and join him, the Commissioner General wrote:

> "The King and the Company have sent me to India to drive out the English. It is with the English that we are at War. It matters little to me that a junior disputes the Deccan with his elders or that such and such Raja disputes with such and such Nabob. When I shall have exterminated the English in all this Coast I shall be in condition to carry out, and without leaving my office and with little expense, operations much more surely than those that have cost up to this point the lives of so many of the King's subjects and so many of the Company's rupees."

He then went on to say that it was now necessary to attack the English at Madras with all the united French forces and, with its fall, to move to the Ganges.

> "It is there where your light is absolutely necessary, it is there where you will partake with me of the glories of success. . . ." [32]

At the same time he called upon Bussy to furnish him with men and horses and also money.

While it is true that, writing in the vein that he did, Lally was carrying out the instructions he had received and also seemed to be on sound military grounds in calling for a concentration of troops against Madras, yet he failed to take into account certain factors in the general problem that were to outweigh in the long run those involved in his decision to recall Bussy. The latter was not a great military man, but he possessed near genius when it came to the use of diplomacy among the native princes. For twenty years he had been at home in India and knew the mind of the people there as few Europeans in the eighteenth century ever did. If France had an indispensable man for a particular task in India it was he. Bussy, however reluctantly, submitted to orders and sent to Lally a bill

---

[32] Lally to Bussy, June 13, 1758, *ibid.*, III, 388–9.

of exchange for a hundred thousand rupees and his assurance of the prospect of securing some two hundred thousand more.[33]

The Commissioner General now reversed himself. Instead of bringing Bussy's little army of six hundred European veterans to assist him against Madras, he decided to leave it in the Deccan and the Northern Circars (Sarkars); he nevertheless recalled Bussy and sent the Marquis de Conflans, quite inexperienced in Indian affairs, to attempt to carry on this delicate work. The results of this shift in leadership in the Deccan as well as in the Northern Circars, as will be later noted, were disastrous.

As for the expedition against Madras, Lally, in subsequently commenting on it, gives it the character of an act of desperation. In his *Mémoire sur le choix d'un commandant*, he declared: "It were better act in destroying the enemy than to expire from want." [34] The force that he possessed for this purpose consisted of some thirty-two hundred Europeans, four thousand sepoys, and a park of twenty siege guns and ten mortars. It was not until late in November that his little army, concentrated just east of Arcot, which had fallen into French hands, was able to move. In advancing in the direction of Madras he seems to have minimized the strategic importance of the fortified city of Chingleput (Chengalpat), on the lower waters of the Palar River and lying between Pondicherry and Madras. Only after it had been heavily garrisoned by Madras troops did he come to realize the fact that it could dominate his inland supply line. Had he taken possession of it, the British would have been left with but two fortified places in the entire Carnatic: Trichinopoly and Madras. After a belated and unsuccessful attempt to acquire it, he left it behind him. By the second week in December he approached Madras. The place was in reality two cities — the one restricted in size, fortified, where the Europeans dwelt, Fort St. George; the other, then somewhat separated from the first, un-

---

[33] Bussy to Lally, July 15, 1758, *ibid.*, III, 390. A letter written by one at Pondicherry to his correspondent at Masulipatam early in September — the day after d'Aché departed for Île de France — which was intercepted by the English, gives a true picture of the French situation on the Coromandel Coast: "They say M. de Bussi is coming; let him make Haste; let him bring Men, and especially Money, without which he will only increase our Misery. The Country, being Ruined, scarce affords us any Provisions . . ." (London advices, October 11, 1759, *Pennsylvania Gazette*, December 20, 1759).

[34] Waddington, *op. cit.*, III, 395.

Southern India in the Eighteenth Century.

(From Henry Beveridge's *A Comprehensive History of India*)

"Plan de Madras." By Bellin.

(From *Le Petit Atlas maritime*, 1764)

fortified, and of great extent, with a population of over fifty thousand natives.[35]

Meanwhile, at Madras Governor Pigot and Colonel Stringer Lawrence had been extremely active in preparing for the anticipated attack by strengthening the fortifications, by gathering munitions and food supplies, and by enlisting military support. With two thirds of the troops of the Presidency still with Clive in Bengal, it was indeed necessary to exhaust every resource to strengthen the garrison, especially with the departure of Pocock for Bombay. It is true that Colonel Draper with a part of his regiment arrived opportunely from England, but the British, numbering about two thousand Europeans, including about one hundred marines, were inferior to the French in numbers. Caillaud, now with the rank of major, was therefore ordered from Trichinopoly with some of his Europeans; two thousand sepoys were also later brought from there under Isouf Cawn and thrown into Chingleput; and, finally, certain friendly native princes were prevailed upon to furnish reinforcements, which, however, could not be much depended upon.[36] But at least a spirit of great unity reigned in the city among those in authority and an equal determination that what had happened in 1746, when the French under La Bourdonnais gained possession of Fort St. George, should not be repeated. Indeed, the Madras fortifications were very different in 1758 from those of the earlier date, with a series of strong outer bastions projecting from an inner wall, with ravelins, counterscarps, covered ways, glacis, and a moat. There was reason, therefore, for confidence on the part of the defenders that they could hold out until the return of Pocock in the spring, especially in view of the fact that food supplies and ammunition seemed to be ample.

Nevertheless, the native city was occupied by the French without difficulty. To protect its inhabitants from plundering and to strike the enemy troops a decisive blow while thus occupied, with many of them drunk on arrack, Draper sallied from the fortifica-

[35] Captain Landevisiau to the Minister, April 24, 1759, *ibid.*, III, 396.

[36] Beatson, *op. cit.*, II, 116. In preparing for the defence of Madras, it may be pointed out, that part of the native quarter — called in the dispatches the Black Town — which lay northward of Fort St. George was demolished in order to enlarge the esplanade and to take away from the enemy a shelter for siege operations (Fort St. George Select Committee to the Company, October 10, 1758, India Office, HEIC's Coast and Bay, 6:258).

tions with a considerable force. Although displaying great personal bravery, he failed, however, in his objective. As a consequence, for two months thereafter the garrison of Fort St. George was obliged to submit to a siege. Early in January Lally had succeeded in erecting batteries for his large siege guns and mortars, whereupon he began to pound the walls of the half bastion on the waterfront and throw shells into the city. Yet the heavy guns of the fort were not silenced; when dismounted they were quickly replaced, as were also the battered embrasures, and by superior fire-power they more than once put the besieging batteries out of action. This was not the only embarrassment faced by the French. A good many of the European troops, with pay long overdue and deeply dissatisfied with conditions in the camp, deserted — not only Swiss mercenaries, but Frenchmen — and found their way into the fort, where, with their needs fully met, they became, for obvious reasons, among the stoutest of the defenders. Further, Captain Preston, operating out of Chingleput with a strong mobile force, called a "flying camp," so interrupted the line of communication with Pondicherry that Lally, after sending out several smaller detachments to check him, was compelled to divert a considerable portion of his troops from the siege operations to deal with him. But Soupire, who commanded them, received so warm a reception in his attack upon Preston, stationed advantageously at Mount St. Thomas, not far from Chingleput, that he was impelled to retreat to the French camp.[37]

Despite all difficulties, the French persisted in the siege and toward the latter end of January had succeeded in setting off a mine that made a breach in the counterscarp by destroying the bastion under attack. Further, bombs lobbed into that quarter of the city created fires that carried out the work of destruction. Much of the city was now in ruins. Moreover, the waters about Madras were patrolled by two French frigates. With the defenders cut off by land and by sea from relief, it seemed that victory was at hand. When Pocock, who had gone to Bombay to refit, as stated, might return could not be determined. Then on the 30th of the month there appeared on the horizon a sail. It was the *Shaftesbury*, an armed Company ship commanded by Captain English. Engaging the two French frigates, he drove one of them ashore and the other disappeared, and thereupon he entered the roadway. English

[37] Fort St. George Select Committee to the Company, February 21, 1759, India Office, *ibid.*, 6:265–7; Entick, *op. cit.*, IV, 186–91.

brought not only a supply of money and munitions as well as some reinforcements, but also news that a British squadron would soon appear.

Vice Admiral Pocock, upon arriving at Bombay on November 25 of the preceding year, had found in the harbour two men of war together with six Company ships that they had convoyed from England, bringing with them the remainder of Draper's regiment, the 64th, as well as money, munitions, and other supplies, all destined for Madras. Realizing the vital importance of sending them forward without delay and yet unwilling to risk his ships of the line, he detached the cruiser *Queensborough* from his squadron and with the Company frigate *Revenge* sent off the relief on December 18 under command of Steevens's flag-captain Richard Kempenfelt. The latter finally reached Madras on February 16, some two weeks after the *Shaftesbury*, one of the convoyed ships, had arrived.[38]

Meanwhile, Lally found himself unable to exploit the breach in the wall for storming the city, for the defenders were able to utilize the ruins of the structures thereabout effectively for their own purposes. Already discouraged, now with the appearance of the British fleet he and his army — after having suffered a loss, it was asserted, of some three hundred officers and fifteen hundred privates killed or wounded, as against a British loss of twenty-eight officers and six hundred privates — therefore determined to give up the siege.[39] On the following day, after spiking their siege guns, the French retreated. Three days before this move Lally, in a despondent mood, had written to the Governor of Pondicherry, M. Leyrit, the following amazing letter:

> "We remain still in the same position: the breach made these fifteen days, all the time within fifteen toises [40] of the wall; and never holding up our heads to look at it.
>
> "I reckon we shall, on our arrival at Pondicherry, endeavour to learn some other trade; for this of war requires too much patience.

· · · · · ·

[38] Pocock to Pitt, December 7 and 19, 1758, Pocock Letter Book. When Pocock wrote on December 7, he had decided that the *Shaftesbury* and the *Rhoda* were not fit to proceed; the former he called "an extreme bad sailor," and the latter he said was "much in want of repair." However, the two ships left and it was, in fact, the *Shaftesbury* that was the first to appear in Madras roadway, as indicated in the text.

[39] Fort St. George Select Committee to the Company, February 21, 1759, India Office, HEIC's Coast and Bay, 6:265–7.

[40] The *toise*, no longer used in France as a term of measurement, was 2.1315 yards.

"I am this day taking my measures to set fire to the Black Town [the native city], and blow up the powder mills.

.   .   .   .   .   .

". . . I renounce . . . meddling directly or indirectly, with any thing whatever that may have relation to your administration, whether civil or military. For I had rather go and command the Caffres of Madagascar, than remain in this Sodom which it is impossible but the fire of the English must destroy sooner or later, even though that from heaven should not.

Lally."

"P.S.   I think it necessary to apprize you, that, as M. de Soupire has refused to take upon him the command of this army . . . you must of necessity, together with the council, take it upon you. For my own part, I undertake only to bring it back to Arcotte or Sadraste. Send therefore your orders, or come yourselves to command it; for I shall quit it on my arrival there." [41]

We must now turn to consider very briefly developments in the Northern Circars and in the Deccan after the departure of Bussy, who was just as ineffective as a member of Lally's staff as he had been a source of strength to French interests at the court of the Subahdar at Aurangebad. The effect of this has been well stated: "Immediately the departure of Bussy was known, the edifice so painfully erected by French influence in the Deccan crumbled like a house of cards." [42] Soon afterward in the Northern Circars a revolt against the French took place at the city of Vizagapatam, an important seaport, from which the English Company had been expelled by Bussy. The local Rajah, having raised the British colours, begged for assistance from Clive in Bengal. The latter determined to run the risk of reducing his forces on the Ganges to a handful, even in the face of opposition on the part of the Council of Fort William, in order to send to his aid Colonel Forde with five hundred Europeans, sixteen hundred sepoys, and an artillery park. Proceeding by water, Forde arrived there on October 20 and early in December supported by the troops of the Rajah met Conflans, whose forces he finally routed, though superior to his own in num-

[41] Lally to Leyrit, February 14, 1759, *Annual Register* . . . 1759 (London, 1760), pp. 224–5. This letter was taken by the British when the courier who carried it was captured.

[42] Waddington, *op. cit.*, III, 402. This point is developed by R. G. Cambridge, *The War in India between the English and French* (London, 1761).

bers as well as in artillery; he also captured on this occasion the enemy's baggage and all of his large guns. Conflans thereupon retreated southward to well-fortified Masulipatam, the most important city in the Southern Circars. There Forde appeared in the spring of 1759 and besieged him for a month, and then, with his munitions running dangerously low, the British colonel determined to carry the city by assault at night. This took place April 9. Although Forde at the time had not more than three hundred Europeans and seven hundred sepoys, and Conflans had upward of five hundred Europeans and over two thousand sepoys, the action was successful and the Frenchman surrendered his force.[43]

The collapse of French power in the Northern Circars had the most disastrous consequences.[44] The Subahdar of the Deccan, Salabat Jang, who was coming to Conflans's aid with a numerous force — but already greatly disconcerted by Lally's failure at Madras — now made a dramatic shift and on May 14 signed a treaty of friendship with the British whereby he granted to the English Company not only the Circar of Masulipatam but that of Nizampatam and certain other districts, the revenues of which had previously been turned over to the French.[45] His example was not lost upon other native rulers, who were made to realize that their connections with the French might be a grave liability and not an asset. By the beginning of the summer of 1759, therefore, the French influence in India had disappeared from Bengal, the Northern Circars, and the Deccan and was to all intents and purposes confined to a few places in the Carnatic and on the Coromandel Coast, in view of the loss likewise of Surat in northwestern India in the spring of the year.[46]

To recover its losses and to stave off irretrievable disaster, the representatives of the Compagnie des Indes could only look to the coming of powerful aid from home. The sending of such aid must, however, include its safe arrival in India; and this involved not only naval power but the solution of a problem in logistics.

When d'Aché had arrived at Île de France from Pondicherry early

[43] Fort William Select Committee to the Company, October 22, November 10, December 31, 1758, and December 29, 1759, India Office, HEIC's Coast and Bay, 6:221, 229, 236–7, and 340.

[44] Waddington, op. cit., III, 404.

[45] Fort St. George, Secret Department, to the Company, July 25, 1759, India Office, HEIC's Coast and Bay, 6:301; Entick, op. cit., IV, 206–7.

[46] Pocock to Pitt, March 22, 1759, Pocock Letter Book; Bussy to Belle-Isle, April 22, 1759, Waddington, op. cit., III, 405.

the preceding October, he had found there a reinforcement of three ships of the line under command of Fragier de l'Eguille, as well as several Company ships. As it did not seem possible to move back to India before the spring and as the food resources of the island were very meager and insufficient to meet the requirements of almost ten thousand people, including the inhabitants, it was determined to send part of the fleet to winter at the Dutch colony of Cape of Good Hope and to procure there the needed provisions for the voyage to Pondicherry and also for the sojourn in the waters of the Bay of Bengal. This inevitably brought about delays in the departure of the fleet, with the result that it was after the middle of July when it finally lifted anchor at Port Louis on Île de France and it was not until the beginning of September that it moved into the Bay of Bengal off the eastern coast of Ceylon.[47]

Meanwhile the situation of the French in India continued to deteriorate. Lally — highly temperamental and weighed down with discouragement after the series of reverses to French arms in India — in the spring of the year turned to Bussy, whom he had previously treated with scant respect. In the words of the latter:

> "He proceeded to offer me the command of his army, all in tatters, dying of starvation, without pay for 6 months, excessively discontented and face to face with the enemy." [48]

But the offer was felt by Bussy to be a trap and, pleading ill health, he refused it. Thereupon relations between the two men gradually became one of unrestrained hostility. By the summer of 1759 Bussy, in the eyes of Lally, was the chief source of all the misfortunes that had overtaken the French in India. In communicating with the authorities at home, the Commissioner General charged that Bussy had not only plundered Salabat Jang but that his operations during the past five years had cost the Company four million livres. He further wrote:

> "What treacheries and abominations I have suffered from Sieur de Bussy since I recalled him from the Deccan! . . . If eight months ago I had sent to you in Paris M. de Bussy bound hand and foot, this colony would today be in a state of defence." [49]

---

[47] Beatson, op. cit., II, 204–5; Waddington, op. cit., III, 408–9.
[48] Bussy to Belle-Isle, April 22, 1759, ibid., III, 405.
[49] Lally to the Compagnie des Indes, August 1, 1759, ibid., III, 407.

In this connection it may be pointed out that the dissatisfaction in Lally's own regiment over lack of money with which to buy the necessities of life was such that it mutinied at Chettiput in July and only by the greatest effort of the officers was brought back to its duty. Even so, the desertions from the French forces by soldiers who entered the English service between December and August amounted to some four hundred Europeans.[50] Then in October came the still more serious mutiny of the Lorraine regiment, which was soon joined by other battalions, the cavalry, and even the artillery; but this also was, fortunately, terminated after Lally was able to gather some funds with which to make a partial payment to the bitterly dissatisfied soldiers.[51] Under these circumstances it is not surprising that the Commissioner General was not eager for an engagement and disposed of his forces so as to cover the road to Pondicherry and that to Arcot, all the while awaiting the arrival of the anticipated and sorely needed relief.

Reference has already been made to the fact that Vice Admiral Pocock, soon after reaching Bombay harbour in November of the preceding year, had sent a small relief squadron to Madras, the arrival of which in February had brought about the lifting of the siege of that city by Lally. With excellent facilities for refitting his ships of the line he was even in a position to recondition the leaky *Cumberland*, making her once again "a tight ship." [52] By April 8 he was able to make sail for his return to Madras with nine capital ships, and by the 19th he was carried by favourable winds to the coast of Ceylon and by the 30th had moored in the roadstead at Negapatam, where he was in position to intercept d'Aché's fleet, which he anticipated would soon appear off the coast from Île de France and which he was determined to face in battle.[53]

The enemy, however, as has already been indicated, was not destined to arrive in the Bay of Bengal until the month of September. It was on the 2nd of this month, while the British fleet was cruising off the northeastern coast of Ceylon, that an outlook saw in the distance fifteen sails. Realizing that here at last was d'Aché's squadron, Pocock immediately gave chase; but the wind died down and he made no progress. The morning of the 3rd the French fleet again

---

[50] Pocock to Pitt, August 12, 1759, Pocock Papers.
[51] Waddington, op. cit., III, 417–19.
[52] Pocock to Pitt, March 22, 1759, Pocock Papers.
[53] Pocock to Pitt, June 5, 1759, *ibid.*

appeared in sight and he spent this and the following day vainly pursuing it before it disappeared in the mist. Persuaded that the enemy was headed for Pondicherry, he now made for this road-stead; but on arriving there early on the 8th, he saw no sign of the French squadron. It did, however, come into view in the distance early in the afternoon of the same day, and he was able to resume the chase. As the result of his perseverance, on the afternoon of the 10th, while off Tranquebar, he succeeded in making the contact with it that he so much desired, when he put his flagship, the *Yarmouth*, almost abreast of de'Aché's powerful reconditioned *Zodiaque*. At musket-shot range the two vessels delivered their broadsides at each other. The cannonading then became general between the two fleets and continued with great fury for two hours. Thereupon, gradually disengaging itself, the French fleet, with all the sail it could crowd, left the scene of battle.[54]

It should be pointed out that when d'Aché engaged Pocock, he had at his command the most powerful fleet that up to that time had ever sailed the waters of the Bay of Bengal. It was composed of eleven ships, all carrying from seventy-four to sixty guns,[55] as against nine British ships of from sixty-eight to fifty guns.[56] Had it been most effectively used and especially had the large guns been operated with maximum efficiency, with its tremendous advantage in fire-power, it might well have all but destroyed Pocock's fleet and established French naval supremacy in the Bay of Bengal.[57] In fact, the British van, including the *Tyger* and the *Newcastle*, which

---

[54] For accounts of the chase and of the battle see Pocock to Pitt, October 12, 1759, *ibid.*; d'Aché's report to the Minister, December 15, 1759, Waddington, *op. cit.*, III, 409–12; and Beatson, *op. cit.*, II, 205–9.

[55] The *Zodiaque*, the flagship, the *Minotaur*, and the *Comte de Province* were all seventy-fours; the *Centaur* was a seventy; the *Actif*, the *Vengeur*, the *Illustre*, and the *Fortuné* were sixty-fours; and the *Duc d'Orléans*, the *St. Louis*, and the *Duc de Bourgogne* were sixties. They carried 728 guns and a complement of 6,500 men (Pocock to the Admiralty, October 19, 1759, Pocock Letter Book).

[56] The *Grafton*, carrying Rear Admiral Steeven's ensign, was a sixty-eight-gun ship, the *Yarmouth*, Pocock's flagship, a sixty-six, the *Elizabeth*, a sixty-four, the *Tyger*, the *Sunderland*, and the *Weymouth*, all sixties, the *Cumberland*, now reduced to a fifty-eight, and the *Newcastle* and the *Salisbury* both fifties. They carried 524 guns and a complement of somewhat over 4,000 men (*ibid.*).

[57] D'Aché attributed his failure at the time to the bad conduct of some of the captains of the Company ships. He later wrote: "Too great speed, too great an interval between the rear division and the centre at the time of the beginning of the combat and our line too close together to permit us to manœuvre, all these things were responsible for our want [of success]" (Waddington, *op. cit.*, III, 411).

were being mercilessly raked by the batteries of five of the French ships, was about to be overwhelmed when Steevens in the *Grafton*, who started to engage the *Zodiaque*, moved forward to help the three ships that formed it.[58] Only in the rear — owing to the inactivity of the *Fortuné* as well as that of some other French vessels during the early part of the conflict — was there any advantage to the British; there the *Illustre*, a sixty-four, commanded by that excellent officer M. de Ruis, was for a time obliged to endure the concentrated fire of several of Pocock's ships. The arrival of the slow-sailing *Sunderland* and its consort the *Weymouth*, both of which also engaged the French rear, at length led to the first French disengagement at that point, with the French center and then the van following suit. French casualties in the action were over 1,500 as against the British casualties of 560.

Had Pocock not suffered so heavily, he could have ordered a pursuit. But, in addition to the loss of personnel, the *Tyger* was demasted and the *Newcastle*, *Grafton*, and *Cumberland*, as well as his own flagship, had received such damage, especially to the rigging, that they could not proceed on such a mission. Returning slowly to Negapatam road, the vice admiral upon arriving set to work to recondition his fleet and by the 26th was able to proceed to sea again in search of the French fleet. This he found anchored under the guns of the fortifications of Pondicherry. Although he lured it out, it showed no inclination to renew the fight, but disappeared in the distance, with the result that he himself sailed to Madras.[59]

Pocock's naval victory of September 10, it is clear, was a contribution of extraordinary importance to the annihilation of French power on the Coromandel Coast. Hardly had d'Aché, after his drubbing, moved to Pondicherry and landed the all too meagre supplies of money and munitions, together with a few soldiers whom he brought, when, to the utter consternation of the Superior Council and Lally, he announced his intention of returning immediately to Île de France. Despite their pleadings not to desert them in the grave emergency and turn over to the enemy control of the water approach to the Coast, he remained adamant in his resolve to depart. A final effort was made to divert him from his plan of departure when a grand remonstrance was drawn up, signed by all the

[58] The *Tyger* suffered 168 casualties, and the *Newcastle* 112 (Pocock to the Admiralty, October 19, 1759, Pocock Letter Book).
[59] Pocock to Pitt, October 12, 1759, Pocock Papers.

military, civil, and ecclesiastical dignitaries, and was presented to the admiral, protesting

> ". . . against your precipitate departure. . . . You alone are respon-
> sible for the loss of this colony. In consequence, it has been agreed
> that complaints will be carried to the King and to the Minister to
> demand justice; the Company never having had any object in ask-
> ing vessels of the King than to save these establishments at the risk
> of these same ships." [60]

When this paper was received by d'Aché, he was already at sea. Sufficiently moved by it, he returned to Pondicherry and was there when Pocock formed his line of battle outside the roadstead on September 27 and, in order to draw the enemy away, put to sea. With the departure of the British fleet for Madras, the French admiral re-entered Pondicherry and then, after landing additional munitions and five hundred Europeans to support the colony, finally sailed for Île de France on October 1. His decision was influenced undoubtedly by the information he possessed that Pocock would receive at any moment a reinforcement of four ships of the line that had sailed from England under command of Rear Admiral Samuel Cornish — among these the powerful *Lenox*, a seventy-four, and the *Duc d'Acquitaine*, a fine French sixty-four, which after capture carried the British colours.[61] As was the case with Admiral des Gouttes at Louisbourg in 1758, he sought above everything else to save his fleet and was able in the face of bitter opposition on the part of the military authorities to do so — something that des Gouttes did not accomplish. It may be added that he was destined never again to appear off the Coast. The French at Pondicherry were therefore to witness the process of the inevitable and rapid attrition of their military power and its ultimate utter disintegration — face to face as they were with opponents of great capacity and equal determination, who in full command of the seas were supplied from England with all that was requisite for them to complete the task in hand.[62]

With d'Aché's departure for Île de France, Pocock, free to return to Bombay to refit, now left Madras with the hearty approbation of the Council and also with expressions of gratitude for his services

[60] Letter of the "Counseil National" to d'Aché, September 17, 1759, Waddington, *op. cit.*, III, 413.

[61] Beatson, *op. cit.*, II, 213; III, 208.

[62] J. S. Corbett, *op. cit.*, II, 126.

during the past two years. Before setting sail he assured the Council that he would at the earliest possible moment dispatch a squadron from the Malabar Coast so that, including the Cornish reinforcement, there would be nine ships of war early the following year on the Coromandel Coast.[63] Meeting at sea with Cornish, who had brought out not only the vice admiral's recall to England but the remainder of Colonel Coote's regiment, he sent the troops on to Madras, and the combined squadrons thereupon entered the Indian Ocean. But Pocock was impelled to prolong his stay at Bombay before setting sail for home. By rushing the work of refitting, he was able to send Steevens southward in December with six ships of the line and, as a result of startling developments in Bengal, even planned to return to Madras in March with five more ships of this class. For it seemed by reports as though the English would be obliged to face in the Bay of Bengal in the spring of 1760 the combined naval forces of the French and the Dutch in the Far East.[64]

With the British in India busily engaged not only in their struggle with the French but repairing the damage done to Calcutta when captured by Siraj-ud-daula in 1758, the Dutch at Batavia, in Java, seized the occasion in June 1759 to send a body of some three hundred Europeans and some six hundred Malays on board seven ships with the purpose of securing military control of Bengal and a monopoly of the saltpetre trade that had been granted by the new Nabob to the English Company.[65] They landed at Nagapatam in August, but not until October did they approach the river and, in the face of the Nabob's prohibition against their introducing troops into the province, attempt the following month to force their way up the Hugli. Clive, who had been appointed Governor of Calcutta by the Council of Fort William, was, as the result of this delay, able to prepare for them. Colonel Forde was recalled from Golconda with his victorious detachment, and three Company ships were heavily armed. The latter, with the movement of the Dutch fleet up the river, dropped down from Calcutta and in a lively engagement on November 24 captured all the Dutch fleet. Before this occurred the troops in it had been disembarked, and they proceeded

---

[63] Pocock to Pitt, October 19, 1759, Pocock Letter Book.

[64] Pocock to Pitt, February 11, 1760, *ibid.*

[65] It was reported by Resident Herbert at Batavia that the Dutch there were planning to send a thousand Europeans and fifteen hundred "Bugguesses" to Bengal (Fort St. George Select Committee, July 29, 1759, India Office HEIC's Coast and Bay, 6:300).

up the river to reach the Dutch center at Chinsura. But Forde was on hand to receive them, as well as those troops at Chinsura which now marched to form a juncture with the invading force. The very day of the naval victory the colonel put to rout the Chinsura detachment of some four hundred men and the following day scattered that from Batavia. As a result the Dutch in India now anxiously sued for peace.[66]

Thus, with the Dutch as well as the French overwhelmed in Bengal, and the Nabob of Bengal quite dependent upon the English for his security, it was now possible for Clive and the Council of Calcutta to grant the maximum support within their power to the Madras Presidency. To this end that excellent soldier Eyre Coote — advanced to the rank of lieutenant colonel of the 84th regiment, which was recruited for the Indian service and was to distinguish itself in this service — had already been sent to Madras in October to join his regiment there and, as senior officer, to take charge of the British military forces along the Coromandel Coast. In the month of November, when Lally proceeded against Trichinopoly to gain possession of that great stronghold, Coots, in order to divert the French general from his purposes, proceeded to invest the town of Wandiwash, under French control, located about sixty miles southwest from Madras, and took it. Other near-by places likewise surrendered.[67] Lally, in view of this ominous development, was led to give up his enterprise to the southward and at the end of the year assumed personal command of the French army that was concentrated under the walls of Arcot.

It was a matter of the most vital importance to dislodge the British from their advanced positions in the direction of Pondicherry. To this end the French general, at the head of some thirteen hundred French foot soldiers, one hundred and fifty French cavalry, and eighteen hundred sepoys, moved rapidly upon Wandiwash. In the absence of Coote he gained possession of that city itself, but the fort, manned by a small body of English and six companies of

---

[66] Fort William Select Committee to the Company, December 29, 1759, India Office, HEIC's Coast and Bay, 6:347–8. For an interesting contemporary letter from Calcutta giving an account in considerable detail of the Dutch aggression see Beatson, op. cit., II, 224–8; see also Entick, op. cit., IV, 217–30, for the English demands of December 1, 1759 and the Dutch answers and the Dutch demands of the same date and the English answer, as well as the memorial subsequently sent by the government of Great Britain to the Dutch States-General covering the incident.

[67] Coote to Pitt, February 13, 1760, London Gazette, September 23, 1760.

"Map to illustrate the Wars in Coromandel, 1744–1780."

(From Henry Beveridge's *A Comprehensive History of India*)

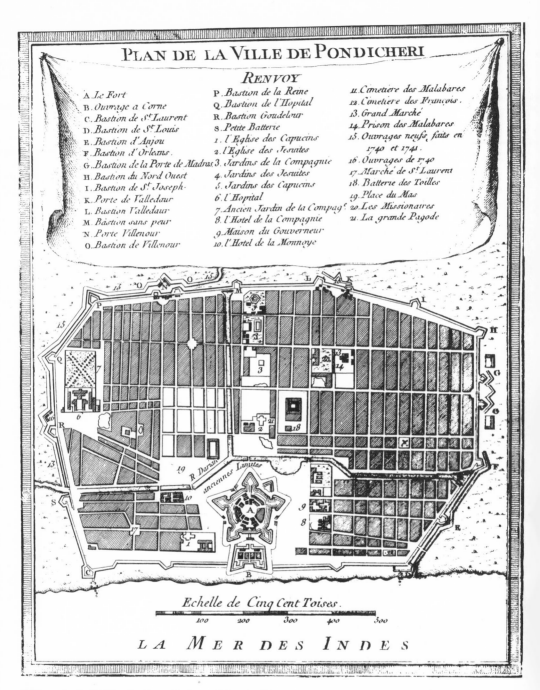

PLAN DE LA VILLE DE PONDICHERI

RENVOY

A. Le Fort
B. Ouvrage a Corne
C. Bastion de St. Laurent
D. Bastion de St. Louis
E. Bastion d'Anjou
F. Bastion d'Orleans
G. Bastion de la Porte de Madras
H. Bastion du Nord Ouest
I. Bastion de St. Joseph
K. Porte de Valledaur
L. Bastion Valledaur
M. Bastion sans peur
N. Porte Villenour
O. Bastion de Villenour

P. Bastion de la Reine
Q. Bastion de l'Hopital
R. Bastion Goudelour
S. Petite Batterie
1. l'Eglise des Capucins
2. l'Eglise des Jesuites
3. Jardins de la Compagnie
4. Jardins des Jesuites
5. Jardins des Capucins
6. l'Hopital
7. Ancien Jardin de la Compagⁿ.
8. l'Hotel de la Compagnie
9. Maison du Gouverneur
10. l'Hotel de la Monnoye

11. Cimetiere des Malabares
12. Cimetiere des François
13. Grand Marché
14. Prison des Malabares
15. Ouvrages neufs, faits en 1740 et 1741
16. Ouvrages de 1740
17. Marché de St. Laurent
18. Batterie des Toilles
19. Place du Mas
20. Les Missionaires
21. La grande Pagode

Echelle de Cinq Cent Toises.

100   200   300   400   500

LA MER DES INDES

"Plan de la Ville de Pondicheri." By Bellin.   (From *Le Petit Atlas maritime*, 1764)

sepoys, held out. Six precious days were consumed by Lally in erecting batteries and in rectifying their location before a breach in the wall of the fort was made. Coote was thus able to come up to assist its defenders and offer battle to Lally on January 22.

The Battle of Wandiwash that followed is rightly regarded as one of the decisive battles in modern history in view of the results that flowed from it, and in importance it rightly takes a place with that of Plassey won by Clive. It is clear that the fate of southern India was at stake. The two sides seem to have been in effective fighting strength about equal.[68] The French were drawn up in line of battle between the reservoirs. The engagement opened with an artillery duel, and then Lally, when its effect upon the English line seemed to be apparent, ordered a cavalry charge. Although neither the commander of the mounted troops nor his second would execute the order, a captain of horse put himself at the head of them and sought to run down his opponents, but was received by such a blast of grapeshot and musketry fire that it broke up the advance.[69] The French general then placed himself at the head of the Lorraine regiment and bore down upon the enemy centre, and the struggle became a hand-to-hand combat. At this critical juncture a shell from the English artillery struck a caisson filled with powder located near a reservoir embankment on the French left. The effect of the blast was such as to impel the French marines posted there to abandon their position. Coote immediately ordered the battery there to be seized, and this was done by Draper's regiment. With his left wing turned, Lally, could no longer hold his army. Leaving behind almost all its artillery, it retreated — at first to its camp just outside Wandiwash, and then headed for Pondicherry, where it arrived four days later. In the course of the battle it not only suffered losses amounting to some eight hundred men killed or wounded, but left in the hands of the British as prisoners the redoubtable Bussy as well as other French officers.[70]

But this was not the most serious consequence of the defeat at

---

[68] Coote in his report to Pitt (*ibid.*) gives the strength of his own forces as 1,700 Europeans, 3,000 sepoys, 13 field guns, and a howitzer, and that of the enemy as 2,200 Europeans, 400 Kaffirs from southern Africa, between 9,000 and 10,000 native troops, and an artillery park. Lally asserted in his letter to Belle-Isle of February 6, 1760 (Waddington, *op. cit.,* V, 3) that he had only 1,200 French soldiers and 4,000 native troops.

[69] *Ibid.*

[70] *Ibid.,* V, 5–6; Fort St. George Select Committee to the Company, February 16, 1760, India Office, HEIC's Coast and Bay, 6:358–9.

Wandiwash. Lally, overwhelmed with despondency, permitted this reverse to develop into a French disaster. One place after another in the Carnatic that he had previously held was captured by Coote: Wandiwash immediately fell; on the 29th, Chettiput; on February 2, Timmery, not far from Arcot; and on the 5th a battery was opened against Arcot itself, where on the 10th the fort surrendered.[71] With the giving up of this vastly important place, the natives considered that the French in India were doomed, and even French soldiers deserted to Coote in such numbers that in writing to Barrington on July 1 Coote was able to inform him that he had been able to establish an effective corps known as the "French volunteers." [72] Other places in the Carnatic also subsequently fell into Coote's hands, including the town of Valdoor, only nine miles from Pondicherry. Then, in a combined movement with Rear Admiral Cornish, who landed some eight hundred marines and infantry under Major Monson near Karikal on the Coromandel Coast, that very important place fell to him on April 5.[73] With the capitulation of the invested fort at Valdoor, which held out until the 16th of that month, all that was really left to the French in eastern India now was Pondicherry and the isolated fortress of Gingy.

One hope alone remained to those who guided affairs at Pondicherry. Should d'Aché return with a powerful fleet, equally powerful reinforcements of land troops, and abundant money to fill the empty treasury, all that had been lost might be regained and even more than that accomplished. But Lally and the Council were destined to look in vain for him. In fact, Admiral Steevens — now in command of the British fleet in the East Indies, with the return to England of Pocock — possessed such strength, with sixteen ships of fifty guns or better,[74] as to permit him without fear of interference to dominate the waters of the Bay of Bengal and not only to support the British land forces in India but to protect the still great trade of the United East India Company.[75] Thus, while the English

---

[71] Ibid.; see also Coote to Pitt, February 13, 1760, op. cit.

[72] Waddington, op. cit., V, 7–8.

[73] Fort St. George Select Committee to the Company, July 31, 1760, India Office, HEIC's Madras, I:10.

[74] For a list of British warships in India waters see Beatson, op. cit., III, 258–9.

[75] When Pocock in the Yarmouth returned to the Downs early in September 1760, he convoyed twenty Company ships that had loaded in China, two at Madras, and one at Calcutta. The convoy was called by the London Gazette of September 23, 1760 "the greatest Fleet of East-Indiamen that ever sailed that place at one Time," and the total value of the cargoes was placed at over nine million pounds sterling.

in India prospered, the enemy at Pondicherry, surrounded by hostile forces on land and sea, was reduced to the greatest want. It is true that after the series of French losses Lally recovered enough energy to attempt to retrieve some of them. Writing on March 4 to Belle-Isle, he had declared:

"I still have about 2000 men, good and poor, of whom I am able to put 1500 in the campaign; the English have 3000, 2000 of whom they can put in the campaign; they are at the gates of Pondicherry and are gorged with money; for six months I have used expedients to pay the troops who already have mutinied three or four times. With all these misfortunes I shall make a strenuous effort . . . if I am able to do it without putting Pondicherry in danger, because it is better to die of steel than of famine. . . ." [76]

But his efforts resulted in only the most temporary successes.

The capture of Pondicherry was, it is needless to suggest, the ultimate objective of the British authorities at Madras. But, in the light of the favourable situation of affairs, there was no disposition to act with undue precipitation, which might adversely affect their gains in the Carnatic. They therefore began to prepare methodically for its investment. To aid in this work over five hundred regulars of Draper's and Coote's regiments opportunely arrived from England late in July. If to the land troops were added Steevens's marines, it seemed that the task could be undertaken. But the admiral was at first reluctant to spare them so long as a French fleet might appear. [77] Nevertheless, toward the end of August he felt at last free to land his marines. With the arrival also of the Company ships at Madras, bringing from England a battalion of Highlanders and additional supplies, [78] serious preparations were now begun for the

---

[76] Waddington, op. cit., V, 10–11.

[77] Steevens to Cleveland, August 6, 1760, ibid., V, 11. Governor Pigot of the Madras Council, writing to Steevens on August 27, 1760 (ibid., V, 11–12), expressed the feeling that the British forces were sufficient to begin investment of Pondicherry. Without counting the garrisons, placed at the various points that had fallen into the hands of the Company, he estimated that twenty-five hundred Europeans and about six thousand native troops were available for the task and that the food and money shortage in the French city, creating distress and increasing desertion among its defenders, would lighten the work of gaining possession of it.

[78] It may be mentioned at this point that when the convoy arrived from England it brought a colonel's commission for Major Monson, which gave him rank over Lieutenant Colonel Coote, who thereupon retired to Madras and took steps to carry his regiment to Bengal, whither he had been ordered (Fort St. George Select Committee to the Company, November 3, 1760, India Office, HEIC's Madras, 1:18–19). He agreed to delay his departure, however, so that Monson could use these troops in his operations. When

reduction of the French stronghold. Siege guns and other matériel were concentrated at Cuddalore, in its vicinity, before the end of September, when the rainy season began.

The following month Admiral Steevens, leaving his marines to support Coote, sailed from Madras with twelve of his ships of the line and headed for the port of Trincomalee in Ceylon to refit and also to coast out the stormy monsoon season that characterized the Bay of Bengal at this period of the year. Before he left, however, a strong detachment of Rear Admiral Cornish's sailors was sent in boats into Pondicherry roadstead which captured two French frigates that d'Aché had sent there from Île de France to carry the disturbing news that he had received strict orders from home not to depart for the Coromandel Coast but to remain at the island to defend it and Île de Bourbon from an anticipated British attack. Thus Lally and the Pondicherry Council were made to realize that the last hope of succour from home had disappeared as had that of naval support from the Île de France.[79]

Despite the rainy season, Coote kept pressing his lines closer and closer about Pondicherry. By December 8 he had established four batteries that could play upon its fortifications, and on the 25th of that month Steevens — assured by the Madras authorities that the danger of great storms on the Coast had passed — joined the blockading division of his fleet that he had left before Pondicherry. Within that place there was little but despair. Lally, bitterly hated by most of the other officers, as well as by the civilian authorities, was physically ill and, what is more, even mentally unbalanced. By the latter part of December he was still once again determined to dissociate himself from all military responsibility and sought to make Brigadier Landevisiau the scapegoat in negotiating a surrender of the place. Convinced as he himself was that a capitulation must soon take place unless unexpected assistance arrived, he looked to an arrangement that would give him a special status. But the brigadier refused to be drawn into this trap[80] and in subsequent correspondence pointed out to the general that the French should wait to see what help the Mahrattas might be able to furnish. Some

the latter was wounded on September 9, Coote was prevailed upon to take command once again of the army before Pondicherry (Entick, op. cit., V, 42–4; H. K. Dodwell, Dupleix and Clive [London, 1920], pp. 186–7).

[79] Corbett, op. cit., II, 133–4.

[80] Lally to Landevisiau, and Landevisiau to Lally, both dated December 24, 1760, Waddington, op. cit., V, 25–6.

steps were taken at this juncture to ease the famine conditions in the town. In this connection the fact may be mentioned that about fourteen hundred natives were driven out of it, were then fired upon by the garrison whenever they sought to return, and were finally permitted by Coote to pass through his lines into the country. Further, as the result of a solemn appeal to the inhabitants of Pondicherry, hidden food supplies were made available to feed the defenders for a period of three weeks. When these were exhausted, however, then the end of resistance would be inevitable — unless the British blockade were lifted.

It was at this critical juncture that the besieged were led to believe that Providence at last had come to their aid. On the night of January 1, 1761 one of the most terrible storms within the memory of men broke upon the Coromandel Coast. According to an unnamed eyewitness at Pondicherry, "along all the shores there was only the wreckage of [English] vessels, and of 13 ships that one saw in the evening in our roadstead only one was at large which appeared in condition, although stripped of one of its masts; three were stranded on the sand almost within cannon shot of the city; three were sunk leaving only visible the tops of their masts; and six others, shorn as a pontoon, appeared on the point of being submerged." The effects of the storm on the besieging army were almost as dramatically demoralizing, according to the same writer: "The violence of the wind . . . had so engulfed the European soldier that he could not move, a great number of sepoys perished, the torrents formed by the rain overwhelmed their camp, the cannon for the most part were buried . . . the batteries had also been overthrown." [81]

Lally immediately dispatched a courier to M. Raymond, the French Resident at Pulicat, which lies north of Madras, calling upon him to induce the Dutch there to send in abundant cargoes of rice: "The English squadron is no more. . . . Tell the Dutch that they have nothing to fear now. . . . Offer great rewards. I expect 17,000 Marattoes within these four days. In short, risk all, attempt all, force all, and send us some rice!" [82] But the messenger was intercepted by the English. Nor was the situation of the Brit-

---

[81] *Ibid.*, V, 29–30. For the British account of the effects of the storm see the letter of the Fort St. George Select Committee to the Company, February 4, 1761, India Office, HEIC's Madras, 1:22.

[82] Entick, *op. cit.*, V, 211.

ish fleet so desperate as the French thought it to be. True it is that the *Duc d'Aquitaine* and the *Sunderland* both foundered and sank, that the *Newcastle* and the frigates *Queenborough* and *Protector* were beached and lost, together with some of the storeships, and that four ships of the line were likewise demasted. But Steevens in the *Norfolk* rode out the storm and returned before Pondicherry on the 4th, where he was soon joined by Cornish in the *Lenox* and by three other ships of the line, all of which had missed the cyclone.[83] Moreover, Coote's army, still enveloping Pondicherry, quickly dug its way out of the debris of the storm and, what is more, by the 13th had placed into action a battery of eleven twenty-four-pounders, firing at close range upon the escarpment of the French fort.

One thing alone was now left to the defenders of Pondicherry: to make the best terms possible with Coote. Therefore on the 14th of January Lally called a council of war and to it invited the Governor of Pondicherry, M. Leyrit. The latter, ignoring the invitation, summoned a meeting of the civilian council, which named a delegation to treat with the British. When the following day it arrived in Coote's camp with a body of proposals, however, it was confronted by a letter already dispatched by Lally which — after demanding the fulfilment of the terms of a cartel tentatively agreed upon before the capture of Chandernagore, in Bengal, but never implemented — declared: "The King's troops and those of the Company surrender themselves, for want of provisions, prisoners of war of his Britannick Majesty. . . ." In this connection the Commissioner General also asked that all the inhabitants of Pondicherry should be embraced within its terms, including the French ecclesiastics, and requested that Coote's soldiers take possession of one of the gates the next day and on the 17th of the other gate. In reply, Coote pointed out that the cartel in question was still a matter of dispute between the two crowns and that while he would not be bound to it, he would nevertheless treat the inhabitants with all the indulgence that was agreeable to humanity.[84] With this understanding, he therefore on the 17th took possession of the town, and on the 18th Lally, escorted by a British cavalry detachment, left it — but with the curses of the people ringing in his ears.[85]

---

[83] Fort St. George Select Committee to the Company, February 4, 1761, India Office, HEIC's Madras, 1:22; Beatson, *op. cit.*, II, 364–6.

[84] For Lally's letter of January 15, 1761, and Coote's reply of the same date, see the *Annual Register*, 1761, pp. 290–1.

[85] Waddington, *op. cit.*, V, 33.

The fall of Pondicherry early in 1761 is an event of the greatest historical importance. For eight months the place had been closely blockaded by Steevens,[86] and from the early part of December Coote, with four British regiments [87] and a large body of sepoys at his command and adequately supplied, had gradually enclosed it by land in a vise of steel. Its surrender at discretion involved some three thousand people who became prisoners of war.[88] Swiftly on the heels of the capitulation came the decision by the Madras Presidency that what the French had done to Fort St. David would be visited upon their own metropolis in India.[89]

The work of destruction of the fortifications of Pondicherry was thereupon begun. On March 6 the Fort St. George Select Committee could report to the directors of the Company in London that much progress was made to that end, and on October 2 that the work had been completed.[90] Indeed, so thorough was the task of demolition carried out by the army engineers that, in the words of an inhabitant of the town proper, "No stone rests on another" where the great French fortifications once stood.[91] Like the ruins of Louisbourg, those of Pondicherry not only epitomize the blasting of the eighteenth-century dream of an expanded French empire but also point to the tremendous significance of the attainment by the British navy, by the beginning of the year 1758, of a degree of supremacy on the high seas that in each instance, working as it did in full harmony with the British land forces, paved the way for the subjugation of the enemy both in the New World and in the Far East. With the surrender of Mahé on the Malabar Coast on February 12 and of the fortress of Gingy (Jingi) in the Carnatic on April 5, the last semblance of French political and military control in India finally disappeared.[92] For even the restorations provided for by the peace treaty of Paris in 1763 in no way altered the fact that from 1761 onward, for almost two hundred years, the fate of that great subcontinent was destined to rest in the keeping first of the United East India Company and then of the government of Great Britain.

[86] Steevens to Cleveland, February 7, 1761, ibid., V, 34.

[87] Drapers, the 79th, S. L. Morris's, the 89th, Monson's, the 96th, and Coote's own, the 84th (Beatson, op. cit., III, 259).

[88] See ibid., III, 260, and the Fort St. George Select Committee to the Company, February 4, 1760, India Office, HEIC's Madras, 1:24.

[89] Ibid.

[90] India Office, HEIC's Madras, 1:34, 44.

[91] Waddington, op. cit., V, 33.

[92] India Office HEIC's Madras, 1:33, 44; also P.R.O., C.O. 77:20.

CHAPTER VIII

Senegal, Belle-Île-en-Mer, and Martinique

IN THE TWO preceding chapters relating to India little has been said about the role played by the government of Great Britain in determining the outcome of the Anglo-French struggle in that part of the world. That this role was of decisive importance is clear. Nevertheless, Pitt — anxious as he was at all times to give every assistance within his power to support the United East India Company in seeking to maintain, or even to improve, its position — was well aware that he himself was not able to prescribe any specific course of action there, as he freely did during the course of the war not only in Europe and its littoral waters but also in the New World, as has already been emphasized in the course of this narrative. Not only was he prevented from doing so by reason of the fact that the distance between London and Calcutta or Madras, and consequently the time-lag in communications, was so great as to make well-nigh impossible the issuing of orders that would be adapted to the existing situation when these were received, but, what is more, he was not prepared at the time to assume the responsibility of injecting himself into the affairs of the most powerful of British incorporated commercial companies, with a background of over a century and a half of experience in dealing with Indian affairs, if one were to include the period before its reorganization in 1708. In a letter dated January 11, 1757 and addressed to Vice Admiral Watson, operating with a squadron of the royal navy in Indian waters, his views of the nature of the position of the government in its relations with the Company, which it had chartered, are clearly expressed; from it the following passage is quoted:

"The Company have, it is to be hoped, a complete understanding of their own affairs, and may therefore make such plans of operation as they deem best suited to secure their possessions, or to inflict loss upon the enemy; the King is therefore anxious to arrange that the commanders of his ships should assist those of the Company's vessels in the execution of their plans; at the same time they are on all suitable occasions to inform the Company's captains of such actions as are practicable and suitable for his Majesty's ships and advisable for the general conduct of the War." [1]

Not only was Rear Admiral Steevens sent in 1757 with additional ships from the royal navy to support Watson and Pocock in Indian waters, but the following year Rear Admiral Cornish was ordered to proceed there with four men-of-war, thus giving the British unquestioned command of the Bay of Bengal. Increments of foot troops were also detached from the regular army at home each year from 1757 to 1760 for the Indian service, so that by 1761, as has already been noted, there were available adequate forces to garrison various places captured from the French before that year and at the same time to carry to a successful conclusion the siege of Pondicherry. What is more, it was the military capacity and team work of those leaders in the army and navy who held the King's commission — Clive, also a Company servant, Coote, Forde, Watson, Pocock, Steevens, and Cornish — rather than those in the Company employ, that were chiefly responsible for the wise planning of the campaigns against French influence in India and its ultimate destruction. With respect to the history of the consolidation of British power there after this had been accomplished, a consideration of these matters must be reserved for treatment in later volumes of this series.

Up to the present point in dealing with the history of the Great War for the Empire almost no mention has been made of the great continent of Africa and particularly of the possessions of the British and the French there. Needless to suggest, these did not remain immune from attack by either party to the conflict. In fact, early in the year 1757 a squadron of four French men-of-war appeared upon the Windward and Gold Coasts and, before sailing for Mar-

---

[1] Albert von Ruville, *William Pitt, Earl of Chatham* (London, 1907), II, 340.

tinique in March, not only captured a large number of British and American ships engaged in slaving, but sought to destroy some of the smaller factories belonging to the Company of Merchants Trading to Africa — which in 1750 had taken the place of the Royal African Company — and even attempted by means of a heavy bombardment to get possession of Cape Coast Castle, the most important and also the most powerfully fortified of the new Company's possessions on the Gold Coast.[2]

But the French themselves had established interests on the west African coast — on the Senegal, on the island of Goree off Cape Verde, and on the Gambia — which were destined to become the object of the attention of the British government in 1758. As early as the year 1756, during Pitt's brief tenure of office in connection with his first administration of public affairs, the minister's attention had been drawn to the importance of depriving France of Senegal. This was done by one Thomas Cumming, called a "sensible Quaker." Cumming, it seems, had acted as a factor on the Gum Coast and claimed to be an acquaintance of the Moorish ruler of Zara. According to the merchant, this King had acquired an utter aversion for the French and had declared that he would never be easy in his mind until they were entirely driven from the river of "Senega." What is more, he indicated that the Moor had promised that should the English King accomplish this, he would grant an exclusive trade to his subjects in those parts and had even presented to him such a charter written in Arabic.[3]

After the above proposal was considered by the Board of Trade, together with a definite plan of action that the Quaker had drawn up, the ministry finally, in 1758, approved them, and Cumming himself was appointed as political agent for a small expedition to be directed against Senegal, and if it succeeded, was promised Pitt's support in obtaining a royal charter for trade to that river for a limited number of years.[4] This expedition, under command of Commodore Henry Marsh, consisting of two ships of the line and some four auxiliary vessels with two hundred marines under Major

---

[2] Letter from Antigua, April 12, 1757; Kingston, Jamaica, advices of May 7, 1757; and New York advices of June 6, 1757, *Pennsylvania Gazette*, May 19 and June 9, 1757 and March 2, 1758.

[3] [John Almon], *A Review of Mr. Pitt's Administration* . . . (London, 1764), pp. 83–4.

[4] Pitt to Thomas Cumming, February 9, 1759, *Correspondence of William Pitt* (ed. W. S. Taylor and J. H. Pringle, London, 1838), I, 221–2.

Mason and a detachment of matrosses, in addition to the crews, arrived off the coast of Africa early in April of that year. On their reaching the native roadstead and coast town of Portendic, acquired by the French in 1717, where Cumming had earlier enjoyed the friendship of the local ruler, to their dismay they found that the suspicious Moors there would grant them no assistance as promised — not even a pilot to help the ships arrive at their destination.[5] In view of this situation, giving up the enterprise was at first contemplated; but it was finally determined to prosecute it vigorously, even with the small resources at hand.

The French Fort Louis was located on an island ten miles above the mouth of the Senegal and was thus protected by a bar of sand that extended some distance along the Senegal coastline. For a sailing vessel to negotiate the bar, against which the billows of the ocean dashed with great violence, required great skill and knowledge on the part of the navigator and was the work always assigned to an expert Negro pilot.[6] It was not until the 29th of April that Marsh succeeded in surmounting this great obstacle; in doing so he suffered the loss of two of his smaller craft.[7] Thereupon he was obliged to face a flotilla of some seven French vessels. But the *Nassau*, a sixty-four-gun ship, and the *Harwick*, with fifty guns, easily cleared the way in moving against the weakly armed enemy shipping, which soon retired. Landing a body of seven hundred men — made up of marines, matrosses, and sailors — and the artillery, Marsh prepared to attack Fort Louis without delay. He was relieved of the necessity, however, for its commandant now raised a flag of truce and agreed to surrender.

Under the terms offered by the French and accepted with little alteration, the English were on May 1 put in possession not only of Fort Louis but of all the other French forts as well as the storehouses on the Senegal, together with the vessels, arms, provisions, merchandise, and bullion belonging to the enemy. The civilians of the town of Senegal were permitted, should they so desire, to take away most of their private possessions and were also promised, should they decide to leave, passage to France within a period of

---

[5] A Review of Mr. Pitt's Administration, pp. 84–5.

[6] Michel Adanson, A Voyage to Senegal, the Isle of Goree, and the River Gambia . . . (London, 1759), pp. 29–31. It may be noted that the river at this period was called the Niger by writers. In fact, it was not until 1796 that Mungo Park was able to prove that the Great Niger empties not into the Atlantic but into the Gulf of Guinea.

[7] John Entick, The General History of the Late War (London, 1765), III, 63–4.

six weeks. They preferred, however, by swearing allegiance to the British monarch, to remain,[8] many of them apparently having inter-married with the native women, who, with their "delicate and soft" skin, small mouths and lips, and regular features, were described by one Frenchman as "perfect beauties."[9] It was calculated that this conquest gave to Great Britain control over the lucrative gum trade that centred on the Senegal, and also of factories that to-gether had provided the French West India islands annually with some fourteen hundred slaves, and the merchants of France with quantities of ivory, gold dust, and beeswax.[10]

After Marsh had taken possession of this conquest,[11] with his force necessarily depleted by reason of the complement of troops left on the river for garrison duty, he dropped down the Senegal and made for the island of Goree. It is small and consists of a rim of low land bordering a precipitous mountain. It may be added that although located in the torrid zone, it has a most salubrious cli-mate. The director or commandant of the island, a M. de St. Jean, had not only adorned it, as a highly valued French possession, with a number of impressive buildings, but had also increased its for-tifications so that, in the eyes of a Frenchman visiting it in 1749, it now had become "impregnable."[12] At least, with Fort St. Michaels and the outlying batteries mounting ninety-four heavy guns, mostly twenty-fours and eighteen-pounders, it was far too strong a place for the commodore to attack with his weak force. He therefore wisely left well enough alone and returned to England.

In view of his success on the Senegal and the fact that Goree sup-plied the French West Indies with some four hundred slaves each year and was therefore one of the props of the empire of the en-emy,[13] the ministry determined to send out a fresh expedition better equipped to get possession of the important island that had been

---

8 [Almon], op. cit., p. 85; Entick, op. cit., III, 65–6.

9 Adanson, op. cit., p. 39.

10 Entick, op. cit., III, 66–7.

11 Although Cumming had been able to make no contribution to the success of the conquest of French Senegal, yet he was rewarded. Pitt, in lieu of an exclusive trade promised to the Quaker, secured for him a pension of £500 a year on the Irish establish-ment "as a reward for his sagacity and zeal in pointing out the object, forming the plan, and attending the execution" ([Almon], op. cit., p. 85). In the pamphlet, A List of Absentees of Ireland . . . Also Some Reasons Why Absentees Should . . . Support . . . the Country . . . (Dublin, 1767), Cumming's pension was given as £300.

12 Adanson, op. cit., p. 103.

13 Entick, op. cit., III, 66.

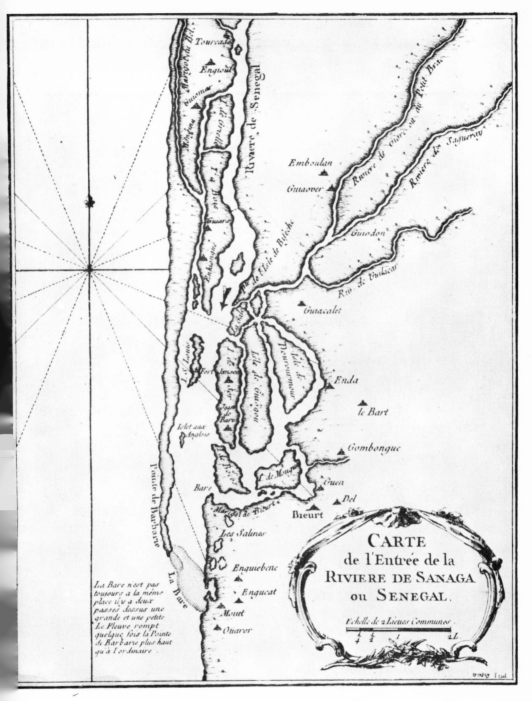

'Carte de l'Entrée de la Riviere de Sanaga ou Senegal," 1764. By Bellin.
(From *Le Petit Atlas maritime*)

PAYS DES MARABOUX

ROYAUME DES FOULES Soumis

habité Par les FOULES

GUIO

ROYAUME.

GUIOLOF

ou Commande le Roy

ROYAUME

DES M

ROYAUME
DE COMBO

DES

SERINS
DOUCKES

ROYAUME D'OUAL
DE BRAC

PAYS DES

Residence du Grand Guiolof
ou Bourgnolof

R de
GNOMY

Mareschancha

ROYAUME
DE BRUSALM

PAYS

ROY me DE JAGARA

ROYAUME DE CAYOR

AU ROY DAMEL

BAOL
DE TIN ou
habité Par les Guiolofs

ROYAL
ROY me
DE SER RES ou CERES

ROYAUME DE BARBESSIN

ROYAUME
DE
R me DE BARRE
ou
MANDINGUE

PAYS DU ROY FOIGNI
qui se du Empereur

Isle et Fort St LOUIS

Cap Verd
Isle de la Madelene

R. de Bassar
R me DE
COMBE

FELOUPES

R de Casamance

Cap Rouge

le Maringoin

le Grand Palmier

captured from the Dutch in 1677 and ceded to the King of France by the Treaty of Nijmwegen the following year. To this end Commodore Augustus Keppel was given command of the new expedition, consisting of four warships,[14] two bomb vessels, and transports carrying six hundred soldiers under Lieutenant Colonel Worge.

Arriving at Goree Bay on December 28, Keppel ordered an attack the next day. In the midst of the bombardment that thereupon took place, the French — in view especially of the terrific fire from the heavy guns of the *Torbay* that drove the defenders from their positions — called a parley and offered to surrender if granted the honours of war. This was refused. With all the ships now in position to deliver their broadsides and bombs against the fortifications, the Governor agreed to surrender at discretion. As a result, the garrison of three hundred Frenchmen and a large number of armed blacks laid down their arms, and with this ceremony Goree passed into the hands of the British, who from this vantage point easily deprived the French of the last foothold in Africa to which they had still clung — a factory on the Gambia,[15] along which river the British also had interests centred at James Fort.

In the eyes of the British, the chief significance of the capture of Senegal, and Goree, the French Gambia post, lay in the fact that it completed "the ruin of the French trade on the coast of Africa, and therewith . . . put the last and finishing hand to the destruction of those colonies, which our enemies could not cultivate without black slaves."[16] It also provided the victors with important additional sources of wealth. In view of all this, it is not surprising that great care was taken that these strategic conquests should not be placed in danger by a surprise counterattack, and to that end three ships of war were so stationed as constantly to patrol the entrance to the Senegal River.[17] Garrisons were also stationed on this river, as well as at the two other African conquests.

By the end of the year 1760 the Great War for the Empire was manifestly reaching a climax. In North America, Montreal, the last of the French strongholds in Canada, had fallen; in the West In-

---

[14] The *Torbay*, a seventy-four, the captured French *Fougueux*, a sixty-four, the *Nassau*, a seventy, and the *Prince Edward*, a forty-four.

[15] Entick, *op. cit.*, III, 271–7; Keppel to Pitt, January 3, 1759, *London Gazette Extraordinary*, January 29, 1759.

[16] Entick, *op. cit.*, III, 269–70.

[17] Letter from Senegal, February 20, 1760, *Pennsylvania Gazette*, June 26, 1760.

dies, French Guadeloupe had been conquered; in Africa, French Senegal, Goree, and Gambia had become British; and in India, Pondicherry was under siege by Coote and Steevens and would soon fall, bringing with it, as has been indicated, the capitulation of Gingy (Jingi) and Mahé and the final disappearance of French political and military might from that great subcontinent. The only important overseas possessions remaining to France were the unprofitable province of Louisiana in North America, the highly profitable St. Domingue, as well as strategic Martinique in the West Indies, and the Îles de France (Mauritius) and de Bourbon (Réunion) in the Indian Ocean lying east of Madagascar. Nor would even these escape were Pitt to fulfil his plans, which now embraced the idea that France must be reduced to the status simply of a continental European power. Nevertheless, the minister was diverted from his task by a more immediate objective, which he screened by rumours that reached Paris to the effect that an expedition was fitting out in England to be directed against "the Maskarenes" — that is, against the Île de France and Île de Bourbon.[18] Acting upon them, the court of Versailles issued orders to Admiral d'Aché, who was refitting his fleet there in order to return to the Coromandel Coast, that he was not under any circumstance to depart from these islands, but to make it his chief business to defend them. There he remained, prepared as best he could to ward off the expected enemy fleet that never appeared. Pondicherry was thus left to its fate.

Pitt, in fact, had had his eyes ever since the fall of 1758, and especially since the British defeat at Saint-Cas in September of that year, upon Belle-Île-en-Mer. This island was strategically located in the Bay of Biscay off the coast of Brittany and commanded not only L'Orient, the port belonging to the great French Compagnie des Indes, but also the estuary of the Loire, as well as to a lesser extent the ports of Brest to the northwest, and Rochefort to the southeast, of it.[19] Admiral Hawke at the time had been by no means favourable to the Pitt suggestion that an attempt be made to seize it.[20] Moreover, the minister himself soon threw all his energies into the Wolfe-Saunders expedition up the St. Lawrence and, with that

---

[18] Very definite plans had been laid to the above end but given up (P.R.O., C.O. 77:20).

[19] See "Heads of a Scheme, planned by an Officer in the last War, for seizing the Island of Bellisle, on the Coast of France," *Pennsylvania Gazette*, June 25, 1761.

[20] Ruville, *op. cit.*, II, 188.

launched, also — as has been brought out in an earlier chapter of this volume — into the conquest of the French West Indies.

It was therefore not until the fall of 1760 — with the prospect of hearing at any moment of the final conquest of Canada with the reduction of Montreal — that Pitt returned seriously to the idea of occupying Belle-Île, as a contribution not only to the war in Germany — by holding large numbers of French troops that otherwise could be sent there — but to the implementation of the plan for a great blockade by Admiral Hawke of the whole French coast of the Bay of Biscay, so that should Spain enter the war on the side of France, it might be possible to prevent the latter country from sending to the New World any important assistance to her ally.[21] It was a strategic conception of vital import. To carry it to successful fulfilment demanded great preparations and also the utmost secrecy. Yet even the *Pennsylvania Gazette* carried news of the preparation of "a prodigious Armament" at Portsmouth, and also the report current at that naval base that it was "designed against Belleisle."[22] To offset such rumours, it is true that other reports were issued that were designed to indicate that the "Grand Expedition" was intended for a hot climate.[23] Seven British battalions of the line, one of guards, a regiment of dragoons, and a great siege train were soon concentrated at this place. Orders were also sent for two regiments in Ireland to embark on transports, and the ships carrying them actually sailed to the Bay of Biscay. But unexpected obstacles to carrying the plan into execution soon appeared. Admiral Hawke — the victor over Conflans near Belle-Île the preceding year — reported adversely upon it, and even George II, who had strongly approved the project, now turned against it.

Then, equally unexpected, came the death of the King on October 27 and the accession of his grandson, which brought strong support for the project from the new King and his adviser, Lord Bute.[24] But the season was by this time too advanced for the haz-

---

[21] Corbett, *op. cit.*, II, 95–8.

[22] Extracts of a letter from Plymouth, December 28, 1760, *Pennsylvania Gazette*, February 26, 1761.

[23] Advices were printed in the *Pennsylvania Gazette* of April 2, 1761, from London, under date of January 5, that the Commissioners of the Navy had purchased for the expedition forty thousand gallons of oil, "which makes it conjectured that they are designed for a hot Climate," and from Portsmouth, under date of January 11, that they were sheathing "nine Ships of the Line for the West Indies."

[24] Corbett, *op. cit.*, II, 99–102.

ards involved, with the result that Pitt decided to postpone its execution until the spring of the year. Then on March 29 Commodore
Keppel, the conqueror of Goree, with ten ships of the line, eight
frigates, and other war vessels, together with transports carrying
nine thousand land forces, some one hundred and fifteen vessels in
all — "said to be designed for the Island of Bourbon" [25] — finally
sailed for Spithead and headed for Belle-Île. By the morning of
April 7 he came in sight of his objective.

Belle-Île-en-Mer is some twelve leagues in circumference and has
an area of thirty-three square miles. With a settled population in
1761 of about five thousand hardy inhabitants engaged in tilling the
soil and in catching and curing pilchards, it had but one strongly
fortified place, the citadel of the little city of Le Palais, facing the
mainland to the northeast. Nevertheless, the island was in a sense
a natural bastion. In character an almost treeless plateau rising
abruptly from a broken and rugged coastline to an average height
of one hundred and thirty feet and covered largely with moors, it
was therefore highly defensible. Of the three nominal harbours,
only that of Le Palais, on the northeastern shore as indicated, was
fit to accommodate ocean-going vessels; almost everywhere the approach is forbidding for ships, and access to the plateau by land
troops could only be secured by scaling the rocky coastal rim, except at those places that had been strongly entrenched. To defend
the island the Governor, the Chevalier de Sainte-Croix, had at his
disposal at the time of the appearance of the British fleet three regiments of regulars and one of militia, together with coast guards,
artillerymen, and musketeers. He was determined, alert, and a dangerous opponent.

To carry out the amphibious assault the British land troops had
been placed under command of Major General Studholme Hodgson, who had served not only under the Duke of Cumberland in
Europe and Scotland, as aide-de-camp, but also under Keppel's
own father, the Earl of Albemarle, at Dettingen.[26] Upon arriving in
the waters off Belle-Île and after reconnoitring its coastline, he and
Keppel agreed to attempt to disembark an attacking force at Port
St. André (Andro), a fishing village near Point Locmaria, the most
eastern extremity of the island. However, to distract the attention
of the French, it was agreed that a naval demonstration and simu-

---

[25] Beatson, op. cit., III, 330–2.
[26] Thomas Keppel, Life of Augustus, Viscount Keppel . . . (London, 1842), I, 298.

lated landings should be made at the harbour of Sauzon, some distance to the northwest of Le Palais. This was done. Very early the next day in furtherance of the plan a number of warships and vessels with the landing troops aboard, rounding Locmaria still in the darkness, gained Sandy Bay. After silencing a fort located on the heights, the soldiers, now crowded into shallops and flatboats, at a given signal rowed for the land in three divisions. Unfortunately for them, Sainte-Croix had divined their intentions and had concentrated most of his forces there. Although landings were made at rather widely separated points — one even to the east of Locmaria — the French were everywhere ready to receive them. Some of the soldiers, nevertheless, with great difficulty gained the plateau, but only to be killed, captured or dispersed as the result of the withering fire directed against them by the French regulars, followed by bayonet charges. After a loss of at least five hundred soldiers and many of the flatboats Hodgson recalled his men.[27] Writing to Pitt on April 12, he declared:

> "I cannot help observing to you that the whole island is a fortification, and that the little nature had left undone to make it such, has been amply supplied by art, the enemy having been at work upon it ever since Sir Edward Hawke appeared before it last winter." [28]

Hodgson and Keppel, though temporarily discouraged, resolutely refused to accept defeat as final.[29] Indeed, with Sainte-Croix securely cut off from any substantial aid from the mainland, they could well afford to wait for a better opportunity to land their men, meanwhile maintaining the strict blockade. During the fifteen days that followed the reverse, the weather was such as to make impossible any new attempt. Then on April 22 came a flat calm and with it a thick fog. Under these favourable conditions, with many of Keppel's ships presenting their broadsides to the shore-line all the way from Port St. André to Port d'Arsic to the southwest of it in such a manner as to sweep with their fire the French batteries and entrenchments located there, Hodgson's second disembarkation took place at two o'clock in the afternoon.

[27] Hodgson to Pitt, April 12, 1761, and Keppel to Pitt, April 13, 1761, *Pennsylvania Gazette*, July 2, 1761; Adjutant General Sir Thomas Spencer Williams to Lord Fitzmaurice, April 13, 1761, Shelburne Papers, 37: 173, in the Clements Library; "Mémoire of Cauchois Feraud," Richard Waddington, *La Guerre de Sept Ans*, V, 46–7.

[28] See the preceding note.

[29] Thomas Keppel, *op. cit.*, I, 306–10.

This time the troops sought out the more inaccessible and consequently the less securely guarded points. A detachment led by
Brigadier Hamilton Lambart (Lambert), moving in their flatboats
far to the right of Point Locmaria, reached the shore at Point Ker-
donis, some distance to the east of the fishing village of St. Foy.
Mounting the forbidding cliff by a path among the rocks so narrow that two men could hardly move abreast, the grenadiers of the
19th Regiment reached the summit and then proceeded to form
themselves behind a wall of stones. Marines and other grenadiers
now swarmed up the height to support them. Completely caught
by surprise, Sainte-Croix too late sought to overwhelm the invaders, and though he led three charges against them in person, he was
repulsed, with the British ships directing a deadly fire against his
exposed columns. As a result, before the close of day all the troops
were safely landed and then proceeded to establish their camp on
an elevation three miles from the coast. In view of this untoward
turn of events the French Governor realized that it was imperative
to concentrate all of his forces, numbering some thirty-five hundred, behind the ramparts of Le Palais. This was done, and with
such precipitation as entailed the loss of much matériel, including
artillery.[30]

Hodgson had thus made good his landing. But by reason of heavy
winds there was now a delay of some five days, and with it a period of deep anxiety before food supplies and the siege artillery
could be placed ashore by Keppel. Despite this fact, the unde-
fended posts along the shore-line were occupied, and with the return of good weather the invading force was soon amply supplied with all that was required for the prosecution of the siege of
Le Palais. Further, when the news reached Pitt of the failure of the
first attempt at landing, he ordered four additional battalions to go
out to reinforce Hodgson and also five ships of the line to strengthen
Keppel's blockade.[31] Meanwhile, Sainte-Croix had swiftly constructed a series of six redoubts on the outskirts of the city. His position there, however, was an exposed one when the British brought
it under heavy mortar fire, and he was impelled to retire to the
heavy masonry walls of the fortress and a series of six more redoubts just outside of these. On May 2 Hodgson, while avoiding
the town of Le Palais proper, began breaking ground on its north-

---

[30] Beatson, op. cit., II, 461; Waddington, op. cit., V, 49.
[31] Beatson, op. cit., III, 331–2.

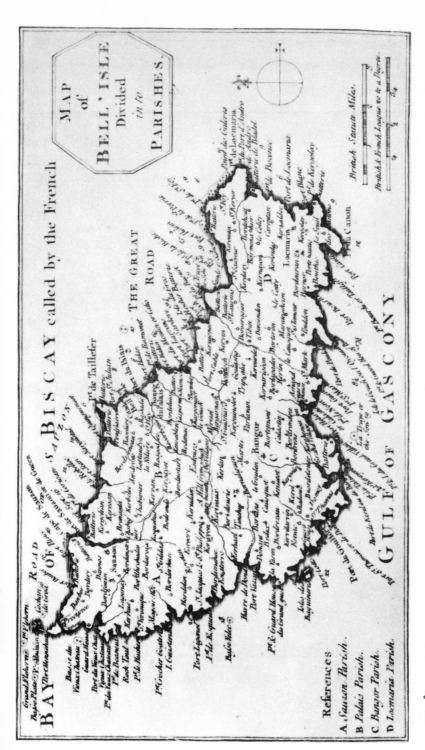

(From the *Gentleman's Magazine*, 1761)

Belle-Île-en-Mer.

"Plan du Siège de Belle-Isle."   (From Richard Waddington: *La Guerre de Sept An*

ern outskirts for the establishment of parallels and five batteries that could command two thirds of the buildings within it.[32] To frustrate this work, the following night a desperate sortie was made from the citadel against an entrenchment established by the left wing of the British army, the defenders of which were thrown into confusion and suffered heavy losses. But the French were unable to capitalize on their temporary success and soon retreated behind their ramparts when faced by a body of British marines that was rushed up to support the hard-pressed grenadiers of the 30th Regiment.[33]

From this time until the 12th of May there is little to record beyond the more or less constant bombardment of the fortress in aid of the British engineers who were engaged in constructing a new parallel. As it was necessary, in order to complete it, to dislodge the enemy from one of their redoubts situated under the guns of the fortress and close to a neck of the sea, Hodgson ordered a heavy concentration of artillery fire against it. This was continued throughout the night. The following morning the entrenchment was assaulted with such vigour that the fatigued enemy, unable to escape, was obliged to surrender. In the panic that now ensued within the French lines, two more redoubts close to the first were carried, the defenders fleeing to the security of the citadel. Nor was this all. For the remaining three redoubts, located near the western approaches of the fortress, were carried that same day with little loss of life by the 69th regiment. With Hodgson's occupation of the town, which now took place, Sainte-Croix was securely locked within the fort,[34] for every avenue for securing aid for escape was cut off by land and sea. The French Governor nevertheless continued a vigorous defence of the doomed place.

On the 16th the British batteries at last were prepared for action, and forty mortars, ten great howitzers, and ten thirty-two-pounders, supported by other field pieces, opened fire and then played incessantly upon the walls, the enclosures, and the inner structure. On the 20th one of the shells ignited a powder magazine located in a casemate, and the explosion that followed seriously impaired the wall; by the 23rd a breach appeared in it "sufficient large," according to an English officer, "for a wagon to pass through"; then other

---

[32] Griffith Williams to Lord Fitzmaurice, May 3, 1761, Shelburne Papers, 37: 175.

[33] Entick, op. cit., V, 124–6.

[34] Sir T. S. Williams to Fitzmaurice, May 16, 1761, Shelburne Papers, 37: 177.

breaches became evident as the result of the ceaseless battering of the heavy guns. Further, by June 4 British sappers had driven a tunnel almost up to the French escarp, and the sounds of their activities could be plainly heard by the defenders.[35]

Clearly, among the leaders of the besieged a decision was imperative whether it were possible or desirable to attempt to hold the place any longer in view of the dire consequences that might follow a successful British storming of it — something likely to occur almost any day. At a council of war that Sainte-Croix called on the 6th, the military engineer Dubouchet laid bare the real situation and the uselessness of further resistance. After more discussion it was unanimously agreed to treat for terms, which were thereupon drawn up. The valiant Governor, however, decided to resist still another day, and great efforts were put forth to repair in a measure the breaches. But the fire of the British, now concentrated upon the bastion of the government house, which was filled with wounded, was so shattering that at nine o'clock the morning of the following day he ordered the drummers to beat the chamade and a white flag to be raised over the ramparts.[36]

The terms granted to the gallant defenders of Le Palais were generous. The garrison was permitted to enjoy the full honours of war — in marching under arms with their baggage through the breach with drums beating and colours flying. It was further agreed that vessels should be furnished to carry the soldiers to the nearest ports of France by the shortest way; nor was any restriction placed upon their further military service in the course of the war, so as to save them from the financial embarrassment of being reduced to half-pay.[37]

With the execution of these terms Belle-Île-en-Mer became the flaunting symbol of British power in the Bay of Biscay and was destined so to remain until its return to France in the treaty of peace of 1763. Its conquest, as was true of other British amphibious military operations in the course of the Great War for the Empire, came as the result of the skilful and harmonious co-ordination of the ef-

[35] Major Charles Veaitch to the Earl of Shelburne, June 4, 1761, Shelburne Papers, 37: 182; Waddington, op. cit., V, 50–4; Entick, op. cit., V, 126–8.

[36] Sir T. S. Wilson to Fitzmaurice, June 7, 1761, Shelburne Papers, 37: 183; Waddington, op. cit., V, 53–4.

[37] For the terms of surrender see Beatson, op. cit., III, 332–5; Entick, op. cit., V, 128–32.

forts of the army and navy.[38] In this connection it should moreover be pointed out that Pitt took good care that the operations attendant upon it would not be disturbed by any interference from the French fleet at Brest. To that end he saw that thirteen ships of the line — some of them, such as the *Namur* and the *Union,* among the most powerful in the navy — placed under the command of Commodore Buckle, should constantly patrol the waters in front of that port.[39]

Thus step by step there was taking place in the course of the war the destruction of the French overseas empire and the strangulation not only of French sea-borne commerce but of naval power as well. While desperately longing for peace, the enemy, nevertheless, continued to resist. Pitt therefore determined to take the next step to reduce the French King to impotence outside of the land mass of Europe. There still remained in the hands of the latter the province of Louisiana and also St. Domingue and Martinique in the West Indies, as well as the so-called Neutral Islands: Dominica, St. Vincent, St. Lucia, Tobago, and, in addition, Grenada.

Although Martinique had been singled out by the minister for conquest in 1759 — as we have noted in an earlier chapter — Guadeloupe instead had been captured. Pitt still continued to regard the reduction of Martinique, the centre of French privateering activities in the Lesser Antilles, as a matter of major importance, especially after the collapse of French power in Canada. At the same time he was aware of the fact that French Mobile Bay and the Mississippi had long been a most important military objective from the point of view of the government of the province of South Carolina, which had shown comparatively little active interest in the campaigns against the French to the northward, though deeply concerned with the Cherokee war, which will be considered in the next volume of this series. Writing on December 17, 1760 to the commander-in-chief of His Majesty's forces in North America, Major General Jeffrey

---

[38] Writing on June 4, 1761, to Fitzmaurice, who had now become the Earl of Shelburne, Adjutant General Sir Thomas Spencer Wilson, serving under Hodgson, declared that it was "impossible for greater harmony to have subsisted" between the two branches of the service (Shelburne Papers, 37: 181).

[39] Beatson, *op. cit.,* III, 338.

Amherst, the minister notified him that he had in the name of the
King communicated with the governors of North America, calling
upon them to raise troops for the year 1762, so that the regular
forces in North America might during the next campaign be free
to be employed "either against Mobile and Mississippi, or Martinico,
and the other French Islands in the West Indies." [40] By the beginning of the new year the decision of the Cabinet Council had been
given in favour of a descent upon Martinique, particularly in view
of the difficulties and hazards involved in any movement of a large
armada into the Gulf of Mexico.

It may be pointed out in this connection that, at the time of the
British attempt to conquer Martinique in 1759, there was so much
dissatisfaction on the part of the inhabitants, and doubtless of the
Minister of the Marine, with the conduct of the Governor General,
the Chevalier de Beauharnois, and the Intendant, M. Givri, that
they were replaced after this event by M. de la Touche and M. de
la Rivière respectively. Plans were also laid by the King's advisers
to strengthen very materially the number of regular troops stationed
there. It was determined in 1760 to send from Rochefort some nine
hundred, convoyed by three ships of the line and three frigates.
But the British blockade of Rochefort was so very close that the
ships had to be laid up. In fact, it was not until early in January
1761 that the new Governor General was able to arrive in the *Tigre*,
which slipped out of the Charente in December of the preceding
year. Nevertheless, about two hundred and fifty grenadiers reached
Martinique from France in August 1760, and in 1761 five hundred
more arrived. As the strength of the militia was placed at twenty
thousand men, it seemed to de la Touche that with this force — in
addition to the reinforcements, together with a new supply of artillery and munitions that were brought to the island — he would be
able to make an effective defence against any force that the enemy
might bring against it, provided that food requirements could be
met.

In fact, to anticipate the need of ample provisions for the troops
and the inhabitants, in case of an attack, large purchases were made
by the Intendant, not only from neutral powers, but even from the
enemy — according to the author of a very long and circumstantial
mémoire prepared with great care and a good deal of objectivity

40 *Correspondence of William Pitt* . . . (ed. G. S. Kimball, New York, 1906), II,
370–3.

and addressed to the Minister of Marine.[41] The same writer, while praising thus far the insular administration, at the same time made clear that de la Touche, a navy man, never really understood the problem of land defence and was also too easy-going and placed too much confidence in certain subordinates who utterly failed to measure up to their great responsibilities. Moreover, instead of embodying the numerous militia early in 1761 into eight battalions and introducing military exercises and discipline among them, as required and expected, he did not bother to assemble them until the 20th of October of that year, and that was the only day that they were ever brought together before the arrival of the British early the following year — and even then only a part of the people owing military service responded, as was equally true when the invasion actually took place. Nor did his Inspector of Artillery, M. de Rochemore, show wisdom and competence in placing his artillery so close to the shore-line at points to be defended that the guns could easily be silenced by the broadsides of the enemy ships and, when captured, turned against the defenders. Thus, from the point of view of the author of the *mémoire* in question, the island, potentially capable of powerful resistance, was destined to fall a victim to the optimism of de la Touche and the incompetence of the men in whom he placed his chief trust.

In turning again to the British project for the conquest of Martinique, it should be stated that it became clear to Pitt and his advisers very early in 1761 that the sailing of the proposed expedition for this purpose must be delayed until the end of the hurricane season — that is, until the end of September. In order to utilize the intervening period so as to secure additional advantages at the expense of the French, however, Pitt was given leave by the King to order Amherst to send without delay two thousand of his men to Guadeloupe, from which island an attempt would be made to take possession of Dominica, provided they could arrive there early in May, before the beginning of the period of storms. As to the plans for the main objective, Martinique, the commander-in-chief was instructed to begin preparations so as to be ready to send from North America, under an officer of his own choosing, between six and

---

41 *Mémoire politique sur l'admininstration du gouvernement de la Martinique, avec réflexions militaire* [sic] *sur sa prise par les Anglois* . . . , Brit. Mus., Add. Mss. 24982, ff. 1–26. For the dispatches sent by the secret intelligence respecting food shortages on the island, see *ibid.*, 32901, ff. 80–1.

eight thousand men and an artillery train whenever the transports for carrying them to their destination should arrive in New York at the end of summer.[42]

Amherst, on the receipt of Pitt's letter, set vigorously to work to prepare for the immediate dispatch of the contingent of soldiers to be used against Dominica. Those selected were all seasoned veterans and were placed under the command of the energetic Andrew Lord Rollo,[43] who in 1758 had overrun Isle St. Jean and in 1760 had brought to submission several French villages on the upper St. Lawrence. On May 3, after being greatly delayed by adverse winds, the expedition set sail from Sandy Hook for Guadeloupe. Unhappily, it ran into a heavy storm that dispersed the vessels. Nevertheless, with the arrival of some of the transports at the island at the beginning of June it was possible for Rollo to set sail for Dominica on the 4th with about seven hundred men in four vessels convoyed by an equal number of warships commanded by Commodore Sir James Douglas. On the 6th the fleet was within a league of Roseau, the principal town on the island.

Dominica, then one of the so-called Neutral Islands, lies only some twenty-nine miles south of Guadeloupe. Less than thirty miles in length and some sixteen in breadth, and of volcanic origin, it presents from the sea the appearance of a confused mass of mountains. But the valleys interspersed among them were and still are very fertile. Of all the islands of the Lesser Antilles, it alone at the period under consideration possessed a considerable number of native Caribs, who had been extirpated from most of the others. Although in 1730 it had been agreed by the governments of Great Britain and France that Dominica, together with St. Vincent and St. Lucia, should not be colonized by either nation and should be considered neutral in their quarrels, settlers from Martinique and Guadeloupe began establishing themselves there. By 1753 it was reported that they numbered some four thousand, who, after driving the Caribs into a narrow corner of the island, had established sugar plantations

---

[42] Pitt to Amherst, January 7, 1761, *Pitt Correspondence*, II, 384–7; see also Pitt to Governor Dalrymple of Guadeloupe, February 14, 1761, *ibid.*, II, 389–90. In a letter dated March 24 Pitt authorized Amherst to contract for six or eight thousand tons of transport in America so that no delay on that score should arise (*ibid.*, II, 407–8).

[43] The regiments selected were Vaughan's, which had served at Fort Pitt, Whitmore's, which had campaigned on Cap Breton Island in 1758 and then on the mainland, and six hundred of Montgomery's Highlanders (Amherst to Pitt, February 27, 1761, *ibid.*, II, 403–6).

and had organized a militia and a regular form of government.[44] It is at least true that in 1761 some two thousand Frenchmen were still living on the island and even cultivating their plantations there, which, with the aid of about six thousand Negro slaves, were producing three million pounds of coffee and vast quantities of cocoa and cotton.[45]

Immediately upon appearing before Roseau, Rollo sent a summons to the inhabitants of the town to surrender without resistance. Although they were not supported by any French regular troops, this demand was refused. The British commander therefore ordered a landing. Thanks to the efficient work of Douglas, the disembarkation was carried out in perfect order, and soon afterward the town was occupied without much interference. But above it were the entrenchments where the French local militia was concentrated and from which a continuous fire was directed against the invaders. Despite the fact that it was very late in the day, Rollo thought it best to storm the enemy's camp without delay. This was done by his grenadiers with such rapidity that even the French commandant, M. de Longpré, and his second in command, M. de la Couche, as well as others, were taken prisoner. As a result, all opposition to the British was soon at an end not only at Roseau but in other parts of the island. The French inhabitants of it instead now flocked to Rollo's headquarters most obediently to deliver their arms and to take the prescribed oath as required of those of Guadeloupe.[46] Soon five hundred had made their submission and were granted full protection and freedom of commerce with England; [47] others continued to submit.

To lead the expedition against Martinique, Amherst had appointed Major General Robert Monckton, a soldier who had campaigned in Nova Scotia and on Cape Breton Island and had fought with Wolfe on the Heights of Abraham, where he had been wounded; he was now recovered and was acting under the King's commission as Governor of the Province of New York.[48] In these

---

[44] Testimony of Captain Pye contained in the letter of the Earl of Holderness to Lord Albemarle, August 24, 1753, *British Diplomatic Instructions, 1689–1789*, VII, France, Part IV, 1754–89 (Camden series, third series, Vol. XLIX), p. 39.

[45] *Acts of the Privy Council, Colonial, 1745–1766*, p. 587; Rollo to Pitt, July 10, 1761, *Pitt Correspondence*, II, 447–9.

[46] Rollo to Pitt, June 8, 1761, *ibid.*, II, 440–3.

[47] *Ibid.*, II, 444.

[48] Amherst to Pitt, February 27, 1761, *ibid.*, II, 403–6.

services he had shown a high order of capacity and, as events proved, his selection for the chief command of the new expedition was fortunate. The chief error involved in the campaign of 1759 to reduce the island was that the total force sent was considered by its leaders to be inadequate to accomplish the task in hand. This error was not repeated. Pitt, in fact, soon revised upward the estimates of the numbers of soldiers needed for this purpose — placed at first at six thousand to be drawn from the army in North America — and gave Amherst the utmost freedom to employ as many of his New World forces as he could safely spare.[49] As a result, he decided to contribute — in addition to the two thousand men sent under Lord Rollo in the spring — seven thousand foot soldiers, which, with the forces already stationed in the West Indies and sent from the British Isles and some twenty-six hundred drawn from Belle-Île-en-Mer that were no longer needed, brought Monckton's total strength to almost fourteen thousand land troops.[50] But in launching the expedition there were unavoidable delays as the result of the shattered condition of many of the transports sent from England. It therefore did not leave New York until November 19.[51]

To support Monckton, Rear Admiral George Brydges Rodney was given command of the fleet to operate against Martinique. This was another excellent choice. Rodney as captain of the *Eagle* had won laurels under Hawke in the naval victory off Ushant in 1747; ten years later he had participated in the Rochefort expedition, and the year following had been under Boscawen in that against Louisbourg; in 1759, now rear admiral, he had, as has already been noted, led a naval force against Le Havre and had bombarded it for two days, and the next year had again cruised along the northern French coast with a squadron engaged in destroying flat-bottomed boats intended for the invasion of England. Sailing from England early in October, Rodney reached Barbados late in November, and with the arrival there on December 24 of the American squadron escorting the transports with Monckton's regiments, he now had at his disposal a very powerful naval force consisting of eighteen ships of the

[49] Pitt to Amherst, July 17, 1761, *ibid.*, II, 452–4.

[50] Beatson, *op. cit.*, III, 363–4.

[51] Amherst to Pitt, November 27, 1761, *Pitt Correspondence*, II, 485–7. On November 10 the Spanish Ambassador in London, Fuentes, wrote to Grimaldi, Spanish Ambassador in Paris, giving details of the British plan for invading Martinique. According to him, Amherst was to remain in America so as to be ready to attack Florida should war take place between Great Britain and Spain (B.M., Add. Mss. 32930, ff. 394–5).

line, fourteen frigates, nine sloops and bomb-ketches, as well as other supporting vessels, with a total personnel of some eleven thousand men.[52] On January 5 the great armada of one hundred and seventy-three vessels left Carlisle Bay and two days later joined the squadron under Sir James Douglas which had been sent ahead of it to blockade the port of Fort Royal and silence the outlying batteries supporting it.[53]

Monckton at first sought to approach the French fort and naval base by landing a force at St. Anne's Bay, just south of that of Fort Royal. From St. Anne's chapel on its eastern shore a road wound around the bay to the main objective. After a landing, however, it was found to be quite impracticable to attempt to move the heavy equipment by that very circuitous route. The plan next considered was to land on the western shore of this bay near the village of St. Lucy and then, by marching across the peninsula, to arrive on the eastern shore of Fort Royal Bay near heavily fortified Pigeon Island. With the capture of the latter it was felt that the warships could then move into the bay sufficiently close to the French citadel to bombard it effectively. This plan was also discarded because of the difficult nature of the terrain to be traversed. Monckton thereupon decided to land troops directly on the eastern shore of Fort Royal Bay so that they would then be in a position to attack Pigeon Island. He placed two brigades at the disposition of two very experienced leaders who had campaigned in the American wilderness: Brigadier General William Haviland and Brigadier Grant, and also gave them a corps of light-armed troops commanded by Lieutenant Colonel Scott, who had fought under Amherst with his American rangers at Louisbourg. But when this force had reached a point opposite Pigeon Island and within range of the fire of its batteries, Haviland found the roads impassable for cannon. In fact, the hills approaching the shore at that point were so steep that it required seventy-five men to move a twelve-pounder gun or a mortar.[54]

With the failure of the third plan, the general, after carefully examining the northern shore of Fort Royal Bay and after having also conferred with Rodney, at length determined to adopt the approach

---

[52] Egremont to Amherst, December 12, 1761, Amherst Papers, Vol. 40, Canadian Archives transcripts; Beatson, op. cit., III, 364–5.

[53] Barbados advices, Pennsylvania Gazette, March 11, 1762.

[54] "Journal of the Siege of Martinique," Ms., New York Public Library; "Account of the Proceedings at Martinico" from January 6 to January 18, Pennsylvania Gazette, March 18, 1762.

that Hopson had used in 1759 — to land at Cas des Navières and then move eastward some four miles against the enemy fortress and town. The most careful preparations to this end were made. Early on the morning of January 16 the ships ranged along the shore began a heavy cannonading, which continued until about three o'clock in the afternoon, when all the batteries of the enemy had been silenced. Thereupon, detachments ready in their flatboats pushed off from the fleet and two hours later reached the beach without the least opposition. By the 18th all of the troops were landed, among these one hundred and fifty Carolina Indians — brought from South Carolina by Colonel Grant — who immediately plunged into the woods.[55] But the French were strongly entrenched on an elevation east of this point, at Morne Tartenson (d'Artanson), and it seemed necessary to bring heavy field guns and howitzers from the ships to dislodge them. This was done.

On the 24th one battery was made ready to go into action; another battery still closer to the French position was completed on the 25th; and the following morning at two o'clock their guns opened up briskly. At four thirty, supported by this fire, British grenadiers under Grant, in the first glimmer of daylight, pressed directly up the heights. On the right a brigade under Rufane moved eastward along the coast to attack the defences there; while on the left Scott with his light-armed troops began a movement to encircle Morne Tartenson. Driven from post to post by the impetuosity of the grenadiers, the enemy's stubborn resistance was finally broken when Scott, about eight o'clock in the morning, succeeded in striking the French flank. Retreating in great confusion, the defenders now concentrated on fortified Morne Garnier, a still greater elevation nearer to Fort Royal and separated from Tartenson by a deep ravine covered with brush.[56]

---

[55] *Ibid.* A letter that the Governor General of the French Lesser Antilles, M. Le Vassor de la Touche, is said to have written on January 18 to the Minister at home is given in translation in the *Pennsylvania Gazette* of July 8, 1762. In it he shows a confidence in his ability, with his four thousand soldiers and three thousand mariners from the privateers in arms, to defend the island. "Let the Attack be ever so severe, both by Land and Sea," he wrote, "Fort Royal will render their deepest Projects abortive. . . . The Gentlemen Inhabitants are resolved to die or save their Isle, having no Inclination to trust to the Clemency of Ravagers to divide their Plantations. . . . In a short Time I hope to return you a large Freight of Prisoners . . . and a particular Detail of our Successes."

[56] Monckton to Egremont, February 9, 1762, *ibid.*, June 10, 1762; the *Mémoire politique sur l'administration du gouvernement de la Martinique, avec réflexions militaire*

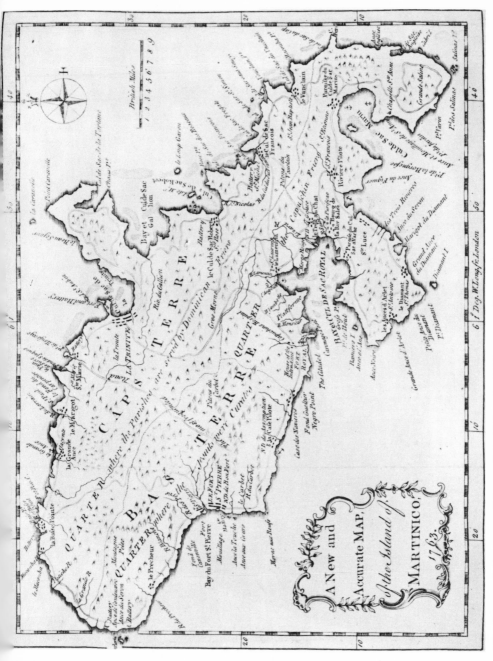

"A New and Accurate Map, of the Island of Martinico."

(From John Entick: *History of the Late War*)

With Morne Tartenson, providing ten well-constructed redoubts furnished with cannon, now in British hands, preparations were made to construct batteries that could play upon the town and citadel of Fort Royal, some fifteen hundred yards to the southeast. But while this work was progressing, the French on Morne Garnier continued by the use of their heavy guns so to harass the engineers as to make the task exceedingly difficult. Monckton therefore determined to storm this stronghold, whatever it might cost. By a fortunate tactical blunder on the part of the enemy, this did not become necessary. For on the afternoon of the 27th the greater part of the French force left this eminence and, in descending it, attacked the British left wing, composed of Brigadier Haviland's brigade, which was busy erecting a battery to fire upon their entrenchments. Instead of routing it, they were received with so deadly a fire that they were impelled to retreat up the sides of the ravine to the security of their outworks. But in doing so they found Haviland's regulars hot on their heels, and before they could recover from this flight and form, their pursuers had seized their outlying entrenchments and were soon supported by other British contingents. Thus by nightfall Morne Garnier, as well as Morne Tartenson, was in the hands of the invader.[57]

The defeat of January 27 quite broke the spirit of the French on Martinique. The militiamen, fleeing from Morne Garnier, deserted to their habitations about the island, leaving the regulars to crowd into the citadel. It is true that the latter continued to resist and that it was necessary for Monckton to complete batteries on both of the newly captured elevations that commanded Fort Royal and to put them into action; also to begin the construction of batteries on Morne Capuchin, only some four hundred yards from the fort, as well as at the quarry (*Carrière*) near by. Yet by the end of January, from reports brought by deserters, it was clear that the common soldiers — as the result of the destructive fire directed against them to which they could not effectively reply — were anxious to surrender. It was therefore not a matter of great surprise at British head-

---

[sic] *sur sa prise par les Anglois* . . . (n.d., Brit. Mus., Add. Mss. 24982, ff. 16–22, Library of Congress transcripts) is a very detailed and critical account by a Frenchman in Martinique of the campaign; it was addressed to the Minister of the Marine.

⁵⁷ *Ibid.* See also a letter from a gentleman in Martinique to a friend in Antigua, January 29, *Pennsylvania Gazette*, April 1, 1762; a letter from an officer in Martinique, February 13, *ibid.*, May 6, 1762; and "Journal of the Siege of Martinique," Ms. N.Y. Public Library.

quarters that on the evening of February 3 the French leaders, also having lost all hope, ordered the beating of the chamade and that the following day they signed articles of surrender of the garrison of some eight hundred men.[58]

The terms for the capitulation of Fort Royal gave to the French regular troops defending it the honours of war, just as was granted to the defenders of Le Palais on Belle-Île-en-Mer. In each case it was provided that the garrison should be transported to France at the expense of His Britannic Majesty. But with respect to the militia and so-called "free-booters," who still remained under arms on Martinique, they were to be considered prisoners of war until the fate of the island had been determined.[59] This was not permitted to remain long in doubt.

It should be pointed out that the Governor General of the French Leeward Islands, Le Vassor de la Touche, had been in charge of military operations about Fort Royal until the capture of Morne Garnier. When most of the troops had retreated to the fort, he thereupon with the remainder of them withdrew from the scene of disaster to two distant eminences called Lamentive and Le Gros Morne. Then when news came that St. Pierre was to be attacked, he made a forced march to that place. Reaching the metropolis of the island, he was determined to continue to resist the invaders. But he was, unhappily, confronted with the same type of determined opposition to his proposal by merchants and planters that the Governor of Guadeloupe finally had had to face on the part of the inhabitants of that island who did not choose to lose everything in a bitter fight to the end. Indeed, despite his wishes, four days after the surrender of Fort Royal deputations from nine districts of the island waited upon Monckton and Rodney with articles of capitulation which the leaders of the people had drawn up.[60] These, with some modification, were accepted. In character they may be compared to the very generous terms previously given to the inhabitants of

[58] Mémoire . . . sur . . . la Martinique . . . , B.M., Add. Mss. 24982, ff. 22–6; Monckton to Egremont, February 9, 1762, Pennsylvania Gazette, June 10, 1762; Ensign Miller's "Memoirs," Amherst Papers, Packet 54, Canadian Archives transcripts; "Journal of the Siege of Martinique," Ms., N.Y. Public Library; Letter from the fleet at Martinique, February 8, Pennsylvania Gazette, April 1, 1762.

[59] For the terms of surrender see Beatson, op. cit., III, 368–70; Pennsylvania Gazette, April 22, 1762.

[60] Monckton to Egremont, February 9, 1762, ibid., June 10, 1762.

Guadeloupe.[61] But St. Pierre, under the control of de la Touche, still held out. Monckton, who had hitherto been busy making repairs at Fort Royal, was now about to launch an amphibious attack upon it when on the 12th two deputies arrived with elaborate terms for a capitulation of the entire island drawn up by the Governor General as the result of the insistent demands of the inhabitants of St. Pierre.[62] Again, with only slight modifications these were accepted, and as a result the opulent metropolis of the island was peacefully occupied by British forces on the 16th, and all resistance on Martinique disappeared.[63]

The conquest of Martinique came not only by reason of the great preponderance of military power enjoyed by the British and the martial spirit of soldiers, marines, and sailors, but also, and perhaps chiefly, was owing to the quality of leadership that Monckton, working in harmonious co-operation with Rodney,[64] brought to the task. In the words of one of his officers: "Never was an Army more happy under the Command of any General than we are under the worthy Mr. Monckton . . . the whole Army would sacrifise their Lives for him; and a General so beloved will ever have Success." [65] The significance of this achievement is well stated by an intelligent participant in the campaign: "Thus a conquest was made of the capital of the French Islands in these seas; it was striking at the root of their strength in that quarter and almost totally annihilated their West India trade." [66]

Since Martinique had served as a lifeline, as it were, for the remaining islands in the Lesser Antilles where the French had colo-

---

[61] For these terms see Beatson, op. cit., III, 370–3. It is clear that the proffered terms of surrender made by the inhabitants of Martinique in 1762 were copied after the terms prepared by those of Guadeloupe in 1759. For the latter see ibid., III, 217–20.

[62] See also ibid., III, 373–9 for de la Touche's terms and those finally granted.

[63] Monckton to Egremont, February 27, and Rodney to Cleveland, February 28, 1762, London Gazette, April 2, 1762.

[64] Rodney to the Admiralty, February 10, 1762, Pennsylvania Gazette, June 10, 1762.

[65] Letter written by an "Officer in Martinique," February 13, 1762, ibid., May 6, 1762. Another, in a letter written from St. Pierre to his correspondent in Philadelphia dated February 28, said: "It is needless for me to say any Thing in Regard of General Monckton's Conduct and Character . . . I shall only observe, that so fit a person could scarcely have been found for this Service, his remarkable Disinterestedness obliging the conquered Inhabitants to love him and revere him as much in Peace, as his Courage and Steadiness made them fear him in War" (ibid.).

[66] Ensign Miller's "Memoir," op. cit.

nized, its capture brought with it their fall in quick succession. St. Lucia, one of the so-called Neutral Islands, lying just to the south of Martinique, upon the appearance of a squadron commanded by Captain Hervey in its principal port, the Carénage or Castries, capitulated on February 26; [67] Grenada, a very fruitful, well-populated small island, the most southern of the Windwards, followed suit on March 5 without the firing of a shot upon the arrival of Commodore Swanton convoying a land force commanded by Brigadier Walsh; [68] and, finally, St. Vincent, another of the Neutral Islands, also soon surrendered to Walsh. By the 12th, deputies from these three islands had repaired to Monckton's headquarters on Martinique and procured for the inhabitants of them the same terms recently granted to those of Martinique.[69] In fact, the lot of the conquered French in the Lesser Antilles was by no means unhappy. They were no longer under the fear of devastation and were privileged, upon taking the required oath of submission, to share all the benefits of commercial intercourse enjoyed by the people of the British West Indies, and without any interference with their religious or social practices. The words of one writing from Martinique on May 11 may here be quoted as indicative of their new situation:

> "The Inhabitants here seem now quite satisfied with their Condition; and indeed they have Reason, for they are indulged in every Thing they desire, and I believe were never so happy before." [70]

[67] Rodney to Cleveland, March 1, 1762, London Gazette, April 2, 1762. It should be noted that on October 9, 1761 Egremont in his letter to Monckton directed him to fall upon and conquer St. Lucia, as well as St. Vincent, Tobago, "the Grenades," and any other French islands in those parts, "in case . . . the enterprise against Martinique . . . should not have the expected success" (P.R.O., C.O. 5:215).

[68] Monckton to Egremont, March 18, and Walsh to Monckton, March 6, 1762, London Gazette, May 1, 1762.

[69] Rodney to Cleveland, March 24, 1762, ibid.; see also the Pennsylvania Gazette, April 22, 1762.

[70] Ibid., June 3, 1762. That the above comment was not far from the truth is evidenced by the fact that the merchants of St. Pierre, as a testimony of the generous treatment that they had received at the hands of General Monckton and of their regard for him, subscribed before his departure for New York "for an elegant service of Plate" to present to him (ibid., June 17, 1762).

CHAPTER IX

Failure of Peace Negotiations and the Fall of Pitt

THE ACCESSION of George III to the throne — an event already considered in an earlier chapter of this volume — was destined to shake the foundations of the vast power exercised by William Pitt since 1757. Yet there were few outward signs that this was to be the case. Referring to the beginning of the new reign Horace Walpole wrote:

> "The administration was firm, in good harmony with one another, and headed by the most successful genius that ever presided over our councils. Conquest had crowned our arms with wonderful circumstances of glory and fortune; and the young King seemed to have the option of extending our victories and acquisitions, or of giving peace to the world, by finding himself in a situation so favourable, that neither his ambition nor moderation could have been equitably reprehended." [1]

It may further be stated that at this juncture no responsible person in public life sought to deprive the Great Commoner of the chief responsibility of conducting the war with France to a successful termination. Nevertheless, the nation now had a new King, who had his own conception of the part he was called upon to play as the occupant of the throne; the young monarch also had his own, though circumscribed, circle of friends who were bound to seek some public recognition. Further, regarding the state of hostilities, there were

---

[1] *Memoirs of the Reign of King George the Third* (ed. Sir Denis Le Marchant, Philadelphia, 1845), I, 15.

many signs that public opinion was becoming increasingly hostile to a continued intertwining of the Anglo-French war with "the German war," as the latter was then called. Finally, it was not hard to discern that divisions in the ministry not only over the kind of peace that must ultimately be made with France but over any extension of hostilities, so as to include, for example, Spain as an active enemy, were apt to occur and thus compel the youthful George to take sides. Thus there were many complex facets to the problem that now confronted Pitt on seeking to retain his position.

The great minister might well with honour have sought retirement from the press of public affairs. Although but fifty-two years of age, physical infirmities had crowded upon him: he was subject to periods of extreme illness, he could not walk, but rather hobbled with his ankles greatly swollen with the gout and "his legs pretty small and almost all the way of a bigness" — to quote a contemporary.[2] What is more, his physical incapacities were to affect his mental health. But his spirit still brightly burned — at times at white heat — and, if the brashness of youth had disappeared, he still had all the overweening confidence, and perhaps arrogance, of the mature man with a fixed conviction that only he could perform the task he had in hand. With much justice he attributed his dominant position in government to the call of the nation and its rallying about him during his years in office. Moreover, he had been permitted to serve it without much royal interference, once he had won the confidence of George II. Thus, while openly disclaiming the title of prime minister, he had, despite the pretensions of the Duke of Newcastle, his colleague, enjoyed all the substance of the power that such a position conferred. Could he continue to do so?

Although still in his twenty-third year, George III, despite his youth and total inexperience in the work of government, had already come to the conviction that his duty to the nation called on him to take steps that would ultimately free it from the control of a comparatively small group of men, who still, under the party label of Whig, continued, as in the days of his great-grandfather and grandfather, to divide among themselves the offices of state and the emoluments attached to them. He would be, in other words, a truly national king and not the so-called "Whigs'" king. After all, he was an Englishman by right of birth; as such he felt that he could de-

---

[2] Jared Ingersoll to William Samuel Johnson, December 22, 1759, Johnson Papers, Connecticut Historical Society.

pend on the loyalty of all Englishmen to a degree not possible for his immediate German-born predecessors of the Hanoverian line. The old Tory Party in the days of George I had had as a basis for supporting the Stuart line the fact that it acknowledged the claims of one born among them rather than those of a foreigner. Now the situation was reversed. Indeed, the support of the foreign-born Stuarts on any computable scale was nonexistent in England in 1760. For the descendants of the Old Tories vied with those of the Old Whigs in paying homage to him as their rightful King and in their willingness to sacrifice their lives, if need be, to protect his person and the kingdom over which he had been called upon to reign. Why, therefore, should these devoted people have the penalties of the sins of their fathers visited upon them? If not, who but the King, pray tell, was in a position under the circumstances to make them feel that what had gone before, in which they had had no part, was now covered with the cloak of oblivion? Who but the King could implement this ideal of true national unity by recognizing, and using for national ends, talent wherever it might be found among his loyal people?

Again, George was the King not only of England and Wales but of Scotland as well — he was a British King. No people had shown a greater readiness to take up arms to support the war against France than had the Scots, once they were given the chance by Pitt. Further, no regiments had displayed greater courage in battle than those recruited from beyond the English northern border. What about the proper recognition of this patriotic, martial nation, as well as that of English families which had been tainted with the name of Tory? The Union of 1707 had brought into existence the Parliament of Great Britain; but the chief government services of the United Kingdom remained in the hands of Englishmen. Of the fifty chief ministerial, administrative, and judicial posts of this Kingdom, what one — outside of the office of Chief Justice of the Court of King's Bench, filled by the eminent jurist Baron Mansfield, called "a mild Tory" — was in the hands of a Scot at the beginning of the new reign? Was this due to Scottish incapacity or unworthiness to fill high office, or to English conceit or selfishness? But, assuming that Scots could be found who were neither incapable nor unworthy of occupying places of responsibility, who but the King could lead the way to break down this monopoly of offices of trust still in the hands of Englishmen who were "Whigs"?

Early in the reign of George III the Earl of Bute, a Lowland Scot, descended from the loyal Archibald Campbell, first Duke of Argyll, and, as has been stressed in an earlier chapter, enjoying to the fullest extent the confidence of the King, sought an English peerage, undoubtedly with the idea that thereby he would be enabled to serve his royal master on the throne as effectively as he had done while the latter was Prince of Wales. But, in the face of Pitt's resistance to this step, it could not be taken.[3] Nevertheless, at the very first meeting of the Privy Council after he was proclaimed, the King named his brother Edward, Duke of York, and also Bute to that body.[4] In other respects the personnel of the ministry, with or without portfolio, remained as it was at the death of George's grandfather, with Pitt and Newcastle entrusted as in the past with the chief responsibility of guiding the government. Although this continued to be the case, inevitably there was speculation as the year 1760 came to a close whether the new King would decide, as it was wittily expressed, to "burn in his chamber . . . Scotch-coal, Newcastle-coal, or Pitt-coal."[5] On March 21 of the new year both Pitt and Newcastle were confirmed to their offices,[6] which seemed to indicate to the public that no great change in administration was contemplated.

Behind the scenes, however, there were developments that portended extensive alterations in government. In organizing his household the King appointed two "Tory" lords, Edward Harley, Earl of Oxford, and Lord Bruce, afterward to become the Earl of Aylesbury, to the Bedchamber, together with others not of that party.[7] William Petty, Lord Fitzmaurice, eldest son of the Earl of Shelburne and soon to succeed to the title, was, as a friend of Bute and Henry Fox, made Equerry much to the disgust of the Whigs.[8] More-

---

[3] George to Bute, November 1760, Letters of George III to Lord Bute, 1756–1766 (ed. R. Sedgwick, London, 1939), pp. 48–50.

[4] Papers of George III (ed. Sir J. Fortescue, London, 1927), I, 18. Walpole (op. cit., I, 17; Letters, ed. Mrs. Paget Toynbee [Oxford, 1904], IV, 442) stated that the two were made members of the Cabinet Council. That the Duke of York ever became a recognized member of this body may be questioned. For a "List of the Cabinet Council, as sumon'd to Attend the Recorder's Reports" in November 1761, a list that may be considered complete, see E. R. Turner, The Cabinet Council of England . . . (Baltimore, 1933), II, 9–10.

[5] Walpole, Letters, V, 8.

[6] Papers of George III, I, 22.

[7] Walpole to Sir Horace Mann, December 6, 1760, Walpole Letters, V, 8. For the use of the terms Whig and Tory under George III see R. Pares, "George III and the Politicians," Royal Hist. Soc. trans. (fifth series), I, 127.

[8] See George III to Bute, November 1760, Letters of George III to Lord Bute, pp.

over, the elderly Duke of Newcastle, who had founded his power under George II in his ability through the use of patronage and by other means to bring into the House of Commons a consistent Whig majority, very soon saw himself cutting a very sorry figure at the royal court and his control over elections so seriously threatened that he was obliged to admit privately that "the Whigs were given up in many parts of England" as the result of active royal intervention.[9] Beyond this, defections now took place in the Whig ranks. The Treasurer of the Navy, George Grenville, who had been previously allied with his brother, Earl Temple, and his brother-in-law, Pitt, deserted to the royal group the following year under such circumstances as to lead Horace Walpole to remark caustically that "Lord Bute was in want of tools; and it was a double prize to acquire them from his rival's shop."[10] As further emphasizing the shift that gradually took place in government, the Duke of Bedford, the leader of the powerful Russell Whig group, was displaced as Lord Lieutenant of Ireland by the Earl of Halifax; the Honourable Henry Bilson Legge, who had refused to support in the Hampshire elections the candidacy of Bute's nominee, Sir Simson Stewart, the Tory, was dismissed as Chancellor of the Exchequer in favour of Viscount Barrington; and Charles Townshend took the latter's place as Secretary at War.[11]

In view of these developments, it is perhaps not surprising that an announcement was made on March 25 that the Earl of Bute had assumed the office of Secretary of State for the Northern Department, replacing in that post Robert D'Arcy, Earl of Holderness. Up to this time Bute had acted simply as the King's most confidential adviser and, as a member of his household, had occupied the post of Groom of the Stole and First Gentleman of the Bedchamber; he had also, as noted, been made a member of the Privy Council. It is clear that he was not a needy fortune-seeker — Lady Bute at this juncture had come into possession of a princely fortune on the death of her father, Wortley Montagu, while the Earl himself by the death on April 15 of his uncle, the third Duke of Argyll, Chief Justiciary, known as the

---

50–2; *Diary of the Late George Bubb Dodington* (ed. H. P. Wyndham, London, 1784), p. 417; Lord Edmond Fitzmaurice, *Life of William, Earl of Shelburne* (London, 1875), I, 96–7.

[9] Richard Rigby to the Duke of Bedford, December 19, 1760, *Correspondence of John, Fourth Duke of Bedford* (ed. Lord John Russell, London, 1843), II, 424–5.

[10] *Memoirs of the Reign of George III*, I, 32.

[11] Walpole's *Memoirs*, I, 34, 37.

uncrowned "King of Scotland," was to become at least the potential heir to the latter's great political influence in that kingdom.[12] On the contrary, as "a man of undoubted honour," to quote the words of the Whig historian Macaulay,[13] his every thought seemed to have centred on the means, at whatever personal sacrifice, to make the reign of his royal master not only easy but memorable in the annals of Great Britain. His willingness to assume public office — when his love of ease could be satisfied and his influence at court was already so powerful — can therefore only be explained, it would appear, by his complacency in acquiescing in George's deep desire to have him actively associated in the work of government, especially that having to do with the re-establishment of a state of peace.[14] Could he have fully anticipated, in other words, the storm of disapproval that would be raised against him in his new character,[15] it is by no means clear that he would have faltered in what he considered to be his duty not only to the King but to the nation — assuming, as we must, that his views on public matters coincided fully with those of George.[16]

It may be said that by the spring of 1761 all contemplated changes in government personnel had been completed and, for the first time since the coming of the Hanoverian line to the throne, a respectable representation of all political groups had been brought into the administration. At the same time, it must be added, those who had failed to secure recognition, and especially individuals who had claimed some inherited right to this by reason of the Whig affiliations of their families, were not easily reconciled and soon became

---

[12] Walpole, *Memoirs of the Reign of George III*, I, 33. The Marquis of Tweeddale succeeded to the office of Chief Justiciary.

Holderness, it is clear, was not highly regarded by either Newcastle or Pitt. The latter on one occasion declared that he "dispis'd Him" and the former had long sought to get rid of him (B.M., Add. Mss. 32899, ff. 5-8, 164-6).

[13] Lord Macaulay, *Critical, Historical and Miscellaneous Essays* (New York, 1860), VI, 20. The above view of Bute is fully endorsed by Albert von Ruville in his *Pitt, Earl of Chatham* (London, 1907), II, 315; see also his *William Pitt and Lord Bute* (Berlin, 1895).

[14] For the arrangements leading up to Bute's appointment as a Secretary of State see George to Bute, March 13, 1761, *Letters of George III to Bute*, p. 52.

[15] Bute, upon becoming a Secretary of State, of course resigned his post as Groom of the Stole.

[16] Walpole, who always kept his ear very close to the ground, indicates that the Duke of Bedford advised summoning Bute to office, as the two saw alike about the question of making peace; he also asserts that both Newcastle and Hardwicke approved of the idea, but with the sinister view to Bute's "destruction" (*Memoirs*, I, 37).

very real in their opposition to the ministry and, particularly, to Bute as Secretary of State. For, with the Duke of Newcastle an aged man and William Pitt very infirm, signs pointed to a new political leadership to mark the new reign. In fact, according to Doddington, both Newcastle and the Duke of Argyll in December had spoken of Bute to the King in flattering terms and had offered to act under him.[17]

Nevertheless, the Pitt-Newcastle ministry, despite the changes that had taken place, did not appear to be immediately threatened with loss of power. Its popularity was, in fact, too great to be in danger at the moment, in view of British victories on land and sea that had brought the nation's military prestige to perhaps the highest point in its history. Yet on certain issues, as was suggested earlier in this chapter, there were divisions of opinion within the Cabinet Council itself that might bring about its downfall. None of these was more pronounced than the question of further participation in the German Seven Years' War. To Bute, the ministry, far from being united on this point, "neither were nor could be." At the same time he thought this body

> "had some glimpse of getting off our system, by setting up that of abandoning Hanover, and of applying the money to distress France into a peace; that they would by their popularity, force this measure upon the King, who must confessedly lose a good deal of his own." [18]

To Doddington, the future Lord Melcombe, not only was this the right course to pursue, but he strongly recommended to the new Secretary of State, as the only sound measure for getting out of the German war, that the King in his speech to the new Parliament should declare

> "that his Majesty found himself involved in this war, to which he had in no way contributed . . . that he was convinced that the present method of defending Hanover would ruin this country, without defending that; and he therefore would no longer expose his regal dominions to such hardships, for fruitless attempts to protect his electoral; but would leave them in the hands of his enemies, and apply the expense to force them to a reasonable peace, by means more probable and proper to attain that end." [19]

---

[17] Dodington, op. cit., p. 420.
[18] Ibid., pp. 422, 424.
[19] Ibid., pp. 422-3.

Bute, however, could not but realize that such a course would be opposed by the nation's idol, Pitt — accepting the fact that Newcastle was so anxious for the re-establishment of peace that he "would go to any lengths to attain it." For Pitt, as has been noted earlier in this volume, had too deeply committed himself to the support of Frederick of Prussia as well as to the defence of Hanover to be able to withdraw from his Continental commitment without loss of honour. He had, moreover, made it abundantly clear to the Earl "that less than the entire direction of the war would not satisfy him." [20] So long as this was the case and so long as the services of the minister were considered to be indispensable, it was impossible to do other than continue to submit to his views respecting the support of the war in Germany. This was done.

But this difference that existed within the Cabinet Council, with the opening of the year 1761, was tied up with the question of the making of peace. It is therefore desirable to summarize developments along this line up to this period.

As early as the spring of 1759, Baron Knyphausen — who was at the beginning of the war the Prussian Ambassador in Paris and who had later been sent to join the Prussian chargé d'affaires in London, Abraham Ludwig Michell — had thought that the dissensions within the British ministry over the question of the termination of the war with France were so serious that on June 8 he and his colleague, doubtless with the privy knowledge of Pitt, had sent a letter to Frederick urging the latter to pray George II to act in concert with him in initiating a peace congress. In this connection he had written:

> "Such a step, which we are assured would be received here with pleasure, would not only prevent precipitous and badly directed overtures of peace but would bar the road to all clandestine negotiations in establishing a formal Congress. . . . All propositions in such an assembly would be maturely weighed and resolved in the [British] King's Council, and the Chevalier Pitt, whose uprightness and zeal for the interests of your Majesty are manifested on so many occasions, would in such a negotiation play a role that the superiority of his talents and the confidence that the nation has placed in him, should necessarily assure him." [21]

---

[20] Sir Gilbert Elliot's "Memorandum," *Bedford Correspondence*, III, xiii.

[21] Knyphausen and Michell to the King of Prussia, Private, June 8, 1759, *Politische Correspondenz Friedrich's des Grossen* (Berlin, 1890), XVIII, 337–9.

Acting upon this suggestion, and in view of the adverse turn of the war in Germany and in order to support the sagging influence of Pitt in England, the King of Prussia had written to George on June 20 that, influenced by considerations dictated by "humanity and the good of mankind" and by a desire to put an end to "an onerous and bloody war," he proposed a joint Anglo-Prussian declaration in favour of opening a congress in order to arrive at an agreement for a peace that would be honourable and useful to all the belligerent powers.[22]

In furtherance of the above plan, a month later a conference had been held in London at which Knyphausen and Michell had outlined to the members of the Cabinet Council the specific steps that should be taken to the end of bringing into existence a peace congress. Although George II had the conviction that the enemy was not ready to make peace without a new campaign, to many who had talked with Newcastle the question had been: can we continue the war?[23] As for Pitt, the possession in British hands of Louisbourg and Guadeloupe, he had held, was the best plenipotentiary that the nation could have in such a congress. Nevertheless, while favouring it, he had sought delays, undoubtedly, so that the results of the St. Lawrence campaign might be received.[24] With Frederick's stunning defeat at Kunersdorf on August 12, the plan of a congress had again been put forward by the Prussian London envoys as a matter of urgency. Pitt, on his part, with the receipt of the news not only of the capture of Fort Niagara and the French destruction of and retreat from Forts Ticonderoga and Crown Point in America but of the annihilation of de la Clue's fleet off the coast of Portugal by Boscawen in August, had thought that France might be in a sufficiently chastened mood to negotiate for peace in earnest. As a result, at another Anglo-Prussian conference held in London on September 26 the words of a declaration to be issued by the two Kings to the heads of the enemy governments in favour of a peace gathering had been agreed upon. It had seemed, however, inadvisable to issue it until news respecting the anticipated capture of Quebec had been received. This came in October. It had meanwhile been agreed that the intermediary who would transfer the text of the declaration

---

22 Ibid., VIII, 341; von Ruville, op. cit., II, 237.
23 Newcastle to Hardwicke, July 21, 1759, B.M., Add. Mss. 32893 ff. 189–92.
24 Newcastle to Stone, August 1, 1759, ibid., ff. 403–12.

to the diplomatic representatives of France, Austria, and Russia should be Prince Louis of Brunswick, commander-in-chief of the troops of Holland, a neutral state. This took place on November 25 — just eight days after the crushing of Conflans's great French fleet at Quiberon Bay by Hawke.[25]

If there had been high hopes in any quarters that such a peace congress as the declaration suggested would be held, these were doomed to be blasted. On December 1 the French Minister Choiseul, in acknowledging the receipt of the declaration, had indicated that His Most Christian Majesty "was proceeding to concert with his allies the terms of the reply." [26] While Louis XV was witnessing the disintegration of his empire and the destruction of his naval power and was therefore really anxious for peace, both the Empress Maria Theresa and Czarina Elizabeth as the result of late military success had looked upon a congress with jaundiced eyes as something that had been devised to save Prussia from irretrievable ruin. Nevertheless, in order not to offend public opinion, the court of Vienna soon afterward had prepared the draft of a counter-declaration that had accepted the proposal for a congress in expressing a desire "to terminate the wars which already for some years have been going on between England and France, on the one hand, and his Prussian Majesty, the House of Austria and her Majesty the Empress of Russia, on the other hand." [27] The only reservation that had been attached was that, during the negotiations, hostilities should not be suspended. As for the Czarina, she had not been prepared to oppose a congress that might award her portions of Prussia.

It was over three months, however, before a reply to the declaration had been framed acceptable to all three powers. In its final form it had confirmed the fundamental distinction between the Anglo-French war and the German war. As to the termination of the former, it had introduced the idea of the mediation of the Spanish King. For with the passing of King Ferdinand VI in 1759 and the coming of Charles III to the throne of Spain, France had acquired a warm friend who, as will be emphasized in the following chapter, viewed with alarm the increase of British power in the New World. To the end of aiding his Bourbon cousin he had tendered his good

[25] For the "Declaration" that bears the date November 25 see *Parliamentary History,* XV, 1019–21.

[26] Waddington, *La Guerre de Sept Ans,* III, 489.

[27] "Projet de contre-déclaration de l'Impératrice-Reine," *ibid.,* III, 490.

offices. Therefore the reply, framed in the light of this development, had declared that

> "his Majesty, the Catholic King having been pleased to offer his Mediation in the War which has subsisted for some years between France and England; and this war having, besides, nothing in common with that which the two Empresses, with their Allies have likewise carried on for some years against the King of Prussia; His most Christian Majesty is ready to treat of his particular Peace with England through the good Offices of his Catholic Majesty whose Mediation he has a Pleasure in accepting."

The declaration thereupon had stated: "As to the War, which regards directly his Prussian Majesty; their Majesties . . . are disposed to agree to the appointing the Congress proposed," but with the proviso that all the powers, great or small in arms as allies against Frederick should be invited to participate.[28]

Pitt, however, had been quite indisposed to any negotiation with France that did not include Prussia. On the other hand, France, not at war with Prussia, had felt quite properly that there existed no proper basis for including the latter country in the proposed separate talks. This led to interminable diplomatic manœuvres to surmount the impasse with neither Choiseul nor Pitt prepared in the final analysis to desert his Continental allies in order to consummate a peace for the two respective countries.[29] A year therefore rolled by without the slightest progress in the direction of the proposed congress, in the course of which Canada had been lost to France and George II had given place to George III. What is more, Pitt had shown his determination not only to make no concessions to French pride but to secure still further gains at the expense of the enemy upon the basis of the principle of *uti possidetis* — which would mean

---

[28] For the counter-declaration see the translation in the *London Gazette*, April 15, 1760.

[29] For these negotiations see Waddington, *op. cit.*, III, 510–44; IV, 442–54.

During the period under consideration Louis XV, it should be understood, held to the position taken by M. d'Affry, French Ambassador at The Hague, in conferring with General Yorke, British Minister at the same place: "His Most Christian Majesty had accepted the Mediation of Spain, and had ever made the King of Spain the absolute Arbiter of these Disputes by sea, and in America . . ." (Yorke to Holderness, March 4, 1760, B.M., Add. Mss. 32903, ff. 63–7). During these negotiations Britain continued at the same time to press the war against France, despite the fact that as early as March 1760 Newcastle was affirming "that it is *impossible* to carry on the War, another year, at the Immense Expence of this year . . ." (Newcastle to Hardwicke, March 15, 1760, *ibid.*, 32903, ff. 294–5).

stripping France of Canada, Guadeloupe, Dominica, Tobago, Senegal, and Goree, without taking into account further losses she might sustain in India.

On the other hand, rumours had been spread from Paris in October — doubtless for the purpose of sowing discord between Great Britain and Prussia — that King Frederick was so anxious for peace that to obtain it he had written to the court of Versailles that he would take it upon himself, if need be, to obtain for France the "Restitution of the greatest Part of the Conquests made by England; provided she would but prevail upon the Empresses to desist from their claim and accommodate matters with him." [30] Throughout this period of stalemate both Austria and France, each for its own purposes, had continued, consistently enough, to stress the point that there were two distinct wars. On December 1, Kaunitz, Maria Theresa's chief minister, in maintaining this position, had advocated, in a *mémoire* sent to Paris, a general congress that could meet in Augsburg or in some other German city. He proposed that at this gathering the termination of the two wars should be considered separately. [31] Thus matters stood at the beginning of 1761.

On March 31, declarations from the rulers of France, Austria, Russia, Sweden, and Poland in favour of a peace congress at Augsburg were presented to the Court of St. James's by the Russian envoy, Prince Galitzin, accredited to that court. [32] This brought on April 3 a counter-declaration by the British Cabinet Council signed by Bute that plenipotentiaries to such a congress should be appointed. Pitt later, however, in an audience with the King, insisted on delays until he was assured that France would be willing to relinquish not only Canada but the Newfoundland fisheries as well. He declared that "if he ever were brought to sign a treaty that did not secure these points, he would regret that he had ever recovered the use of his right hand." [33]

But no such preliminary conditions were or could be agreed upon.

[30] Extract of a letter from Paris, October 12, 1760, *Pennsylvania Gazette*, February 12, 1761.

[31] Waddington, *op. cit.*, IV, 465–6.

[32] For this Declaration see *Parliamentary History*, XV, 1021–2.

[33] *Memoirs of the Marquis of Rockingham* (ed. Earl of Albemarle, London, 1852), I, 23. "When a Congress was proposed some days ago, Mr. Pitt declared he could not enter on the Subject, till the French first agreed to give up all Pretensions to Canada and the Fishery, And by the Mail To-day I am informed they have agreed to the former, but struggle to keep the latter" (Letter from London, April 11, 1761, *Pennsylvania Gazette*, June 25, 1761).

The British public, nevertheless, was well satisfied with the sharp differentiation that the enemy powers had made respecting the two wars. As one writer put it:

"It is to be observed, there are two distinct treaties of pacification to be considered; namely, that between their Britannic and Most Christian Majesties, with which none of the other contending powers have anything to do; and that between the Empress Queen and the King of Prussia."

This distinction, he felt, was highly advantageous to Great Britain. He then went on to state a view held widely, if not universally, in England, which was prophetic of what was destined to happen:

"Whatever parties are made to suffer by the terms of the pacification, Great Britain, who has contributed so largely to the support of others, while she has, without any kind of assistance, been the achiever of her own signal conquests, has a right to consult her individual interests and security. The only justifiable motive for going to war [was] to obtain that security which representations could not effectuate, or justice maintain; which was our case with respect to North America. Providence and our own valour have placed this security in our hands." [34]

Here we find stated with clearness the basis of the dilemma that faced Pitt. He himself had been the great champion of the security of the Empire; he was demanding that this security must be amply provided for in any treaty of peace. However, he had committed himself beyond reversal, even for one who had repeatedly reversed himself, in promising Frederick to stand by him to the very end. Yet, granted these circumstances, was he prepared to risk the national interests in an effort to satisfy the ambitions of the King of Prussia, who had started a Continental war that in no respect had received the approval of the government of Great Britain? This risk he was apparently ready to face, according at least to Prince Galitzin, who in writing to Choiseul on April 28 from London counselled him to be on his guard against the British minister, whose secret aim was to procure a "glorious peace" for the King of Prussia." [35]

With the proposals of the coalition that were, as stated, handed to the British government on March 31, there came a letter to Pitt

[34] London advices, April 28, ibid., July 9, 1761.
[35] For this letter see Waddington, op. cit., IV, 509–10.

from Choiseul together with a *mémoire* that related exclusively to the particular war between Great Britain and France.[36] The letter stressed the point that, since the objects that occasioned this war were quite foreign to the dispute in Germany, it was necessary to come to an agreement on the principal points in their own negotiation in order to promote as much as possible the conclusion of a general peace. It further fully accepted the idea that peace between the two powers should be based on *uti possidetis* and suggested terminal dates for various parts of the world where it would go into effect. On its face the communication showed the French minister to be in a most yielding light. But upon further reflection Pitt arrived at the conclusion that what the French government had in mind was balancing its conquests in western Germany, particularly its conquest of Hesse and of the canton of Göttingen, against the overseas losses [37] — in other words, that there was a "hidden sense" in the offer that bade fair to deprive Britons of much of the advantage they had gained in the course of the Great War for the Empire, despite the French avowal that the war in Germany was quite distinct from the former.[38] It was therefore necessary for Pitt to use great caution in replying to Choiseul.[39] His letter with an accompanying memorial made clear that His Britannic Majesty accepted "as a fundamental principle that the nature of the objects which have occasioned the war between England and France, is totally foreign from the disputes in Germany." In order to facilitate the negotiations that would be consummated between the two powers at Augsburg, France was therefore invited to send a representative to London.[40]

Choiseul, in answering the Pitt letter and memorial, was careful to point out that His Christian Majesty did not mean to imply "that the peace of Germany could be concluded distinctly from that of France and England, and he only proposed to the King of England to separate the discussion of the two wars, in order to bring about a

[36] For the letter and the *mémoire* see *Parliamentary History*, XV, 1023–5.

[37] Newcastle to Devonshire, April 2, 1761, B.M., Add. Mss. 32921, ff. 272–4.

[38] Comte de Choiseul to the Duc de Choiseul, April 5, 1761, Waddington, op. cit., IV, 499–500.

[39] That great care was exercised by Pitt is clear. See the Earl of Granville to Pitt, April 5, 1761, *Correspondence of Chatham*, II, 113–14.

[40] For the Pitt letter and the memorial under date of April 8, 1761 see the *Parliamentary History*, XV, 1025–8.

general peace for all parties." At the same time he notified the British minster that, in responding to the invitation, his royal master was sending the Sieur de Bussy to London and hoped that His Britannic Majesty would in turn accredit a representative to the court of Versailles.[41] This latter request was accepted, in spite of the difficulties inherent in such a dual exchange of views, and Mr. Hans Stanley, a member of Parliament and one of the Lords Commissioners of the Admiralty, was selected for that delicate post. At the same time the Earl of Egremont, Sir Joseph Yorke, Ambassador to The Hague, and Lord Stormont were designated to represent the government at Augsburg when the congress should convene there.[42]

The making of peace between two belligerents is not a simple thing unless one of them has been reduced to the point where resistance cannot be continued. Such was not the case with France, heavily as that nation had suffered in the loss of overseas possessions and of sea power. For it was still formidable on land, despite the many checks its armies had suffered in western Germany, and was fighting in Europe in combination with allies that were still powerful. Nevertheless, it desired peace very sincerely and to attain it — one must believe upon the basis of existing evidence — was willing to make many real sacrifices. But not to the point of dishonour.

As for Great Britain, there existed the sharpest divisions of opinion within the government as to how far it was safe and proper to show an unyielding attitude with respect to the terms of accommodation with the enemy. Pitt, before the arrival of M. Bussy, presented to the Cabinet Council what to him were the essential concessions that must be secured from the French before concluding a peace. According to Newcastle's memorandum of April 10, he stated that he would not permit the situation of the Electorate of Hanover to enter into the calculations of compensations; at the same time he would demand not only the cession of Canada but the relinquishment of all French fishing rights along the coasts of Newfoundland. In order to compel France to accept these conditions, he indicated his willingness personally to continue the American war, if need be, for six or seven more years. Yet, realizing that he was in disagreement with

---

41 For the Choiseul letter and *mémoire* of April 19, 1761 see *ibid.*, XV, 1028–30.

42 See Stanley's letter to Pitt under date of April 18, 1761, *Chatham Correspondence*, II, 116–19. For Pitt's letter of April 28 to Choiseul together with the accompanying memorial see *Parliamentary History*, XV, 1031–3.

other members of the Council, who were willing to seek a peace on somewhat milder minimum terms, he declared that he would request to retire.[43] This threat to resign his post, and with it the management of the war, was, however, not acted upon at the time by the great minister. In fact, it was not to occur until the fall of the year, when differences with his colleagues reached such a point that they could not easily be composed.

In light of what has been said, it is perhaps not surprising that the subsequent course of the Anglo-French diplomacy did not flow smoothly. Nevertheless, Stanley was given a warm reception in Paris. As he wrote to Pitt, "a peace is here the general wish of the people; it is most excessively wanted. . . . I am courted, caressed, and invited on all sides." [44] But Pitt was wary of falling into a trap. De Bussy's movements in London were therefore closely watched.[45] Further, while the French, by reason of their weakness on the sea, could not enhance their bargaining power by striking at British possessions during the course of the negotiations, Pitt at this very juncture not only set on foot the Belle-Île expedition, the success of which was considered in an earlier chapter, but was already laying his plans to seize Martinique, an enterprise that was consummated the following year, as has already been made clear. In view of these objectives he was naturally in no hurry to bring on an armistice and therefore saw fit to raise numerous objections to the French proposals, especially those concerning the date when the principle of *uti possidetis* would come into operation in various parts of the world.[46] On the other hand, there is every indication that Choiseul was most anxious, as previously suggested, to arrive at a settlement. To that end, to a surprising extent he took Stanley into his confidence and, in view of what is now known of the complicated diplomatic situation in Europe in 1761, it may be stated that he frankly bared to him his true attitude respecting many delicate points. He even spoke to him very slightingly of the Sieur de Bussy, *"le pauvre diable,"* and revealed to him the arguments advanced by the Austrian Ambas-

---

[43] B.M., Add. Mss. 32921, ff. 381–2.

[44] Letter of June 9, 1761, *Chatham Correspondence*, II, 124–7.

[45] For a memorandum endorsed "Movements of M. de Bussy," see *ibid.*, II, 126–7 n.

[46] For the various letters and memorials that were exchanged between London and Paris in the course of the futile negotiations of 1761 and covering the period from March 26 to September 20, see Francis Thackeray's A *History of the Right Honourable William Pitt, Earl of Chatham* (London, 1827), II, Appendix V. Additional letters are in Volume I, Chapters xvii and xviii of the same work.

sador, Count Starhemberg, against the type of "insidious negotiation" in which France had become involved with her enemy.[47]

Stanley's instructions were so framed as to give him very limited
powers and were largely those designed to clarify the basis for the
real deliberations that the Cabinet Council doubtless hoped would
be carried on in London.[48] He therefore could conclude nothing
without referring the matter to London and without the specific approval of one of the Secretaries of State. In reporting to Pitt his first
conversation with Choiseul he stated that "we carefully distinguished
that war of which the causes were merely British and French, from
the war of the King of Prussia." This was in line with his instructions. But when the French minister sought to uncover the crucial
point respecting "the ideas of our court upon the quality and nature
of future compensations," or, in other words, the prospective losses
or gains that the peace between the two countries might involve,
the British envoy had to confess his "total ignorance" — particularly
in view of the fact that nothing was said of British demands in these
same instructions. Still referring to the first interview, it may be
noted in passing that when the discussion turned to the capture of
French ships as a cause for the Anglo-French war, and Stanley had
made clear that this came as a reprisal for the "sufferings of British
subjects in North America" as the result of French military action
there, Choiseul admitted "that the Governor of Canada had in many
instances acted contrary to the intentions of his sovereign," and thus
by implication seemed to agree that this war, in part at least,
stemmed from French aggression in the New World.[49]

As for the instructions provided for the Sieur de Bussy, he was
given in some respects much more leeway than Stanley enjoyed.
While he was not to commit himself in writing to any proposition,
he was at the same time to seek to obtain from England categorical
propositions on paper. His mission was to secure for France, if possible, a "reasonable peace"; in doing so he was to understand that
His Most Christian Majesty would not sacrifice his own interests to
"the ambitious and often chimerical ideas" of his imperial allies. He
was, in line with this approach, to make clear that France did not
seek any augmentation of territory in Europe, not even Ostend and
Nieuport, but rather proposed — as a proper basis for the final treaty

[47] See Stanley's letter to Pitt of June 28, 1761, ibid., II, 524–8.
[48] For the principal articles in these instructions see ibid., I, 506–9.
[49] Stanley to Pitt, June 8, 1761, ibid., II, 514–19.

of peace — not only the exchange of Minorca for Guadeloupe, Marie Galante, and Goree, with the recognition of her claims to St. Lucia and Tobago, but also the restitution of her conquests in western Germany, made at the expense of the Elector of Hanover and his allies, for the return of Canada and Isle Royale (Cape Breton Island), and, finally, the restoration of all prizes taken by the English marine before the declaration of war or an equivalent payment for them. Here then, he was instructed, was that "reasonable" foundation for the framing of a peace treaty between the two great maritime powers. In case he found that the government of Great Britain was not reasonable, he was to understand that the court of Madrid had proposed to France the conclusion of an offensive and defensive alliance. This project — presented by Spanish Ambassador Marquis de Grimaldi, who was accredited to the French court — he was informed, was considered to be subject at present to great inconveniences; therefore, in place of such an alliance the King was proposing to His Catholic Majesty only "a treaty of friendship, of mutual guarantee," which would be purely defensive and in the nature of a family compact. Nevertheless, should the British minister (Pitt) "carry his pretensions to an insupportable degree," His Majesty, he was warned, would seek to preserve the good will of Spain so that she might "join . . . in the part that will remain: to secure justice by force of arms." With these facts in mind, de Bussy was therefore called upon to exert himself in every way to keep the good will of the Spanish Ambassador at the Court of St. James's, the Count Fuentes, and not to hesitate to ask for his passports and return to France should he find that the English were playing with him.[50]

As to the negotiations that thereupon ensued, it may be pointed out that Choiseul by no means sustained the French reputation for logic and precision.[51] This inevitably led to some retractions of statements, with a resulting loss of confidence in him by the British ministers.[52] In view of this fact Sieur de Bussy was more than once placed in an embarrassing position with respect not only to the French *mémoires* but also to letters forwarded to him that he

---

[50] For de Bussy's instructions see Waddington, op. cit., IV, 512–17.

[51] Stanley, writing to Pitt on August 6, 1761 (Thackeray, op. cit., II, 582), says that, as the result of personal observation, he finds the French minister "uses his pen with extraordinary rapidity, but with little attention or accuracy; he undertakes more affairs than any man can execute exactly . . . his rough drafts come incorrect into the hands of his secretaries, and he very often does not sufficiently revise them."

[52] See Waddington, op. cit., IV, 599; von Ruville, op. cit., II, 375, 389–90.

was called upon to sign and to submit to Pitt. Moreover, the French envoy could never establish intimate friendly relations with the latter. He not only was intimidated in his presence but throughout his stay in London was dominated by the views of the Spanish Ambassador.[53]

In contrast, the communications addressed to the French court by the British Cabinet Council, while in places obscure in meaning, were much more carefully framed. Stanley, moreover, though not trained as a diplomat, executed his delicate mission with a high degree of competence that brought commendations from his superiors at home.[54] Although it is quite true that he was not able to ferret out the fact of the actual signing of the Bourbon Family Compact in August, he suspected at least that the two powers were in such complete accord as to future actions that little remained to be done beyond the final signatures. Nor is it quite fair to intimate, as has been done by writers, that he was led to give full credence to Choiseul's sometimes facile explanations.[55] If he forwarded these explanations in terms in which they were given to him by the French minister, he was nearly always careful to make clear that there might be other explanations. If, for example, he was led to place too much importance on the fate of the ancient French right to the Newfoundland fisheries, it was doubtless because at that particular juncture in the course of his discussions with Choiseul the latter seemed to have really had more at heart the preservation of this right than any other thing, and was equally persuaded that if this were successfully arranged, all other issues, which were of lesser importance, could likewise be resolved.[56] Nor was the British envoy in any doubt as to the gradual waning of his influence with Choiseul, as against the growing ascendancy of Grimaldi and Starhemberg, both very critical of Choiseul's negotiations with the British.

Whether or not there existed the possibility of an accommodation that would have granted to the two powers at the time the minimum requirements respectively for ratifying a treaty of peace, it is difficult to say. Certainly a close perusal of the correspondence and the

---

[53] Waddington, op. cit., IV, 599.

[54] For the praise of the Cabinet Council bestowed on Stanley see Pitt's letter of August 27, 1761 (Thackeray, op. cit., II, 604).

[55] See, for example, von Ruville's statement (op. cit., II, 397).

[56] Stanley reported to Pitt on August 6 that Choiseul had stated to him that should he give up the fisheries, "no company would speak to him or receive him, and that the populace would mob him or stone him in the streets" (Thackeray, op. cit., II, 578).

memorials that were exchanged does not clarify the mind of the student on this difficult point. It is true that by the ultimatum submitted on September 13 France was prepared to surrender Canada with the widest acknowledged limits; she was prepared to give up Cape Breton Island and Isle St. Jean, to restore Minorca, to submit to the loss of Senegal and Goree, to divide the so-called Neutral Islands of the West Indies, to forgo the acquisition of Ostend and Nieuport promised by Austria, and to acquiesce in the destruction of all the fortifications at Dunkirk.[57] Great Britain, on her part, indicated in a memorial signed on August 16 that she was prepared not only to restore to her rival the Newfoundland fisheries rights and to provide a shelter for French fishermen by turning over the island of St. Pierre but also to give back Belle-Île-en-Mer, Guadeloupe, and Marie Galante, and to consider favourably the granting of some slaving post on the African coast. Nor did the problem of the respective interests of the two countries in India seem to present serious difficulties.[58]

On certain points, however, no solution was presented, such as the issue relating to prizes taken after the beginning of hostilities and before a formal declaration of war, that having to do with the delimitation of the eastern bounds of Louisiana so as to protect the rights of the Carolinas to their hinterlands and of Virginia's claims to the Ohio Valley, and, particularly, that concerning the future relations with their allies respectively involved in the German war. But it was, after all, the Spanish issue, to be considered in the next chapter, that loomed as the most formidable barrier to an accord. The British position was clear and unmistakable: that the Spanish disputes with England must not be intermingled with those the latter had with France. The French position, at least by the middle of July if not at the time that de Bussy was instructed, was equally clear: that no settlement could be made by Great Britain with one of the Bourbon powers without a like settlement with the other — upon the basis of an understanding arrived at between these two powers even before the signing of the formal Franco-Spanish alliance in August. Therefore, when de Bussy in London handed Pitt the French *mémoire* of July 15 embodying this understanding and covering the Spanish complaints against the English,[59] Pitt's action

---

[57] For the French propositions of September 13, 1761, see *ibid.*, II, 619–23.

[58] For the British propositions of August 16, 1761, see *ibid.*, II, 591–7.

[59] For the *mémoire* of July 15 see *ibid.*, II, 552–3. According to a memorandum made by Newcastle, Bussy in an extraordinary interview with him on July 29 began "by

in rejecting it with great warmth [60] certainly carried with it the support of the nation. Although after this rejection Spain and Spanish affairs are not mentioned in the subsequent formal exchanges of documents between the two belligerents, the basis for a compromise on other points became increasingly difficult to reach. In view of this situation it is perhaps not surprising that with the delivery of the French *mémoire* on September 13,[61] rejecting in part at least the final British offer and seeking additional advantages, Pitt should have notified Stanley to demand a passport and to return to England.

The reality of the stalemate to a peaceful settlement seemed to lie in the fact that Britain's minimum terms were too high for France to pay with the prospect dangled before her of receiving the full support of what was still considered to be a powerful ally in case she determined to proceed with the war. This brings us back to the activities of the British Cabinet Council.

On June 8 Stanley, after conferring with Choiseul the preceding evening, wrote to Pitt describing faithfully the conversation and with it the spirit of concession and manifest desire for a separate peace displayed by the minister. This letter arrived in London on the 12th. To Lord Bute the position taken by Choiseul was much more conciliatory than de Bussy's and showed differences in point of view between the two; [62] to the Duke of Newcastle, the Choiseul-

blaming his Court extremely," especially for the mémoire relating to Spanish affairs, and indicated "how improper it was in every Respect." With regard to the issue of the fisheries, he stressed the point that France herself was interested in them and insisted "That Spain should not have any Share in the Fishery of Newfoundland"; and that as to the other Anglo-Spanish issues, he observed that after peace had been restored, "France might very naturally propose her Good Offices, but not before." Further, in view of the suspicion "that this affair of Spain had been concerted between Fuentes [the Spanish Ambassador] and Him, He protested that there was not the least Foundation for it; And that it was, he believed, Grimaldi's [the Spanish Ambassador in Paris] doing. . . . He blamed the conduct of his Court in every thing" (B.M., Add. Mss. 32926 ff. 47–52). This indicates that if Choiseul had a poor opinion of Bussy, as suggested earlier in this chapter, Bussy had an equally low opinion of the former, at least as a diplomat. Choiseul, in reality, was not in favour of this move but had to give way to Louis XV's desire to support openly the Spanish claims (*Revue historique*, LXXI [1899], "Choiseul et l'Angleterre").

[60] Pitt to de Bussy, July 24, 1761, Thackeray, *op. cit.*, II, 553–4. In his conversation with Choiseul, Stanley presented a devastating analysis of the absurdity of the idea "that France would do for the Bay of Honduras, in the hands of another power, more than in defence of her own Canada and Goree" (Stanley to Pitt, August 6, 1761, *ibid.*, II, 584).

[61] For the *mémoire* of September 13, see note 57.

[62] Bute to Bedford, n.d., *Bedford Correspondence*, III, 11–12.

Stanley conference was an "unexpected happy beginning" of the negotiations that at least hinted a "security for his Majesty's German dominions," with the possibility of a suspension of arms; [63] to the Duke of Bedford, the terms for an accommodation proposed by the French were "so advantageous to this country, that I think no one should hesitate a moment in giving his assent to the conclusion of it, upon the very terms chalked by Monsieur Choiseul himself." In fact, the only difficulty that he saw was that these terms were so highly advantageous to England that he was hardly able to believe that France was in earnest to conclude a peace upon the basis of them.[64]

As for Pitt, his attitude has already been indicated in his determination to add to the number of British conquests by preserving them all, with the exception of Belle-Île. To that end, and knowing well the more moderate attitude of most of his colleagues in the Cabinet Council, he was secretive in his attitude toward them, especially with respect to divulging the contents of Stanley's dispatches to him. Even Bute's secretary, Charles Jenkinson, was led to complain that "Mr. Pitt endeavours to keep from us here everything that he can." [65] His leadership in the government, as the result of the series of British victories, was at the moment, however, unchallengeable. He therefore not only was responsible for the rejection of Choiseul's definite and not ungenerous proposals forwarded by Stanley under date of June 17 [66] but was even determined to deprive the French of the right to fish in Newfoundland waters, as has previously been stressed, and only Bedford had the hardihood to oppose him in the Council on this extreme position.[67] The instructions to the British envoy under date of June 26 were, therefore, in line with his own views as to the advantages the nation must secure from any peace treaty.[68]

Nor did his fellow ministers fail to feel the lash of his imperious will when they seemed to cross his purposes. Bute, who was guilty of this, expressed his great resentment at the "insolence" displayed by Pitt toward him in a session of the Council over the negotiations, and complained to Newcastle that he was not given proper support

---

[63] Newcastle to Bedford, June 13, 1761, ibid., III, 13.

[64] Bedford to Bute, June 13, 1761, ibid., III, 14–17.

[65] Charles Jenkinson to George Grenville, June 16, 1761, Grenville Papers . . . (London, 1852), I, 365.

[66] For the Choiseul proposals in French see Thackeray, op. cit., I, 343.

[67] Von Ruville, op. cit., II, 377.

[68] Pitt to Stanley, June 26, 1761, Thackeray, op. cit., I, 543–9.

on this occasion by his colleagues.[69] The Duke, writing to Bedford, indicated that he himself had assured Bute that "we should be very ready to concert previously with his Lordship the measures to be taken: our point was to do nothing that might prevent or delay the peace." He went on to say: "I find Mr. Pitt's letter neither pleases the King nor My Lord Bute and I doubt he [Pitt] will not forward our negotiations of peace."[70]

The idea of the moderates in the Council coming to an understanding in order to oppose Pitt's extreme views was again pressed upon Bedford by Newcastle on July 6.[71] To further that end Bedford on July 9 addressed a long letter to Bute in which he raised the question as to whether by another year of war Great Britain could hope to obtain more advantageous terms of peace than at the present. In this connection he affirmed that to attempt to deprive the French of their fishery rights was an attempt to deprive them, despite their long coastline, of their naval power, something that "is fighting against nature, and can tend to no one good to this country; but, on the contrary, must excite all the naval powers of Europe to enter into a confederacy against us." He also gave his hearty approval to the words of the Lord President of the Council, Earl Granville, that the proffered terms for a peace that His Most Christian Majesty seemed willing to grant were "more advantageous to England than any ever concluded with France since Henry V's time." In fact, the Duke felt so deeply about the matter of "carrying on a bloody and expensive war, when the object for which it was begun ceases," that he made clear that should Pitt decide in the face of these honourable terms to continue the war, he himself would wash his hands "from all the guilt of the blood that may be spilt, [and] the treasure wasted," and therefore hoped that His Majesty would dispense with his further attendance at the meetings of the Council, where he could no longer be useful.[72]

---

[69] Newcastle to Bedford, July 2, 1761, *Bedford Correspondence*, III, 17–20.

[70] *Ibid.*

[71] *Ibid.*, III, 22.

[72] *Ibid.*, III, 22–9. The Earl of Hardwicke was also very critical of Pitt's handling of the diplomatic correspondence with France. With respect to his letter to Stanley and his "Paper of Points," sent on July 25, the Earl wrote: "I was never less satisfied with any Performance, that have come from *that* hand." The "Paper of Points," he complained, was in a "very haughty & dictatorial Stile, more strongly so than any which I remember to have seen of Louis the 14th in the height of his Glory & Presumption" (Hardwicke to Newcastle, August 2, 1761, B.M., Add. Mss. 32926, ff. 140–2).

While Bute in his reply indicated that "our ideas are nearly the same," he also affirmed that the real intentions of France were only to be inferred from the conversations between Choiseul and Stanley and that many things were not clear. Among these were the questions whether the enemy had in mind erecting a new Louisbourg in the Gulf of St. Lawrence and whether they would really agree to the terms regarding Dunkirk, Nieuport, Ostend, and Westphalia. As to Canada, he called it a "barren country, not equal in value to the duchies of Lorrain and Barr," and asked: "Why not . . . out of all our rich conquests, reserve to posterity something that will bring in a clear and certain revenue, to enable them to pay the interest of the enormous debt we have by this most expensive war laid upon them?" [73]

Indeed, in the beginning of August, Newcastle was persuaded that both Bute and the King were disposed to support Pitt's warlike policy and therefore to ignore his own recommendations, even to the point of permitting him to resign his office.[74] Yet the situation with respect to the peace negotiations had been sufficiently clarified, according to the Duke, so that the "point of the fisheries is and has been almost the sole obstacle to our peace." [75] But still the Cabinet Council was sharply divided. Bedford, so thoroughly disgusted with Pitt's intransigence, frequently stayed away from the meetings. The Duke of Devonshire was almost equally so, especially in view of the fact that the Great Commoner refused to submit his letter to de Bussy of August 16, in reply to the French memorial, to any modification on the part of his colleagues of the Council on the 14th.[76] As a result, Devonshire walked out of the meeting when it was accepted by a majority of one. In unburdening himself to the King thereafter, he made clear his personal desire, as a gesture in the right direction and in opposition to Pitt's position, to offer to the French some small island for carrying on their cod fishery — a proposal that met with George's approval.[77] Further, the Duke of Newcastle, weary of having his advice ignored and deeply concerned with the tremendous expense that the war was bringing to the nation, was determined to

[73] Bute to Bedford, July 12, 1761, Bedford Correspondence, III, 29–34.

[74] Newcastle to Devonshire, August 5, 1761, and Newcastle to Hardwicke, August 6, 1761, B.M., Add. Mss. 32926, ff. 187–93, 269–70.

[75] Newcastle to Bedford, August 9, 1761, Bedford Correspondence, III, 35.

[76] For Pitt's letter to Bussy under date of August 16, 1761 see Thackeray, op. cit., II, 589–91; English Historical Review, XXI, 328.

[77] Devonshire to Bedford, August 16, 1761, Bedford Correspondence, III, 36–9.

resign unless he was treated with the respect due to his high position at the head of the treasury.[78] To that end he invited Bedford as well as others to Newcastle House, which led the Pitt group, taking it as a symptom of "faction," according to the young Earl of Shelburne, to issue a warning that it was prepared "to conquer the company who dined there." [79] Shelburne, for his part, was persuaded that Pitt and Bute were firmly united, but Devonshire was able to inform Bedford on August 18 that the Earl, irrespective of any former opinion he had held, would now be "with us," in stating the terms on which the country would make peace. He therefore begged his Grace to swallow a bitter pill and return to the Council.[80]

Although Pitt was not easily shaken, it nevertheless appears that, as the result of the influence of the King and Bute and the exertions of the Duke of Devonshire, he was impelled at this juncture not only to offer to the French the right to the fisheries, which he already had grudgingly conceded, but to agree to give them, as Devonshire had urged, an *abri*, or small island. Thus by August 22 a certain unanimity in the Cabinet Council had been restored.[81] This harmony, however, was short-lived. The spectre of a new war with Spain now loomed to add to the burdens of supporting not only the Great War for the Empire against France but the German Seven Years' War. Whatever chance there had been for terminating hostilities with France by an advantageous peace had by the end of August disappeared in view of the signing of the Bourbon family offensive and defensive alliance. Indeed, the climate of opinion in England had not been such as would encourage the government, and especially Pitt, to act with great moderation toward the enemy. While men expressed a wish for peace, at the same time, according to Richard Rigby, a Bedford supporter, "they will tell you in the same breath, that you must keep every thing which you have taken from the

---

[78] Albemarle, op. cit., I, 30.

[79] Rigby to Bedford, August 18, 1761, Bedford Correspondence, III, 39–41; Newcastle to Hardwicke, August 17, 1761, B.M., Add. Mss. 32927, ff. 68–73.

[80] Bedford Correspondence, III, 41–2.

[81] Earl of Hardwicke to Lord Royston, August 22, 1761, P. C. Yorke, Life and Correspondence of Philip Yorke, Earl of Hardwicke . . . (Cambridge, 1913), III, 321. It may be pointed out that the Duke of Bedford, while willing to restore to the French their old fishery rights, was at first strongly opposed to granting them any island in the Gulf of St. Lawrence. This he thought would lead to a revival of their military power in that area (Bedford to Newcastle, August 10, 1761, B.M., Add. Mss. 32926, ff. 358–9). For Pitt's explanation of the change in his own attitude with regard to the sharing of the fisheries with the French, see the English Historical Review, XXI, 328.

French, and have every thing returned to you which you have lost by the war." It is therefore not surprising that the same observer should state: "Mr. Pitt, it is plain, does govern; and the worst of it is, that he governs not only in the cabinet council, but in the opinions of people too." [82] It would, in fact, appear that in the course of the deliberations that took place toward the end of August in the Council, Pitt was impelled to deliver "a strong speech" against the position taken by the former Lord High Chancellor, the Earl of Hardwicke, who as a member of that body, though without portfolio, favoured in general a policy of moderation. [83] By such means he swept aside all opposition.

When Stanley's letters, giving the French minister's reactions to England's last proposals for peace, arrived on September 11 and Bussy two days later had presented a new French *mémoire* indicating that Choiseul expected other advantages than those offered, Pitt determined to break off negotiations. Although Bedford, the ardent advocate of peace, absented himself from the Council as a rebuke to him, and Newcastle still favoured as an active member a continued effort to find an acceptable basis for peace even by further concessions, Bute, Devonshire, and Hardwicke sided with Pitt on the proposition that Stanley should be immediately recalled. To have done otherwise would have placed the government in jeopardy. For the Great Commoner was now openly expressing a desire, if not a threat, to leave office — something his colleagues were not prepared to face at the moment. [84] He therefore was given permission to direct the British envoy to return home, as has already been observed.

This was Pitt's last major triumph in the Cabinet Council. On September 18 he appeared before that body with a demand for an immediate declaration of war against Spain. Although he urged the advantages of such a step in that Spain still needed time to prepare for hostilities and that the Spanish plate fleet would thus fall victim to British sea power, his proposal was firmly opposed by Bute and Granville as "rash and unadvisable." [85] Only Earl Temple came to

[82] Rigby to Bedford, August 27, 1761, *Bedford Correspondence*, III, 42.

[83] George Harris, *Life of Lord Chancellor Hardwicke* . . . (London, 1847), III, 256–7.

[84] Newcastle to Bedford, September 13, 1761, *Bedford Correspondence*, III, 43–6.

[85] Thackeray, *op. cit.*, I, 589–90. By the beginning of August, according to Newcastle, both Pitt and Bute had come to feel that by beginning hostilities with Spain, Britain would through sea captures be better able to carry on the war with France than otherwise. Writing to Hardwicke on the 7th of that month, the Duke declared: "My

his support. Doubtless anticipating strong opposition to such a move, the two now brought forth a statement they had prepared in advance to be presented to the King, embodying their views on this issue.[86]

The gravity of the ministerial crisis was evident. Bute conferred on September 19 at Devonshire House with Newcastle, Devonshire, and Mansfield, vainly seeking some way of preventing Pitt's resignation. He himself was convinced, however, that war with Spain would require the abandonment of the German war and that if Pitt was permitted to have his way as to the former, he would surely resign when German affairs again came up for discussion.[87] On the 21st an indecisive meeting of the Cabinet Council was held. The majority took the position that no action against Spain should be contemplated until Stanley, who had been recalled, as has been noted, was heard from.

The next day two letters from the Ambassador arrived. One of them indicated that Choiseul was still desirous of a peace settlement. This determined the majority of the Council to refuse to be involved in precipitate action. Another indecisive meeting was held on the 28th with Pitt still holding firm to his position that there must be a declaration of war or he would not continue in office. Then, on October 2, with all members present except Bedford, the decisive meeting was held.[88] At this meeting Pitt in a long address affirmed, it was reported, that

---

Lord Bute depends upon the certain success of that measure, which I was once very nearly impeached for, viz. The stopping their Galeons & preventing their coming to Europe" (B.M., Add. Mss. 32926, f. 281). Bute, as noted above, had drawn back from this drastic course in favour of Newcastle's position respecting the Spanish crisis. For various memoranda made by the Duke having to do with it see *ibid.*, 32928.

[86] For the Pitt-Temple paper see the *Grenville Papers*, I, 386–8.

[87] B.M., Add. Mss. 32928, ff. 248–50, 259–62. The minutes of the meeting at Devonshire House and Newcastle's letter to Hardwicke, written September 20, are printed in the *English Historical Review*, XXI, 121–4. It should be pointed out that Hardwicke was absent from the conference on the 19th because of the death of Lady Hardwicke, and Newcastle's letters to him of the 21st, 23rd, and 26th, also printed in the *Review* (pp. 224–30), are therefore of especial interest.

[88] Those present were the Lord President, the Earl of Granville, the Dukes of Newcastle and Devonshire, the Earl of Hardwicke, who had been kept from earlier meetings by the illness and death of Lady Hardwicke, Lord Anson, Viscount Ligonier, the Earl of Mansfield, Earl Temple, and Lord Bute (Newcastle to Bedford, October 2, 1761, *Bedford Correspondence*, III, 46–7). For an admirable summary of the arguments of the ministers, based on Newcastle's full notes, see B.M., Add. Mss. 32929, ff. 18–28; *English Historical Review*, XXI, 130–2.

"this was the moment for humbling the whole House of Bourbon; that if he could not prevail in this instance, this would be the last time he would sit in that council: he thanked the ministers of the late King for their support; said he was himself called to the ministry by the will of the people, to whom he conceived himself accountable for his conduct, and that he would not remain in a situation which made him responsible for measures he was no longer allowed to guide." [89]

In a cutting reply, as presented by the *Annual Register*, the Lord President of the Council is said to have declared:

"I find the gentleman is determined to leave us, nor can I say I am sorry for it, since he would otherwise have certainly compelled us to leave him; but, if he be resolved to assume the right of advising his majesty, and directing the operations of the war, to what purpose are we called to this council? . . . However, though he may possibly have convinced himself of his infallibility, still it remains that we should be equally convinced before we can resign our understandings to his direction, or join with him in the measure he proposes." [90]

This purported statement doubtless expressed the sentiments not only of the King but of all the other members of the Council, outside of Temple. There was therefore no retreat before the meeting came to an end. The majority were doubtless inclined to echo Lord Waldegrave's characterization of Pitt in 1758 in his *Memoirs:*

"At present he is the guide and champion of the people, — whether he will long continue their friend seems somewhat doubtful. But if we may judge from his natural disposition, as it has shown itself, his popularity and zeal for public liberty will have the same period; for he is imperious, violent, and implacable — impatient even of the slightest contradiction, and, under the mask of patriotism, has the despotic spirit of a tyrant." [91]

Two days later Pitt waited upon the King and tendered to him the seals of an office in which he had rendered such distinguished service to the nation. Significantly, George did not refuse to receive them. Nevertheless, on accepting them he offered no word of rebuke

---

[89] *Annual Register,* 1761, p. 43.

[90] *Ibid.,* p. 44. In its issue of November 2, 1762, No. 25, the *North Briton,* published by John Wilkes, denied the authenticity of this statement.

[91] George Harris, *op. cit.,* III, 261.

for Pitt's departure from the ministry at this critical juncture of affairs; on the contrary, he gave expression to his own deep appreciation of Pitt's incomparable achievements and thereupon proceeded to shower him and his family with honours and monetary rewards.[92]

In reflecting upon this historic episode, one may be permitted to take issue with Pitt, who in later years asserted that his demand for an immediate declaration of war against Spain was refused by "a trembling council."[93] The Cabinet Council — very justifiably, it would seem, upon the basis of evidence then in its possession — was not prepared to have the nation rush into such a war, at least until some official explanation of what all conceded were very unjustifiable and unfriendly steps taken by the Spanish court had been given. While the ministers agreed "that to shun war upon a just occasion was cowardice . . . to provoke or court it was madness. And . . . to desire it with Spain, if possibly it could be avoided, was to overturn the most fundamental principles of the policy of both nations." Yet they were prepared to go so far as to indicate that if Spain, "blind to her true interests . . . should . . . obstinately refuse a reasonable satisfaction, it would then be the true time to declare war," but that that time had not yet arrived and until it had, it was senseless to add "war to war, and enemy to enemy."[94] Such a view was not "trembling"; it was statesmanship in the best sense. Could Great Britain, moreover, wisely embark upon this war until it had at least disengaged itself from financial commitments to support Frederick in the German war? Would Parliament, already unhappy about this commitment, easily vote great supplies for a new commitment? So pondered Newcastle.

As for George III, faced with this crisis within the ministry, his actions not only represented sound political strategy, but were fully in harmony with the role that the nation's Patriot King should play as a constitutional monarch: on the one hand, in supporting the position of an overwhelming majority of his official advisers on a great principle that certainly seemed to involve the moral standards of the state; and, on the other hand, in giving concrete expression to the nation's sense of gratitude to its great war-time leader.

---

[92] B.M., Add. Mss. 32929, ff. 80–1.

[93] For Pitt's speech of November 22, 1770, in which he uses this expression, see *The Speeches of the . . . Earl of Chatham* (London, 1848), p. 117.

[94] The position of the Council is well outlined in the *Annual Register*, 1761, (p. 43), from which the above extracts are taken.

In summarizing the contents of this chapter it may be stated that an effort has been made to emphasize two lines of British political development during the early years of the reign of George III: one was internal in nature, having to do with the conduct of government within the constitutional framework; the other external in nature, concerned with efforts to come to an understanding with France and bring to a happy conclusion the Great War for the Empire. With respect to the internal situation, all that need at this point be stated is that George III from the time of his accession to the point of Pitt's retirement had done much to implement his ideal of what a "national" king, as against a "Whig" king, should be. But he was hampered by the fact that the nation was at war. With respect to the effort in the direction of the termination of hostilities, in weighing in the balance all factors for and against its success in 1761, it is difficult to arrive at any clear-cut conclusion. There is no doubt that the people of France and that Choiseul were sincerely desirous of a return to the ways of peace; so were the people of Great Britain and even Pitt, their leader. But France understandingly sought a peace without national disgrace, while Great Britain sought a peace in terms of the recognition of her commanding successes. When the British government attempted to press what the French government considered extreme demands, it had the effect of driving the French, however reluctantly, into the embrace of Spain as an ally in order to chance another throw of the dice of war. If this step was taken in the absence of a cool analysis of the realities of the situation, it at least demonstrated that French national pride still weighed heavily in the scales. Waddington, the French historian, in placing upon the shoulders of Pitt the chief responsibility for the failure of the negotiations, wrote not without some justice respecting this minister's inflexibility (*raideur*):

> "To humiliate France, to ruin her commerce, to take away her colonies, to destroy her marine, he had no other end and did not hide it. He delayed making concessions which, if accorded at the beginning, would have assured the signing of the preliminaries, combatted them with energy, and, when they were torn from him by his less intractable colleagues, transmitted them with expressions, commentaries, and restrictions that narrowed much their effect." [95]

---

[95] Waddington, op. cit., IV, 600. Both Stanley and Newcastle were convinced that peace with France could have been made in 1761 if concessions had not been made too late. Stanley, after his return from Paris, declared to Lord Bute "that if he had been

But we must now turn to examine with some care the history of the relations of Great Britain and Spain, not only during the period when the latter was still neutral in the Great War for the Empire, but also when she joined France as a belligerent.

empowered to offer the last Terms early, he would have made Peace" (B.M., Add. Mss. 32928, f. 440). Writing to General Yorke at The Hague in October, Newcastle affirmed: "That M. Choiseul seriously meant peace at first, I am fully convinced. That he doubted of our Sincerity for it here, I verily believe; and that that put him upon his Negotiation with Spain, & renewing, and perhaps extending his Engagements with the Court of Vienna" (ibid., 32929, f. 220).

In view of the fact that the chapter entitled "The Peace of Paris" contributed by the late H. W. V. Temperley to the Cambridge History of the British Empire (I, 485–506) presents a rather different interpretation of the history of the peace negotiations than is to be found in this chapter, the student would do well to read it with care.

CHAPTER X

Spain as a Neutral Power

IN THE PRECEDING chapter repeated reference has been made to
Spain as a neutral power. It is therefore desirable at this point
to consider in some detail the position of this country in the presence of the mighty conflict that was being waged between Great
Britain and France.

The War of the Spanish Succession, as is well known by all students, resulted, on the one hand, in seating upon the throne of Spain
a member of the French Bourbon dynasty and, on the other, in conferring upon Great Britain not only title to the island of Minorca in
the Mediterranean and the stronghold of Gibraltar in Spain itself
but also for a term of years the famous Asiento, which previously
had been enjoyed by France and earlier by Portugal. By the Anglo-
Spanish treaty signed on March 26, 1713, it was agreed that for a
period of thirty years the British should enjoy the exclusive right of
supplying the Spanish colonies in the New World with slaves. To
this privilege was soon added the additional right of sending annually to Puerto Bello, on the Isthmus of Panama, a ship of five hundred tons loaded with commodities to be sold at the great fair held
there each year.[1]

These concessions were in turn transferred by the government of
Great Britain to the South Sea Company, organized originally in
1710 to operate in the Pacific Ocean, but never destined to do so.
Great expectations of vast wealth to be acquired by the Company
through trade with Spanish possessions sent its stock soaring in
value. But in 1720 a panic took place — the bursting of the South

---

[1] Jean O. McLachlan, *Trade and Peace with Old Spain* (Cambridge, England, 1940),
Chapter iii.

Sea Bubble — which seemed bound to wreck it. Although it survived the crash, its trade to Spanish America never became profitable, at least to the stockholders, and by 1733 its directors were seriously considering the idea of securing a treaty with Spain whereby these privileges could be advantageously surrendered.[2] In fact, the cost of maintaining its so-called factories for the sale of slaves at eight or more places, and the credit terms for the sales, gave it little but bad debts;[3] what is even more important in explaining its unfavourable financial situation was the contraband activities of "free traders."[4] They not only brought to the Jamaica slave market vast numbers of slaves, which were thereupon sold to the Company or to others for export to the mainland or to the Spanish islands, but, in contravention of the exclusive rights of the Company, also entered into direct trade with the Spaniards, despite the activities of the *guarda costas*. The Company, moreover, seems to have greatly abused the privilege of the annual ship. As a result of these lawless activities, the government of Spain was led to take stringent measures against them. Inevitably ships flying the British colours that were engaged in perfectly legitimate trade to the West Indies were made to suffer together with those which were not. This interference with the right of British merchantmen to move in the Caribbean Sea brought British counter-measures and in 1739 an open declaration of war.

The War of Jenkins's Ear, as it is commonly called, was soon fused into the War of the Austrian Succession. But, outside of the British destruction of Puerto Bello and the neighbouring fort of Chagre, there was little effective action. Admiral Vernon's costly failures first against Cartagena, then Santiago de Cuba, and finally Panama saw the conclusion of Anglo-Spanish New World hostilities, and the Treaty of Aquisgran in 1748 brought peace again to the two nations

---

[2] South Sea Company, Minutes of the General Court, April 17, 1733, Vol. 3:21, B.M., Add. Mss. 25, 545.

[3] See the Court Minutes for April 10, 1734, 3:60-2, *op. cit.*

[4] Vera Lee Brown, "The South Sea Company and Contraband Trade," *American Historical Review*, XXXI, 662–78, and "Contraband Trade: A Factor in the Decline of Spain's Empire in America," *Hispanic American Historical Review*, VIII, 178–89. G. M. Nelson in an article entitled "Contraband Trade under the Asiento, 1730–1739" (*American Historical Review*, LI, 55–67) points out that during the years under consideration the South Sea Company made profits of one hundred per cent, but only by means of illicit contraband activities carried on by an inner circle of the directorate of the Company and presumably therefore not for the benefit of all the stockholders.

and with it the surrender by the South Sea Company to Spain of the Asiento and the right to the annual ship.[5] Unhappily, the restoration of peace did not bring with it the establishment of harmony between the two peoples in the New World. The free trader was still active and continued to be a thorn in the side of Spanish government.

Beyond this there was the unresolved issue of the exploitation of the logwood of Central America by British subjects. At least as early as 1638 English buccaneers resorted to the bays in that area to secure this valuable dyewood. At first they plundered the native logwood-cutters and then by 1662 they began to settle there and engaged in cutting this product and in carrying it away. Most of these intruders came from the colonies in North America, and though repeatedly driven away from the inhospitable area by the Spaniards, who were themselves unwilling to settle there, would return. As a result, they finally acquired what may be called a prescriptive right to carry on their activities there. The Anglo-Spanish peace treaty of Madrid of 1670 laid down the general principle of *uti possidetis*, and this was confirmed in the treaty of commerce and navigation of 1713.[6] But as to the application of this principle to the logwood region there arose sharp differences of opinion between the two governments.[7] These differences continued after 1748. In 1751, for example, four Spanish warships entered Honduras Bay, where some thirty-three British vessels, mostly from the Northern colonies, were anchored, and seized four of them, and in 1754 the settlers on this bay received two destructive Spanish visitations: one overland from Guatemala and another by a fleet of *guarda costas*.[8] But war did not break out between the two powers. What is more, though hostilities between Great Britain and France began in 1754, there was no immediate rapprochement between the latter country and Spain such as took place in 1740 for the purpose of uniting their forces in the New World against a common enemy.

The determination of King Ferdinand to remain neutral in Britain's Great War for the Empire was based on a variety of factors. To

---

[5] L. H. Gipson, "British Diplomacy in the Light of Anglo-Spanish New World Issues, 1750–1757," *American Historical Review*, LI, 627–48.

[6] *Archives of British Honduras* (ed. J. A. Burdon, London, 1931), I, 50, 62.

[7] *Ibid.*, I, 64–5.

[8] *The Scots Magazine*, May 1752; a letter from Bristol, B.M., Add. Mss. 33029, ff. 152–5.

begin with, Queen Maria Barbara of Braganza possessed, as a Portuguese, strong sentiments of friendship for the English. She was supported in these sentiments on occasion by the Spanish Minister of Foreign Affairs, Don Carvajal y Lancaster, with the blood of John of Gaunt flowing through his veins. With Carvajal's death in 1754 his place in the ministry was taken by Don Ricardo Wall, Irish Jacobite exile, who had become naturalized and as a faithful servant of the Spanish Crown had been sent to England as Ambassador, where he had won the respect and friendship of the Duke of Newcastle and others in high places in the government. Both General Wall and Newcastle were committed to the idea that all differences between the two countries, including those over the logwood business, could and should be peacefully accommodated. Their efforts in this direction were supported by a remarkable diplomat, the British Ambassador at Madrid, Sir Benjamin Keene, whose astuteness, charm, and familiarity with the Spanish language proved to be invaluable assets.[9] Opposed to them were the powerful Minister of State for the Marine and the Indies, Marquis de la Enseñada, and the Jesuit Father Ravargo, Ferdinand's confessor, both with strong French sympathies. It was, in fact, Enseñada who had been responsible for the attacks on the British logwood-cutters and ships, with his orders to "exterminate" the English and their logwood establishments.[10]

Keene had been led to think at one time that the ticklish logwood issue would be settled amicably upon the basis of a proposal that Enseñada himself had made, which involved the formation of an Anglo-Spanish company for harvesting and selling the wood. But the minister, according to the British Ambassador, dropped the project in favour of the policy advocated by Don Juan de Isla, "which carried violences and the interruption of Harmony between the two Nations."[11] When a copy of the hostile orders that he had sent in 1750 to Don Heredia, captain-general of Nicaragua, came into the hands of the Duke of Newcastle early in July 1754, the latter tactfully wrote to Wall in terms of close intimacy and yet with a veiled warning:

---

[9] Sir Richard Lodge, "Sir Benjamin Keene, K.B.: A Study in Anglo-Spanish Relations . . . ," Royal Hist. Soc. Transactions, fourth series (London, 1932), XV, 1–43, and by the same author The Private Correspondence of Sir Benjamin Keene, K.B. (Cambridge, England, 1933).

[10] Captain Hodgson to the Earl of Halifax, February 22, 1752, C.O. 137:48, and M. J. de Aranda, El Marques de la Enseñada (Madrid, 1898).

[11] Keene to Sir Thomas Robinson, July 31, 1754, B.M., Add. Mss. 32849 ff. 441–52.

"I am frightened out of my Wits at these *Ensenada* Orders And the *Voyes de fait* which are probably begun. . . . How often have I beg'd that the Affair of Logwood might be settled — we are entitled to that Privilege by the Word & meaning of the Treaty of Utrecht. . . . Let it not be said that Gen¹ Wall has Either not Inclination or not Power, to prevent these. If a stop is not put to them, without Delay, I know, what must be the Consequence — Our Enemies will tell the rest with Pleasure." [12]

As for Keene, as soon as he became aware that such orders had been sent, he secured a conference with Wall. He seized this occasion to give a history of the negotiations between the two nations over the logwood activities of the English and to go into detail respecting Enseñada's relations with the French Ambassador, the Duc de Duras.[13] Wall had no love for his Spanish colleague and was especially indignant that the latter without express royal permission should have issued orders that might well involve Spain in war. What is more, Enseñada's conduct seemed to convey a certain contempt for the King in thus ignoring his supreme authority in all matters relating to the Indies.

Determined now to get rid of his rival, General Wall sought an interview with Ferdinand and Barbara, at which he insisted that it was only France among the powers of the world that desired "the Oppression and Abasement of the Spanish Monarchy" and that Enseñada by his usurpation of power was assisting in this abasement. Unfortunately for Enseñada, it was discovered that he had not only issued the orders complained of, but was carrying on secret negotiations with the court of Naples and was also engaged in an intrigue with the Jesuits of Paraguay directed against Brazil, in clear violation of a Spanish-Portuguese treaty that had recently been signed. Angered by this conduct, Ferdinand placed the minister under arrest.[14] Moreover, the hostile orders were recalled and the captured logwood ships returned to their owners.[15] Thus the logwood dispute, for a time at least, was allowed to rest — with the log-cutters once

---

[12] Newcastle to Wall, July 4, 1754, *ibid.*, 32849.

[13] Keene to Robinson, July 31, 1754, B.M., Add. Mss. 32849, f. 452.

[14] *Ibid.* For King Ferdinand VI and Queen Barbara see William Coxe, *Memoirs of the Kings of Spain of the House of Bourbon, from the Accession of Philip the Fifth to the Death of Charles III* . . . (London, 1813), III, 67–231; and Rines A. Garcia, *Fernando VI y Doña Barbara de Braganza* (Madrid, 1917).

[15] *Archives of British Honduras,* I, 80, 85.

again resuming their former activities. For the next six years, in fact, there was peace in Honduras Bay.

There were other points in dispute, however, between the British and the Spaniards. One of these had to do with the settling of claims against Spain for the seizure of English ships after the cessation of hostilities in connection with the late war. In fact, Enseñada's successor as minister of the Indies, Don Julian Arriaga, in the eyes of Sir Thomas Robinson, Secretary of State for the Southern Department, showed such a "cavilling disposition" over this issue that he despaired at arriving at any settlement until Arriaga had followed Enseñada into retirement.[16] But neither Keene nor General Wall were in any position to disturb the new minister. The Spanish court was torn by faction, and under the weak King the four Secretaries of State were permitted, unless they offended him, to operate in their respective departments without much check or interference.[17] If Arriaga could not be reached, Father Ravargo, Enseñada's friend, could be. Keene very quietly collected evidence against him — some of it furnished by the court of Portugal — that so deeply implicated the Jesuit in the Paraguay intrigue that he was dismissed from the King's service the following year and "a very mild and worthy person" was made confessor in his stead.[18]

The court of Versailles, according to the British Ambassador, the Earl of Albemarle, was "thunderstruck" at the news of the fall of Enseñada.[19] The Duc de Duras, deeply involved and in an effort to remove from the mind of the Spanish King his prejudices against France shrewdly suggested in the fall of 1754 that Ferdinand be called upon by both the English and the French to act as the mediator in all outstanding disputes between the two nations. But the British position on this delicate matter was made clear to Wall by Keene. For the latter pointed out that it would be considered very improper for the King of Spain to charge himself with this mediation while he had disputes of his own to adjust with the British; nor could His Britannic Majesty under these circumstances be expected to leave so many difficult and important points to the decision of the

16 Robinson to Keene, November 4, 1754, B.M., Add. Mss. 37851, f. 132.

17 Richard Waddington, *Louis XV et le renversement des alliances* (Paris, 1896), pp. 118–19.

18 Keene to Robinson, October 15, 1755, Coxe, op. cit., III, 185–6.

19 Albemarle to Robinson, August 21, 1754, Shelburne Papers, 36:26, Clements Library.

house of Bourbon.[20] Duras, though checked in his plan to sow suspicion and discord between the courts of Madrid and London, bent every effort to revive the old entente between the two Bourbon thrones. He was made to realize, however, that General Wall was the chief obstacle between him and his goal. Writing to the French minister, he declared early in 1755:

> "The Minister of State (Wall) is in the camp of our enemies. But his giddiness and his rashness in showing such zeal in favour of a foreign court will deliver him into our hands." [21]

To achieve that end he spent lavishly.[22] These facts were not hidden from the British ministry and, in order to strengthen Keene's hands, Robinson sent to the Ambassador a group of carefully drawn papers covering the British case respecting the North American territorial disputes with France, with the idea that these were to be presented to His Catholic Majesty.[23] In an accompanying letter he suggested that Keene should

> "particularly point out to M[or] Wall the Dangers which the immense Claims of France in America threaten the Rights & settlements of the Spaniards themselves, as those Claims, & Pretensions under Colour of M[or] de la Salle's Discoveries, may extend as far on the Western, as on the Eastern side of the Mississippi & embrase all Mexico itself, a consideration so alarming, that the bare mention of it, is surely sufficient to excite the utmost jealousy in the Court of Spain, and to show all Europe, that the Pretensions of France are circumscribed by no Line or Limits whatsoever." [24]

That the Spanish government became ever more suspicious of the aims of France rather than of those of Great Britain in the New World and regarded the French as the real aggressors in North America is indicated by the very cordial and intimate relations that were maintained throughout the year 1755 between the Spanish Ambassador in London, Marquis d'Abreu, and Newcastle. In fact, Abreu was apparently given very confidential information as to the purpose of Boscawen's expedition that year into the Gulf of St. Lawrence. At least the Ambassador wrote to Wall that this expedition

---

[20] Keene to Robinson, October 25, 1754, B.M., Add. Mss. 37851, f. 110.
[21] Duras to Rouillé, January 7, 1755, Waddington, op. cit., p. 118.
[22] Ibid.
[23] Copies of these papers are in the British Museum and are among the Additional Manuscripts in Series 32853.
[24] Robinson to Keene, March 11, 1755, ibid., 32853:183.

was projected solely for the purpose of preventing the landing of more French regular troops in Canada. Upon receiving the latter's reply, Abreu waited upon Newcastle and indicated that the minister "entirely approv'd that Measure." [25] Moreover, before leaving, the Spaniard seized the opportunity "to extol" the British King's prudence for confining the war to North America.[26]

Further evidence of the existence of an informal Anglo-Spanish entente in that year is indicated by the rebuff administered to the French Ambassador by the royal court. Duras, having secured an audience with the King and Queen, not only denounced Wall in the most violent language but made a dramatic appeal for the support of Ferdinand's kinsman of the French house of Bourbon.[27] The reply was a polite refusal. French policy respecting Spain as well as the French Ambassador had failed in the eyes of the French government. There was only one thing therefore to do. The French Minister of Foreign Affairs, Rouillé, wrote icily to Duras:

> "It seems to me that you have only one position to take and that is to request your recall as something that you have sought for a long time." [28]

It may be noted also in passing that at the very time when Duras was having his fatal interview, Keene spent some three hours with General Wall in further elucidating the nature of the Anglo-French crisis in North America. Indeed, Newcastle was able to write late in August:

> "As to our War, our Friend Wall does most astonishingly well; They [the Spaniards] have declared in Form, that the King of Spain will adhere to His Friendship with us, the Queen of Hungary, and the King of Sardinia. *Wall* says, That what Boscawen did in America, was the *Suite* of Hostilities begun there *by the French;* And, that the Repair of the Fortifications of Dunkirk authorized any Thing That Hawke may do here." [29]

Moreover, the Secretary of State gave Keene permission at this period to confide to Wall the secret that the British government was

---

[25] Newcastle to Holderness, July 18, 1755, B.M., Add. Mss. 32857, ff. 182–3.

[26] *Ibid.*

[27] A copy of the Duras address is to be found in the French Archives des Affaires Étrangeres, Espagne, 518:104–6.

[28] Rouillé to Duras, August 13, 1755, Waddington, *op. cit.,* p. 123.

[29] Newcastle to Harrington, August 30, 1755, B.M., Add. Mss. 32858, ff. 352–3.

making an effort to secure a promise from the King of Prussia that he would remain quiet in the midst of the Anglo-French war.

Thus the prestige of the British government seemed to mount rather than to wane at Madrid during the early critical years of the Great War for the Empire and at a time when most of the leading powers of Europe were determining the part that each should play in a struggle that the French had warned would not be limited to North American hostilities. Although the Abbé de Bernis was appointed to take over the post made vacant by Duras's hurried departure from Madrid, he did not go to Spain. Only the secretary of the French embassy, Abbé Frieschmann, remained there to represent French interests in the Spanish capital, and he was quite without influence. In fact, the period, covering the years 1750–7 has been described as the Anglo-Spanish "Seven Years' Peace." [30] It was, unhappily, to be shaken to its foundations with the disappearance of one after another of those who had been the main pillars of good understanding. Newcastle in 1756 gave way to Pitt, who had no friends in the Spanish court; in the fall of 1757 Keene, who had been an ailing man for some years, died at Madrid; and in August 1758 Queen Barbara also passed away, leaving behind Ferdinand, a mental as well as a physical wreck, who outlived her but a year.

Pitt, it is true, sought in August 1757, at a time when the situation in Europe looked dark, even desperate, to build upon the foundations of Anglo-Spanish good will that Newcastle had bequeathed to him. In a "Most Secret and Confidential" letter addressed to Keene and "unanimously approved" by all those in the government who were entitled to be consulted in such matters, the Ambassador was asked to sound out with utmost circumspection the disposition of the court at Madrid as to the possibility of "a more intimate Union with the Crown of Spain" in this period of "violent and dangerous Crisis" so that a solid system could be re-established again in Europe. The idea was that the Anglo-Spanish entente of 1755 should now be extended into an alliance of such a nature as to bring Spanish arms to the assistance of the forces of Great Britain, particularly for the purpose of recovering Minorca. Clearly Spain would require certain conditions to be fulfilled before this suggested alliance could be implemented. The issue over establishments by the logwood exploiters made by British subjects on the Mosquito Shore and in the

---

[30] Jean O. McLachlan, *op. cit.*, p. 144.

Bay of Honduras since the Treaty of Aix-la-Chapelle would un-doubtedly have to be settled to Spanish satisfaction. But it was felt that this would not be enough to bring Spain squarely into the Brit-ish camp. If the prospect of regaining Gibraltar should also be held out, the Spanish government might, however, be willing to attempt to drive the French from Minorca, which, if successful, could then be turned back to Great Britain in exchange for the Rock. Espe-cially would this be true if, in addition, Great Britain would agree — as another means of reviving the "Lustre of the Spanish Mon-archy" in Europe — to support the claims of the second son of Charles, King of the Two Sicilies and presumptive successor to the Crown of Spain, to succeed his father on the throne at Naples. Keene's instructions therefore comprehended all these inducements to Spain for accepting a British offensive alliance.[31]

But by the summer of 1757 the *entente cordiale* of 1755 had in reality disappeared, as Keene could not but realize. He neverthe-less did his best to attempt to restore not only "the old Friendship & Confidence between Mo[r] Wall & myself" but the former harmony between the two governments. But he found this to be impossible. Wall in a long interview in September exhibited a good deal of pas-sion and resentment and expressed great feeling over the fact that in all his efforts to cement friendship between the two nations he had not been given any solid support in England by acts of justice to satisfy Spanish complaints. Referring to the disposition of the court at Madrid to remit all points in dispute to a friendly deter-mination of the two courts, he asked: "What had been done for the past two years by the government of Great Britain?" He had now become bitter over British usurpations on Spanish New World ter-ritory, involving the harvesting of logwood, and even more so over the insults that Spain had met with at the hands of British priva-teersmen, especially in view of the fact that not one of them to his knowledge had been punished for unfriendly acts. Therefore he declared that with respect to the proposal of an alliance whereby Spain would join with Great Britain in the war against France even to secure the return of Gibraltar, he would not give it the slightest support nor would he so much as mention it to the court. He like-wise brushed aside the question of the succession to the throne of the Two Sicilies. Keene, in fact, was so discouraged as a result of his

---

31 Pitt to Keene, August 23, 1757, Hist. Mss. Comm., *Tenth Report*, pp. 212–16.

failure to bring Wall into a more co-operative attitude of mind that, in view of the precarious state of his health, he begged Pitt, in writing to him very fully of the interview, that he would give him leave to return home.[32] Not long after penning this letter the exhausted man reached the end of his human resources, but lingered on until, in the month of December, he died.

Nor was the British ministry left in doubt of the changed atmosphere in the relations between the two nations before Keene's letter reached London. In September 1756 a Spanish memorial covering the complaints had been presented to the British ministry by Marquis d'Abreu; not until the following September was it answered. The British reply was considered to be so very unsatisfactory by the Spanish Ambassador that, according to Pitt, it was returned not only in an unfriendly but even in an "offensive" manner.[33] As a result, d'Abreu became *persona non grata* at the British court, apparently much to his embarrassment and surprise, and as such was rather ostentatiously snubbed by the King at his levees.[34] But Wall and d'Abreu had a right to be concerned over the treatment that Spaniards were receiving at the hands of British colonials and to protest this treatment as members of a neutral nation.

We have already dealt with the dispute over British settlements in the logwood area of Central America. Still more dangerous was that over the treatment of Spanish ships in the New World. For an understanding of the period it is important to refer to certain examples of this treatment in some detail.

There was, for example, the notorious case of the *St. Joseph and St. Helena*, which left Havana for Spain in October 1752, and after springing a leak sought a North American port to refit. The vessel, loaded with an unusually valuable cargo, valued at some four hundred thousand Spanish milled dollars, was picked up by the New London ship *Susanna* and carried into that port by her Captain Simpson, who, it would appear, unsuccessfully tried to wreck the *St. Joseph* on the reefs outside the harbour; the ship's cargo was thereupon transferred to a warehouse and subject to such constant pillage by the inhabitants of this Connecticut seaport and by others that her supercargo, Joseph Miguel de San Juan, finally, failing

[32] Keene to Pitt, September 26, 1757, *ibid.*, pp. 216–21.

[33] Pitt to the Earl of Bristol, August 1, 1758, Francis Thackeray, *History of William Pitt, Earl of Chatham* (London, 1827), I, 380.

[34] See d'Abreu to Pitt, September 11, 1758, *Correspondence of Chatham*, I, 350–2.

to secure for it any protection from plunderers or from the court of vice-admiralty in New York, left New London and appealed to the High Court of Admiralty in London. In 1754 the British government intervened and sent a warship to New London to assist another Spanish merchant ship that had gone there to try to recover the cargo. But this was all in vain. The Connecticut authorities were helpless in face of the lawless conspiracy of silence on the part of those guilty of thievery and their abettors. Nor did repeated sharp notes by the Secretary of State for the Southern Department to Governor Fitch of this little republican British commonwealth bring any results, though Fitch, it must be said in justice to him, was a man of high honour who deeply deplored the shameless conduct of the New London inhabitants. Even as late as the year 1758 Pitt was insisting that justice be done to the Spanish owners of the cargo by the people of the colony. All that the government of Connecticut would do, however, was to attempt to prove that what had occurred had not been done as a result of the negligence of the officers of the colony itself, without regard to the gross negligence of the New London authorities. Indeed, it is far from clear that in this gross violation of every standard of decency in human relations the owners of the *St. Joseph* ever received any compensation for the almost total loss of the cargo of gold, silver, indigo, sarsaparilla, and balsam.[35]

When war between Great Britain and France had let loose a swarm of British colonial privateers, as already mentioned in an earlier chapter, there took place acts of violence, even of piracy, against the ships and subjects of neutral Spain.

For example, in 1756 a Captain Haddon commanding the *Peggy* of New York, of twenty guns, seized the *Virgen de Rosario*, commanded by Philip y Banes, who had sailed from Havana for Trinidad and was at the time south of Jamaica. On the ship were some British subjects as well as Spaniards. The New York privateersman, after stopping the *Rosario* by a warning shot, boarded her and proceeded to loot her of money and other valuables to the sum of over seven thousand Spanish milled dollars, "contrary to all Humanity and good Faith," in the words of Secretary of State Holderness, and also contrary to the general royal instructions given to all privateers and particularly those instructions issued relating to Span-

---

[35] For this episode see L. H. Gipson, *Jared Ingersoll: A Study of American Loyalism in Relation to British Colonial Government* (New Haven, 1920), pp. 61–8.

ish ships.[36] The news of this outrage and of other lawless acts on the part of the American privateersmen against the persons and property of a benevolent neutral power was received with indignation in London, after a complaint was lodged by Spanish Ambassador d'Abreu. Immediately the Earl of Holderness wrote to Governor James de Lancey of New York instructing him to issue a proclamation for the apprehending of Haddon. This was issued on July 16, 1757.[37] But the privateersman was at the time out of reach of the New York authorities. Nevertheless, early in 1758, doubtless assured that he could do so in safety, he returned to the province. His brazen conduct could not be overlooked. Advocate General William Kemp of the New York court of vice-admiralty on February 17 was brought to enter a claim in his court in the King's name and in behalf of Don Banes and other injured parties.

When the case came to trial, however, the lawyers for the defendant filed a very skilfully drawn demurrer against this claim. In this it was stated: that the King ought not to attempt to recover property that is expressly declared to belong to a Spanish subject; nor should His Majesty by law sue for himself and for a subject in this suit, as that would deprive the defendant of rights guaranteed, in that while damages might be awarded against the securities of the latter, he himself would still be liable to a new suit on behalf of our Lord the King to bind him to good behaviour; further, that a decree upon this claim would not bar Banes from filing another claim in his own name, especially since divers persons were parties to the claim in question; finally, that no British subject was obliged by law to answer to the King for an injury done to another subject by criminal prosecution.[38]

On April 19 the court of vice-admiralty allowed the demurrer and dismissed the claim, even in the face of affidavits transmitted from England and laid before it in the name of the King to substantiate the charges against Haddon. Whatever may have been the merits of the legal principles involved in the case, it is clear that

---

[36] Deposition of Philip y Banes, October 27, 1758, N. Y. Col. Mss. 86:95, New York State Archives; Holderness to Vice Admiral Holburne, May 20, 1757, Loudoun Papers 81:3671, Huntington Library; Holderness to the Lieutenant Governor of Jamaica, May 20, 1757, P.R.O., C.O. 5:215.

[37] For de Lancey's proclamation of July 16, 1757 see N. Y. Col. Mss. 86:101, New York State Archives.

[38] For the demurrer see ibid., 86:15.

the court's decision was a gross miscarriage of justice; it is equally clear that Haddon did not stand alone, but was supported by powerful New York privateering interests. The *Peggy*, in fact, was the property of the merchants Nathaniel Marston and Jasper Framer; [39] they also owned the privateer *True Briton*, of fourteen guns, [40] while Marston and John Alsop, another great merchant, owned the *Hunter*, of eighteen guns; [41] in 1759 Marston also acquired the *Relief*, of six guns, and in 1760, in company with five other New York merchants, came into possession of the privateer *De Lancey*. [42] What influence such a man as Marston could bring to bear upon the court is not hard to surmise.

It is true that the Lieutenant Governor, doubtless in view of the international importance of the decision, called upon Kemp to report the proceedings of the case to him and that the advocate general replied in a memorial, [43] which was then submitted to the Provincial Council by de Lancey on May 25 with an order to give its judgment upon the same. This was done on June 2, when the council rendered its opinion "that the Rights of his Majesty and the Honour of his Crown and Government are greatly interested and Concerned in the present matter"; it also advised him to secure a certified copy of the proceedings of the court and, in particular, the reasons that induced the said court to dismiss the claim. [44] Although on October 6 Captain Banes petitioned the Lieutenant Governor for justice [45] and on the 27th of that month signed an extended deposition covering the whole scandalous episode of the seizure of his vessel, [46] it was apparently as difficult for a Spaniard to secure his rights in New York as the subject of a friendly nation as it was in Connecticut.

Nor were the North American privateersmen alone to blame for attacks upon Spanish shipping. Early in 1757 the *Nuestra Señora de los Remedios*, en route from Teneriffe, one of the Canary Islands, to the port of La Guaira in what is now Venezuela, was over-

---

[39] *Ibid.*, 83:70.
[40] *Ibid.*, 84:100.
[41] *Ibid.*, 85:13.
[42] *Ibid.*, 88:21.
[43] *Ibid.*, 86:15.
[44] *Ibid.*, 86:19.
[45] *Ibid.*, 86:85.
[46] *Ibid.*, 86:95.

hauled and plundered by two Barbadian privateers and the crew put to torture. In a memorial directed to Pitt by Ambassador d'Abreu it was declared:

> "The circumstances of this capture are of such a nature as to excite every nation that has honour and generosity. Up to the present the English privateers have been content to act against treaties subsisting between the two crowns, against the friendship subsisting between the two Kings, and, finally, against international Law. Now they commit cruelties against the subjects of my master the King which are shameful and shocking to humanity." [47]

Even when the colonial privateersmen refrained from acts of brutality against the Spaniards, they frequently hampered the legitimate commercial activities of the latter. This may be illustrated by the case of the *St. Joseph* — not to be confused with the *St. Joseph and St. Helena* with which we have been concerned — that early in 1757 left Campeachy and sailed to the Mississippi, where she took on some indigo and bills of exchange. Proceeding from there to Spain, she was stopped by the Rhode Island privateer *Black Snake* and carried into the harbour of Providence in that colony for condemnation. Released there by the court of vice-admiralty in July, she then sailed for the Spanish West Indies, where she received a cargo of sugar and then was stopped on her return to Campeachy by the New York privateer *Oliver Cromwell*, commanded by a Captain Nicholls, who, however, after examining the ship's papers freed her. But soon afterward the *Revenge*, commanded by James Griffiths, also of New York, seized the vessel and sent her to that port as lawful prize. Before reaching that place, the ship and cargo were, unfortunately, stranded late in December off Martha's Vineyard and lost. This led to a memorial addressed to New York authorities on the part of Captain De La Rosa protesting against "these violent and unjust Proceedings . . . contrary to the Friendship subsisting between His Brittanick Majesty and His Catholick Majesty." The Provincial Council very properly ordered the advocate general to proceed against Griffiths.[48] But, again, one is left in the dark as to whether any relief was given to the owners of the ship and of the cargo. In fact, the only evidence that Pitt could furnish by the summer of 1758 to show that any real effort was be-

---

[47] For the memorial of d'Abreu dated August 1, 1757 see P.R.O., C.O. 5:215.
[48] N. Y. Col. Mss. 85:84, New York State Archives.

ing made to protect legitimate Spanish commerce was the execution of four people at Antigua for flagrant crimes against it.[49]

In making this brief review of certain typical examples of the bad conduct of American colonial privateersmen, if not the colonial governments as well, toward Spanish merchant ships, it might be pointed out that the Spaniards themselves, after the close of the late war and before the outbreak of the Great War for the Empire, not only had seized British ships while on the high seas — upon pretence of their having contraband goods on board — but had sold them and their cargoes at public auction. When the owners thereupon applied to the Spanish governors for restitution, this was not possible to make nor was the value of the ships and cargoes made good out of the Spanish treasury. This may help to explain why Spaniards did not receive greater protection from British colonials than might have been expected. Yet, to balance things, it must be added that doubtless an equal number of Spanish ships were taken during the same period of peace by ships flying the British colours.[50] But putting these incidents into the prewar background where they properly belonged, it may be affirmed that the conduct of British colonials in no way supported the efforts of government to encourage the development of harmony and good understanding with Spain. No one deplored these irregularities of the privateersmen more than did Pitt, and in writing to Keene's successor, the Earl of Bristol, before the latter set out for Madrid from Italy, where he was at the time, Pitt declared that no opportunity that the nature and constitution of the government offered had been neglected to give Spanish sufferers all possible satisfaction.[51] But all this could be but cold comfort to the suffering Spaniards.

Bristol arrived in Spain early in the fall of 1758 and set himself to work to mend the diplomatic fences. He was a man of real ability, worthy to take up Keene's weighty task. Perhaps to his surprise, he found General Wall most cordial and apparently very anxious to restore the confidential relations that had once subsisted between

---

[49] Pitt to Bristol, August 1, 1758, Francis Thackeray, op. cit., I, 384.

That the treatment of neutral Spanish ships was the chief reason for Charles III's actions that led to a declaration of war in 1762 is emphasized by Jean McLachlan in her scholarly article, "The Uneasy Neutrality . . . 1756–1759," Cambridge Historical Journal, VIII (1938–40), 55–77.

[50] See William Beckford's address in the House of Commons on the King's speech of November 14, 1754, Parliamentary History, XV, 352–3.

[51] For this letter see Thackeray, op. cit., I, 380–5.

himself and the official representative of the government of Great Britain.[52] But none of these issues between the two powers were settled, and new disputes arose. Yet, despite these and Wall's strong support of the Spanish position in connection with them, Bristol was convinced, after spending a year at Madrid in rather intimate association with the general, that the latter had a real attachment for Great Britain, which was based on his patriotic conviction that only in close union with that country could Spain remain a great and independent nation.[53]

With respect to the disputes, the British position as outlined by Pitt to Bristol in the summer of 1758, when the Earl was about to take up his duties, remained the official position. A distinction was made between the privilege, which British subjects had long enjoyed and practised, of resorting to the uninhabited region of Yucatán to cut logwood, and the violation of the territorial jurisdiction of the Crown of Spain in the setting up of British settlements. With respect to the latter, the Secretary of State affirmed that His Britannic Majesty was anxious to give relief and satisfaction, provided that this did not involve the infringement of the logwood privilege. As to British interference with Spanish vessels, his position was set forth fully in the answer that he presented on September 1, 1760 to the new Spanish Ambassador, the Conde de Fuentes, to a memorial presented by the latter in June of that year against the treatment of these vessels. In this connection he emphasized the point that when Spanish vessels were seized and brought to a British port for condemnation by a court of vice-admiralty, this court gave its judgment solely on the basis not only of the recognized maritime law of nations but of treaties subsisting between Great Britain and other powers — and not upon any national law passed by Parliament except as it reinforced these bases for determining what was lawful prize. He therefore denied the validity of the complaint that the inferior courts of vice-admiralty, the High Court of Admiralty, or the Lords Commissioners of Prize Appeals were improperly influenced for national ends.[54] It may be added that when cases involving the seizure of Spanish vessels for unneutral acts came

---

[52] Bristol to Pitt, November 1758, Chatham Correspondence, I, 371–4.

[53] Bristol to Pitt, December 19, 1760, ibid., I, 473–4.

[54] See Pitt's long "Answer to the Spanish Memorial" (in French), Thackeray, op. cit., II, Appendix, 486–95. For a very full and scholarly treatment of the work of the English prize courts for the period under consideration see Richard Pares's Colonial Blockade and Neutral Rights, 1739–1763 (Oxford, 1938), Chapter ii.

before the court in England, especial efforts seem to have been made to do full justice to the owners of the ships and the cargoes.[55] As to acts of robbery and piracy, Pitt assured the Ambassador that these were capital crimes and that everyone sought to see the perpetrators of them brought to exemplary punishment.

It should now be pointed out that in the fall of 1760 a third issue was added to the two disputes referred to above. This involved the question of the right of Spaniards to go to the Banks of Newfoundland in order to catch cod. The claim was asserted in a memorial, delivered by de Fuentes on September 9, that also significantly contained an appeal to France with respect to Spanish fisheries rights, which so restrained a man as the Earl of Hardwicke was impelled to call both "extraordinary" and "unprecedented."[56] On this new issue Pitt was not only firm but even uncompromising. Writing to Bristol later in the month, he set forth "the unquestionable right [of the British] to the sole fishery of that island . . . excepting only the liberty . . . granted to the French . . . by the treaty of Utrecht." He added that this was held to be "so sacred" that it would be impossible for His Majesty to make a concession "so destructive of the true interests of Great Britain."[57]

The injection of the Newfoundland fisheries into the disputes already clouding Anglo-Spanish relations, and with it the unfriendly act of sending a copy of the Spanish memorial addressed to the government of Great Britain to that of France, shows a significant departure in Spanish policy. It is by no means difficult to fathom the reason for this. On August 10, 1759, that pathetic figure King Ferdinand VI passed away and was succeeded on the throne of Spain by his half-brother Charles, the King of the Two Sicilies. The new King was strongly inclined to support his Bourbon kinsman on

---

[55] *Ibid.*

[56] The Spanish memorial, supported by four documents dated between the years 1553 and 1639, took the position that the fishermen of northern Spain were the first to resort to the Banks of Newfoundland, where their rights to catch the cod had long been acknowledged by both France and England, and particularly by Great Britain in Article XV of the Treaty of Utrecht and in Article II of the Anglo-Spanish treaty of 1721 (the documents, all in French, are among the Chatham Manuscripts, Bundle 93, P.R.O., and in transcription in the Canadian Archives). What Hardwicke took exception to was the statement "que la copie de ce Mémoire leur [that is, to the court of France] est communiquée" (Hardwicke to Pitt, September 29, 1760, *Chatham Correspondence*, II, 68. It will be noted that I have corrected Hardwicke's quotation so as to make it conform to the original note).

[57] Pitt to Bristol, September 26, 1760, Thackeray, *op. cit.*, I, 487–92.

the throne of France; further, he was disposed to rule as well as reign, consigning his ministers to a subordinate role. Here we have in Charles a man of reticence, who usually kept his views to himself until he was ready to act; also one of great industry, methodical, of simple habits and manner of dress, except on state occasions, and who seemed destined to revive the prestige of Spain.[58] Nevertheless, with the war by this time going so badly for France, he, unfortunately for his kingdom, sought to intervene. Even before he reached Madrid — on his journey from Naples to assume the Crown of Spain — with a precipitation that belied his habitual caution, he offered, in a surprising memorial that the Spanish Ambassador in London was directed to deliver to Pitt, to mediate all the differences between Great Britain and France that had brought on hostilities. In this, Charles frankly indicated that he could not view with indifference British successes in the New World, which had destroyed the balance of power purposely established there by the Treaty of Utrecht; at the same time he very inconsistently avowed that, in his position as "a disinterested equal friend," he held to "a pure neutrality" as between the two warring powers.[59]

Pitt, after reading this remarkable document, was placed on his guard and tactfully indicated to d'Abreu, in reply to the memorial, that the "good offices" of his King would be gladly embraced. With this warning he doubtless was less surprised than he otherwise would have been when the Spanish government the following year injected, as has been noted, the Newfoundland issue into the Anglo-Spanish discussions and in such a manner as could hardly seem proper for a nation determined not to take sides in the war. Moreover, at the time it did so, by means of the memorial referred to above, the new Spanish Ambassador presented another memorial on the logwood dispute that demanded, in "a most peremptory

---

[58] See the long letter of Stanier Porten addressed to Pitt under date of April 28, 1760 (*Chatham Correspondence*, II, 31–40); Porten had spent some years in Naples, a British resident there; his view of Charles is reinforced by a letter written by the French minister at the court of Naples, Ossun, to Choiseul on September 10, 1759 (Waddington, *La Guerre de Sept Ans*, III, 431). For a careful study of Charles III see F. Rousseau, *Règne de Charles III d'Espagne* (Paris, 1907).

[59] D'Abreu to Pitt, December 5, 1759, B.M., Add. Mss. 32899, ff. 303–4; Pitt to Bristol, December 14, 1759, Thackeray, *op. cit.*, I, 461–3. It may be pointed out that Charles in referring to the pretended balance established by the Treaty of Utrecht in the New World merely repeated the substance of a *mémoire* that was drawn up by the French court and presented to the King of Spain on September 21, 1759 (for this *mémoire* see Waddington, *op. cit.*, III, 432–4).

and arbitrary tone," that not only should the government of Great Britain send positive orders for the immediate and complete evacuation of all British subjects engaged in gathering this valuable dye-wood, but that the King should also issue a proclamation disclaiming any protection to those among them found on the Honduras coast.[60] But Charles III was not prepared at the time to act up to the words that his obedient Foreign Minister, General Wall, who held him in "the greatest awe," had placed in the memorial certainly in response to the King's desires as well as those of the avowedly pro-French ministers, if not his own.[61] Nor was Pitt for a moment intimidated by the scarcely veiled threats.

Meanwhile the Franco-Spanish *rapprochement* became ever more evident to the British ministry. Thus by the spring of 1760 the French, as has been made clear in the preceding chapter, had openly accepted the offer of the King of Spain to be the mediator in all issues that divided Great Britain and France, while Pitt, with the support of his colleagues, was not prepared to see Charles go beyond the mere exercise of his good offices. The Marquis Grimaldi, one of the most avowed members of the French party at Madrid,[62] was, moreover, sent to Paris as Ambassador and set to work to bring about a Franco-Spanish alliance.[63] By the spring of 1761 he was able to report to Conde de Fuentes in London that seeds for this had already been sown. In this connection he observed:

> "It appears to me of the utmost importance for us to assure ourselves of France, and engage her, before she makes her peace; for after-

---

[60] Pitt to Bristol, September 26, 1760, Thackeray, *op. cit.*, I, 487–92. It may be mentioned that Bristol wrote to Pitt from Turin in June 1758, congratulating him that the Conde was to displace d'Abreu in London (Chatham Manuscripts, 30. 8. 24, P.R.O.). As to the matter of mediation, Bristol pointed out to Wall the great difficulties involved in it and stressed the fact that an offer of good offices was free of them (Bristol to Pitt, December 19, 1759, B.M., Add. Mss. 32900 f. 178).

[61] Bristol, writing to Pitt on August 31, 1761, was still persuaded that England had a true friend in General Wall, but that the latter, fearful of being denounced as pro-British by his colleagues at the Spanish court, felt compelled to speak and act in a manner diametrically opposed to his personal sentiments and convictions (Thackeray, *op. cit.*, I, 564).

[62] Bristol to Pitt, March 5, 1759, *ibid.*, I, 389–90.

[63] Grimaldi to Conde de Fuentes, February 26, 1761 (English translation from the Spanish cipher), *Chatham Correspondence*, II, 93. At the same time Ossun, now French Ambassador at the court of Spain, was busy and was able to assure Choiseul, in writing to the latter on November 14, 1759, that the King of Spain was ready to take his part if the English did not come to a reasonable accommodation with France (Alfred Bourguet, *Le Duc de Choiseul et l'alliance espagnole*, pp. 48–9).

wards I do not know what inclination she may have to go to war again for our sake." [64]

Fuentes was equally persuaded that an offensive alliance would be the greatest of boons to both France and Spain. In replying to Grimaldi's letter of March 5 he declared buoyantly:

"France will lose nothing by continuing the war, if Spain enters into it . . . nor do we risk a great deal, if we assure ourselves by an alliance. . . . If this is done, at the end of the year we shall have a peace to our liking and France's." [65]

By the beginning of 1761 France — as has already been emphasized in the earlier part of this volume as well as in the preceding volume of the series — had suffered complete defeat both in Canada and in India, had also lost the fair island of Guadeloupe in the West Indies, was threatened elsewhere, and was anxiously looking for peace. But the chance of retrieving her losses by making common cause with Spain was too alluring to be rejected when proffered. In fact, as early as November 1760 the French Ambassador at Madrid had been authorized to broach the question of an alliance; though Charles was wholeheartedly in favour of it, he felt that he needed time to put his army and navy in proper shape. Nevertheless, a full understanding was ultimately reached, and in line with it the French envoy in London, Sieur de Bussy, on July 23 of the following year presented to Pitt the famous memorial from his court which not only proposed that the King of Spain should be invited to "guarantee" the proposed Anglo-French treaty of peace, but also held out the threat that Spain might enter the war unless the three issues existing between that country and Great Britain over Spanish shipping, logwood harvesting, and the fisheries should be settled in a manner agreeable to her. [66] Pitt very naturally re-

---

[64] Letter of March 4, 1761, also translated from the cipher, *Chatham Correspondence*, II, 95.

[65] Letter of March 10, likewise translated from the cipher, *ibid.*, II, 96–7.

[66] For the memorial, dated July 15, 1761, see Thackeray, *op. cit.*, II, 552–3. It should be pointed out that de Bussy could not get up his courage to present the memorial until the Conde de Fuentes had persuaded him to act (Waddington, *op. cit.*, IV, 561–2). The memorial, if not framed in Spain, was at least submitted to King Charles and, according to General Wall's admission, was "verbatim what had been sent by Order of the Catholick king to Versailles" (Bristol to Pitt, August 1761, *Papers Relative to the Rupture with Spain . . . Published by Authority* [London, 1762], p. 23, Newberry Library; Bourguet, *Le Duc de Choiseul et l'alliance espagnole*, pp. 222–3).

ceived with great indignation this interjection of France into the course of Anglo-Spanish negotiations. He suspected that a formal alliance between the two powers was already in existence, but was in no way frightened by the prospect of the consequences of it and rejected the memorial while overwhelming Bussy with reproaches.[67]

The summary rejection by Pitt of the French communication led to the rapid transformation of what had been an "understanding" between France and Spain into a firm alliance. For when the news of this incident had reached Paris, Choiseul placed in the hands of Grimaldi a *mémoire* to be conveyed to Madrid which pointed out that

> "the insult that France had met with relative to the Spanish *mémoire* demands some act of resentment on the part of his Catholic Majesty, without which the court of France will be taxed by all Europe with having taken an indiscrete and imprudent step in affirming something that would have the appearance of being a falsehood. . . . The time for the union of the two crowns has arrived; if therefore his Catholic Majesty is as much Concerned as is the King [of France] over English pride and despotism, and has as little fear of that power, he [His Most Christian Majesty] can regard the treaty and convention between him and his cousin as concluded and in consequence invites him [the Catholic King] to confide in him what are his intentions relative to a declaration of war against England. . . . At the moment of the declaration, we shall turn over to him, according to the convention, the island of Minorca and we shall propose to him arrangements relative to Louisiana." [68]

With the additional French assurance sent to Spain that a rupture of negotiations with Great Britain was inevitable and that the war would begin anew and "with greater fury than ever," His Catholic Majesty no longer hesitated. On August 15 the Bourbon Family Compact, as well as a secret Convention, was signed in Paris and on the 25th of the month was ratified at San Ildefonso. The compact was designed to be limited to members of ruling Bourbon families, which included, in addition to those of France and Spain, those of Naples and Parma, and looked to a close union in the future of all these families in both war and peace. Under its terms any power that was the enemy of one of the members became au-

---

[67] Albert von Ruville, *William Pitt, Earl of Chatham* (London, 1907), II, 388; Waddington, *op. cit.*, IV, 562.

[68] For the French *mémoire* to Spain see *ibid.*, IV, 570–1.

tomatically the enemy of the others.[69] As to the secret Convention, this provided, firstly, that Spain would agree to declare war on Great Britain not later than May 1, 1762, unless the latter power had made peace with France in terms that took care of the specified Spanish grievances; and, secondly, that Portugal should be compelled, by force if need be, to make the Franco-Spanish cause her own.[70]

It will be noted that over eight months were to elapse before the secret Convention would become automatically operative, and it therefore seemed desirable, until that time had arrived, for both the French and the Spanish court to dissemble respecting the existence of an offensive alliance. This was particularly true of the court of Spain, which needed the interval to bring back from the New World the register ships and to complete all military preparations for what was now regarded an inevitable war — in view of the fact that all hope of an Anglo-French peace had by this time been dissipated, as was indicated by the French *mémoire* to Spain quoted above. The position taken by General Wall, in a series of friendly interviews that took place late in August with the Earl of Bristol, illustrate this dissimulation. As the Minister of Foreign Affairs he must have participated in the consummation of both the Family Compact and the secret Convention, yet no word was dropped by him that would lead the British Ambassador to think that Spain even had in contemplation deserting her position of neutrality. He had a ready and satisfying answer to the question of the connection that Spain had with the delivery of the French *mémoire* and also to the question relating to Spanish military and naval preparations.[71] In fact, it was not until the safe arrival at Cádiz of a *flota* from the New World in the middle of September [72] that his tone gradually changed. Yet even as late as September 28 Bristol was still able not only to write that "General Wall has ever acted in too ingenuous a Manner, for me to suspect the least Duplicity in his

---

[69] For an extended analysis of the Bourbon Family Compact and the secret Convention see Waddington, op. cit., III, 606–10; see also Jean Lemoine, "The Reversal of Alliances and the Family Compact," *Cambridge Modern History* (Cambridge, Eng., 1909), VI, 344–6. The text of the alliance is in the appendix of Bourguet's *Le Duc de Choiseul et l'alliance espagnole.*

[70] Jean Lemoine, op. cit., VI, 346.

[71] See Bristol's long letter to Pitt under date of August [31], 1761, with enclosures, *Papers Relative to the Rupture with Spain,* pp. 21–65.

[72] Bristol to Pitt, September 21, 1761, *ibid.*, pp. 69–71.

Conduct . . ." but even to present to Pitt a sympathetic case for Spain — in the face of British territorial encroachments in the log-wood regions — trying to save the dignity of the Crown by seeking, before further negotiations were carried forward with respect to disputed matters, the withdrawal of British settlers.[73]

By the end of October, nevertheless, as reports continued to reach the British Ambassador of an approaching rupture between Great Britain and Spain "grounded upon several authentick Assurances . . . that some Agreement had been settled and signed between their Catholick and most Christian Majesties," Bristol in alarm sought further assurances from General Wall. Instead of giving them, the latter in great heat denounced England's unwarrantable conduct in the New World aimed "to ruin the French Power, in order . . . to have an easier Task in seizing on all the Spanish Dominions." What is more, in his excitement he admitted, it would seem inad-vertently, "that his Catholick Majesty had judged it expedient to renew his Family Compacts . . . with the most Christian King."[74] It should be mentioned in this connection that this avowal hap-pened after the last two great register ships expected from America had safely arrived at Cádiz.[75]

The final break between the two courts was now not long in coming. Bristol's letter of November 2 relating the substance of the above interview and carrying so different an import from that of the previous dispatches was received with "Astonishment" by the British ministry. After careful deliberation it was agreed that the time had come to instruct the Ambassador to call upon the Spanish government for "a precise and categorical Answer . . . relative to their Intention with regard to Great Britain in this critical Con-juncture."[76] In a "most secret" letter that accompanied this demand, Bristol was requested that, in case the Spanish minister made a peremptory refusal to provide such an answer or was un-willing to disavow any intention on the part of his nation of tak-ing part on the side of Britain's enemies in the war, it would be

---

[73] Bristol to Pitt, September 28, 1761, ibid., pp. 71–7. Wall, as Foreign Minister, was fully acquainted with every diplomatic move, it would seem. In fact, late in June in handing to the French Ambassador the papers sent from Paris by Grimaldi that embod-ied the alliance, he said to Ossun: "You see, Mr. Ambassador, the Rubicon has been crossed" (Alfred Bourguet, op. cit., p. 221).

[74] Bristol to the Earl of Egremont, November 2, 1761, ibid., pp. 99–119.

[75] Ibid.

[76] Egremont to Bristol, November 19, 1761, ibid., pp. 119–31.

considered not only "an agression," but "an absolute Declaration of War." [77]

On December 6 and 8 there took place the final fruitless interviews between the British Ambassador and the Spanish Minister of Foreign Affairs.[78] On the 10th General Wall, after visiting the King, then wrote to Bristol refusing the desired information. In doing so he insisted that the "Spirit of Haughtiness and Discord which dictated this inconsiderate Step, and which . . . still reigns so much in the British Government, is what made, in the same Instant, the Declaration of War, and attacked the [Spanish] King's Dignity." [79] But in writing to Grimaldi in Paris two days earlier Wall indicated that the King of Spain, in order to put Great Britain in an indefensible position before the public, had agreed with him to postdate the offensive secret Convention of August 15 "so that it would appear to have been made after the rupture of relations between the French and English." [80] In line with this a *mémoire* was sent to London, to be presented to Egremont by the Conde de Fuentes and also to be published, bitterly attacking Pitt, who, though now out of office, as the result of the Cabinet Council crisis considered in the preceding chapter, was still regarded, and perhaps not without good reason, as the one most responsible for determining British foreign policy.

Thus Spain's friendly neutrality of 1755 toward Great Britain as a belligerent had, as has been stressed, begun to show serious strain by the fall of 1757; by the fall of 1760 it had become an unfriendly neutrality, especially with the coming of Charles III to the throne; and by the summer of 1761 it had shifted to an offensive as well as defensive alliance with France based upon the conception of the fundamental solidarity of interests of the Bourbon family.

---

[77] *Ibid.*, pp. 131–3. In anticipation of the necessity of taking strong measures with Spain, Bute, Egremont, and George Grenville framed the letter referred to above in October. Newcastle was much disturbed by its contents. Writing to Hardwicke on the 22nd, he declared: "I suppose you see that every thing comes to us cutt & dry'd by the *Three Ministers*, And that Mr. Grenville is *the author*. . . . I never can, nor will agree to my Lᵈ Egremont's Letter as it now stands. They breathe War as much as Mr. Pitt did. But from the principle for fear of Mr. Pitt's popularity, which they would endeavour to gain but will never obtain . . ." (B.M., Add. Mss. 32929, f. 472).

[78] Bristol to Egremont, December 11, 1761, *Papers Relative to the Rupture with Spain*, pp. 163–9.

[79] General Wall to Bristol, December 10, 1761, *ibid.*, pp. 169–71.

[80] Waddington, *op. cit.*, III, 625.

CHAPTER XI

The Bursting of the Spanish Bubble

BRITISH DECLARATION of war was issued against Spain on January 4, 1762; this was followed on the 18th of the same month by a Spanish declaration. The two nations were now at war, and for reasons that have been entered into rather fully in the preceding chapter. With all the facts before us it is not difficult to appreciate how suicidal was the foreign policy pursued by Charles III from the time he landed in Spain to claim the throne up to the final break with the British government when its Ambassador, the Earl of Bristol, asked for his passports and returned home. By it the King sacrificed the good will of a victorious belligerent and the commanding position of his own country as the most important neutral in Britain's Great War for the Empire. In doing so, he not only ignored the great restraint that Pitt had shown in his triumphant sweep against the French Empire by not permitting the navy or army to operate in any area where it might justly alarm the Spaniards by reason of its proximity to their own possessions, but actually invited attack. Further, in signing the secret offensive and defensive alliance with France under the terms of which Spain would automatically become a belligerent in 1762 should a peace by that time not have been made, he committed himself to support a nation that had already lost the war in the New World and in India, whose armies were hopelessly bogged down in Germany, whose navy had been shattered beyond repair, and whose use of the high seas for that most essential service of supply to its surviving colonies was at best fugitive as well as sporadic in nature — limited to speedy single ships fortunate enough to escape the vigilant British patrol of the waters off the French coast and elsewhere. It is true that he had a navy and an army, but neither was first-class and neither had behind it able leadership or seasoned battle experience, as events in every phase of the war would prove — when the chimera of a miraculously revived France moving invincibly shoulder to shoulder with an eager, resolute Spain, prepared for every emergency, was to vanish and leave in its place the stark reality of disaster.

In entering the war, Charles sought to punish the British for what he held to be their contempt of the neutral rights of Spanish ships and of their claims of equality in the Newfoundland fisheries, and also of his sovereignty over the logwood area of the New World. What is more, his eye was on Gibraltar, taken from Spain and then ceded by that country to Great Britain in the Peace of Utrecht, and even more so on Portugal, ruled by the kings of Spain for a considerable period of time before the little kingdom had in 1640 succeeded in regaining its independence. As for Gibraltar, Pitt himself, as has already been noted in the preceding chapter, had sought to win over Spain by holding out the prospect of its recession to that country under certain conditions. Its possession by a foreign power since 1704 not unnaturally gnawed at Spanish pride; its location, moreover, circumscribed the full use in time of war of Spain's military and, especially, naval power. Since, however, it was powerfully fortified and its land approaches were dominated by batteries of cannon served by those who could use them with deadly effect on an invading force — as was proved when in 1726 Count de las Torres sought in vain, with twenty thousand soldiers, to capture the Rock — it seemed wise to await first the anticipated destruction of British naval superiority when the Spanish navy of over one hundred warships was added to that of France. With Governor Cornwallis in command there, once it was cut off from all succour, his starving garrison would inevitably fall into Spanish hands without risk.

Portugal was quite another matter. The country was almost lacking in forts, and its army of some twenty thousand poorly armed and poorly disciplined soldiers was hopelessly ineffective as a fighting force — scarcely a man had ever faced an enemy in battle. What is more, it was miserably poor; the terrible earthquake in 1756 had levelled its fair capital, Lisbon, taken the lives of thirty

A portion of "A Map of Portugal."

(From the *Gentleman's Magazine*, 1762)

thousand of the inhabitants, and ruined the merchants and many of the nobility. To add to its woes, the nation had lately been distracted by conspiracies directed against the King, by terrible reprisals, the setting up of the Inquisition, and the driving of the Jesuits from the country.[1] Although participation in the war in progress was the farthest removed of all ideas in the mind of the Portuguese court, although the long-standing defensive treaty with Great Britain did not require the country to aid the latter, involved since 1754 in hostilities, and every effort was made to maintain a strict neutrality during their course, there had, unhappily, occurred in 1759, in connection with the naval battle between Boscawen and de la Clue, a violation of its neutrality by the burning of two French vessels and the capture of two others at the seaport of Lagos, when the British, eager for the kill, had disregarded the country's neutral status and had followed the fleeing enemy vessels into its territorial waters there. It is true that the court of Portugal complained in good earnest to that of Great Britain at this hostile action. But nothing came of it except apologies and the expressions of regret brought by the Earl of Kinnoul, who was sent to Portugal in 1760 as British Ambassador.[2]

It was at this juncture that the question of the fate of Portugal came under discussion between France and Spain. Writing in April to Pitt, Kinnoul indicated that France was attempting to persuade Spain to launch an attack upon the hapless country. In reply Pitt expressed disbelief that "Spain at the instigation of a Power actuated by despair, could wantonly stain the beginning of a reign by designs of the most flagrant and odious violence." [3] Hans Stanley, British envoy in Paris, warned as early as the fall of 1761 that, as

---

[1] The Earl of Kinnoul to the Duke of Newcastle, May 3, 1760, B.M., Add. Mss. 32905, ff. 252-5.

[2] Kinnoul to Newcastle, March 29, 1760, ibid., 32905, ff. 90-3. "You will see by my secret letters to Mr. Pitt, that there is to be a demand in form of the restitution of the French ships taken at Logos," wrote Kinnoul to Newcastle on April 14 (ibid., 32904, f. 354).

[3] Pitt to Kinnoul, May 30, 1760, Lord Mahon, History of England from the Peace of Utrecht, IV, Appendix, pp. xxxviii–xli.

That Choiseul had in mind not only the conquest of Portugal but also Brazil is clear from a letter that he wrote to the French Ambassador at Madrid in November 1760, in which for the first project he offered fifteen thousand troops to support Spain and for the second a fleet (Bourguet, Le Duc de Choiseul et l'alliance espagnole, p. 161). In the Franco-Spanish alliance of the following year provision was made for an attack upon Portugal unless the latter would enter the alliance against Great Britain.

soon as Spain had declared war, Portugal would be singled out for attack;[4] by November of that year reports were spread abroad that a combined Franco-Spanish assault upon the country was planned in order to compel England, by coming to the rescue, to divide her forces.[5] By the middle of December the court of Lisbon began to take alarm, orders being sent out to prevent any of the handful of Portuguese warships from leaving the harbour; and by the end of that month rumours were in circulation that in order to induce Portugal to side with him, Charles was to send thirty thousand of his Spanish troops in three armies over the border.[6]

Stirred to action, the British government — after issuing a declaration of war against the King of Spain early in the new year, as already stated — began to consider seriously the steps that must be taken to prevent Portugal from falling into the hands of the enemy. Lord Tyrawly was ordered there, with eight thousand troops drawn from Ireland and Belle-Île-en-Mer to follow. The decision was taken none too soon. On March 16 the Spanish Ambassador and the French minister at Lisbon presented a joint note to the Portuguese King, Don Joseph I, in the name of their masters calling upon him to unite his country firmly with France and Spain in the war and to break off all relations with Great Britain;[7] a categorical reply was requested in four days.

In acknowledgment, the King, acting through his Secretary of State, pleaded the innocent nature of the ancient Anglo-Portuguese defensive alliance, the inability of the people of his country to support a war, and the bad faith that the government would display if, without proper provocation, it entered upon a course of hostility against Great Britain. Instead, he offered his mediation.[8] An answer to this was presented on April 1, in which it was denied that the alliance with England contracted at the beginning of the century was innocent in character and affirmed that the presence of a British general and staff in Lisbon was proof of the lack of neutrality as well as the conduct of the Portuguese government in the face of the violations of its territorial waters by British warships at Lagos during the late engagement. It also repeated the demand of

[4] B.M., Add. Mss., 32928, ff. 389–93.
[5] London advices, November 12, 1761, *Pennsylvania Gazette*, February 4, 1762.
[6] *Ibid.*, March 11 and April 15, 1762.
[7] The memorial is printed in translation in the *Annual Register*, 1762, pp. 203–5.
[8] For the Portuguese reply, dated March 20, see *ibid.*, pp. 205–7.

the earlier note, with the warning that, unless it was complied with, Spanish troops now on the frontier would enter the Kingdom in order to secure its ports from interference by the enemy.[9] Faced by this ultimatum His Most Faithful Majesty again pleaded his peaceful intentions and those of his people toward his neighbour; he affirmed that, as for the capture of de la Clue's ships in Portuguese waters, he expected to secure their restitution through friendly negotiation with the King of Great Britain; and as for the threat against his kingdom he declared:

> "that it will affect him less (though reduced to the last extremity, of which the Supreme Judge is the sole arbiter) to let the last tile of his palace fall, and to see his faithful subjects spill the last drop of their blood, than to sacrifice, together with the honour of his crown, all that Portugal holds most dear, and to submit to such extraordinary means."[10]

A third and final note was thereupon presented by the French and Spanish envoys, still more threatening in tone, with the demand for their passports if the reply to it was not satisfactory. In the letter handed to them, the King of Portugal adhered firmly to his position that only if attacked would his people take up arms, but they must be expected to do so to preserve their right to neutrality; they were also orally informed that if they insisted on their passports, these would be ready. On March 27 they left the Kingdom.[11]

Spanish forces poised on the borders entered Portugal early in May. As a result, on the 18th her King issued a declaration of war, which was soon followed by counter-declarations by the rulers of Spain and France.[12] In the British Parliament the issue of the support of Portugal came to a debate over the King's message recommending aid to that country, and a resolution of the Committee of Supply that a million pounds be granted for this purpose. It was Pitt, no longer a member of the government, who after various members of the Commons had spoken adversely against this measure,[13] made the principal speech in its favour, stressing, as he did,

---

[9] *Ibid.*, pp. 207–10.

[10] *Ibid.*, pp. 210–13.

[11] *Ibid.*, pp. 213–17.

[12] *Ibid.*, pp. 217–22.

[13] "Some few minutes respecting what passed in the House of Commons on Wednesday 12th May 1762," Walker Papers, I, 69, New Hampshire Historical Society.

at the same time the importance of keeping the French armies in Germany fully occupied so that these could not be utilized against the Portuguese.[14]

Despite the utter weakness of Portugal, the delay that ensued before British armed forces were in a position to render any effective support to her people, and the temporary successes scored by the Spaniards, the latter were not to attain their great objective. Their broad strategy was not, however, at serious fault. The plan was to converge upon the two chief seaports of Oporto and Lisbon by means of a threefold drive moving against these centres from the northern, the central, and the southern frontiers. The northern Spanish army under the Marquis de Saria, entering Portugal at the northeast angle of this country in May, on the 9th laid its hands on Miranda, the defences of which were ruined by the accidental explosion of a powder magazine. On the 15th the populous city of Braganza fell, to be followed by the surrender of both Mincorvo and Chaves. Before the end of the month the enemy was in control of practically all of the northeast province of Tras-os-Montes. But in attempting thereupon to cross the Douro River in their drive westward upon Oporto, they were checked by the armed peasantry, whose activities were directed by British officers. In this area, in fact, the war by the beginning of July had reached a stalemate with the Portuguese and Spaniards practising barbarities on one another. What is more, the Spanish troops were beginning to feel the pinch of hunger, operating as they were in a rather destitute area and well removed from any base of supply.[15]

It was at this juncture, early in July, that Count William von der Lippe-Bückeburgh, a man of great military prestige as an artillerist, arrived in Portugal to become commander-in-chief of the allied troops. Lord Loudoun, who had campaigned in North America, soon afterward appeared with six thousand troops, largely from Belle-Île-sur-Mer, to reinforce those already there under Lord Tyrawly. As for the latter, he had twice been British Ambassador at Lisbon, where he had enjoyed great popularity and had come to have an understanding of the people. In this connection it may be pointed out that for reasons not difficult to fathom, he received from Ireland at least a battalion of troops, Roman Catholic in religion, who were called upon soon after landing to show by their conduct

[14] *Parliamentary History*, XV, 1222–25.
[15] London advices, July 1, *Pennsylvania Gazette*, September 16, 1762.

their appreciation of the relaxation in Ireland of the anti-Catholic laws by the King, as well as due regard for the people of Portugal, with whom they were now joined in arms.[16] Little, however, was accomplished by Tyrawly, who possessed neither the youth and proper military experience nor the essential forces; he also came to have serious differences with some of those at the Portuguese court. But with the appearance of von der Lippe the situation improved. Aided by Loudoun, he was able to take steps to strengthen considerably the defensive position on the Tagus and therefore the approaches to Lisbon. With the Spanish campaign bogged down in northeast Portugal, the elderly Marquis de Saria was displaced as commander-in-chief and the Count de Aranda took over. In August, by utilizing the central army that had been assembled in order to enter the province of Estremadura and move down to Tagus, he laid siege to the important city of Almeida in the eastern part of the Kingdom and, upon being reinforced by a body of eight thousand French, brought about its surrender on August 25. Now moving to both the south and the west, he soon had the territory of Castel Branco in his grip and then advanced in order to cut the Tagus at Villa Velha.

But Aranda soon ran into difficulties. Lower down the river, von der Lippe had securely entrenched himself at Abrantes with a strong force of British and Portuguese. Furthermore, while the Spaniards and French were besieging Almeida, he had detached Brigadier John Burgoyne against the Spanish supply town of Valencia de Alcantara, lying close to the border and on the upper Tagus. Moving rapidly across the mountains, with a force far below his expectations and requirements, in five days Burgoyne struck the town without warning on August 27, captured a general and a considerable body of officers, and cut to pieces a regiment before retiring to resume his watch on the middle course of the Tagus.[17] Early in October the energetic brigadier gave the Spaniards an-

16 For a speech delivered to an Irish Roman Catholic battalion upon their landing in Portugal see the *Gentleman's Magazine*, XXXII (1762), 360–1.

17 In view of the fact that Burgoyne was destined to lose his military reputation in the course of the War for American Independence it may be of interest to quote from Lippe's orders of the day of August 29: "The Field-Marshal thinks it his duty to acquaint the army with the glorious conduct of Brigadier Burgoyne, who having marched fifteen leagues without halting, had taken Valencia d'Alcantara sword in hand, made the general who was to have invaded Alentejo prisoner, destroyed the Spanish regiment of Seville, taken three standards, a colonel, many officers of distinction and a great number of soldiers" (*ibid.*, XXXII, 498).

other surprise when he ordered a force under Colonel Charles Lee, also later to participate in the War for American Independence, to cross the river and strike Villa Velha. It surprised and put to rout a Spanish force there and destroyed magazines.[18] Burgoyne thereupon settled down at Niza to watch the Spaniards and especially to prevent any movement of the enemy to the south of the Tagus, where in the level country the Spanish cavalry could have been used to deadly effect. Lippe meanwhile had concentrated fifteen thousand British and Portuguese troops at Abrantes, called "the pass to Lisbon."

With the coming of the autumnal rains and with his army not only ravaged by disease and other ills but greatly reduced as the result of desertions,[19] General Aranda found it impossible to remain in the desolate mountainous country that he had gained and to which he was confined. He therefore began to withdraw his "half-starved, half-naked" troops, to Spain, and so precipitously, as to leave, according to reports, his sick and incapacitated behind.[20] Although he thereupon took post at Albuquerque just over the border and gave out reports he would return the following spring, the Portuguese war had really ended — and as ingloriously as it had auspiciously begun.

But this was not the only humiliation suffered by the Spaniards before the year 1762 came to a close. Both in the Caribbean Sea and in the Far East disaster of a major order overtook them; they saw, moreover, their navy in ruin, their communications with Spanish America cut and the flow of precious metals from the New World cease, and their merchant marine, unable to move, rotting in the security of their harbours.

In bringing the Great War for the Empire to a victorious conclusion the British plans for 1762 — after Spain had been declared an enemy — called not only for the conquest of Martinique, which has already been considered, but also for the capture of Havana, the

---

[18] William Coxe, *Memoirs of the Kings of Spain, 1700–1788*, III, 277; *Annual Register*, 1762, p. 32.

[19] According to letters written in July by English officers, three Spanish regiments — one Swiss and two Irish — came over in a body to the defenders; later reports gave the number as four thousand who deserted the invading army to enlist under Lippe (*London Gazette Extraordinary*, August 12, 1762; London advices (*Pennsylvania Gazette*, October 28 and November 11, 1762).

[20] Lisbon advices, November 14, *ibid.*, February 17 and 24, 1763.

metropolis of Cuba, from the Spaniards, and of the province of Louisiana from the French.[21] In connection with these latter enterprises it was expected that the colonials would make an important contribution by supplying recruits to fill up both the depleted regular British regiments serving in the New World and provincial contingents. For, as the Earl of Egremont had pointed out to Amherst in command of the armed forces in North America, Britain was "drained, by the great numbers of men furnished for the various services . . . not a man can be got to supply deficiencies." [22] To encourage the colonies, the liberal inducements that Pitt had held out were repeated by Egremont. As was the case during the earlier years of the war, the northern colonies made a ready response, especially with respect to raising provincial troops; but Pennsylvania and the colonies to the southward put certain local issues and considerations above that of bringing the war to a speedy conclusion, and therefore did little or nothing.[23] Outside of the troops that had been concentrated at New York early in the year to aid in the attack on Martinique, which soon proceeded on that mission, Amherst's regular forces were widely scattered. Some were doing garrison duty at Quebec, Montreal, and Trois Rivières in Canada; others were in Nova Scotia, Cape Breton Island, and Newfoundland, or in the Lakes George-Champlain area; some were settled at posts about Albany, up the Mohawk River, at the former French posts both in the Great Lakes region and on the Maumee and the

---

[21] Earl of Egremont to Sir Jeffrey Amherst, February 13, 1762, Amherst Papers, Packet 40, Canadian Archives transcripts.

[22] Egremont to Amherst, December 12, 1761, and Egremont to the Governors of North America of the same date, *ibid.* The letter was sent to eleven governors; that sent to the Governor of Maryland and to the governors serving south of that province was worded somewhat differently from that sent to those in the more northern colonies. As for intractable Maryland, the letter declared that His Majesty expected that this province "will not obstinately persist in refusing to comply with their duty to the King on this head." Each of the more southern colonies — with weak Georgia omitted from consideration — was called upon to raise "as large a Body of Men as the number and situation of its Inhabitants may allow." Pennsylvania was asked to raise two thirds of the men raised for the campaign of 1761; the more northern colonies were called upon to raise the number supplied the last year (*ibid.*).

[23] As for Pennsylvania, the Earl of Egremont, in writing to Deputy Governor Hamilton on November 27, 1762, declared that the conduct of the Assembly could only have proceeded from "a premeditated Resolution not to afford any Assistance to the Services in General now the immediate danger is removed from their own Doors" (*ibid.*). Maryland maintained its attitude of smug recalcitrance, even in the face of a royal rebuke (Egremont to Governor Sharpe, July 10, 1762, *ibid.*).

Wabash rivers as well as at the forks of the Ohio; still others were in South Carolina and Georgia.[24]

The four thousand provincials requested for service in the West Indies were slow in assembling, and in order to secure two thousand regulars for the same purposes Amherst had to cut to the bone the defences of Canada and Nova Scotia. Anstruther's regiment at Quebec and Murray's at Trois Rivières and Montreal were ordered to march to New York City; [25] a part of Gorham's Rangers in Nova Scotia were brought down, and the four New York Independent Companies were ordered in from the upper country.[26] But with every exertion it was not until June 11 that the transports, having at last received the troops, set sail for Havana, and not until the 30th of that month that the second division left Sandy Hook on the same mission. Going by the most direct way, which was through the Bahama Straits, the first division had the misfortune to lose the *Chesterfield* and four transports while entering those dangerous waters; happily, all the soldiers and seamen were saved and landed in Cuba. The second, was less fortunate in that three transports were captured by a French squadron.[27] By the time of the arrival of the first division on July 28, the campaign on the island had reached a critical stage. We must therefore turn our attention to its inception and progress.

With the declaration of war against Spain the Earl of Albemarle was designated "Commander in Chief of all . . . Forces [to be] employed . . . on a secret Expedition" and given the rank of lieutenant general.[28] His instructions called upon him to proceed to Portsmouth and there place on board the men of four regiments,[29] a train of artillery, and a corps of neutral Protestant prisoners, after which he was to proceed to Barbados under convoy of a fleet un-

---

[24] "Disposition of His Majesty's Troops serving in North America, 1st January 1762," *ibid.*

[25] Writing to Viscount Ligonier on May 12, Amherst declared that "the force remaining in Canada will be so small and what remains in the Ports and on the Communications so separated and thin, that I hope it will not be expected that a man more can be taken out of this country" (*ibid.*, Packet 11).

[26] *Ibid.*, and also Amherst to Egremont, April 6, 1762, *ibid.*, Packet 41.

[27] Amherst to Ligonier, September 23, 1762, *ibid.*; Pocock to Cleveland, August 16, 1762, Pocock Letter Book, p. 279, Huntington Library.

[28] Albemarle was notified on January 7, three days after the declaration of war, that he was to command a secret expedition; his full instructions were dated February 15, 1762 (P.R.O., C.O. 117, 1:24–36).

[29] Whitman's, Cavendish's, Keppel's, and Richmond's.

der Admiral of the Blue Pocock, who was to be in command of the
ships on the expedition. He was, moreover, to be reinforced not
only out of the regiments of regulars sent from England against
Martinique, but also by other British regiments in America that had
been ordered to move against that island under Major General
Monckton. This was designed to bring his numbers up to fourteen
thousand. In addition, he was upon his arrival in Cuba to receive,
as has already been noted, four thousand additional troops from
Amherst's command.

With his force thus strengthened in the Lesser Antilles, he was
to proceed in one or two divisions to the neighbourhood of Cap
Nicolas on the island of Hispaniola as a rendezvous, and with the
vessels assembled — not awaiting the ships sailing from North America — was to move to attack Havana by land and sea. In case of
success he was thereupon, in co-operation with Pocock, to proceed
against one or more of the following Spanish centres: Vera Cruz,
Pensacola, St. Augustine, St. Jago de la Cuba, or any other part of
the Spanish dominions that seemed to offer opportunities for further successes. He was also instructed to note that as soon as the
Havana expedition "had had its issue," General Amherst was to
lead another with eight thousand troops against French Louisiana
and that he must have for that purpose returned to him as many
troops as he was to send to Havana — that is, four thousand. In this
connection Albemarle was advised to take particular care that the
American provincials should be treated with "all such proper attention and humanity, that they may not return home disgusted
with the Service." Finally, he was informed that an endeavour
would be made to furnish him with a corps of Negro troops raised
in Jamaica whom he would arm and clothe [30] — as was also done in
connection with the conquest of Martinique. In fact, the ministry
was fully aware from past experience that a campaign on a tropical
island, such as Cuba, presented great hazards to those not accustomed to the climate and especially to those undertaking exhaust-
ing labours such as are involved in siege operations. It may be
added that this forethought, nevertheless, did not prevent great
losses of soldiers who by overexertion or for other reasons fell victim to the insidious distempers of the island.

Held up by adverse winds, Pocock, convoying sixty-four trans-

---

[30] P.R.O., C.O. 117, 1:24–36. For the steps taken to raise the Negro corps see also
ibid., pp. 1–7.

ports and supply vessels, was not able to sail until March 6 and therefore could not arrive at Barbados until April 20. There he and Albemarle got the inspiriting news of the surrender of Martinique and also were impressed by the reports of the great service rendered during Monckton's campaign on that island by the corps made up of three thousand slaves.[31] This led Albemarle to procure what blacks he could at Antigua and St. Christopher — especially in view of reports of the lack of success in securing them in Jamaica [32] — before Pocock, convoying now some two hundred ships, set sail for Cap Nicholas. On May 23 the general made a return of available troops, which indicated that he had in all somewhat over twelve thousand, over twelve hundred of whom were sick. This put his number far below the specified fourteen thousand effective men. But no time could be lost in waiting for Monckton's ill soldiers to recover, in view of the information that had reached him that Don Juan de Prada, the new Captain General of Cuba and Governor of Havana, was busy strengthening the defences of the city.[33]

After the concentration off Cap Nicholas — in connection with which one of his ships of war took a look into the harbour of Cap François, where a number of "flags of truce" that had brought supplies to the French enemy from America were observed — Pocock, dividing the great armada into seven divisions, set sail for Havana by way of the treacherous Bahama passage and, moving through it without incident, on June 6 appeared in the neighbourhood of the great Spanish seaport. Taking most of the ships of war together with the storeships, he moved to block up the Spanish navy resting in the harbour and also to make a feint off the coast to the west of it. While the major part of the fleet was thus occupied, Commodore Keppel, Albemarle's brother, with a squadron watched over the disembarkation of the troops that occurred next day some miles to the east of Havana.[34] Although the landing took place between two forts located near the beach, Keppel's ships silenced their guns, and his marines then took possession of them, dispersing in the process

[31] Albemarle to Egremont, May 27, 1762, ibid., 1:69–72; Pocock to the Admiralty, March 6 and May 24, 1762, Pocock Letter Book, pp. 221, 229, Huntington Library.

[32] Ibid. and Governor Lyttelton of Jamaica to Albemarle, May 4, 1762, P.R.O., C.O. 117, 1:73.

[33] Return of troops, May 23, 1762, ibid., 1:77; Albemarle to Egremont, May 27, 1762, ibid., 1:69–72.

[34] Pocock to the Admiralty, May 26 and July 14, 1762, Pocock Letter Book, pp. 229–37, 249–55.

the local inhabitants, white and black, that had appeared in arms. Pushing in the direction of Havana, when some six miles from the landing-place Albemarle was confronted on the 8th by a Spanish force of about six thousand men advantageously posted on high ground. The enemy cavalry — including, it may be mentioned in passing, the so-called "Regiment of Edinburgh Dragoons" — now incautiously left the security of its position in charging down the hill against the British infantry and was received by such a deadly fire of small arms that it recoiled and then retreated. With this reverse the morale of the Spanish army disappeared and all units of it fled from the scene of battle. Thus the way was opened for an unimpeded approach to the defences of Havana.

With the communications to the landing-place secured, the investment of the chief citadel of the city, El Morro Castle (El Moro as it was written), was begun on the 10th by Colonel Guy Carleton with his light infantry and grenadiers. After a careful reconnoitre of the ground about it, the construction of batteries of heavy siege guns and mortars was begun at a distance of some two hundred and fifty yards from it. Unhappily for the British, the batteries could be protected only by fascines and earth brought in baskets from a distance; for it was found impossible to throw up entrenchments owing to the nature of the ground. While this vastly laborious work progressed, Colonel William Howe landed with a force seven miles to the west of Havana in order to get a footing in that area and to draw the attention and fire of the enemy away from Carleton's troops. Other batteries were also begun and completed, all directed against the Morro stronghold, and, wherever possible, parallels leading up to them — each new battery and parallel ever closer to it.[35] At daybreak on June 20 the Spaniards tried to drive the besiegers back by means of a sortie staged by landing from boats on either side of the Morro, but they were soon dispersed as they likewise were when another sortie was made on July 22.[36]

Until July 1 the firing on each side continued with slight effect; for the great mass of masonry of the fort received and absorbed, apparently without much damage, the discharge of the most powerful of the British siege guns. On that day Admiral Pocock therefore ordered Captain Hervey to move in against the Morro with the *Cambridge,* an eighty-gun ship, the *Dragon,* a seventy-four, and the

---

[35] Engineer Patrick Mackellar's "Journal," C.O. 117, 1:89–93.
[36] Ensign Miller's "Memoir of an invalid," Amherst Papers, Packet 54.

Marlborough, a sixty-six, and to bombard it at grapeshot range. For six hours — from eight in the morning until two in the afternoon — Hervey blasted its walls while at the same time receiving a steady and well-directed fire from the Spanish guns, and then withdrew, with the first two of his ships badly crippled. Although the direct effect of the bombardment on the towering walls was not evident, it nevertheless so diverted the attention of the defenders of the Morro from the British land batteries that the latter were able, by concentrating their fire, to dismount and put out of action a number of the Spanish guns.[37] To offset this, however, the day following, because of the extreme drought, the great mass of fascines that screened the main battery — the carriages of which were of wood — took fire and burned furiously. Immediately new batteries were erected, so that by the 14th of the month twenty guns were able to play at close range upon the Morro, which could only reply with some four or six.[38] Thus it became quite evident that the ability of the enemy to resist was steadily waning.

The great exertions of the British troops in the intense heat, the scarcity of good drinking water, and the excessive consumption of ardent spirits, together with the fevers that lurked in the wooded places, were taking their heavy toll. When a return of troops was made on July 17, it was clear that over two fifths of the troops were either ill or missing; their total had now been reduced to something over eleven thousand men.[39] Writing to the Earl of Egremont on that day, Albemarle expressed his deep concern at the failure of the American forces to appear and his feeling that without them he knew not how to proceed as the result of the stubborn resistance at the Morro. His supply of ammunition and provisions was also getting very low and he was obliged to appeal to the Governor of Jamaica for aid.[40]

At the same time, as great assets in favour of the successful outcome of the expedition, there was the full harmony that prevailed

---

[37] Pocock's Letter Book, p. 253.

[38] Mackellar's "Journal," *op. cit.*

[39] C.O. 117, 1:95. "The fatigues on shore were excessive; the bad water brought on disorders that were mortal. You could see the men's tongues hanging out like a mad dog's; a dollar was frequently given for a quart of water, in short, by dead, wounded or sick the army was reduced to two reliefs and it was supposed that we should be obliged to re-embark without taking the place" (Ensign Miller's "Memoir" *op. cit.*).

[40] Albemarle to the Governor of Jamaica, July 16, and Albemarle to Egremont, July 17, 1762, C.O. 117, 1:96–8.

"A Plan of the Siege of the Havana, Drawn by an Officer on the Spot, 1762."   (From the *Gentleman's Magazine*, 1762)

between the land and naval forces and the constancy and courage of the men, possessed by a "Noble ardour to Conquer." [41] To lighten the excessive exertions of the soldiers called upon to erect screens for the advancing batteries, bales of cotton were now secured and used to great effect.[42] Then, on the 28th, eight ships loaded with provisions arrived, and also eleven sail of transports with the soldiers of the first division sent from New York, and on August 2 the same number of transports of the second division from the same port.[43] With this welcome relief and support it was possible to send back to North America two battalions of the Royal Highlanders, Montgomery's Highlanders, and Monckton's regiment — all so stricken with sickness that they were no longer fit for duty — and also to bring the campaign against the Morro to a climax.[44]

Even before the arrival of the second North American division Albemarle had determined, with the fresh and healthy American corps now available, to storm the fort. This was carried out on July 30 under the direct command of his brother, Major General Keppel. In preparation for this, pioneers had succeeded in getting a lodgement under the walls and with great effort had drilled the solid rock and planted mines. About one o'clock these were exploded and created a break wide enough for a file of men to penetrate. The pickets, fully prepared, rushed over the debris, through the break, and formed a line of fire before the bewildered Spaniards were prepared to receive them. In their first volley the Governor of the Morro, Don Valesco, was killed, sword in hand, defending the Spanish colours. Some four hundred of his men therefore laid down their arms; others, refusing to surrender, were forced over the precipitous rock to their death; still others were drowned seeking to escape to Havana across the waters of the inner harbour. With resistance over, the King's standards were raised over the castle.[45]

The next step, preparatory to the assault on Havana, was to put out of action the Puntal Fort lying across the entrance to the harbour. Despite every effort to prevent their erection, batteries were

---

[41] Pocock to Cleveland, July 17, 1762, Letter Book, p. 256.
[42] Ibid., p. 259.
[43] Pocock to the Admiralty, August 16, 1762, ibid., pp. 279–80.
[44] Ibid.
[45] "Journal of the Siege," C.O. 117, 1:110–21; Albemarle to Egremont, August 21, 1762, ibid., 1:100–1; Pocock to the Admiralty, August 19, 1762, Pocock Letter Book, p. 287; Ensign Miller's "Memoir," op. cit.

formed against it and also against the city on the heights overlooking it. On August 11 the Puntal Fort was silenced, as were the guns in the North Bastion. Fearing the effects of permitting the British to deliver an assault on the city, the Spaniards now raised the white flag and beat a parley to request a cessation of arms while a capitulation could be agreed upon. Pocock thereupon landed and with Albemarle agreed to grant one up to the 13th at noon. Articles were drawn up by the Spaniards, and an agreement was reached before the expiration of the truce.

The terms of surrender were generous. On the one hand, the Spanish troops and sailors — in consideration of their gallant defence, especially of Morro Castle — were permitted the honours of war and after depositing their arms on the beaches were to be taken to a port in old Spain on ships provided by His Britannic Majesty. On the other, all military articles were to be turned over to the British, including the warships, and also all merchant ships as well as warehouses with their contents, together with the public treasury and all public papers. As for the inhabitants of the city, they were to be permitted to continue to enjoy their property and public offices and to exercise their religion without "hindrance" — with the one reservation that in the appointment of priests by the Bishop of Cuba, this should be done with the approbation of the British Governor.[46] Thus passed into possession of the victors the key Spanish port in the New World, interdicting trade between Spain and the most important possessions of its King; into their hands also fell some of the best ships of the Spanish navy: six ships of seventy guns, one of sixty-four, and five of sixty, as well as frigates, which, in the words of Admiral Pocock, "will leave all their settlements in this part of the World exposed."[47]

Only in one other area of Spanish America did the British attempt to make conquests, and in doing so they were to suffer defeat and disaster. That was in connection with the small "private" expedition launched against Buenos Aires late in 1762. Under command of an experienced and brave sailor, Captain Macnamara, three frigates and some smaller armed vessels and storeships, with

[46] The terms offered by the Spaniards and those accorded by the British are given in the *Annual Register*, 1762, pp. 259–65. It is to be borne in mind that the surrender related only to the so-called jurisdiction of Havana, which extended sixty leagues eastward from the city border and to the westward as far as Capes St. Antonio and Corruntes ("Jurisdiction of Havana," C.O. 117, 1:102).

[47] Pocock to the Admiralty, August 19, 1762, Letter Book, pp. 284–6.

a combined force of five hundred British and Portuguese troops on board, set sail from the Tagus in Portugal at the end of August. Upon entering the great Río de la Plata early in November, they were faced by a violent tempest and also found the approaches to Buenos Aires obstructed by shoals. Learning that the Spaniards there had taken the initiative to conquer the Portuguese settlements of Nova Colonia or Sacramento, near at hand, they therefor? decided to recover these first of all. In making the attack, which occurred at the beginning of the new year, it was necessary to silence a Spanish battery. This had been almost accomplished by the guns of the frigates when Macnamara's frigate, the *Clive*, took fire and soon was a roaring furnace. Men cast themselves into the water; others perished by their own hands; Macnamara himself was drowned. Of three hundred and forty men aboard the doomed vessel, seventy-eight escaped and were picked up by the Spaniards on shore and treated with humanity. The second largest frigate, the *Ambuscade*, almost a wreck now with her hull pierced by sixty shot, left the scene of disaster and only managed to limp into Rio de Janeiro. The rest of the ships of the expedition, with but a handful of soldiers surviving, thereupon fled.[48]

Outside the occupation of Nova Colonia, long in dispute between Spain and Portugal, the Spaniards were incapable of any positive undertaking in the New World. Their allies, the French, however — doubtless with the idea of distracting the attention of the British from such important objectives as Havana and Louisiana — decided to seize the island of Newfoundland, the successful retention of which to the time of making the peace could be an asset of great value in connection with the negotiations. In this connection it may also be emphasized that the vastly lucrative French cod fisheries on the western and northwestern coasts of the island had disappeared in the course of the war and, as a consequence, Frenchmen naturally cast longing eyes in that direction.

It was estimated in 1759 that Englishmen, now monopolizing the Great Banks and other cod fisheries, were taking as many as forty-

---

[48] David Ramsay, *Military Memoirs of Great Britain* . . . 1755–1763 (Edinburgh, 1779), pp. 459–61; William Coxe, op. cit., III, 274–5; *Annual Register*, 1760, pp. 15–18. The fighting spirit of British sailors was strikingly illustrated at the time of the burning of the *Clive*. Some of them serving on this frigate could not swim. Realizing that they were doomed, they went down to the lower guns and there kept up a constant fire on the enemy until they met their fate (*ibid.*, p. 17).

three million cod from the water each year and that they had gained a million and a half pounds sterling by the elimination of French competition.[49] The great island had a population of hardly more than eight thousand people, most of them living at St. John's and other places along the southeastern and eastern coast. They were almost without land defences. To guard them and this valuable possession there was scattered at various places on the island but a handful of soldiers, totalling about two hundred and forty foot soldiers and officers and seventy artillerymen; of these, one hundred and forty-seven footsoldiers and thirty-seven artillerymen were on duty at St. John's, the one town of any importance.[50] While it is true that St. John's possessed some fortifications, these were badly decayed. In 1759 the Ordnance Board had ordered that certain repairs on these be undertaken, and the following year strong recommendations were made by Governor Webb that other improvements should be made; [51] yet little enough had been done in this direction, doubtless because of the great demands before the board in connection with military operations on a very large scale taking place elsewhere. It is clear that to Pitt the real defence of the island must rest upon superior sea power in that area and not in fortifications or land forces. But he did not bring about, while in office, any naval concentration there, though it is true that shortly before his retirement from office he urged the necessity of sending four ships of the line to it.[52] The need for them was such in other quarters, however, that it was doubtless felt that they could not be spared.

Under these favouring circumstances a French expedition was launched against St. John's almost simultaneously with that of the British against Havana. When General Amherst on July 15 received information from Governor Bernard of Massachusetts Bay of the presence of a strange fleet in the neighbourhood of the island, he at first thought that it must be a group of British victuallers bound for Quebec; [53] as other intelligence was forwarded to him his doubts

[49] Pennsylvania Gazette, January 10, 1760; for a computation of the importance of the French cod fisheries, without date but probably about the year 1761, see the Chatham Mss., 85:184–7, P.R.O.; for that of the English cod fisheries see C.O. 194:15.

[50] "Return of the Troops," in Governor Webb's report of February 23, 1761, ibid.

[51] Ibid.

[52] [John Almon], Review of Mr. Pitt's Administration (London, 1764), pp. 134–5.

[53] Amherst to Bernard, July 16, 1762, P.R.O. War Office, 27:517.

of the presence of an enemy fleet were cleared, but he was left with the impression that it was a Spanish squadron; by the 25th, however, it was made plain to him that it was French colours flying from the ships.[54] In fact, late in May M. de Ternay's squadron of four men-of-war and a bomb-ketch, with Count d'Haussonville, commanding some eight hundred picked troops taken from four regiments, sailed from Brest and by reason of a fog eluded the British blockading squadron. On June 24 it was off the coast of Newfoundland.

At the time of the appearance of the French, Captain Thomas Graves, who on May 14 had been appointed Governor in place of Webb, had not reached the harbour of St. John's and, as a result, Captain Douglas in the *Syren* was sent to look for him, for he was expected at any moment. When Graves in the *Antelope* was at length found and the situation reported to him, he immediately dispatched a group of marines to help protect the Isle of Boÿs, which with its sixteen guns was reckoned to be a strong post capable of successful defence. He thereupon sailed for Placentia, arriving there on July 22, in order to put it also in condition to ward off an attack — reasoning that if it fell to the French, who already had control of the northern part of the island, and if kept by them in a peace treaty, it would mean that both passages to the Gulf of St. Lawrence and therefore to Canada would be under their control and the trade to Halifax and the homebound trade from the West Indies passing over the Banks would likewise be continuously imperilled.[55]

But to return to the French invaders. Count d'Haussonville with about five hundred of his regulars were, first of all, landed at the Bay of Bulls in Avalon and burned the fishing flakes; thereupon de Ternay with his marines and the remainder of the troops sailed northward to St. John's and appeared there June 27. The town surrendered without opposition and the seventeen vessels in the harbour were also seized. The invaders now occupied in succession Conception, Trinity, and Bonavista bays all to the northward of St. John's, destroying in the process fishing boats, flakes, and stages and at Carbonear and Trinity also the artillery that fell into their hands. With this accomplished, and collecting all the cattle that they

---

[54] The same to the same, July 21 and 25, 1762, *ibid.*, 27:521–3.
[55] Graves to the Board of Trade, August 18, 1762, C.O. 194:15.

could find, they concentrated at St. John's, where they proceeded to erect batteries to cover the harbour and other approaches in anticipation of an attempt to retake it.[56]

The advantage that would accrue to the French should they be permitted to retain possession of the great island over the winter was quite evident to Amherst at New York. At the same time it was clear to him that Lord Colville's diminutive Gulf of St. Lawrence squadron — with but one vessel that could be classified as a warship and useful only for general patrolling activities, such as were indicated in the preceding volume of this series — was not strong enough to interfere with them, nor were the possibilities at all bright that a British fleet convoying transports with troops on board bound for Canada would appear off Newfoundland. The American commander-in-chief therefore determined that an expedition must be organized without delay in America to retake the town, whatever be the risk. Gathering together what troops he could, he placed them under the command of his brother, Lieutenant Colonel William Amherst. They consisted of units drawn from the light infantry that Gage had organized, the second battalion of Montgomery's Highlanders, and the 45th Regiment, later supplemented by men drawn from the Massachusetts Bay provincials posted at Halifax. To convoy the transports carrying these contingents, he called upon Governor Bernard to place at his brother's disposal the Massachusetts Bay warship the *King George*, with the understanding that it would, upon the completion of this task, join Colville's ships.[57]

On August 14 Colonel Amherst moved out of the port of New York; by the 26th he had reached Halifax and on September 4, Louisbourg, at which place he strengthened the force that he brought with him. Sailing then for Newfoundland on the 11th, he was joined by Colville's flotilla to the southward of St. John's. The intelligence that he now received of the activities of the enemy led him to change his proposed landing-place from Kitty Vitty, a narrow entrance close to the town, in favour of Torbay, some three leagues to the northward. On the 12th the transports, protected by Colville's *Syren*, moved into the bay, and next day the troops were disembarked — with the light infantry, accustomed to hand fighting

---

[56] *Ibid.*

[57] P.R.O., W.O. 34, 27:531–2; Amherst to Ligonier, August 15, 1762, Amherst Papers, 11:95–6; "Orders issued by Colonel Amherst," n.d., *ibid.*, Packet 39.

on the continent, driving the enemy before them when it now appeared and tried to break up the landing.

Thereupon came the march of four miles toward St. John's, much of it along a narrow path in the dense woods, during which the seasoned light infantry again showed their expertness in wilderness fighting. Arriving at the mouth of the Kitty Vitty River, they cleared this on the 14th of the shallops that had been sunk to obstruct its entrance by ships, and very early next day some of Montgomery's troops and a contingent of the Royals, supported by grenadiers, drove the enemy from a dominating hill where it was entrenched. On the 16th, while the military stores were being conveyed from Torbay to the Kitty Vitty, the main force advanced close to St. John's and captured another high hill, and that evening, in face of the approaching peril, the French fleet departed from the harbour, leaving Count d'Haussonville and the French infantry to shift for themselves.[58] It was also on this day that Amherst sent a summons to the French general to surrender, with a warning that if the fort was blown up, as it was reported the French intended, every man of the French garrison would suffer capitally for it.[59] D'Haussonville returned a note of defiance.[60] By the evening of the 17th the British had erected a mortar battery and had begun one for twenty-four-pounders about five hundred yards from the fort.

The French troops at St. John's were manifestly caught in a trap of their own making. For there was no possibility of escape now that the fleet had left them. The town could not possibly be defended against land troops in view of the fact that it was all quite exposed to the latter because of the great slope rising behind it. As a result, d'Haussonville early in the morning of the 18th sent to Amherst a rather enigmatic note, which, despite its very defiant tone, intimated his willingness to consider terms of surrender and later in the day sent terms, which proved to be acceptable. Under these the French soldiers were to be embarked on British ships and carried to Brittany.[61] This was done.

With the end of the campaign in Newfoundland and in Cuba, the Great War for the Empire came to a close in the New World — outside of the so-called "private" and abortive expedition against

---

58 William Amherst to Egremont, September 20, 1762, *ibid.*
59 The summons is printed in the *Annual Register*, 1762, p. 264.
60 *Ibid.*, pp. 264–5.
61 For the terms of the surrender see *ibid.*, pp. 265–6.

Buenos Aires, already considered. For by the time these operations were terminated, it was realized that the plan to conquer Louisiana could no longer be executed. This had called for the employment of eight thousand troops, which, upon the conclusion of the operations at Havana, would be placed under the direct command of General Amherst and were to consist of the four thousand sent there from North America and the same number out of those Albemarle had brought with him.[62] In outlining his plan of campaign in the spring, Amherst had thought in terms of the reduction not only of New Orleans but of the entire province, including the Illinois country. To accomplish this he had suggested two methods. By the first, the troops at his disposal would be divided into two distinct corps. One of these could penetrate the Illinois country by way of the Great Lakes during the period of high waters in the springtime; the other could make its approach by way of the mouth of the Mississippi. The second method called for the use of the entire force at his disposal for a direct attack on New Orleans.[63] This latter was, of course, the only practicable project if the attempt were still to be made in 1762, and it was the one that the general adopted.

The conquest of Louisiana did not, in fact, seem to be a difficult thing at the beginning of the year. That the province had been sadly neglected by France for many years was not open to question. It was evident to the British in 1758 — as the result of capture of intercepted documents — that no reinforcements had been sent there since the outbreak of hostilities in 1754.[64] Governor de Kerlérec, in a letter breathing despair and addressed to the Commissary General of the Marine in the month of February 1757, had declared that his condition was such that unless the latter would take pity on him and send him aid, he would be obliged "to put the key under the door." [65] In the latter part of 1758 a British mariner, who had been a prisoner at New Orleans but had been exchanged, reported in his examination at Philadelphia that the force of French regulars at that place numbered only about two hundred and that the militia in the lower Mississippi amounted to only about four hundred men.[66] The only real obstacle that faced a respectable force

---

[62] Egremont to Amherst, February 12, 1762, Amherst Papers, Packet 40.
[63] Amherst to Egremont, April 6, 1762, ibid., Packet 41.
[64] Ibid., 21:53–4.
[65] Loudoun Papers, 61:508, Huntington Library.
[66] "Examination of William Perry," Chatham Mss., Bundle 96, P.R.O.

in order to take possession of the city appeared to be a small battery on La Balise at the mouth of the river, which could undoubtedly be silenced easily by bombardment.

But the enterprise had to be put aside in face of certain grim realities. With the capitulation of Havana, Albemarle, it is true, carried out in part his instructions by proceeding promptly to send back to North America some of the units that had come from there to support him. However, when the transports bringing them appeared in September at the port of New York, Amherst was aghast at the spectacle. Writing to Viscount Ligonier on the 23rd he declared: "These troops are arrived here in such a Deplorable Melancholy State as is not to be conceived without seeing them." [67] A month later he informed Ligonier that other units that he had expected from Cuba could not leave on account of the great mortality among Albemarle's regulars since the time of the capitulation.[68] Thus the very men upon whom he was dependent for his Louisiana expedition either were stricken with fevers and fluxes — many of them unto death — or were required to act as garrison troops in Cuba. He was therefore compelled to give up all thought of launching it during the remainder of the year and, as a result of this decision, proceeded to discharge the pilots who, acquainted with the waters of the Gulf of Mexico, had been for that reason taken into his pay and detained at New York. Nevertheless, in another part of the world there were developments that demand our attention.

At the very time that the British were proceeding with the reduction of Havana and the recovery of St. John's, they were also on their way to Spain's prized possession in the Far East, the Philippine Archipelago. The possibility of the capture of Manila, its capital, was presented to the minister upon the declaration of war against Spain. Lieutenant Colonel William Draper, who had been serving in India, as indicated in an earlier chapter of this volume, had returned to England and had strongly urged that the contemplated expedition against the French Île de France and Île de Bourbon, in the Indian Ocean — as first planned be launched from England but now from India — should be put aside in favour of one against the Spanish Philippines. Draper, while in China in 1760 — where he went with Captain Howe of the *Winchelsea* to recover his health — had gathered considerable information relating to these

---

[67] Amherst Papers, 11:97–9.
[68] *Ibid.*, 11:102–5.

islands and especially as to the state of the defences of Manila, all of which indicated that the capture of the city would be possible. His recommendations were tentatively adopted, with the understanding that should the attempt be made against it, he was to command the land forces.[69] Promoted at this juncture to the permanent rank of colonel and then commissioned — with the temporary rank of brigadier while thus engaged — Draper was ordered to proceed at the earliest possible moment to Madras. Having arrived there, he was, according to his instructions, to seek the advice of the military, naval, and civilian leaders at Fort St. George respecting the enterprise and to govern his future movements accordingly.

Draper boarded the speedy frigate *Argo* and set sail as soon as it was possible; early in March he touched at the Madeiras; [70] and on June 27 he arrived at Madras. His instructions directed him to confer with Rear Admiral Steevens, in command of His Majesty's ships in the Indian Ocean, and with his second in command, Cornish, as well as with Major General Stringer Lawrence, at the head of the land forces at Madras, and Governor George Pigot, representing the United East India Company at Fort St. George. As a group they were to determine whether the resources at hand were sufficient to justify an attempt against Manila.[71] Steevens, however, had died, as has already been pointed out in this volume, and Rear Admiral Cornish had taken over the command; so he and his second, Captain Tiddeman, were called to the conference, which was held early in July.[72] After a careful review of the situation in India, all but Lawrence voted in favour of the expedition.[73] It was there-

---

[69] Egremont to Major General Lawrence, January 23, 1762, P.R.O., C.O. 77:20; *Annual Register*, 1763, p. 4.

[70] Draper to —— , March 11, 1762, P.R.O., C.O. 77:20. This paper and other papers in this collection are not separately numbered.

[71] For Draper's "Instructions" see *ibid*.

[72] When the *Argo* arrived at Madras, Cornish with his fleet was at anchor in a harbour of Ceylon. The frigate thereupon sailed to find him. On July 7 he returned to the Madras road (Draper to Egremont, July 27, 1762, *ibid*.).

[73] Writing to the Earl of Egremont on October 13, Lawrence gives the basis of his refusal to approve of the expedition in the following words: "In my own Opinion indeed I thought the present state of our effective military force made it too hazardous to spare as great a Part of it to make and preserve so distant a conquest and that while Mauritius [Île de France] continues in the hands of the enemy and we are ignorant of what force may be collected there" (*ibid*.). Speaking for the rest of the group, Draper stated in his letter to Egremont of July 27: "With us his [Lawrence's] objections had but little weight as he reasoned only from a possibility of danger rather than from any probability" (*ibid*.).

upon determined to bring it to realization at the earliest possible date.

When Draper left England he had had visions of being able to gather together possibly fifteen hundred British regulars on duty in India and some five hundred of the Company's troops in order to execute his daring *"coupe de main,"* as he called it, against Manila. In fact, outside his own battalion, then in India, and an artillery company, amounting all together to nine hundred and seventy-four men, all that Lawrence could be prevailed upon to spare were mostly natives of Asia and deserters from the French forces made up of people of various nationalities whom Draper declared he took with him "more to ease the Fears and Apprehensions of the People of Madrass [by their absence], than from any service I can expect from them. . . . Such a Banditti never assembled since the time of Spartacus." [74] He had, however, a few highly gifted and energetic land officers, such as Colonel Monson, second in command, who, despite his wounds and impaired health, displayed remarkable efficiency and energy; he could also depend upon Cornish and the other naval officers. Most of the troops, with the supplies, were embarked on two large ships used in the China trade, and between July 29 and August 4 the little flotilla of some fifteen sail in all set out in three divisions.

It was realized that the work in hand must be done rapidly, as the monsoon season customarily arrived in the China Sea toward the end of September and the squadron was not in condition to battle hurricanes. [75] On August 19 Cornish reached Malacca, where he took on a supply of fresh water and a large quantity of rattans — which Draper desired to use for gabions, once he had landed his artillery on shore — and then proceeding on his way on September 22 sailed into Manila Bay.

The Spaniards were caught quite unaware of the fact that a state of war existed between Spain and Great Britain and were therefore totally unprepared for an attack. [76] In fact, the great annual galleon

[74] *Ibid.* In addition to his regulars and the artillery company of thirty men, Draper had six hundred sepoys, a company of coffrees and one of topazes, two companies of French deserters, several hundred unarmed Lascars, and a company of pioneers (Draper's "Journal," *ibid.*).

[75] Draper to Egremont, July 27, 1762, *ibid.*, Lawrence to the Directors of the United East India Company, July 31, 1762, P.R.O., India Office, HEIC's, Madras, 1:59–61.

[76] Manila, November 10, 1762, *ibid.*; Draper's "Journal," C.O. 77:20.

from Acapulco, Mexico, with a large supply of bullion for the Manila trade and bearing the nephew of the Governor to the islands as well as letters telling of the state of hostilities, had not yet reached Manila, though it had arrived in the archipelago. Cornish, having secured information of its presence, on the 27th with the approval of Draper detached two ships of war to secure it. While this was not accomplished, the galleon that was bound for America was located and captured after a hard fight. This constituted the first serious blow against the Spaniards in the Pacific.[77]

To take full advantage of the surprise, it was decided to change the plan of attack — which had called for the capture, first of all, of the fort of Cavite at the entrance of the bay — and to storm the city. While preparations for this were being rushed, however, a summons to surrender was sent to the city the morning of the 24th. This was refused. That morning, after Cornish and others had examined the coast, it was decided to land two miles south of Manila in three separated divisions — Draper himself leading the centre one, Colonel Monson at the head of that closest to the city, and Major More, the eldest field officer, with the third. While the frigates moved as close to the shore as possible and poured their fire into the Spanish foot soldiers and cavalry that assembled to oppose the landing, the three divisions moved abreast in longboats manned by sailors. With the retirement of the enemy out of range of artillery fire and despite the violent surf that dashed many boats to pieces, the troops landed at their assigned places without loss of life and then assembled at a village called Malata. That night, as the invaders slept on their arms, the Spaniards busied themselves burning part of the suburbs of the city. The approach began the following day. An abandoned outer fort was seized that permitted Draper to cover the landing of military supplies; then Colonel Monson occupied a great church with massive walls, located but nine hundred yards from the city enclosure. While this was proceeding, the monsoon broke with a tremendous downpour of rain accompanied by wind and a very dangerous surf, which only the intrepidity and great expertness of the British sailors overcame in order to get essential supplies, such as food and ammunition, to the troops on land, as well as a reinforcement of sepoys and regular troops. Some of the latter were, however, lost in the highly hazardous task.[78]

---

[77] *Ibid.* and the *Annual Register*, 1763, pp. 13–14.
[78] C.O. 77:20.

By September 26 the waters of the bay were sufficiently quiet so that the rest of the Company's troops were landed and also a battalion of Cornish's sailors. That day the Spaniards in fair strength, supported by artillery, made a sortie from the city, but were driven back by Monson. A second summons was then sent to the Governor, but he returned a most spirited reply. It was clear that the only way Manila could be won was by storming it — to besiege it, with its great extent, was quite impossible with the handful of soldiers. What is more, an assault had to be made without much delay as the Marquis de Mediana, in direct command of the Spanish troops, numbering some eight hundred, was bringing to his aid thousands of fierce natives, who were entering the capital by way of the more distant city gates.

Towering in front of the British were the great bastions of St. Diego and St. Andrew. These were provided with orillions, retired flanks, and ravelins and were designed to cover the so-called "Royal Gate." In addition there were a wet fosse, a covered way, and a glacis; and from the bastions and these supplementary defences bristled a large number of fine brass cannon. It was decided that the St. Diego should be stormed. With the rattans secured at Malacca, soldiers began feverishly to make fascines and gabions for the protection of batteries that others were also busily opening up. To secure an adequate breach in the walls, the admiral sent ashore eight of his twenty-four-pounders and some eighteens, and by the 30th the engineers — though they worked with great difficulty through lack of entrenching tools — had traced out a battery for the heaviest guns. But the next day the monsoon again broke in all its fury, endangering the flotilla in the bay and cutting all communication between it and the shore. Nevertheless, the battering cannon were put in place and a mortar battery for heavy ten- and thirteen-inch shells was also installed in the midst of the downpour, so that, with the subsidence of the storm, it was possible on October 3 to begin firing upon the left trace of the St. Diego bastion at the salient angle. The Spanish guns there were silenced after a few hours of bombardment and the defenders driven from them. That same day another battery opened up on the St. Andrew's bastion, and throughout the night, while the mortars dropped their bombs into the gorges, the two bastions continued under heavy fire. To put a stop to this systematic destruction of the city's defences, early the morning of the 4th, in the midst of an incessant rain, a thousand

Filipinos, armed chiefly with bows, arrows, and lances, poured out of the Royal Gate and attacked the seamen's cantonment, advancing again and again with reckless ferocity up to the very muzzles of the guns. Another party of them also attacked the sepoys and dislodged them from a church; but when they came up against Draper's regulars, the latter not only held their ground but finally drove them back. This was the last offensive action on the part of the defenders of Manila.

With the morale of the natives shattered as the result of the two defeats, most of them now left the city and returned to their homes in the country. What is more, the batteries firing night and day were bringing about the disintegration of the fortifications, besides making it impossible for the defenders to repair them. By the evening of the 5th the breach in the walls was considered adequate for the purpose in hand, and at four o'clock the following morning the British soldiers began concentrating about St. Iago's Church. With daybreak a large body of the enemy appeared on the St. Andrew's bastion; when, however, the shells from the mortars began falling upon them, they dispersed. Taking advantage of this confusion and screened by a dense smoke that slowly drifted toward the city, the assaulters now rushed forward, led by a party of volunteers supported by some of Draper's grenadiers; the engineers and pioneers followed, in order to clear the way, enlarge the breach, and make lodgements in case of enemy resistance; and behind them pressed the main body of troops under Monson, followed by the battalion of seamen. The Spaniards on the bastions disappeared; but at the Royal Gate a group of them and Filipinos who refused to surrender were put to the sword, and from the galleries of the lofty houses that surrounded the great city square there was firing for a time. The Governor, with his principal officers, had retired to the citadel and, since the place offered little defence against Draper's guns, they wisely decided to capitulate.[79]

The capture of Manila was a military and naval achievement of a very high order, resulting from skilful planning, a high degree of co-ordination of the respective tasks of the two branches of the service, and the resourcefulness and intrepidity of both soldiers and sailors. It constituted the final humiliation visited on the head of the Spanish house of Bourbon. To the honour of the British arms, the same humanity displayed toward the inhabitants

[79] "Journal," *ibid.*

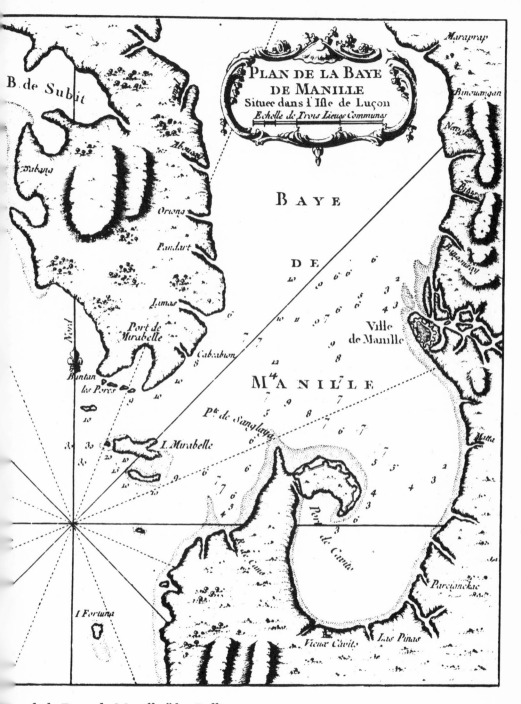

n de la Baye de Manille." by Bellin.   (From *Le Petit Atlas maritime*)

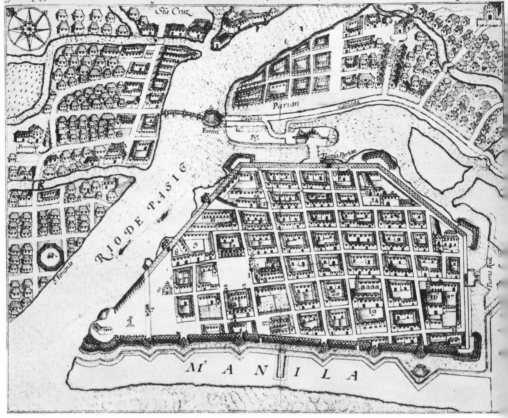

1 La Cathedral: 2. 3. y 4. Palacio, Real Audiencia, y Contaduria: 5. Almazenes: 6. Capilla Real: 7. Castillo de S. Tiago: 8. Santa Clara: 9. Hospital Real: 10. Cassis de Cavildo: 11. Collegio de Santo Thomas: 12. Santo Domingo 13. S. Juan de Dios: 14. S. Francisco: 15. Recoletos: 16. La Compañia de Jesus: 17. Real Collegio de S. Joseph: 18. La Fundicion: 19. S. Augustin: 20. Santa Isabel: 21. Collegio de San Phelipe: 22. Casa Arzobispal: 23. Santa Potenciana: 24. Beaterio de Santo Domingo: 25. Collegio de San Juan de Letran: 26. Recogidas.

"Manila. Descripcion de plazas, prendos y fuertes de las Filipinas" (1777?).

(From the Library of Congress map)

of Havana was likewise in evidence in the treatment of those of Manila.

As soon as Cornish could come ashore he and Draper laid down the conditions under which the city would be preserved from plunder. These provided that the Spanish officers should be prisoners of war on their parole of honour, with the liberty of appearing with their swords, that all military stores should be turned over, that Fort Cavite and other forts dependent upon Manila should surrender, and that four million Spanish dollars should be paid — one half immediately and the rest at a time to be agreed upon, with hostages and other security given to that end.[80] This was agreed to by the Spanish Governor and his Council. Thereupon, the Archbishop of Manila, who was also the Captain General of the Philippines, Don Arzpe de Mande, together with the Royal Audiencia of the Philippines and the officials of the city of Manila, were permitted to offer terms of surrender.

The terms, indicated under twelve articles of the proffered capitulation, included the following requests: the preservation of individual effects and possessions; the maintenance of the Roman Catholic church; the unobstructed return to Manila of families that had fled to the country; the freedom of commerce within the islands; the guarantee by the British of peace and quiet within the city and suburbs; freedom of ecclesiastical authorities to instruct the faithful, and especially the natives; the retention of the "economical" government of the city, as well as the authority not only of the Royal Audiencia, but of the ministers and royal officers in their posts, with sufficient stipends for their support, and with the understanding that His Catholic Majesty would be answerable for the latter. With some explanatory comments these reasonable conditions were accepted by Draper and Cornish.[81] Thereupon the British took over Manila, a city, according to Draper, of "vast opulence," and on the 10th Cavite was also surrendered.[82] Finally, on October 30 a formal surrender of all the Philippines took place in the following terms:

"All the islands (subordinate to Luconia [Luzon] and Manila its capital and which are at present under the dominion of his Catholic Majesty) must be ceded to his Britannic Majesty, who must be ac-

---

[80] "Conditions on which the city of Manila shall be preserved from plunder," *ibid*.
[81] "Proposals of October . . . made by the Archbishop . . . ," *ibid*.
[82] Draper to Egremont, November 9, 1762, *ibid*.

knowledged Sovereign, 'til the Fate of these Islands is decided by a Peace between the two Kings. Their Religion, Goods, Liberties, Properties and Commerce shall be preserved to the inhabitants of these islands who are the Subjects of Spain in as ample a manner as they are confirmed to the Inhabitants of Manila and the Island of Luconia."

To this was added the proviso that all the inhabitants were to be allowed honours of war, and that in consideration thereof they were to give their parole, as had been done at Manila and Cavite, not to take up arms against His Britannic Majesty.[83]

That the formal surrender of the Philippine Archipelago failed to bring about the pacification of the natives and that British soldiers' and sailors' dreams of riches from the ransom of Manila, and those of the United East India Company officials of the widening of its sphere of influence in the Far East, were not to be fulfilled, may best be considered briefly in the concluding chapter of this volume.

---

[83] "Surrender of the Philippine Islands," *ibid.*

CHAPTER XII

The Return of Peace

Britain's Great War for the Empire reached a truly amazing culmination in the fall of 1762, though it is true that news of the conquest of the Philippine Archipelago only reached England early in April 1763 and therefore too late to affect the terms of the treaty that was destined to restore peace.

The war had begun in 1754 with the first of an all but unbroken series of military successes on the part of the French. But finally the tide turned and in place of victories one humiliation after another was visited upon their arms. By the end of the year 1762 they had lost everything in North America east of the distant Mississippi River outside of New Orleans: their forces had been in turn overwhelmed on Cape Breton Island, on Isle St. Jean, to be renamed Prince Edward Island, and in Canada; in the West Indies they were unable to save from conquest the opulent islands of Guadeloupe, Martinique, and Grenada, nor could they continue to hold the so-called "Neutral Islands" of Dominica, St. Vincent, and St. Lucia that they had colonized, despite a solemn agreement between France and Great Britain that neither nation would settle them until their status had been determined. As for Tobago, the fourth Neutral Island, inhabited only by natives, this too had passed under British control.

Nor did France fare any better in other parts of the world. Her two prized African possessions of Senegal and Goree had fallen to British arms. In India, while for a time, it is true — as the result of Bussy's almost uncanny ability to win the confidence of native princes and great concessions for the Compagnie des Indes — it looked as though the United East India Company might be ejected from its precarious footholds in that vast country, yet by the year in question the chief French centre on the Coromandel Coast, Pondicherry, with its once pretentious government buildings and fortifications, lay in complete ruin, as did the chief French centre in Bengal, powerfully fortified Chandernagore. Indeed, with the surrender of the factory at Mahi on the Malabar Coast and the fortress of Gingy in the Carnatic, both of which events occurred during the first half of 1761, the last evidence of French control had disappeared from India and with it the visions of a vast accretion of military and economic power. Moreover, right at home, Belle-île-en-Mer in the Bay of Biscay had been lost. Nor was it possible to retain even St. John's in Newfoundland, which, after falling into French hands in the summer of 1762, had been as quickly lost as it had been gained.

Nowhere, in fact, had the French cause prospered as the war drew to a close. The navy, which during the early years of the war had displayed excellent fighting qualities, was by the autumn of 1762 hopelessly shattered. The ships of the merchant marine could only move out of home waters at the risk of being captured by alert blockading fleets; and when reaching the high seas, especially with the fall of Martinique, they were faced with extraordinary difficulties of attaining in safety any harbour where French products could be exchanged for needed foreign commodities. The great ports of France, as a result, were stagnant and the merchants there either ruined or facing ruin. What was even more ominous, throughout the Kingdom people had become extremely restless, if not mutinous, under the heavy load of war taxation with no victories any longer to buoy up their spirits. With only depressing news of one defeat after another they had become quite disillusioned over the supposed glories of their empire as the latter disintegrated under the blows that it had received. They could, it is true, point to the fact that Minorca in the Mediterranean and the insignificant trading posts of Natal and Tapanooly on Sumatra, also taken from the British, were still held. Yet these were small consolations for their immense losses. Of the overseas empire that they had so hopefully built up at great cost, there only remained to them Louisiana in North America, secretly pledged to Spain under certain conditions — a vast area, thinly populated, that had been unsuccoured for years and for all practical purposes abandoned, owing to the strain of war elsewhere; St. Domingue in the West Indies, subject to capture at any time the British were disposed to assault it in force; and, finally, lying to the east of Madagascar in the Indian Ocean, the impoverished and weak but strategic Îsle de France and Îsle de Bourbon.

As for Spain, the inflated anticipations of Charles III had only too soon been cruelly blasted, once the war had been proclaimed that he had so eagerly sought. For the wealth of the flota and the register ships that had reached the safety of Cádiz in 1761 had not availed him. He had to witness helplessly the sweeping of the commerce of his empire from the seas, the sealing up of his fleets at Cádiz and Havana, the assault on that jewel of the Caribbeans, Cuba, and the utter prostration of the island with the loss of its metropolis and with it many of the best ships of the Spanish navy. Thereupon most of his New World possessions stood all but naked of defence, with no prospect of material aid from any quarter. This was particularly true of Santo Domingo and Puerto Rico in the West Indies, St. Augustine, the capital of the province of Florida, Vera Cruz, the chief port of the Viceroyalty of New Spain, and on the Isthmus of Panama the great emporium, Puerto Bello, the key to the Viceroyalty of Peru. Moreover, the one enterprise that had seemed to offer to him an easily obtained and extraordinarily valuable prize — the conquest of an all but helpless Portugal, lying just over the Spanish border and with important overseas possessions, including Brazil — had, with the marshalling of British forces, hopelessly bogged down in barren, mountainous country far removed from Lisbon and Oporto, his immediate military objectives. Gibraltar, which he also had expected to reclaim in his victorious stride, he likewise had found was impregnable to any assault his army could deliver against it. Nor was he to learn until the new year of the minor success when the small British-Portuguese force was prevented from recapturing Nova Colonia, in the delta of the Río de la Plata, chiefly as the result of the loss by fire of one of the three frigates carrying most of the invading force, or of the major defeat with the capture of Manila and the surrender of the Philippine Archipelago.

The Seven Years' War in Europe had also reached a climax in the fall of 1762. So far as western Germany was concerned, the outstanding event was the capture of Cassel, capital of Hesse, by Prince Ferdinand's allied army on November 1, with the surrender of the large French defending force. With this event the prolonged and confusing struggle in Westphalia really came to a close, with the French army still smarting under defeats administered to it earlier in the year when it was outfought and outmanœuvred in that area. In eastern Germany, King Frederick — at last relieved of the pressure that Russia under Elizabeth had brought to bear upon him, now that that country under Catherine had assumed the role of a neutral — was able early in October, as already indicated, to retake, after a prolonged siege, the great fortress of Schweidnitz and, in so doing, to capture an Austrian army defending it. This was followed late the same month by the decisive victory of his brother, Prince Henry, over a combined Imperial and Austrian army at Freiberg. Henry thereupon, in the absence of any serious resistance, proceeded on a triumphal march through Bohemia, Saxony, and Franconia, everywhere levying enormous contributions. Thus at the very time when Great Britain, France, and Spain were about to reach a decision to terminate their own war, the Seven Years' War had reached a stage highly favourable to Prussia as well as to Hanover, Hesse, and Brunswick.

With the above facts before us it is now desirable to turn our attention to political developments in Great Britain in 1762 in so far as these are germane to the problem of the termination of the Great War for the Empire.

To the nation — and also far beyond it — William Pitt in a sense had epitomized in his person the dominating position in world affairs that Britain had attained before the coming of the memorable year 1762. If her power had come to be feared and respected, so had he been, as an individual. When France and Spain had watched every move of the embattled island kingdom with apprehension, their eyes had really been on him. But he no longer was a minister, for he had retired from the direction of the Great War for the Empire the preceding October when he had found that his plan to deliver a sudden attack upon truculent Spain could not obtain the support of most of his colleagues in the Cabinet Council. But, in retiring, his unprecedented services to his country and his King had been suitably recognized, as was made clear in an earlier chapter, by rewards showered upon him and his family.

In the reorganization of the ministry with the retirement of the Great Commoner his post of Secretary of State for the Southern Department, though not his unique place in the Cabinet Council, was taken by Charles Wyndham, Earl of Egremont, a brother-in-law of

Pitt's brother-in-law George Grenville, and his position as leader of the House of Commons by Grenville himself, who was given a place in the Council. There was, however, little or no immediate change in policy, outside of the fact that Pitt's plan of an immediate attack on Spain was laid aside in favour of a more conventional method of bringing that country to account. With respect to the war with France, the King's speech to Parliament — prepared by Hardwicke and finally approved by his colleagues in the Council with little amendment — had called for its most rigorous prosecution.[1] Further, the letter that Egremont had addressed to the Earl of Bristol, Ambassador at Madrid, which was sent on October 28, had, in the words of the Duke of Newcastle, breathed "war as much as Mr. Pitt did."[2] It was clear that Pitt's continued popularity had had the effect upon Bute, Egremont, and Grenville of determining them to carry on negotiations with Spain with great firmness and the war with France with unabated zeal.[3] As has already been noted, the attack on Martinique was made early in the new year with overwhelming force and, with the receipt of an unsatisfactory reply from Spain, war had been declared against that power and every exertion made to press hostilities against the Bourbon powers to a victorious conclusion.

Indeed, the country by the beginning of 1762 had been in almost every respect so well prepared to wage war against both France and Spain — so outstanding were the capacities of its military and naval leaders, so seasoned by the ordeal of battle its soldiers and sailors, so formidable its sea power, and so adequate the logistic arrangements, including the sources of all necessary supplies — that it is hard to believe that the absence of Pitt at his old place of command adversely affected in any respect the final outcome of the year's campaigns. For, as has been stressed in the preceding chapter, more than was actually accomplished could not, under the given circumstances, have been undertaken in the New World by the conquerors of Havana and the retrievers of St. John's in Newfoundland, and more was not required to tip the balance in favour of sincere overtures of peace on the part of both the French and the Spanish governments.

---

[1] Philip C. Yorke, The Life and Correspondence of Philip Yorke, Earl of Hardwicke, III, 294.

[2] Newcastle to Hardwicke, October 27, 1761, ibid., III, 335.

[3] Hardwicke to Newcastle, October 23, 1761, ibid., III, 335–6.

Not only was Britain's Great War for the Empire to be concluded, however, but it was necessary for the country to extricate itself from the European Seven Years' War. The growing unpopularity of continuing British participation in it has already been dealt with rather fully earlier in this volume. Further to illustrate this point, when on November 13, 1761 the address to the King had been moved in the Commons, George Dempster, representing Perth for some thirty years, "censured the German War, as having neither object nor end . . . and said, he was pleased to see that his Majesty had emancipated himself from the chains that had been prepared for him" — with manifest reference to Pitt.[4] Another member, Elias Harvey, also condemned Britain's connection with this war. The views thus expressed were apparently openly supported by other members newly chosen in the recent general election. Thereupon Pitt rose to defend his policies as late minister. Although in the lengthy speech that followed he dealt with other matters, it is with his attitude toward the continued support of what he himself called the "German War" that we are concerned. On this point he declared, according to Horace Walpole, that in view of the "many arraignments" of this war by members of the House and the failure of any of the ministers of state to speak in support of it, especially by reason of the fact that reports of the debate would be carried abroad, he must affirm that he would feel himself

> "robbed of his honour, if our troops were recalled from Germany. . . . The way to peace was not by lessening our efforts. England was equal to both wars . . . and if continued, nothing but conquest would follow — all owing to the German War. If we abandoned our allies, God would abandon us. *America had been conquered in Germany.* Prince Ferdinand had been the saviour of Europe, and had shattered the whole military power of that military monarchy, France. It was not from what young members had said against the German War, but from what had *not* been said for it, that . . . augured ill for this country (and) though every other man in the House should be against the German war; he would stand single, and undergo the shame."[5]

[4] In November, Devonshire warned the King that Bute and Newcastle must work together lest Pitt return to power "and take possession of his Majesty" (*Letters of George III to Bute* (ed. R. Sedgwick, London, 1939), pp. 69–70).

[5] *Memoirs of the Reign of King George the Third* (London, 1845), I, 96–7. The words italicized were underlined by Walpole. The author of these *Memoirs* assures his readers (p. 107) that "what I give was faithfully taken down from his own mouth in the House of Commons."

The points to be particularly noted in Pitt's address are: first, that he had committed the country to support the German war to the end and that his personal honour was therefore involved should there be a withdrawal from it; second, that there were two distinct wars and not simply one, and that the success of the Anglo-French war was due to Britain's participation in the German war, and also that further participation would make possible further conquests at the expense of France; and, finally, that it was Prince Ferdinand, leader of the allied troops defending Hanover, who had shattered the power of France.

Pitt, it is true, had earlier committed himself so openly and so definitely to a continued support of the war in Germany, and with it the cause of the King of Prussia, that no government that he led could have easily withdrawn from it except under terms acceptable to Frederick. It is equally true that he and every other statesman in Europe agreed that there were *two* distinct wars going on at one and the same time, in *both* of which Great Britain and France were involved, while, in contrast, Prussia, Austria, the Empire, Russia, and Sweden were concerned in only *one* of them, as was also true of Spain and Portugal when they became belligerents. This distinction is of great importance for the understanding of developments during this period, a distinction that has been all but lost as the result of the lack of sufficiently high standards of precision in nomenclature and in some other respects on the part of those concerned with writing its history.

As to the famous dictum that the success of the war in America was to be attributed to Britain's participation in the German war and to Prince Ferdinand's achievements in arms, there is lack of evidence that this was true. It must be borne in mind that the chief reason that France lost Canada, Cape Breton Island, most of her islands in the West Indies, with the Neutral Islands there, Belle-Île-en-Mer and her hold in Bengal and in the Carnatic and along the Coromandel Coast in India, was not lack of supplies and soldiers, but her inability, as already emphasized in this and the preceding volume of the series, to obtain command of the high seas. For sea control was essential not only to transport funds, supplies, and reinforcements urgently required to strengthen the French position in these places, but also to interdict by aggressive action the use of British sea power in the enterprises launched against them. This required, among other things, the building of more and bet-

ter warships and supply ships than could be constructed in the shipyards of Great Britain and New England, where great and sustained
efforts to the end of preserving the British Empire's sea supremacy
had been going on ever since the beginning of hostilities. Under
the most favourable conditions, when not as yet involved in a continental European war — as when Machault in 1755 turned all the
available resources of France to the strengthening of the navy —
the country while building very good ships could not match the
rate of British production, which rate was increased under Pitt. In
this connection it should be pointed out that the art of a shipwright
demanded a high degree of skill born of experience — mere numbers of men in shipyards could not answer the need. Such a program of tremendously accelerated ship construction also called for
vast supplies of the necessary materials: seasoned oak for hulls,
pine for the great masts and yardarms, together with other naval
stores such as resin, pitch, and tar, as well as other materials, much
of which were foreign-produced commodities, which could be denied to France by a blockading power, and which were, in fact,
denied, at least in quantity.

In other words, France had a logistical problem of the first mag-
nitude which she never was in a position to solve. In contrast, the
British Empire was, by the period in question, independent of the
rest of the world for every article required in the building and
equipping of both war ships and merchantmen even in war-time —
with masting and naval stores flowing from America — and, what
is more, had the men at hand with the skill to utilize those resources. Again, France was faced by an even more serious lack than
that of shipbuilding supplies — that of a large seafaring population.
The desperate effort to supply a sufficiently large number of good
sailors for the French navy and the failure to do so, for example,
before that splendid Brest fleet moved out of the harbour to its destruction in the Battle of Quiberon Bay, are but another illustra-
tion of the fatal handicaps that faced the nation in seeking to challenge on the high seas a country blessed with the greatest crop of
sea-fighters that any nation up to that time had ever nurtured and
that in quality measured up to the best of the Elizabethan "sea-
dogs." No number of discharged soldiers without previous long
service before the mast could have hoped to take out the great ships
of the line with any chance of being able to perform the exacting
duties required of sailors called upon to manœuvre them with suffi-

cient expertness to bring about the destruction of the British navy — a navy superbly manned, as it was, from top to bottom. Nor could any amount of money saved by failure to participate in the German war have made good the glaring deficiencies; indeed, the extent to which British resources could be diverted to this war, as against the other, was a clear gain to France. We must therefore believe that Pitt, on the one hand, erred in his statement that "America was conquered in Germany," and that George Grenville, on the other hand, was more nearly correct when, in answering Pitt in the same debate, he declared: "It had not been the German war but the want of seamen that had disabled France from prosecuting the war in America and from invading England."[6] He should, of course, have added to the phrase "want of seamen" the words "and of a sufficiently large number of warships." But a myth, once it has been created, dies slowly, and most writers of history have uncritically accepted this one and have consequently embodied it in their treatises.

The issue over the further support of the German war had by the beginning of 1762 become one of first importance and involved the highest echelons of government. In the Cabinet Council meeting of January 6 Bute raised the question of withdrawal from it and was opposed by Newcastle. As for George III, the King patriotically took the position that as for himself he was quite willing to sacrifice his private interest by ordering the British troops from Germany; he even went so far as to declare to Bute that if the Duke of Newcastle would "not hear reason concerning the German war it would be better to let him go than go on with that."[7] In fact, the Cabinet Council came to the decision to inform the British minister in Berlin, Andrew Mitchell, that he should warn Frederick that he must make peace with his enemies on the best terms possible, since Great Britain, faced with a new war in Portugal, could not continue indefinitely to be involved in the German war.[8] What is more, if George II had been deeply angered when the news reached him in 1756 that the King of Prussia had suddenly sent his army across the borders of Saxony to take over that country, the inhabitants of which were dwelling in peace with no warlike designs on any of their neighbours, and had been only persuaded by his min-

---

[6] Ibid., I, 104.
[7] George III to Bute, January 6, 1762, Letters of George III to Bute, pp. 78–9.
[8] Ibid., pp. 79–80.

isters from publicly denouncing what seemed to him a most ruth-
less act, how much more sensitive must George III — a man of much
nobler qualities — have been in continued support of that predatory monarch who was determined to suffer no penalty as payment
for an international wrong and, logically enough, to ensure the ab-
sorption of Saxony, continued to demand British support to that
end. In fact, the King had little use for "that *too ambitious monarch* . . . that *proud, overbearing Prince*," as he called Frederick.[9]

Fortunately for the Prussian King, at the beginning of 1762, when
the darkest clouds of a desperate situation were hanging menac-
ingly over him, one of his bitterest enemies, Elizabeth of Russia, as
already stated, died and was succeeded by the Prussian King's devoted friend, the weak Peter, who ordered his armies to cease all
hostilities against Frederick immediately. A letter from the British
Ambassador at St. Petersburg, Sir Robert Keith, containing this
momentous news reached London on February 5.

That same day the Duke of Bedford, Lord Privy Seal, despite the
entreaties of the Duke of Cumberland,[10] rose in the House of Lords
to move a resolution deploring the expense of the German war —
very much, it may be added, secretly to the delight of the King.[11]
According to the Earl of Hardwicke, a scrupulous recorder, Bedford, in referring to this war, declared that Britain's participation
in it,

> "unnecessary and unjustifiable at first, is become much more so
> since the Spanish war; which has no connection with Germany. A
> continental war [is] never proper for England, unless attended with
> a grand alliance. Now we are in [such] a war without allies — the
> King of Prussia is not so in effect to us — He [is] not at war with
> France." [12]

In reply to an objection voiced by one of the Lords, "That this is
a war of diversion," the Duke replied: "We have a much better diversion than that — a superiority at sea," and added: "France does
not mean to crush the King of Prussia." [13] Bedford, it should be em-

---

9 George III to Bute, February 5, 1762, *ibid.*, p. 81. The words italicized are so in
the King's letter.

10 Walpole, *op. cit.*, I, 136.

11 George III to Bute, February 5, 1762, *op. cit.*, p. 81.

12 *Parliamentary History*, XV, 1218–19. For the exact wording of the Bedford resolution see *ibid.*

13 *Ibid.*

phasized, was not speaking for the Cabinet Council, though a member of it, but simply in his private capacity. In fact, had his resolution been adopted, it is clear that it would have meant a break in that body, since both the Duke of Newcastle and the Earl of Hardwicke, members of it as well as of the government that had been responsible for sending troops to Germany, were still strongly committed to a continued participation in this war. Bute, well aware of the danger to the ministry that he now led and in order to extricate it from this embarrassing development — doubtless also not unmindful that Pitt in the House of Commons might spring into action and pour consuming scorn upon him and his colleagues — finally rose and declared, again according to Hardwicke:

> "Was I to study my own security, I should perhaps shelter myself under such a resolution. I will not procure safety to myself at the expense of my country — This motion is not only improper, but highly dangerous. . . . Calling away the troops now would be attended with disgrace, infamy, and destruction. Let us lessen our expenses, and in due time bring the war within a proper compass." [14]

He thereupon moved the previous question, which in parliamentary usage had the effect of shutting off debate. His motion was carried by a vote of one hundred and five to sixteen.[15] To the King this scene in the House of Lords was a "most extraordinary affair," with which expression most people would agree; it serves to underline the fact that the political solidarity of the Cabinet Council had as yet not been achieved as a binding principle controlling the conduct of the ministers of state.

If — in view of the indirect but tentative approval given in the House of Lords to a continued support of the war in Germany by voting in favour of Bute's opportune motion — it was made clear there would be no immediate withdrawal of British troops that had the chief responsibility of protecting Hanover, it was equally clear that in the course of the debate leading to the vote not one word had been said in favour of continuing to aid the King of Prussia in his particular war. Indeed, the Earl's advice: "Let us lessen our ex-

---

[14] *Ibid.*

[15] It may be pointed out that seven peers, among them Bedford, signed a protest against the rejection of the latter's resolution. The protest declared, among other things, that adoption of the resolution could be "in no degree construed as a breach of faith to our allies, or a stain to the honour of the nation, as we are bound by no treaties to keep an army in Germany" (*ibid.*).

penses, and in due time bring the war within a proper compass," meant more than the casual listener in the visitors' gallery might have inferred. For it undoubtedly was aimed against the continued support of the Pitt-Newcastle policy of subsidizing Prussia. Already four subsidies — each of them amounting to six hundred and seventy thousand pounds — had been paid. When the peace negotiations with France came to an abrupt end in the summer in 1761, Frederick had sought to renew his subsidy treaty. Each treaty — the first signed on April 11, 1758 — was valid for one year only. It therefore meant that if a new treaty were entered into, it would run from April 1762 to April of the following year.

Before the rupture with Spain, Bute had intimated that the King of Prussia might expect to receive a fifth subsidy. But after hostilities had been entered with that power, thus extending the scope of the Great War for the Empire, the Earl — especially in view of the growing unpopularity within Parliament of the German subsidy policy as well as the added financial burden that the war with Spain had brought — was reluctant to agree to a further renewal of the subsidy treaty, which embodied, it should be emphasized, the following pledge:

> "That neither of the contracting powers shall conclude any peace, make any truce, or enter any treaty of neutrality, of what kind soever, without the participation of the other." [16]

Instead, Bute seems to have had in mind, at least for a time, simply providing Frederick's subsidy out of the general grant by Parliament for war purposes.[17] This would have two decided advantages: the estimate for this grant would not have to be brought before that body with the possibility that it would be refused and, if not, with the probability that a debate on it would evoke many hostile and bitter expressions by members; again, were the subsidy given without a treaty, the hands of the ministers would at length be freed so that, without the slightest taint of moral obliquity, they could enter into whatever arrangements seemed best to promote the re-establishment of peaceful relations with France. The Earl at the same time sought, but without success, early in 1762 to induce both hostile Austria and Russia, now a neutral, to take such steps

---

[16] For the wording of the Anglo-Prussian subsidy treaty see John Entick, *General History of the Late War*, III, 74–5.

[17] C. W. Eldon, *England's Subsidy Policy toward the Continent during the Seven Years' War* (Philadelphia, 1938), pp. 145–6.

as would influence Prussia to bring to a close the Seven Years' War.[18] The Cabinet Council, what is more, decided that it was high time to ask Frederick, in view of his continued demand for another subsidy, to "lay his whole thoughts and plan" respecting the coming year before the King. The latter, acting upon this advice, wrote to him to that effect.

Instead of getting the sort of reply that would encourage the ministers to feel he was disposed to make any concessions in order to re-establish peace in Germany, the King of Prussia's letter was very abrupt — "breathing war more than ever" — and imperiously demanding an answer, *"oui ou non,"* whether a subsidy of the same proportions as previously granted would be paid to him. Added to this, Frederick in a dispatch to his envoys in London declaimed in passionate anger against Bute and his colleagues in the Cabinet Council, declaring they ought to be sent *"a la petite maison, to Bedlam."* A copy of this, secured by the secret service, was made available to the ministers. This did not add to the confidence of the majority of them in his intentions.[19] The King called the letter addressed to him "the most cavalier, and I may say the most impertinent one ever wrote by a subsidized monarch." [20] Hardwicke, however, did not think the subsidy could be honourably refused.[21] As for Newcastle, his view respecting the question of granting or withholding it seemed to fluctuate, but was finally determined by Hardwicke's arguments.[22] Bute also seemed to have fluctuated in his opinions until in the spring he came to the King's view that the subsidy should not be granted. George III's words embodied in a letter to the Earl are important:

"The more I consider the Prussian subsidy the more objections arise in my mind against it, and as to the German war, I am clear that if France is not willing for peace, we must instantly nock [knock] it [that is, the German War] in the head, and if men will leave my service because I love this country preferably to any other, it will be they that will be run at and not me." [23]

---

18 *Ibid.*, pp. 146–7. See also W. L. Dorn, "Frederick the Great and Lord Bute," *Journal of Modern History*, I, 535–9.

19 Newcastle to Hardwicke, February 22, 1762, B.M., Add. Mss., 32935, ff. 9–10.

20 George III to Bute, February 20, 1762, *op. cit.*, p. 86.

21 Hardwicke to Newcastle, February 25, 1762, B.M., Add. Mss., 32935, f. 76.

22 See, for example, Newcastle's letters to Hardwicke of February 25 and 27 and of April 10 and 17, B.M., Add. Mss., 32935, ff. 74 and 94; 32937, ff. 13 and 183.

23 George III to Bute, the middle of April 1762, *op. cit.*, pp. 92–3.

By the latter part of March Frederick had become aware of the measures that had been undertaken by members of the Cabinet Council, including Bute and Newcastle, to ease tensions in Europe and, always suspicious, he was sure that he was being betrayed and therefore ordered Michell and Knyphausen to stop negotiating for the subsidy.[24] That was just as well. For early in April George Grenville seemed to have decided that the time had come not only to get rid of it but as soon as possible to get out of the German war, and apparently he had Bute's full support [25] as well as that of the King, though the Earl's attitude had remained outwardly at least for a time one of hesitation, as has been suggested. Nevertheless, when the issue over the Prussian subsidy came up for the final determination of the Cabinet Council on April 30, he, joined by Grenville, Egremont, Granville, and Ligonier voted against it — the Earl of Granville, in fact, said that Frederick was really "the greatest enemy the King had." [26] Mansfield, while he remained silent, was also opposed to it; Bedford would likewise have strongly opposed it had he been present. Only three members supported it: Newcastle, Hardwicke, and Devonshire.[27]

With this weighty matter now disposed of and Prussia thus cut off from further British aid, the additional question — raised, as has already been pointed out, by Bedford in the House of Lords — involving further support in any form of the German war, came up for determination. Tied up with this matter was the further question of the ability of the treasury to stand the strain of this when added to the weight of the demands created by the Spanish war. To Newcastle the two issues were secretly determined by Bute and Grenville when they tentatively agreed to ask for a credit of but one million pounds as a subsidy to be used solely for the support of Portugal. The Duke, still at the head of the treasury, on the other hand, insisted that it should be two millions, one of which would be utilized to support the German war.[28] Yet he was opposed by

[24] The above point has been developed by Professor Dorn in his article previously cited.

[25] Newcastle to Hardwicke, April 10, 1762, B.M., Add. Mss., 32937, f. 13.

[26] Hardwicke to Newcastle, April 14, and Newcastle to Hardwicke, April 17, 1762, ibid., ff. 103 and 183.

[27] Newcastle to Sir Joseph Yorke, May 14, 1762, B.M., Add. Mss., 32938, f. 239; Correspondence of John, fourth Duke of Bedford, II, 76–7; P. C. Yorke, op. cit., III, 352 n.

[28] Newcastle to General Yorke, May 14, 1762, B.M., Add. Mss., 32928, ff. 239–41.

the King, who agreed with Bute and Grenville.[29] As a final indignity to the elderly Newcastle, his opponents secured a report from the treasury from one of his subordinates that supported their views of the absolute necessity for financial retrenchment, as against his own. He thereupon informed both Bute and the King of his determination to give up his place in the government. How far he was removed from being prepared to adopt the policy that Bute and the majority of the Cabinet Council now had at heart is clear from the statement of his position in a letter he wrote about the middle of May to Major General Yorke at The Hague telling of his resignation:

> "My Lord Bute's schemes for foreign affairs are very different from ours [that is, from those of himself, Hardwicke, and Devonshire]. Popular maritime expeditions in war and a total dislike of all continental measures, are the basis of his politics. . . . My scheme was to make our push this campaign, whatever it might have cost; and I would have carried it on everywhere, whatever might have been the expense." [30]

The formal resignation of the Duke of Newcastle took place on May 14, two days after the King had requested of Parliament but a million pounds, which that surprised body had gladly granted. It may be added that when the message was read recommending this grant, stress was placed on the dangerous situation of that "ancient and natural ally" Portugal, and no reference at all was made to the war in Germany, except the very oblique one to the effect that measures "may be necessary to disappoint or defeat any enterprises . . . of his enemies, against his Majesty, or his allies, as the exigency of affairs may require." [31] Thus the reorientation of foreign policy was given further emphasis. Not until March 1, 1763 — after the ratification of the Treaty of Paris — is there mention of the payment of a subsidy to any German principality. It is true, however, that, under cover of general appropriations for the army, large sums were either directly or indirectly granted and lesser sums continued to be provided, after the signing of the peace treaty, for the liquidation of all obligations to the rulers of Hesse-Cassel and Brunswick-Wolfenbüttel — without reference to payments made to Hanover,

---

[29] George III to Bute, May 6, 1762, op. cit., pp. 99–100.
[30] Newcastle to General Yorke, May 14, 1762, B. M., Add. Mss., 32938.
[31] Parliamentary History, XV, 1215 and 1222.

over which the King ruled as Elector.[32] It is also true that the allied army, facing the French army under Soubise and d'Estrées, continued to be so adequately supported by these general appropriations that it was possible for Prince Ferdinand and the Marquis of Granby not only to inflict defeats on it in June at Wilhelmsthal and in July at Lutternberg, but also to compel the evacuation of Göttingen in August and later, as already observed, the surrender of Cassel.

The passing of the old Duke of Newcastle from the centre of the political stage and the assumption of his key office by the Earl of Bute had, undoubtedly, large international implications. His statesmanship in the field of foreign affairs — and no one who has examined with care the papers of this busy man would deny that he possessed statesmanship — was based during the earlier period upon maintenance of the so-called "system," involving the subsidization of Austria and lesser European states, in order to guarantee the safety of Hanover and to strengthen the position of Great Britain in the Council of Europe. Although this system broke down under the stress of movements on the Continent that led to the realignment of the leading powers, he remained sincerely devoted to the principle of the subsidization of European states as a vital instrument for maintaining the prestige of his country. He therefore became as deeply committed to the maintenance of the new system that substituted Prussia for Austria as he had been to the old. His truly amazing correspondence, together with the accumulation of reports regarding European developments — even when head of the treasury — are not only a rich quarry today for the student of diplomacy, but a testimony of his vital and intelligent interest as well as influence in this field. But his grasp of international realities was limited to Europe and even to that part of Europe with the policies of which he had been primarily concerned when Secretary of State for the Northern Department. He simply could not see that Great Britain, not because of anything that had happened in the course of the German war, but rather elsewhere and far beyond Europe — with Canada firmly under British control and India, politically prostrate, destined likewise to be — was by 1762 about to assume a new role, a peculiar position, in world affairs, which would by no

---

[32] *Ibid.*, XV, 1315–19; C. W. Eldon, *op. cit.*, pp. 159–62.

means be promoted if she were preoccupied with the troubles of central Europe — in other words, acting as but another European power.

The extrication of the nation by King George and the Bute ministry from the web of commitments in Europe, as the result of the personal union of Great Britain and Hanover, was undoubtedly a major contribution to British statesmanship, and even the degree to which the nation was later — and rightly — to be concerned in warding off the menace presented by a dynamic Revolutionary and Napoleonic France does not seem to invalidate this view, any more than does the nation's still later immersement in the First and Second World Wars. In other words, whatever undoubted merits the Newcastle diplomacy respecting Europe had previously possessed, it was no longer valid in 1762. It was better therefore for the Duke to leave. He had served well two Kings. Not the least of his contribution to the quiet of their reigns had been his efforts to bring into the House of Commons as members those who could be expected under normal circumstances to give their loyal support to measures designed to promote the welfare of the state. His distribution of patronage was and has been the subject of much careless criticism. Obviously someone — whether the King himself or a subordinate — had to assume the responsibility for this — as onerous as it was important — and Newcastle's correspondence, involving both ecclesiastical and lay appointments, indicates his solicitude that worthy men who had a real claim to preferment should be recognized.

With the elimination from the Cabinet Council of the ardent defender of the old European diplomacy as well as the intractable Pitt, who wanted to make no concessions to France but strip that country of every overseas possession and humble it in the dust; freed likewise from interference and threats from the King of Prussia, who, as intractable as Pitt, was determined not to yield an inch of territory he had plundered from Austria or any other territory, whatever it might cost him or his allies, the atmosphere became sufficiently clear to permit George III and his advisers to begin to take really effective steps to end Britain's war with France.

It should now be pointed out that upon the resignation of Pitt the preceding fall and through the instrumentality of Comte de Viry, Sardinian minister in London, and his colleague, M. Bailli de Solar

in Paris,[33] feelers were put forth respecting the resumption of negotiations that had ended with the recall of M. Bussy to France and
of Hans Stanley to England in 1761. Although Choiseul had not
been prepared to carry on any further interchange of ideas with
Pitt, he showed his willingness to do so now with the Earl of Bute.
It was therefore suggested — with Viry and Solar acting, as indicated, as the mediums for the interchange of views — that the British ultimatum of July 25 and that of France of August 5, 1761 be
used as bases from which to approach a solution. Each of these
memorials had agreed to the cession of Canada and a division of
the so-called four Neutral Islands of the West Indies; each also
agreed, under certain conditions which differed, that Guadeloupe
should be returned to France. As for the fisheries, the British note
denied to France any right to engage in them or to occupy any island in the River or Gulf of St. Lawrence, while the French note
insisted on the restoration of this right and some land shelter for
French fishermen operating in that area. Other matters, likewise
involving different points of view, had to do with the restoration
of all lands conquered by the French in Germany and occupied by
the French in the Austrian Netherlands, the cession of Minorca and
Belle-Île-sur-Mer, the destruction of the works at Dunkirk, and the
indemnification of France for captures at sea made before the declaration of war.[34]

To clarify the situation further, Egremont indicated — in line
with the British final concessions of August 16, 1761, by one of
which the French right to share the cod fisheries had been at length
conceded, despite the opposition of Pitt, with also the right to a
land shelter [35] — not only that the fishing rights would be restored
but that the two small islands of St. Pierre and Miquelon would be
granted for the furtherance of that interest. In the course of these
diplomatic exchanges and after tentative agreement had been
reached in April that both Guadeloupe and Martinique might be
restored to France — provided France made large concessions in
other matters — the thorny question of the ultimate fate of little
St. Lucia, also located in the Caribbean Sea, came up for consideration.

---

[33] This correspondence between Viry and Solar is preserved in three volumes of
Shelburne Papers (Volumes 9, 10, and 11) that are in Clements Library at Ann Arbor,
Michigan, where I was able to examine them while working there.

[34] For the English and French Memorials see *Parliamentary History*, XV, 1047-54.

[35] For this document see *ibid.*, XV, 1061-7.

It is hard for anyone today quite to appreciate the importance attached in the eighteenth century to tiny St. Lucia, then one of the Neutral Islands. But it is strategically located just south of Martinique and only a comparatively short distance to the northwest of Barbados and possesses superb harbour facilities. In 1687, in negotiations carried on between England and France, it was coupled with the vast Hudson Bay region in importance; in 1750 the rival claims involving it received almost as much attention on the part of the Anglo-French commissioners meeting in Paris as did those respecting the limits of Nova Scotia.[36] While Choiseul was willing to divide the Neutral Islands and to make important sacrifices elsewhere he was determined to secure St. Lucia. This was indicated to the British early in June through dispatches exchanged through Solar and Viry, and later in that month Solar was able to assure the latter that were Great Britain prepared to give up the island the French government would make peace.[37] Although at a Cabinet Council meeting held on June 21 it was decided to reject the claim, Bute and Egremont secretly agreed to permit Viry to reassure Choiseul orally. As a result, Egremont – to protect himself from Grenville and other colleagues who were opposed to giving up St. Lucia – asked the King "to order him to give Viry a hint that St. Lucia will be yielded, if all other articles are agreed to." [38] Choiseul's favourable and confidential reply to the secret offer reached Egremont, to the delight of the latter, on July 8.

Nevertheless, a curious situation had arisen. Bute and Egremont had been making momentous decisions, unknown to the other ministers of the King, and Louis XV had likewise taken an equally momentous step, unknown to Charles III of Spain, with whom he was bound in the Bourbon Family Pact and as an ally in the war. To relieve the embarrassment of Bute and Egremont, Choiseul, at the request of the latter, sent a second and open letter that arrived on July 24 in which – without reference to the secret offer – he insisted that there could be peace only if St. Lucia were given up.[39]

Meanwhile, thought was being given by the Cabinet Council to

---

[36] For the history of the rivalry over St. Lucia see Volume V of this series, pages 223–30 and 305–14. It may be pointed out that the question whether Canada or Guadeloupe should be retained, which had been the subject of discussion among the British, was no longer an issue by the spring of 1761.

[37] George III to Bute, June 4 and 20, 1762, op. cit., pp. 113 and 118.

[38] The same to the same, June 21, ibid., pp. 118–19.

[39] The same to the same, July 25, 1762, ibid., p. 124.

the termination of Anglo-French military activities in Germany. It may be recalled that in the French memorial of August 5, 1761, assurances were given that all territories that French arms had conquered in western Germany would be restored, outside of the lands of the King of Prussia. This problem of freeing Cleves and Guelders was considered by the board as well as that of a suspension of arms in Portugal.[40] There came up in this connection the question of how to make Spain withdraw from that country. This involved Franco-Spanish relations. As has been noted, the French minister had been negotiating for peace behind the back of the Spaniards. Bute had attempted to open up *pourparlers* with the latter, but had been rebuffed by the "extreme arrogance of the Spanish *mémoire*." He was therefore disposed to bring matters to a conclusion with France and to wait until the campaign in Cuba had been terminated before resuming negotiations; he therefore made this proposal to his colleagues at a meeting on July 26. It was strongly opposed, however, by Grenville and Granville as well as by other members of the Cabinet Council. They insisted that the ministers of Louis XV must be induced to bring pressure upon those of Spain to join in the work of framing a peace treaty that would, among other things, care for Portugal. Writing to Egremont after this meeting, the deeply distressed Bute expressed the feeling that the obstacles obstructing peace could only be surmounted by the two working alone with the French ministers — as they had already been secretly doing — in "a perfect confidence . . . founded not only on our honour and integrity, but on our weight in the Government." He also affirmed that Choiseul had now not only accepted all the British terms but "agrees even to what we most wished: to sign our Spanish Peace, leaving the Spaniards to themselves . . . and presses our naming ambassadors to finish the business at once." [41] The King on his part was so outraged at the obstructionist tactics of the majority in the Council that he expressed a strong desire to dismiss most of them and, unless peace could otherwise be concluded, to send the Duke of Bedford without delay to France.[42]

The crisis in the Cabinet Council, happily, was only temporary. Egremont, on the one hand, expressed his willingness to take the step demanded by Grenville and Granville in order to bring Spain

40 The same to the same, July 9, 1762, *ibid.*, p. 122.
41 Bute to Egremont, July 26, 1762, *ibid.*, pp. 126–8.
42 George III to Bute, July 26, 1762, *ibid.*

into the picture; the Council on July 28, on the other hand, agreed to accept the French proposals, including the insistence on possessing St. Lucia, and to send Bedford to conclude the peace with France — provided the latter power would agree to give no further assistance to Spain and would also come to an accommodation with Portugal should Charles III not be prepared to sign a peace treaty. The news of this development turned the King's anger into joy.[43]

Preparations for the exchange of ministers plenipotentiary were now pressed. France decided to send a nobleman of eminence who was a patron of the arts, the Duc de Nivernais, and in the person of the Duke of Bedford Britain was represented by one of the most powerful and wealthy of the peers of the realm. In the Pitt-Newcastle ministry he had been the leading advocate of a settlement with France that represented a departure from the type of dictated peace that Pitt had demanded, with few, if any, concessions. For he had become convinced by the summer of 1761 that Choiseul had made every concession that could justly be demanded of his country in order to re-establish peace, and therefore, as was made clear in an earlier chapter, Bedford refused to attend further meetings of the Cabinet Council in view of Pitt's continued uncompromising attitude. He had also been bitterly opposed to other views of Pitt and Newcastle, both of whom attached great importance to the German war; for he felt that Britain's future would best be cared for by extricating the country from it. In general he was, it may be affirmed, well qualified to represent the views of the King and of many other people of weight and importance in Great Britain who had come to feel as he felt. For, despite his strong desire to help achieve peace, he did not lack firmness in the course of the negotiations when the necessity arose of protecting what were held by the King and his counsellors to be the country's essential interests. That the best terms that he or any other man could be expected to obtain would be bitterly opposed at home he also must have realized, and he therefore must have been prepared for the denunciations bound to follow. Not only were rumours respecting the terms to be accorded to France being "whispered about" late in August 1762, but papers began publishing statements regarding the reported "Preliminaries." As these implied a serious British diplomatic defeat, great expectations were voiced "that a certain illustrious

---

[43] The same to the same, July 28, 1763, ibid., pp. 128–9.

commoner will expose the principles on which the Preliminaries are founded." [44] Indeed, before the Duke left for France a violent spirit of opposition to the anticipated terms was manifested among certain London groups.[45] According to Newcastle, the reputed agreement to cede St. Lucia would be especially the subject of attack; [46] this was also the feeling of the Duke of Cumberland.[47]

Although Bedford expressed to the King the feeling that his instructions bound him too tightly, he nevertheless did not seriously object and was in good humour on his departure.[48] He determined, doubtless largely for the impression that would be made on the minds of the French people of the power and wealth of Great Britain, to go to Paris in state.[49] We are told that he took with him "a most magnificent equipage and service of plate, and a very numerous retinue," and that when he started for Dover, he had in his train twenty-three coaches and thirty horsemen. This, it would seem, had the desired effect. For when the brilliant procession arrived at the outskirts of Paris, it was escorted into the city by four hundred of the King's own household troops amidst great acclaim of the people.[50] However, it did not mean that Bedford was not faced with difficulties.

The French, through the Duc de Nivernais, raised objections about the evacuation of Cleves and Guelders, both a part of the King of Prussia's dominions. Egremont therefore had to inform the Duke of this new development. What is more, the French envoy presented a *mémoire* in which "all the Articles already refused them were again named." [51] Bedford himself was handed a copy of the same *mémoire*, which was in form a French redraft of the tentative preliminary treaty. This he described as "extraordinary and surprising," and he was so much displeased that he began making preparations to return to England. When the King in London read it he was inclined to agree with him, and recommended to Egre-

---

[44] London, August 27, Pennsylvania Gazette, November 18, 1762.

[45] P. C. Yorke, op. cit., III, 413.

[46] Newcastle Papers under date of September 4, 1762, B.M., Add. Mss., 32942, ff. 145–57.

[47] George III to Bute, September 6, op. cit., pp. 133–4.

[48] The same to the same, September 5, 1762, ibid., pp. 131–3. For Bedford's instructions see the Grenville Papers, Diplomatic Correspondence, Stowe Collection, Huntington Library.

[49] Bedford Correspondence, III, 93.

[50] London advice of September 5 and 15, Pennsylvania Gazette, November 25, 1762.

[51] George III to Bute, September 19 and 24, 1762, op. cit., pp. 135–7.

mont that a meeting of the Cabinet Council should be held to secure the advice of the members before final instructions were sent
to the Duke.[52] These instructions were finally embodied in a letter
that Bute wrote to Bedford late in September. In it he stressed the
point that before the latter should sign any preliminary treaty, the
document should be sent home to be approved by the Cabinet
Council — a safeguard, he declared, that he himself had agreed to
out of pure friendship for the envoy, so that should a clamour be
raised about the terms embodied in it, the odium would not fall on
Bedford alone but on the ministers as well. The Duke was further
informed for his future guidance that after his dispatches had been
read in the Council and after those articles in the preliminaries
upon which no concessions to France were to be made had been
clearly designated by that body, he would have power to sign —
provided the treaty was then acceptable to both the French and the
Spanish courts. This precaution, the Earl pointed out, has been
taken by reason of "the ungenerous attempts made to elude the fundamental agreement" already reached before the Duke had left
England, as was clearly indicated by Nivernais's "Project" [53] and,
one may add, in other ways.

In face of an inflexible attitude on the part of the British with respect to what were felt to be the essentials for an accommodation,
the French government gave way. In fact, before Bute's letter had
arrived, Bedford had been able to reach an agreement in line with
his earlier instructions and on September 24 forwarded a copy of
the draft treaty. After the Cabinet Council had studied it, that
body was faced with another crisis. Grenville and Egremont demanded both Florida and Puerto Rico in exchange for Havana,
while Bute felt strongly that Florida was a fair equivalent. As for
the Duke of Devonshire, he was so bitterly opposed to Bute's foreign policy in general that he had for some time refused to attend
meetings of the Council.[54] In view of this situation, the King for a
time played with the idea of bringing Newcastle back and did introduce Fox into it to strengthen Bute's position.[55] Still another
step finally taken to this end was to give to the Earl of Halifax the

[52] The same to the same, September 26, 1762, ibid., pp. 137–8.
[53] Bute to Bedford, September 28, 1762, ibid., pp. 138–40. Copies of Bedford's
letters to Egremont and of many other important documents relating to the peace negotiations of this period are in the Stowe Collection, Box 103, Huntington Library.
[54] Newcastle to General Yorke, May 14, 1762, P. S. Yorke, op. cit., III, 357.
[55] George III to Bute, October 2, 1762, op. cit., pp. 142–3.

post held by Grenville while still leaving the latter in the Cabinet Council. This was done on October 14, and also before the end of the month Devonshire was dismissed from his office of Lord Chamberlain and his name removed from the list of the King's councillors.

Meanwhile, the draft treaty sent on by Bedford continued under consideration. It was suspected that the French ministers had succeeded in introducing alterations into it that were not in harmony with previous understandings. Egremont therefore wrote to the Duke to prepare the court of France for the rejection of all such changes. In his reply of October 23 Bedford insisted that none whatsoever had been introduced, nor had Grimaldi, the Spanish Ambassador, acted in a haughty manner, as had been reported. But before his letter reached London the Council determined to send an ultimatum to the French government and with it Richard Rigby, long closely attached to the Duke, so as to calm the latter when he received it in order to hand it to Choiseul.[56] As the result of this continued firmness on the part of the British government and the intense desire of the King of France to reach an agreement, the work of reconciling minor points and of clarification moved along rapidly. By the end of October the only obstacle that remained to be surmounted, so that a general agreement could be reached, was that having to do with compensation Great Britain would receive for the return of Havana to Spain. The Cabinet Council had at length agreed to embody in its ultimatum to Spain that this must be the cession either of Florida or of Puerto Rico.[57] Therefore when Bedford made clear that Havana would be given up only on this condition, Grimaldi felt compelled to consult his government on that point. This involved delay. At length the reply came that authorized him to offer Florida in exchange. The British envoy was now quite prepared to attach his signature to the preliminaries, which were signed on November 3.

The Duke of Bedford, it may be pointed out, in helping to bring to an end the Great War for the Empire exercised a good deal of freedom in the interpretation of his final instructions — something that a man of less weight in public life would hardly have ventured to do.[58] Yet the King, while blaming the Duke for his independence,

---

56 George III to Bute, October 24, 1762, op. cit., p. 151.

57 Bedford Correspondence, III, 142–3.

58 For Bedford's letter explaining the differences between the draft that had been sent home and the preliminaries that he signed see the Bedford Correspondence, III,

was disposed to call the preliminaries "a noble Peace," [59] and Granville on his death-bed referred to the war now ending and the outcome of it as "the most glorious war and most honourable peace this nation ever saw." [60] Charles Townshend, however, was critical in view of the fact that the Spaniards had, in exchange for Havana, handed over Florida, "an uninhabited country," rather than well-settled Puerto Rico, which he called a "weighty objection" to the peace.[61] Yet, according to Bute, when there were rumours that Puerto Rico was to be given up rather than Florida, all the cries were for the latter country, and he added: "now the same mouths vomit out curses against Florida." [62]

It had been agreed that the preliminaries should be submitted to Parliament for approval. Although this was not a constitutional requirement, it was a statesmanlike move, especially in view of the bitter attacks that continued to be made upon them in the city. The degree of animosity directed against Bute, who was held to be the master mind in what was asserted in some quarters to have been a betrayal of the country, was indicated by the rough treatment that he received on his way to the opening of the new Parliament on November 25: he was hissed and his coach was pelted by the mob, which seemed even disposed to destroy him. Even the King, driving to Parliament House in magnificent array, was likewise insulted.

On November 29 the preliminaries were placed before the two houses, where they were read and ordered to be presented.[63]

Newcastle — quite unable to adjust himself to the new orientation of British policy, and also in no way reconciled to his loss of power to the Earl of Bute — was hoping fervently that a powerful oppo-

---

144–9. The King's chief complaints against Bedford were that he had expanded somewhat the article relating to Honduras; he had also extended the time allowed for Canadians to leave before automatically becoming British subjects, as well as the time for evacuating Florida. With respect to the cod fisheries, he had reduced the distance from six to three leagues off British territory within which the French were not allowed to fish; and he also had changed the clause, relating to right of British inspection of St. Pierre and Miquelon for possible violations of the treaty, to one providing for the royal parole that the provisions would be strictly observed respecting the fortification and garrisoning of the islands (George III to Bute, November 8, 1762, op. cit., p. 160).

[59] Ibid.,
[60] Basil Williams, Life of William Pitt, II, 141.
[61] George III to Bute, November 8, 1762, op. cit., p. 161.
[62] Bute to Bedford, November 10, 1762, Bedford Correspondence, III, 152.
[63] For the preliminaries see the Journal of the House of Commons, 1761–1764, XXIX, 361–7. I am following the Journal (p. 360) for the date when these were presented to the House of Commons.

sition would arise in both houses to overwhelm the administration. When the debate took place on December 9, Pitt, in spite of extreme illness, appeared in the House of Commons and spoke for over three hours. He was temperate but critical in his opposition to accepting such a treaty and charged that it "obscured all the glories of the war, surrendered the dearest interests of the nation, and sacrificed the public faith by an abandonment of our allies"; he also emphasized the fact that when he himself was in the government and had consented to conclude a peace — with reference to the abortive attempt during the preceding year to end the war — he had not "made a sacrifice of any conquest; he had neither broken the national faith, nor betrayed the allies of the crown." [64] In other words, Pitt was still the statesman who would have made no concessions and would have clung to the Continental connections that once he had denounced but for the preservation of which he was now the chief British champion. Those who spoke against him and in favour of the treaty, such as the Earl of Shelburne,[65] stressed the point that Great Britain had not entered the war in order to make conquests of the lands of other nations, but simply for "the security of our colonies upon the continent [of North America, threatened by French encroachments]." The treaty now before them, these speakers affirmed, provided amply for this security — with the inhabitants of the colonies "now freed from the molestation of enemies and the emulation of rivals, unlimited in their possessions, and safe in their persons." Therefore, "having made very large demands in North America, it was necessary to relax in other parts [of the world]." They predicted also the growth and future wealth of the colonies and the "real grandeur" that awaited such an empire.[66] In the course of the debate in the House of Lords, the principal speech against the peace preliminaries was made by the Earl of Hardwicke, who among other things declared that "by this desertion of the King of Prussia, we are left without any system or connection at all on the continent." [67]

The resolution that brought on the debates called upon the two

---

[64] Parliamentary History, XV, 1259–71.

[65] H. W. V. Temperley, "The Peace of Paris," Cambridge History of the British Empire, I, 504 n. Shelburne in 1761 entered the House of Lords and his speech was therefore delivered there.

[66] Parliamentary History, XV, 1271–2.

[67] Ibid., XV, 1251–8; P. S. Yorke, op. cit., III, 372–4.

A plan of Dunkirk as it was in 1757.

(From the *Gentleman's Magazine*, 1763)

"A New Map of the British Dominions in North America, with the Limits of the Governments annexed thereto by the late Treaty of Peace and settled by Proclamation—October 7th, 1763."

houses "to express to His Majesty their Approbation of the Advantageous Terms upon which His Majesty hath concluded Preliminary Articles of Peace." In the voting in the House of Commons that occurred at the end of the speeches, sixty-four members voted in opposition to them as against three hundred and nineteen supporting them; in the House of Lords the opposition was so weak numerically that no division was demanded. Thus Parliament gave the government a resounding vote of confidence, to the dismay of Newcastle in the House of Lords and Pitt in the House of Commons. The significance of this goes far beyond the mere endorsement of the specific terms of the draft treaty.

The Preliminary Articles and the Definitive Treaty of Peace signed on February 10 of the following year,[68] provided among other things of minor importance: that Canada and all its dependencies should be ceded to Great Britain, together with all islands in the River and the Gulf of St. Lawrence; that the dividing line between the British continental colonies and Louisiana should be the centre of the Mississippi River — outside of the enclave to the east of that river comprehending the town and environs of New Orleans — and that the free navigation of that river should be guaranteed to British subjects; that three of the four Neutral Islands of the West Indies — namely, St. Vincent, Dominica, and Tobago — and also the islands of Grenada and the Grenadines should remain in British possession, as well as Senegal in Africa; that Minorca should be restored as well as the two East India Company posts on Sumatra; that in India all French acquisitions made there since the beginning of the year 1749 should be renounced; and, not least, that no recompense should be demanded for the vast number of French ships captured after hostilities had begun but before an open declaration of war in 1756 — an acknowledgment by the French that the war began in 1754 and not in 1756 as previously insisted. As for the continent of Europe, the articles specified that the fortifications of Dunkirk should be destroyed; that the possessions of the Elector of Hanover, the Landgrave of Hesse, the Duke of Brunswick, and the Count von der Lippe-Bückeburgh should be evacuated, as well as "the fortresses of Cleves, Cassel, Guildres [Guelders], and . . . all the countries belonging to the King of Prussia." This was to be accomplished by the simple device of the withdrawal of both the Brit-

---

68 The two are all but identical, outside two or three articles no longer applicable to the final treaty.

ish and French armies out of every part of the Holy Roman German Empire.

In return for the acceptance of the above demands Great Britain agreed to permit the French to share the cod fisheries on the same basis as provided for in the Treaty of Utrecht; and, to make this possible, to return to them the two small islands of St. Pierre and Miquelon in the Gulf of St. Lawrence — provided that these should remain defenceless, and that outside of the western and northern shores of Newfoundland, where their fishermen might dry their catch, they were not to approach within three leagues of any British possession in the gulf and were not to come within fifteen leagues of Cape Breton Island, where the great fortress of Louisbourg once stood. Further, France was to receive back the West India islands of Guadeloupe and Martinique with small dependent islets; the neutral island of St. Lucia there was also conceded; Belle-Île-en-Mer off the coast of France and Goree off the coast of Africa were also to be returned, as well as the factories in India possessed by the Compagnie des Indes at the beginning of the year 1749, but with the clear understanding that the French were to construct no fortifications nor to keep any troops in Bengal and were to recognize the present native rulers of the Coromandel Coast, Orissa, and the Deccan as the lawful rulers and to respect their authority.

Spain, according to the articles, was obliged to cede Florida in all its extent, to renounce any pretensions to a right to participate in the cod fisheries, also to agree not to disturb British subjects who resorted to Honduras and "other places of the territory of Spain in that part of the World" for the purpose of cutting and carrying away logwood, and, finally, to submit to the decision of courts of admiralty in Great Britain with respect to the legality of the capture of Spanish vessels at a time when the two nations were not at war. In return for accepting these demands Great Britain agreed to evacuate Cuba and to destroy all fortifications that had been erected for the defence of the logwood-cutters; she also agreed to return any conquests made that were not specifically mentioned in the treaty, and thus was obliged to renounce without compensation the Philippines.

Here we have before us the terms of the Treaty of Paris. The cessions made to Great Britain by the articles were vast in relation to those concessions granted in return. The future security of the French islands in the West Indies depended almost wholly upon the ability of the French to control the seas — as was clearly indicated by the loss of St. Lucia in the course of the War for American Independence and the subsequent use made of the island as a naval base by Rodney. The same precarious tenure was true of Belle-Île-en-Mer and Goree; and the defenceless condition of St. Pierre and Miquelon only emphasized the degree to which Great Britain after the peace remained in position, with commanding naval superiority, to exert pressure on France in a number of other areas bordering the high seas. As for Spain, that proud country by the terms of the treaty was compelled to repudiate every pretension and every demand made during the period of negotiation before war was declared. Finally, with respect to Germany, the treaty blazoned forth the fact that the real Hanoverians had ceased to reign in Great Britain after the passing of George II and the coming of George III to the throne. A truly British rather than a Hanoverian policy toward the continent of Europe and particularly toward the confused affairs of Germany was gradually substituted. Never again would Hanover, as the Electorate of the King, loom as it had so long done in the eyes of the ministers of state. Instead, the ministers' attention was increasingly focused on the problems evoked by a widespread British Empire.

The wise decision no longer to underwrite what an increasing number of people felt were the predatory activities of the King of Prussia by refusing to renew the subsidy treaty and the equally wise decision as embodied in the terms of the Peace of Paris, to leave him to settle as best he could his war with the Empress Queen and the other states of the empire supporting her, signalize the fundamental shift that was taking place in British policy. To say that these decisions represented a breach of international good faith is a charge that must be dismissed by the historian as baseless. In fact, it could be better argued that the yearly subsidy treaty entered into with Frederick to save him from the penalties sought by his enemies for his aggressions was a much more dubious act, however necessary to Great Britain it seemed to be at the time. Indeed, there is little doubt that the pressure exerted by the British government on France to withdraw all financial as well as military support from the Empress Queen had the effect of making it impossible to bring the retribution upon the King of Prussia that she had vowed to exact. At the same time, Frederick, though to the very last he "clung with passionate longing to the idea of acquiring Saxony," [69] was at length obliged to realize that it was equally impossible for him to fulfil his

---

[69] Emil Daniel in the *Cambridge Modern History*, VI, 300.

ambition. As a result, the Peace of Hubertusburg was concluded on February 15 — only twelve days after the Peace of Paris. It provided as a basis for territorial arrangements the *status quo ante bellum*. Thus came to an end the two wars. In view of the fact that each had its own distinct origin in time and place and was waged for objectives equally distinct, it was quite logical that each should be concluded by a distinct treaty of pacification.

People in Great Britain — thoughtful people, that is — were asking questions in 1763 — questions that may well be raised by the student today who is concerned with the history of that period. First of all, they asked, what sort of war had Great Britain and her Empire been fighting between the years 1754 and 1763? Was it proper to call it, in reality, nothing much more than a series of plundering forays launched for the purpose of stripping the rivals of the Empire of their possessions, in connection with which the law of the jungle ruled? For that is how many Americans viewed the war by 1774. Or had it been, rather, a war based on considerations that could be openly proclaimed with honour and pride to all the world? In other words, had warlike measures been resorted to by Britons only most reluctantly in 1754 in order to protect the colonies in North America from violent acts of aggression on the part of the French in derogation of the most solemn covenants? Was it in reality begun as a war for *the Empire* and not a war for empire — with all this implies? If so, had the objectives of providing security for the Empire been changed — outside of the broadening, in the course of the war, of the original security objectives so as to include Canada and the equal determination that a fair indemnification should be made by France and later by Spain for those British losses which were of such a nature as could be made good by that means? If these objectives had really been changed, if the coming of Pitt to power meant that the war for the protection of the Empire had been transformed into a war for maximum territorial acquisition, the question may be raised to what extent did the government and the nation accept the views of this dynamic leader?

A victorious peace treaty is almost certain to disclose to a greater or lesser extent the true motives that in the first instance impelled those in control of the destinies of the nation achieving it to embark upon hostilities. What kind of a treaty, after all, was offered to France and Spain by triumphant Britain? Did it reflect fairly faithfully the original aims of the British government at the beginning of the war? In other words, was the war in 1762 still as in 1754 viewed as a War for the Empire, as the Earl of Shelburne affirmed it to be, or was it a war to conquer and to keep whatever the nation could, as Pitt in opposing the treaty had boasted had been his aims when in office? There would seem to be little doubt, in view of the vote in Parliament, that Shelburne more faithfully reflected the sentiments of responsible statesmen on this issue — as well as those of the nation — than did Pitt and the London mob. But granted the spirit of moderation and compromise implicit in the treaty of peace of 1763, it is clear that its terms not only embodied every reasonable British demand, but were patterned in such a fashion as to have had ultimate effects so far-reaching for the English-speaking people and for the world at large as were surely quite beyond the range of the imagination of any man of that generation to predict. Thus ended what one may, with due regard to the meaning of words, call very properly, as for the sake of accuracy I have felt impelled to do in this series and elsewhere, Britain's Great War for the Empire.[70]

---

[70] The best book concerned with the treaty of peace is by Dr. Zenab Esmat Rashed: *The Peace of Paris, 1763* (Liverpool, 1951), with a foreword by Professor Mark O. Thomson of the University of Liverpool. Dr. Rashed carried on her researches in the Public Record Office and the British Museum in London, but also drew on the resources of the Archives des Affaires Étrangères in Paris, the Simancas in Madrid, and the Lansdowne House manuscripts that are in the Clements Library at Ann Arbor. The student should also read the scholarly article by Walter L. Dorn entitled "Frederic the Great and Lord Bute," *Journal of Modern History* I, 529–60, which like the above volume calls into question the wisdom of the Bute diplomacy. This will be the subject of consideration in future volumes of the present series.

Index

Abrantes, Portugal, von der Lippe concentrates forces at, 259; called "the pass to Lisbon," 260

Abreu, the Marquis d', Spanish Ambassador in London, intimate relations established between Newcastle and, 234; receives confidential information respecting Boscawen's expedition, 234; presents the Spanish memorial of complaints of 1756, 238; refuses to receive the British answer, 238; becomes *persona non grata* at the British court, 238; protests the piracy of Captain Haddon, 240; Pitt indicates to, that the good offices of the King of Spain would be accepted, 246

Acapulco, Mexico, arrival in the Philippines of Spanish galleon from, 278

Aché, Anne Antoine, Comte d', chef d'Escadre, at Île de France, 140; arrives on the Coromandel Coast, 140–1; weakens his squadron, 141; first engagement of, with Pocock, 141–2; adheres to French naval tactics, 142–3; disciplines the captain of the *Duc de Bourgogne*, 143; refuses to renew the engagement, 143; prevailed upon to remain at Pondicherry, 147; importance of the activities of, along the Coromandel Coast, 147–8; second indecisive engagement of, with Pocock, 148; return of, to Pondicherry, 148; losses sustained by, in the naval engagement, 149; return of, to Mauritius to refit, 149; unfavourable opinion of Lally held by, 150; complains of the hostility against French navy personnel held by army officers at Pondicherry, 150; problems facing, at Île de France, 157–8; sails for Pondicherry, 158; Pocock pursues the squadron of, 159–60; third naval engagement between Pocock and, off Tranquebar, 160–1; refuses to renew the engagement, 161; determination of, to return to Île de France, 161–2; factors in the decision of, to leave the Coromandel Coast, 162; not to return to Pondicherry, 166; ordered to remain at Île de France, 168

Act of Settlement, the, and the Hanoverian dynasty, 48

Actif, the, French ship of the line, in the third engagement with Pocock, 160

Adolphus Frederick, King of Sweden, signs Treaty of Hamburg with Frederick, 62

Æolus, the, British frigate, sails in pursuit of Thurot's squadron, 26–7; duel between the *Maréchal de Belle-Isle* and, 27

Affry, Louis August d', French Ambassador at The Hague, on the King of Spain as final arbiter between France and Great Britain, 207

Afghans, the, terrorize the territories of the Great Mogul, 108

Africa, British trading posts in, attacked by the French, 173; French trading posts in, captured by the British, 176–7

Aiguillon, Duc d', to command the French invasion army, 4; plan of operations of, when reaching Great Britain, 5; waits at Quiberon Bay for naval support, 19

Akbar, founder of the Mogul Empire in India, 108

Alamgir II, the Great Mogul, in 1754, weakness of, 108

Albany, New York, British regular troops stationed about, in 1762, 261

Albemarle, George Keppel, 3rd Earl of, commander-in-chief of the British forces directed against Havana, 262; instructions of, 262–3; number of troops placed at the disposal of, 262–3, 264; the emphasis on black troops given by, 264; lands troops near Havana, 265; invests Havana, 266; suffering of the troops under, 266–7; arrival of reinforcements for, 267; troops under, storm El Morro Castle, 267; surrender of Havana to, 268; sad condition of soldiers who served under, in Cuba, 275

Albuquerque, Spain, Aranda withdraws his army from Portugal to, 260

Alexander, Captain, of the *Hawke*, seizes the Philadelphia *Friendship* seeking to enter Cap François, 80

Alinagar, new name of Calcutta, given by the Nabob, 120

'Ali Wardi Khan (Alivirdi Khan), Nabob of Bengal, almost independent of the

A NOTE ON THE TYPE

This book is set in Linotype Caledonia. Caledonia belongs to the family of printing types called "modern face" by printers — a term used to mark the change in style of type-letters that occurred about 1800. Caledonia is in the general neighborhood of Scotch Modern in design, but is more freely drawn than that letter.

This series was designed by W. A. Dwiggins, and composed, printed, and bound by The Plimpton Press, Norwood, Massachusetts.

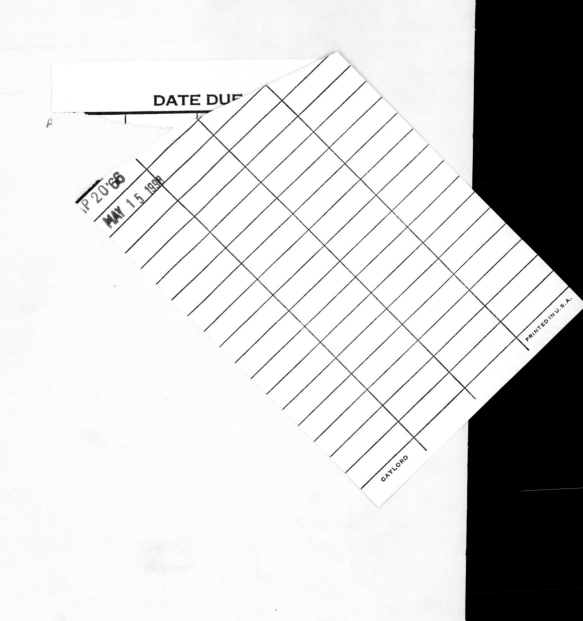